Hume's Politics

Hume's Politics

Coordination and Crisis in the *History of England*

ANDREW SABL

Princeton University Press

Princeton and Oxford

Copyright © 2012 by Princeton University Press

Requests for permission to reproduce material from this work should be sent to Permissions, Princeton University Press

Published by Princeton University Press, 41 William Street, Princeton, New Jersey 08540

In the United Kingdom: Princeton University Press, 6 Oxford Street, Woodstock, Oxfordshire OX20 1TW

press.princeton.edu

Jacket art: John Byam Liston Shaw (1872–1919), Queen Mary (1516–58) and Princess Elizabeth (1533–1603) entering London, 1553, 1910 (fresco), Houses of Parliament, Westminster, London, UK. Courtesy of the Bridgeman Art Library.

Paper ISBN: 978-0-691-16817-3

Cloth ISBN: 978-0-691-13420-8

The Library of Congress has cataloged the cloth edition as follows:

Sabl, Andrew, 1969–
   Hume's politics : coordination and crisis in the history of England / Andrew Sabl.
       p.   cm.
   Summary: "Hume's Politics provides a comprehensive examination of David Hume's political theory, and is the first book to focus on Hume's monumental History of England as the key to his distinctly political ideas. Andrew Sabl argues that conventions of authority are the main building blocks of Humean politics, and explores how the History addresses political change and disequilibrium through a dynamic treatment of coordination problems. Dynamic coordination, as employed in Hume's work, explains how conventions of political authority arise, change, adapt to new social and economic conditions, improve or decay, and die. Sabl shows how Humean constitutional conservatism need not hinder—and may in fact facilitate—change and improvement in economic, social, and cultural life. He also identifies how Humean liberalism can offer a systematic alternative to neo-Kantian approaches to politics and liberal theory. At once scholarly and accessibly written, Hume's Politics builds bridges between political theory and political science. It treats issues of concern to both fields, including the prehistory of political coordination, the obstacles that must be overcome in order for citizens to see themselves as sharing common political interests, the close and counterintuitive relationship between governmental authority and civic allegiance, the strategic ethics of political crisis and constitutional change, and the ways in which the biases and injustices endemic to executive power can be corrected by legislative contestation and debate"—Provided by publisher.
   Includes bibliographical references and index.
   ISBN 978-0-691-13420-8 (hardback)
   1. Hume, David, 1711–1776.   2. Great Britain—Politics and government.   I. Title.
JC176.H9S23 2012
320.01—dc23   2012028874

British Library Cataloging-in-Publication Data is available

This book has been composed in Minion Pro

Printed on acid-free paper. ∞

Printed in the United States of America

To Miriam

Contents

Preface

In his own time, Hume's religious opinions and his largely naturalistic treatment of morality made him a controversial figure. My own encounter with Hume has, perhaps surprisingly, retained a hint of forbidden knowledge.

My only formal education in Hume (two sessions in an undergraduate survey course) in effect assured me that Hume, as a quasi-relativist whose moral theory appealed to sentiment, could safely be ignored as irrelevant to political theory's real task: seeking rational standards for evaluating political and moral obligations. That portrayal, though extreme, only radicalized what, I later learned, many philosophy departments still teach: Hume's theory, however intelligent and original, fails to give proper accounts of normativity, practical reason, or the authority of moral requirements—fails, in short, to be Kant's. Harvard's Government department, where I earned my undergraduate and graduate degrees, lacked this neo-Kantian dogmatism. But it had a canon of its own that also left little space for Hume, or Hume's questions, among its roster of ancients who sought the Good Life (or, depending on whom one consulted, apprehended natural Right) and moderns concerned with the origins and limits of political obligation in the face of natural liberty and equality. When, after my graduate training, I began to read Hume seriously, he seemed to me much as he must have seemed to his contemporaries, though for different reasons. What made his work bracing, both shocking and liberating, was not just what he said but what he claimed a license to ignore. Hume showed me—and can still show others who encounter him in his native, wild habitat—how many icons can be shattered if one merely presses good sense and observation where they lead, with a constant sense of sanity and humanity but without regard to reigning myths.

Approaching Hume as a special-purpose autodidact has had costs, but also advantages. Not knowing at first that Hume scholars were supposed to read only the "philosophical" works and ignore the *History of England*, I encountered that book as a revelation, as the unparalleled synthesis of statecraft, scholarship, human science, rhetoric, and philosophy that it seemed to Hume's contemporaries and to generations of later admirers. Never before and never since has the best philosopher of an era written a book about the varieties of political choice and about the institutions that arise from the stealthy aggregation of political choices. The result remains an inexhaustible source of both joy and instruction. Not knowing that even eccentrics who read the *History* were supposed to take only the Stuart volumes seriously, I took up the whole and found that some of Hume's best political theory, and best writing, occurs in the last volumes he wrote: the ancient and medieval ones. Finally, while the secondary literature on Hume has been of enormous help to me, and I hope I have given it proper credit, I have been free—too free, some will think—to take my own approach to Hume's fiercely independent thought via a set of questions suggested by politics, not by the literature.

Those who have read my first book, *Ruling Passions*, may wonder how the two relate. The books are very different in style, subject matter, and approach. And on an obvious level, while my first book admittedly displays the child-of-immigrant's determination to understand my own country, this book tries to understand politics through the greater distance allowed by an encounter with another. (Here I feebly imitate Hume himself, who wrote about England as a Scot.) But there are also continuities. Both books aim at a political theory that treats not ideal institutions but real politics, seen as a realm of action and strategy. Both show some sympathy toward rational choice theory (greater now), though in a non-sectarian and non-exclusivist form. Both aim to vindicate a kind of liberal and democratic theory that is grounded in politics rather than starting from legal or philosophical alternatives to politics. Both are concerned with the interplay between political reform and constitutional conservation. One way to understand the connection between that book and this is through this last theme. In my first book I largely took constitutional forms of politics for granted, as being both durable and desirable. In this one I seek more fundamental explanations of where they come from and what they accomplish.

This work has profited from what Hume called (in a different context) "the force of many sympathies." Among countless interlocutors who have shaped its arguments through their comments and advice, I would like to thank particularly Jim Barr, Mary Barr, Eric Beerbohm, Ross Carroll, Mary Dietz, Michael Frazer, Bill Galston, Russell Hardin, Frits van Holthoon, Sharon Krause, Harvey Mansfield, Neil McArthur, Dan O'Neill, Michael Rosen, Nancy Rosenblum, Lucas Swaine, and Richard Tuck. My UCLA colleagues Joshua Dienstag, Kirstie McClure, Anthony Pagden, Carole Pateman, Giulia Sissa, and Brian Walker have been particularly helpful, insightful, and patient, though the prize in all these events goes to Mark A. R. Kleiman. Ben

Berger, Marc Hanvelt, and two anonymous Princeton reviewers deserve special gratitude for reading the whole manuscript and suggesting crucial improvements, as does Gerry Mackie for his searching responses to chapter 1. For their comments on earlier versions I thank the panelists and audiences at the political theory workshops at Harvard, Northwestern, and UCLA; the University of Toronto's "Hume at 300" conference in 2011; and the annual meetings of the American Political Science Association, the New England Political Science Association, and the Western Political Science Association. I have never presented anything directly from the book at the Hume Society's annual meeting, but have drawn both wisdom and happiness from an atmosphere there that combines ardent scholarship with good cheer.

A fellowship from Harvard's Program on Constitutional Government made possible very early research on this book. A grant from the Earhart Foundation enabled the final research and drafting. I thank them both. To the extent (in any case exaggerated) that both those entities are perceived to have ideological leanings, they merit particular praise for supporting a scholar who was unlikely to share them. A sabbatical leave from UCLA allowed the manuscript's completion.

At various stages of this project, LaMonica Andreoff, Matt Crow, Chenelle Idehen, Tara Norris, Melissa Salm, and Will Stahl provided able research assistance and proofreading. Copyeditor Karen Verde deserves special thanks for her careful attention and keen eye.

At Princeton University Press my editor, Rob Tempio, deserves heartfelt thanks, not only for his ability, but for his patience in the face of missed deadlines and unreasonable demands. Also at Princeton I thank former editor Ian Malcolm for his support and confidence in the project's early stages, and Leslie Grundfest, Julia Livingston, and Ryan Mulligan for managing the production.

I could not have completed this project if Hume's work had not been available in digital—and searchable—form. I am duly grateful to the Online Library of Liberty (oll.libertyfund.org) and the InteLex Corporation's CD-ROM edition of Hume in its Past Masters series.

My son Benjamin Sabl, a bit younger than the book project, not only tolerated weekend work sessions but came up with the deepest and most penetrating question anyone has posed about the project: "Who *was* David Hume anyway?"

What I owe to my wife, Miriam Laugesen, is not only inexpressible and incalculable but inconceivable (and unlike the character in *The Princess Bride*, I know what that means). In words, on these pages, a dedication is all I can repay her with. Fortunately, there is much more to life than words and pages—as one married to Miriam could never forget.

Los Angeles and New York
March 2012

Hume's Politics

Introduction

In the particular exertions of power, the question ought never to
be forgotten, *What is best?* But in the general distribution of power
among the several members of a constitution, there can seldom
be admitted any other question, than *What is established?* . . . If
any other rule than established practice be followed, factions and
dissentions must multiply without end.[1]

Many find David Hume's writings on politics agreeable. This book will argue
that they are also astonishingly useful. Hume's political ideas illuminate a
host of questions in political theory, political science, and practical politics
that would otherwise seem intractable, as well as calling into question some
political assumptions that would otherwise seem easy. And if Hume's ideas
are crucial to students of politics, distinctly political forms of analysis are
just as crucial to students of Hume. Aspects of Hume's work that might seem
either hard to understand or of questionable modern relevance when treated
with the methods of philosophy or history both fall into place and prove their
continuing importance when viewed through the lens of political theory.

Political theorists can find in Hume an innovative, unfamiliar way of understanding and addressing political disagreement. It is common to assume
that political order rests, or must rest, on a normative consensus, given that
our political, social, and economic interests would normally place us at odds.
What I shall call Hume's "liberalism of enlargement" suggests that the opposite
is the case. Moral factions divide the members or potential members of polities; political interests, suitably defined and creatively accommodated, unite
them. Conventions of authority need not rest on moral agreement. In fact,
their great attraction is that they can arise in the absence of such agreement
and persist, to the benefit of peace and good government, even as the social
and moral foundations of society shift radically. To the extent that Hume can
be labeled a "conservative" in matters of constitutional authority (and the label
should be disputed even there), this conservatism, if such it be, extends to no
other realm of life. In fact, stable constitutional authority not only is proof
against social and moral change but can even facilitate change. When social
change carries no deadly implications for basic political order, it is harder to

1

oppose such change by appealing to fears for personal security. Nor does the fact that political order is a very good thing imply for one instant that it is the only good thing. Hume valued England's distinctive mixed government precisely for its ability to unite authority with liberty. His modern admirers need not overstrain his theory in order to make room as well for equality and democracy, as things that not only are consistent with authority but make it more durable. Hume is often compared with Burke, and may in fact have much in common with the Burke who prized liberty and restraints on arbitrary power (whether traditional or revolutionary). But he in fact has fewer affinities with the cartoon Burke (drawn from a few unfortunate passages of his *Reflections on the Revolution in France*), the peddler of an aristocratic constitutionalism founded on chivalry and reverence for political myths, than with a more populist constitutional tradition that enjoys exploding rather than cultivating myths of origin and of ancient virtue, and that judges structures of constitutional authority according to their ability to check unduly powerful social actors and to be challenged in turn by emerging social forces.

Political scientists, whether students of domestic or comparative politics, can find in Hume's work a comprehensive account of political change, both from one regime to another and within regimes that stay formally the same while their effective governmental powers alter drastically. This account is grounded in a familiar set of ideas: what we now call coordination problems and their possible solutions. But it applies in situations in which familiar formal or mathematical treatments of those problems yield answers whose use is limited because those treatments abstract away from features of the real world that are crucially important (sometimes more important than what the models include). Formal models typically assume that the relevant actors are fixed and known; Hume treats situations in which they are uncertain, ever-changing, or the occasion of political controversy. Classic game theory assumes that the actors know how much they stand to gain from each outcome; Hume treats cases in which the gains from huge and durable changes in political structure are potentially vast but massively uncertain, making payoff matrices impossible to draw up.[2] Formal theory purposely leaves out proper names so that conclusions about human behavior can be stated in scientific or general form; Hume treats the ubiquitous real-world situation in which reaching peaceful and generally acceptable political outcomes requires precisely such proper names or context-specific signals (common traditions, precedents, and tacit agreement on customary solutions). Finally, game theory assumes that the agents' preferences are given and unchanging; Hume treats cases of long-term social change in which the question of how agents will in the future define their purposes and desires is a central object of the game, not external to it. Hume's political science shows that coordination explains even more of politics than first appears. But the kind of coordination theory that does the explaining only works by being open to historical and contextual approaches, not just formal ones. Moreover, the theory only works if it is willing to break down the barrier between ideas and interests that much contemporary political science—and from the other side, political theory—has made great efforts to erect.

Finally, students of Hume can learn that there are systematic lessons in Hume's *History of England*, a work that until recently everyone but historians ignored altogether, and that many Hume scholars still prefer to dip into selectively rather than take on as a whole. Coordination theory unlocks the structure and logic of this massive work and brings out its unifying themes: the development of social interests, the role of fundamental or constitutional conventions of authority in accommodating those interests; the way in which individual actions must be understood and evaluated in the context of those conventions; the role of parliaments in correcting (imperfectly and partially) the biases and corruptions of power to which any fundamental convention is subject. The *History* in particular provides substance and depth to treatments of coordination that in Hume's *Treatise* might seem too spare to satisfy—or too socially complacent, since in the *Treatise* Hume is trying to explain how his own institutions might have arisen, not how they might change.

Hume praised history for keeping us interested but not too interested. Unlike philosophy, whose "general abstract view" leaves us "cold and unmoved," history engages our passions, makes us care about our political and moral judgments rather than just nodding our assent. Unlike discussions of present politics or society, history remains distant enough (because the events it relates no longer affect us) to allow for cool judgment, relatively free of the partisanship and prejudice that "pervert [our] judgment" (E: SH, 567–8). The good news is that Hume succeeded in practicing what he preached. Hume's *History* contains a careful logic that belies its reputation for lacking a system: for being colorful, and perhaps important in historiographical context, but of little continuing theoretical value. But it also contains a humanity, dynamism, and engagement with the full variety of human interests that belies Hume's reputation for detachment. Its subject is life in full—and, above all, politics in full.

Hume as Political Theorist: Praised on the Shelf

David Hume was quite possibly the greatest philosopher of his time. In his own lifetime, he was more commonly known as the greatest historian. He had succeeded in becoming England's Tacitus; he narrated the sweep of events before his own time in ways that simultaneously judged past actions, engaged current readers, and imparted timeless lessons.[3] His first literary successes, and still the source of many non-experts' knowledge of his work, were his *Essays*, in which he applied to a genre characterized by randomness of voice and subject the rigor of the philosopher, the insight of the social scientist, and the discipline of a literary craftsman who never stopped revising. Very few would deny Hume's status as a philosopher, as a giant of British and European historiography, and as a transformative figure in English letters.

But very few read Hume seriously as a political theorist. In the United States, his work is rarely even included in the canon. In Commonwealth countries, it generally is included but rarely the occasion of advanced research; it is, implicitly, regarded as worthy but uninspiring.[4] There are many understandable reasons for this. First, and most crucially, Hume wrote no single treatise about politics that is easily slotted into a set curriculum (for reasons canvassed later, the third book of the *Treatise of Human Nature*, the obvious candidate, will not do).[5] Second, Hume is not attached to a useful summary idea, a compelling label for the doctrine or theory that he epitomizes and with which one might reckon: Hume was neither Theorist of the Social Contract, Patron of Absolutism, Ideologist of the State, Genealogist of Morals, Defender of Human Flourishing, nor Prophet of Revolution. The most prevalent labels are probably "skeptic"—long rejected by scholars as completely misleading when applied to Hume's social and political thought, which is empirical to the core[6]—or else "conservative," which is, in contemporary academe, even more fatal.[7] These two facts feed on each other. Since there is no work by Hume one should automatically read (or assign), there is no need to develop an opinion regarding his contribution; since he is not thought to have made any particular contribution, we need not worry about neglecting his work. Bertrand Russell's observation, by now not at all true in philosophy, is still largely true in political theory: "Rousseau was mad but influential, Hume was sane but had no followers."[8]

If political theory (which integrates philosophy, history, and political science) has no firm portrait of what Hume's political writings said and no clear sense of why we need them, its component disciplines are not nearly as helpless—but only add to the theorist's confusion, as they stress different works and divergent lessons. In Philosophy departments the *Treatise* remains, with few exceptions, the work treated as an authority on Hume's politics. But the *Treatise* on its own tells a compelling but narrow political story, about how familiar human institutions of property and authority could have arisen in quasi-evolutionary fashion without the need for divine guidance, natural law, or (to some extent) deliberate human agreement or planning.[9] This story was in Hume's time both radical and offensive—to Christians because it did without God, to Whigs because it did without social contracts, to Francis Hutcheson because it did without sentimental rhetoric—but is now routine. And it is a story that reduces society to jurisprudence, the genealogy of general and settled private and public laws—while leaving out *politics*, an account of why people might disagree and fight over such things, and what to do about that. As a result some studies of Hume's political and social thought portray it as an exercise in the history of jurisprudence.[10] But when it comes to jurisprudence, Hume's importance can only be of historical interest: the view that justice is a matter of social convention is, to put it mildly, no longer unique to Hume.[11]

In recent years a great many scholars have gone beyond the *Treatise*, rightly treating Hume's political essays and his *History of England* as containing his main insights into politics, as opposed to morality or law.[12] But this effort comes up against its own limitations: the work was started by historians of ideas and continues to reflect that frame. Hume is seen as providing an innovative ideological defense of the Establishment of his day in the face of inadequate alternatives. Whether one sees Hume as a "philosophical" or judicious composer of quarrels between Whig and Tory;[13] as a particularly clever contributor to the Court vs. Country debate (where Hume, to a first approximation, supported the Court position of strong national institutions, the Hanoverian settlement, the post-Glorious Revolution system of government, and a politics of interest, against the Country program of a politics based on the "independent" landowner and reliant on civic virtue);[14] or as a brilliant philosopher whose particular political judgments relied fatally on conservative ideological prejudices,[15] the resulting picture—intentionally or not—is the same. It is a picture, strongly based on the famous Allan Ramsay portrait showing Hume as very well dressed, very obese, and smiling, of a philosopher willing to question all principles except the principle that the foundations of his own society, which had done well by him, were not to be disturbed.[16] Contextualists' attempts to identify Hume's significance have too often served to teach his irrelevance. If Hume is significant for political history because he put to rest party quarrels now forgotten and cleverly justified institutions long abandoned, and significant for historiography because he exploded the party myths of his day and created a way of looking at English history that we now take for granted, Hume becomes a figure to be respected but forgotten, just as we respect in principle but forget in practice the inventors of vacuum tubes. As a proponent of the latter thesis puts it, Hume was the "author of his own neglect."[17] Hume's *History* is, writes another, a "tract for the times, . . . worthy to be examined briefly in histories of history"—a book useful for educating his contemporaries, not ours.[18]

A third, though smaller, school, has attempted to rehabilitate Hume as a political scientist by stressing his political and economic essays. It treats Hume as one of the founders of pure and applied social science, a harbinger of a practical and progressive approach to policy that rested itself on (what became) social science, rather than expecting political goods to arise out of customary principles, folk wisdom, civic virtue, or religious faith.[19] This view, though more accurate than the view that Hume recognized no standard other than custom and "common life," likewise bears the danger of making Hume into a mere stepping-stone. If policy analysis, economic history, and empirical political science are what we are looking for, nobody doubts that two and a half centuries of scholarship have produced better social science than what Hume discovered. Again, this account provides reasons to praise Hume, not to read him.

The political theorist vaguely aware of these traditions will take away the impression that Hume's contribution is dispensable. There is little reason to read a theorist who provided modern foundations for creaky institutions, composed party quarrels that no longer exist, or helped invent social and policy sciences that have long since passed him by. We may, it seems, safely judge by slight acquaintance and move on. Among political theorists, one can say of Hume what Hume said of Spenser, that he "maintains his place in the shelves among our English classics: But he is seldom seen on the table" (H 4.386).

This neglect is not only Hume's loss, but ours. This book aims to clarify Hume, and shine light on his contributions. But it also aims to help us better understand the political world. It is a study not only in what Hume says but in what political theory can do. A form of inquiry that integrates normative and empirical judgments can do full justice to the multiple ends that political actors pursue as well as the institutional solutions for taming clashes among those ends. And just as the limitations of a medium perfect the work of the artist, the need to make sense of the messy material of history renders the claims of philosophy and political analysis alike more acute, more powerful, and above all more cognizant of the ways in which politics is fundamentally about change.

Hume's Political Theory: Dynamic Coordination

Hume's great contribution to political thought is an account of *dynamic co-ordination*. That Hume was an early and profound student of coordination has in recent years been widely recognized. Hume understood, far ahead of his time, the ways in which the goods of human society stem largely from doing as others do, in certain limited but crucial matters, so that each person's purposes in all other matters will mutually further others' purposes instead of crossing them. In some of life and a great deal of politics, the right thing for each person to do is that which he or she has reason to think others will do: speak the same language, meet at the same rendezvous, use the same measurements, accept the same authority for choosing officers and making laws. Hobbes saw this with respect to one limited case (governmental authority) and gave one blunt and largely unworkable solution (unquestioning, universal, and permanent consent to sovereign power). Hume generalized Hobbes' limited insight to all of political and social life and saw that coordinated action in all these realms—including the power of the most absolute sovereign—rested not on command but on convention.

As said, many have portrayed coordination as Hume's central contribution. The case has been made in different disciplines by David Lewis (in the terms of philosophy of language), David Gauthier and Annette Baier (moral philosophy), David Miller (normative political theory)—and, most recently and with great force, by Russell Hardin in the name of positive political science.[20] All of these writers, however, largely focus on equilibrium cases that are relatively *static*. They explain how, on Hume's account, rules in a given sphere may have arisen, and can maintain themselves, merely through the fact that the people who live under them have a common interest in observing the same rules (with the *current* rules being a natural, often surprisingly strong, default). Explicit contracts or sovereign command, as many of these authors note, buttress or restate conventions but do not create them. For Hume, in fact, both promises and government authority are the results of convention, not their cause.

Politics and government, however, represent a special case. For one thing, their central concern is not the convention of property, which is supported by the artificial private "virtue" or maxim that Hume calls justice, but *authority*, whose supporting virtue is called allegiance (or sometimes obedience). And because politics is constituted by authority, disputes over the conventions that govern politics are inherently both ultimate and dynamic. Disagreements over the meaning of other conventions, or over proposals that they be changed or adapted to new circumstances, can often be settled by appeals to authority, which does not establish the lesser conventions but can adjudicate disputes concerning them (most explicitly, concerning property: EPM 3.2.33–4, SBN 196–7). Disputes regarding authority can appeal to no higher judge; they are settled not by "lawyers and philosophers" but by "the swords of the soldiery" (T 3.2.10.15, SBN 562). And this fact renders authority conventions not just crucial but unstable. Those who want reforms in conventions of property, or who want to switch (as Sweden did in 1967) from driving on the left to driving on the right, can accomplish substantial but peaceful change through government (and that alone). Those who want to change the *government* in fundamental ways must, it seems, wait for the kind of massive imbalances between politics and social or economic forces that will lead a great many people simultaneously to risk toppling an old equilibrium in the expectation of finding a new one.

The big questions of politics are thus fights over *dynamic conventions of authority*: what Hume called "the confusions incident to all great changes in government" (H 2.338). These are treated in Hume's *History* and nowhere else in his work. Without denying that the *History* is a massive work about all topics under the sun, "from the martial to the marital,"[21] this book will treat it as if it were a treatise on this one subject: how conventions of political authority arise, change, improve by various measures, and die. Hume's morals and jurisprudence may be all about consensus, about discovering and articulating the foundations for virtues, sentiments, and institutions whose substance may now be taken for granted. Hume's *History* is all about disagreement, misjudgment, misunderstanding, unnecessary enmities that thwart potential cooperation, and the struggle for power. What most interests Hume in the *History* are cases in which conventional solutions to coordination games are theoretically possible but not yet present: "[t]he convulsions of a civilized state usually compose the most instructive and most interesting part of its history" (H 2.338; 1.3). Thomas Schelling has said that economics is about equilibria, about what happens "after the dust has settled," and that disequilibrium is interesting only if one "is particularly interested in *how* dust settles."[22] (Jurisprudence, one might add, is much the same way.) But if seeing the world from the perspective of jurisprudence and economics entails focusing on equilibria, seeing the world *politically* entails seeing it as clouds of dust. Political scientists might prefer things clean but know that something usually stirs them up—partly because the payoffs to stirring them up can be so high. Politics is a story of incessant, usually deliberate, disturbances in common life. And to study politics is to study the disturbances.

Seen this way, the concerns of the philosophers, historians, and political scientists do not disappear but acquire a larger context and greater importance. For instance, in the field of political philosophy (as opposed to political theory), those who focus on that field's most central, classic question—that of political obligation—often read Hume (in vain) in search of a general theory of when one may rebel against the government.[23] A focus on coordination suggests different questions. In real life, almost nobody deliberately rejects "government" in the name of anarchy. The actual dispute over whether a given government properly exerts authority is not between anarchists and statists but between weak actors seeking shelter under government and warlords who like their chances under personal violence. And civil wars, i.e., disputes over *which* government properly exerts authority, are not clashes between those who "appeal to heaven" and those who stick by the police, but clashes among armed groups who all acknowledge the desirability of governmental authority but have different ideas about whom they take to *be* the government, and in virtue of what. Even our most obvious and customary categories of moral philosophy may, on a Humean view, be superstitions. In one sense, the Humean answer to the question of when we may rebel against the government is that the question is badly posed: we *are* the government. State authority is shorthand for citizens' propensity to acquiesce in decisions by designated officers. When the citizens lose that propensity, they don't need to take arms against the government; they have already imagined the government out of existence.[24]

Similarly, the reading of Hume as social science-wielding reformer may be limited to the extent that it assumes we can distinguish the "validity of political ideals" from "the wisdom of actually implementing them."[25] If we take seriously the idea that authority comes from convention, the fact that an attempt at abrupt change would cause "factions and dissentions"[26] is a fundamental and fatal flaw, not an incidental one, since policymaking authority itself presupposes the universal belief that one's authority will end such dissentions. Saying that a certain policy "would be best" if not for the fact that implementing it would discredit governmental authority and perhaps cause a civil war is like saying that it would be best for me to assert "Marshmallows dance she apodeictic under" if only that were proper English, or that it would be best for the official currency to change every hour if only that wouldn't cause economic chaos.[27]

What happens when we re-interpret historians' insight in coordination terms is perhaps the most surprising. Hume's "coalition of parties" solution to the dispute between Whig and Tory will turn out to be not a special and time-bound case but an example of Hume's general policy of "enlarging" disputes. Political peace and progress in general require that the actors discover, or be shown, unexpected ways in which partisans can gain more by concurring on institutional solutions to their dispute than by pressing their own side to extremes, and unexpected ways in which such solutions, based on coordination, may be possible when they seem elusive. Though Hume was concerned with the parties of his time, his method of reconciling them has lessons for all times.

Method

Every second spent discussing the methods of political theory is stolen from time that could be spent learning about politics. Fortunately, much of what we can learn from Hume's political theory does not depend on resolving our partisan disagreements on what political theory is or how to study it. If we start with "formal" analysis or seek explanations that appeal to the behavior of instrumentally rational individuals, we will end up with principled reasons for why politics depends on language, history, and tradition. Conversely, studying Hume's concepts and theoretical innovations in their historical context will yield two conclusions that seem to jump outside that framework. First, that Hume's own intention, what he saw himself as doing, was to seek progressive and scientific forms of truth. Second, that he had some hope of finding that kind of truth, because his object of study was not politics' (changing) substantive concerns but the permanent regularities in how political conventions, including language but not limited to that, arise and change.

While it is sometimes thought that coordination problems are best explored through game theory, one could argue—as coordination theory's modern inventor, Thomas Schelling, did argue—that doing so obscures the most fundamental aspect of those problems: *names matter*. Whether those facing a problem can agree on a solution will depend on what the game is being called, whether relevant solutions have familiar proper names, and so on—all matters inherently obscured by a discussion that posits players named A and B and rows called I and II. But if solving coordination problems requires traditions, symbols, a sense of "naturalness," visual or rhetorical prominence, or interpersonal intuition, game theory may be a counterproductive way of exploring coordination, not (as often assumed) the best or only way. In the most important real-world case in which more than one coordination solution or "equilibrium" is possible, game theory will lead us to ignore the solutions most likely to coordinate real-world actors, and to focus on the solutions (based on mathematical learning in a sterile laboratory) least likely to do so.[28] It is *rational* for instrumental and partial actors who stand to gain from doing as others do to study rhetoric, languages, traditions, laws, local pastimes, and good manners.[29] As noted in the next chapter, the special circumstances of very-long-term constitutional politics render the technical approaches of game theory even less likely to yield useful insights.

Conversely, a "Cambridge school" or contextual approach to Hume that stresses his attempts to shape the political debates of his time oddly yields, in this particular case, much the same lessons as an analytic approach. There are two reasons for this. One involves the substance of Hume's thought; the other, the fact that he thought it. On the first point: the Cambridge school characteristically makes timeless theoretical and methodological claims regarding political language, though its members differ on what political language is and what methods should be used to study it.[30] But while language may on some views (including the Wittgensteinian view that so influenced Quentin Skinner) be a unique realm of human consciousness and one not subject to comparison, another view, familiar since the work of David Lewis, sees it as an instance of a larger category: convention.[31] If that holds, no one who believes there is a proper philosophic or scientific method that enables permanent insights into political language (in the case of science, progressively better insights) can consistently deny that some such philosophic or scientific method might also illuminate other human conventions: promising, property, or authority.[32] But such insights are *precisely what Hume aims at*: perennial truths about the formal conditions for conventions' arising and changing, though the substantive content of those conventions be indeterminate, a matter of history more than logic. Because of what Hume thought politics was—convention all the way down, a matter of forms endowed with meaning and utility—his particular interpretation of what it means to study politics in an experimental or scientific manner does not contradict the Cambridge school, but merely generalizes it.[33]

An autobiographical accident—but not really an accident, as Hume intended a unique and radical program—points in the same direction. Historians' studies of Hume in context have tended to find that one of his central aims was to dispel partisan and superstitious explanations of human behavior in favor of a viewpoint that stressed individual interest, causal rather than teleological explanations, and the study of institutions that would manage interests toward public ends. The study of formal regularities in human passions and the institutions that might productively channel them would be, *Hume himself* hoped, sufficiently subject to general rules to be the proper objects of science. Thus, historians of ideas differ with analytic readers of Hume in what they think Hume was against, but largely agree regarding what he was for: the search for, and promulgation of, timeless truths of politics founded on self-interest, sympathy (with its good and bad effects), and institutional design.[34] If we stipulate for argument Skinner's dicta that "no agent can be said to have meant or achieved something which they could never be brought to accept as a correct description of what they had meant or achieved," and that no "acceptable account of an agent's behaviour" (including a political theorist's behavior when writing) can "survive the demonstration that it was dependent on the use of criteria of description and classification not available to the agent,"[35] reading Hume as a political scientist who aims at timeless truths is not untrue to Hume's own professed, contemporary self-image and intention but precisely *true* to it. Even those who doubt that timeless truths, even formal ones, can be found in politics should admit that Hume failed to share such doubts. Of course, the historian will differ from the political theorist in the conclusion drawn from this. The former may try to explain what led Hume to get everything wrong—though it is not clear from what timeless perspective it might be called wrong—while the latter can proceed to what he got right.

There remains the question of whether the current work intends to interpret Hume's thought or to reconstruct it. The answer is some of both. Hume's observations on dynamic coordination, I submit, add up to a coherent theory and quite a profound one. But Hume did not draft them *as* a coherent theory. They must be assembled into such from a larger narrative that Hume arranged chronologically, not systematically. Except where explicitly noted, I will not intentionally add anything to what Hume said, but making sense of this piece of Hume's work requires radical disregard for the order in which he said it. One may ask why, if Hume had a systematic account of dynamic coordination in him, he did not present it explicitly. One answer, a bit blunt but not therefore wrong, is that no thinker lives long enough to write every possible book that he or she might have written. Another, more satisfying but not necessarily more true, is that Hume was unable to put forth a systematic solution to coordination problems because the problem itself was only properly formulated two centuries after his death.[36] One could go further and say that the posing of the question required an intellectual atmosphere that Hume helped create. In order to ask the question how individuals coordinate on authority, one had to stop believing what most people in Hume's time very strongly believed: that political institutions resulted from some combination of a divinely ordained system of rank and order, a Providential history that looked toward the good of all human beings, and perfect ancient plans of liberty that corrupt contemporaries are in danger of losing through lack of virtue.

Here the fact that Hume wrote his *History* in reverse order, drafting the chronologically latest volumes first, may explain why some of the material most useful for reconstructing his theory of dynamic coordination comes from Hume's account of ancient and medieval England rather than the much more famous Stuart volumes.[37] Hume suggests that his own rejection of the ancient constitution hypothesis was gradual: each successive revision of his work expressed it more confidently.[38] Perhaps as Hume gained assurance that the prevalent myths of his own time were false, he also became ever more curious to provide an account of authority and its limits that might be true.

Hume's Two Sciences

Of the two possibilities just mentioned, Hume's political science is clearly most useful to those who take up the second: who actually believe in political science, in our ability to make generalizations about political actions and institutions that are supported by evidence and that become over time ever more helpful in providing explanations, predictions, or (in practical mode) evaluations or suggestions. Here we must distinguish between two different kinds of social or political science that Hume practiced and had a key role in founding. Hume made a much more permanent contribution to one than to the other.

The first kind of social science, which we may call science (1), became the *causal* social science we are accustomed to: large-scale, large-N, hostile to proper names, data-driven, progressive. Hume numbers politics, along with physics and chemistry, among the "sciences" that "treat of general facts . . . where the qualities, causes and effects of a whole species of objects are enquired into." On occasion he refers to historical events as "collections of experiments" that establish scientific principles, just as naturalists and chemists derive principles from experiments on plants and minerals.[39] In Hume's time a proto-social-scientific approach to history was called philosophical history. Whatever the rest of the *History* may have been doing, Hume's famous Appendices (and similar passages in the text, self-consciously labeled digressions), in which he abandons the chronological narrative and discourses on the state of economics, public administration, trade, arts, and manners, are often regarded as exemplifying this kind of history, a "macronarrative" of "systemic change."[40] How far we should regard this part of Hume's program as scientific in the modern sense is controversial.[41] In any case, we know what this kind of science came to look like, and it is clear that its further progress rendered Hume obsolete. In matters of constitutional design, economics, and the other social sciences, Hume laid the groundwork for those who would gather much more data than he had available and would take their ambitions for making law-like generalizations much further.

There is, however, another kind of social science that studies the choices of individuals, regarding larger social forces as the setting rather than the plot. Sociologists speak of structures that condition agency; political scientists, of institutions that determine actors' most rational strategy; economists, of constraints under which the agent exercises choice. The study of agency, strategy, or choice might be called science (2): a microscience of explaining—or, in normative or "strategic" mode, evaluating or recommending—human actions in a context when others are also free to act but all actors face certain limits.[42] No reader of Hume's *Treatise* can doubt that it was largely if not exclusively about *this* kind of science. It aimed to study human nature through isolating the various causes of "men's behaviour in company, in affairs, and in their pleasures," very much on the level of microbehavior rather than macronarratives (T Intro.10, SBN xix). (As Hume writes explicitly in an early essay, "a nation is nothing but a collection of individuals . . . ," and "the character of a nation" is shorthand for that of its individuals [E: NC, 198].) And certainly no reader of Hume's *History*—except one who reads the Appendices and skips the text, as used to be distressingly common—can doubt that Hume's latest works had this much in common with his earliest. The narrative, very far from being impersonal, uses every reconstructed "situation" or "circumstance" to praise, blame, excuse, understand, evaluate, or in the most general sense account for the actions of individuals.[43]

This is the kind of social science—or whatever one chooses to call it—noted by many of Hume's interpreters under different names. Some call Humean explanations "moral causal" (giving the "reasons an agent had for acting") rather than "covering-law" (Donald Livingston); others speak of Hume as providing "narrative-historical" explanations that portray us as "conscious beings with purposes . . ." (Nicholas Capaldi); still others see Hume as a historian in the traditions of Butterfield and Collingwood, who uses the formal uniformity of human motives not to derive quasi-Newtonian laws but to render apparently inexplicable actions intelligible and to articulate the dynamic circumstances within which they might make sense (S. K. Wertz).[44] On this view generalizations about large-scale causes, however valuable, cannot capture the logic of every circumstance. As Hume puts it, "What is most probable in human affairs is not always true; and a very minute circumstance, overlooked in our speculations, serves often to explain events, which may seem the most surprizing and unaccountable" (H 6.287).[45]

Capaldi, Peter Jones, and others have noted the similarities between Hume's method of understanding motives and correcting our over-hasty judgments of others' actions and the German interpretive or *Verstehen* school of history.[46] Indeed, the links between rational choice explanations in economics or political science and that kind of history are very strong. Weber of course linked the two explicitly. Instrumental rationality was to be posited in the "ideal type" not because agents always act rationally but because pursuing the hypothesis that they do act rationally forces us to distinguish cases in which they really do act irrationally—which will then drive the study of why they do so—from those in which actors merely seem irrational to us because we have failed to research their situation.[47]

Contemporary political scientists treat this nexus between interpretive history and rational choice theory more rarely, largely because methodologies in a specialized age serve not just intellectual but factional purposes.[48] Iain Hampsher-Monk and Andrew Hindmoor's recent article is an exception, and raises the interesting question of whether there is anything that rational choice techniques can do that excellent interpretive evidence cannot do. They note that if the point is to reconstruct the reasons for which agents did things, attributing preferences and strategies to them would seem less efficient and less credible than simply asking them what they were aiming at, or examining evidence (e.g., memoirs) regarding that. But they do cite three instances in which rational choice explanations will improve on *Verstehen*-type history: when there is reason to think that actors are either unaware of their motives or prone to lie about them; when results turn on unintended consequences of individual behavior; or when interpretive evidence is equivocal. (One might add Carl Friedrich's law of anticipated reaction, which does not require game theory but does call interpretive methods into question: people often do not articulate why they refrain from certain actions because they take for granted the fact that doing so would involve huge costs or sanctions.)[49] *All three* of these conditions obtain in Hume's *History*—and, to be frank, in the large-scale history of high politics generally. In the affairs of great powers, politicians lie, and lie more the more is at stake; historical irony and unintended consequences are arguably the great themes of Hume's *History* and his social theory generally; and in matters of history, interviews are of course impossible and reliable memoirs often unavailable—missing altogether for the ancient and medieval periods that make up a third of Hume's *History* and arguably the most instructive third.[50] Deception and self-deception, unintended consequences, and insufficient sources of reliable information as to motives are arguably the conditions of political life generally. But they certainly are the conditions of Hume's *History*, and explain why the most conscientious historian can benefit from theories of coordination and convention in the cases he treats.

If interpretive and rational choice approaches sometimes dovetail in practice, they would seem to diverge sharply in principle—but least so, I would argue, during circumstances of dynamic coordination. Social scientists generally think that agents' typical motives and the choices that flow from them, in particular their response to economic and social incentives, are predictable enough to yield, over time and given large numbers, general social laws. The interpretive historian, anthropologist, or literary critic denies this. The only time Hume takes up something like this question, he endorses the first view. Given that each decision we take in a complex society requires the action of others for its success, anyone aiming at (or interpreting) intentional action must assume that others' actions will be both explicable (science [2]) and prone to follow the same patterns as they did in the past (science [1]). The most fervent believers in free will and human spontaneity, Hume claims, de facto endorse "necessity" in this sense (EHU 8.1.17, SBN 89).

But when conventions are contested, in flux, or lacking altogether, the assumption that others' behavior is rational does not entail that the result will be predictable. Everyone, while trying to do the conventional thing, that is, what others do and expect one another to do, will be unsure of what that thing will be—precisely the conditions of a coordination game. In such circumstances, the scientific attempt to explain regularities collapses into the sociological or historical attempt to explain the origin of social norms, since a whole host of different outcomes are equally rational.[51] Even charisma fits perfectly into a rational choice explanation in these circumstances (and no others). The charismatic leader is followed as a source of safety, identity, or ritual behaviors when and only when conventions of law, national manners, and religion have broken down.[52] Charisma is so powerful precisely because life without conventions is so unpleasant; when we do not know what others around us will do, we can accomplish almost none of what we want.

In general, conventions represent a bridge between science (2) and science (1), between the kind of social explanation that explains "situations" and choices within them and the kind that tracks "trends."[53] If one seeks microfoundations, one can explain large-scale social forces in terms of them. It is in everyone's interest to observe a pattern of behavior that then becomes the context for others' decisions. In that sense, the pattern, especially a durable, constitutional pattern of laws recognized as authoritative, becomes a "cause" of later decisions (in the sense of a factor that determines the feasible set, though not the specific choice taken from it): "Effects will always correspond to causes; and wise regulations in any commonwealth are the most valuable legacy that can be left to future ages" (E: PRS, 24). If one wants to stress the primacy of social causes, one can emphasize that such causes determine the constraints that make most actions impossible and often inconceivable. "New situations produced new laws and institutions: and the great alterations in the finances and military power of the crown, as well as in private property, were the source of equal innovations in every part of the legislature or civil government" (H 2.101).[54] A causal science explains why the circumstances of political choices change. A science of rational choice, and/or the interpretive understanding of such choices, makes sense of what people do in the context of change—and makes sense of it in a way that collapses "rational" and "cultural" explanations into one another. For it will be in the interest of agents to observe cultural conventions where they exist and to manipulate or change them when they don't.

In different languages, many scholars have considered the interaction between individuals and conventions to be the central story of Hume's *History*.[55] They are right. J.G.A. Pocock may put it best, portraying Hume as updating the ancient Thucydidean or Tacitean practice of drawing from narrative history lessons of political strategy:

> [H]e is able to show the speech, thought and actions of his characters as performed under certain historical conditions, as produced by those conditions, and as failing to keep pace with change in those conditions; with the result that the *arcana imperii*, which explain or at least dramatise how it is that human actions produce undesired results, cease to be only the *arcana* of state, of fortune, of the passions of the heart, and become the *arcana* of historical change or continuity.[56]

In Hume, as Pocock sees him, a "history of social and cultural change," accomplished through "generalisations" and the formulation of rules (with due exceptions), takes place alongside a "narrative of actions . . . written with the aid of the maxims of reason of state, designed to explain the anomalies of human behaviour rather than subject them to covering laws and predictions."

Hume's history is written in a "double key"[57]—a key that blends two kinds of social science, whether one calls them that or not.

This book will focus overwhelmingly on the micro level of choice and situation, not the macro level of social, economic, and political causes, because only on the micro level does Hume still have much to teach us. When it comes to large-scale social science or social and economic history, Hume could not possibly be of more use than his successors. Quite aside from methodological innovations and new archival research, history itself allows for a range of data (what Hume called "experience") regarding society, economics, and politics unimaginably superior to what Hume could draw on.[58] Later accounts necessarily improved on Hume's. Even when they confirmed Hume's speculations, they had much better grounds for believing in them than Hume did.[59]

But Hume's account of micromotives, their contexts, and their collective (often unintended) effects was neither taken up nor developed. Though his account of large-scale social causes is stale, this is fresh. Hume's account of convention and coordination anticipated theories only articulated two hundred years later and not yet fully worked out: in Hardin's words, Hume's "strategic categories of moral and political problems are still advanced beyond almost anything else in moral and political theory."[60] In our age, the kind of history of ideas that explains political theory writings in terms of the writers' political intentions and the intellectual situations they faced was developed as an antidote to "perennial questions" approaches to political theory. But ironically, the kind of history that explains *political decisions* with reference to agents' intentions and the political situations they face is more likely than other kinds to yield permanent insights into recurrent predicaments— though perhaps not the insights that the student of political theory "in context" is used to. Though the substantive questions of politics change greatly over time, the *formal* study of how actors move from one equilibrium to another, or how they make other decisions while this is happening, never goes out of style, and we may make steady progress in our understanding of these processes. These are the "general truths . . . invariable by the humour or education either of subject or sovereign," that can be distilled (or as Hume says "reduced") from our study of politics (E: PRS, 18).

In turn, if the "perennial questions" kind of political theory is to be anything other than bad empirical history or political science (asserting questions to be perennial without any evidence that they are so), it may have to redefine those questions in formal terms. "Authority" will become a question of coordinating on ways of designating political officials and lawmaking authorities. "Liberty" will be restated in terms of strategies and institutions for limiting the power that accrues to those who hold power under conventions of authority. The ethics of revolution will become a matter of the advantages and hazards of shifting from one convention to another. The content of the conventions of authority, strategies of liberty, and maxims of revolution will then be largely empirical matters. They will be subject to change (possibly improvement) through reflection on experience rather than deduction from first principles. This work can partly be seen as a call for such transformation.

Only two things need be added. First, conventions are not separate things from actions and intentions; rather, they are a verbal shorthand for regularities in action caused by common interests. If enough people decide that a certain pattern of ownership counts as property, it at some point *becomes* property and those who try to challenge the pattern become thieves. If enough people decide to recognize a given form of government, it *becomes* "the government" and those who hold positions under it will be able to get people to do things without threatening physical harm each time. The interaction between agents and conventions is an interaction between individual actions and the past and present collective results of those actions—not between individual actions and something else. Second, Hume's *History* frustrates attempts to explain its methodology because it focuses on very odd historical moments in which conventions are *not* predictable, in which property, authority, and even religion face large, unstable changes. In these situations everyone would love to respond rationally (and boringly) to incentives—so as to live and prosper, rather than starving or going to prison—but is uncertain how to do that. The question of whether Hume considers human motives unique and "personal" or, on the contrary, caused and predictable has frustrated readers of the *History* for generations and will continue to frustrate them because the question is badly posed. In the cases of dynamic coordination that the *History* covers—and in no others—it is essentially impossible to tell the difference between observing a convention and flouting it.

Audience and Style

This book is not intended only for Hume specialists. It is a book about political order and its discontents, about political change and its risks. It claims that Hume's insights into these matters are superior to our own in crucial respects. In fact, it assumes that neither Hume's political theory nor anyone else's is worth reading except to the extent this is true. The questions raised here are both positive and normative—or better, normative in the sense of that word that straddles empirical and moral claims by recommending as good unexpected ways in which a multiplicity of agents can achieve their interests.[61] A work that is directed at such an audience and treats a book that few have read—or, alternatively, asks those who have read it to read it very differently—must be as accessible as possible and must make the fewest possible assumptions about what readers know or take for granted. For that reason, this work will inflict on both Hume experts and connoisseurs of coordination problems quick, introductory discussions of matters they already know well. With apologies, I can only advise that those who do not need these explanations skip them.

Beyond this, the goal of teasing out a coherent political theory story from a 1.3 million-word book of (mostly narrative) history requires quick treatments of matters that deserve long ones. I will skimp on long and repeated textual citations (or place them in notes); focus more on Hume's own views than on their importance as contributions to philosophical, political, or historical debates in his time or ours; assume in the absence of clear evidence to the contrary that Hume's views in one work provide clues to what he means in another; and focus on those parts of Hume's story that can be translated into more general and timeless claims about politics to the exclusion of those that cannot. The result will look analytic—though non-technical—rather than humanistic. The choice is driven by the project, not by general conviction. When it comes to other work on Hume, a more humanistic approach may be much more appropriate; I salute those who have used it, and I have used it myself.

Outline of the Book

Using dynamic coordination as a key to Hume's *History* allows one to unify many of the *History*'s disparate concerns in a remarkably coherent and logical story. Conversely, taking the *History* as a key canonical work about dynamic coordination allows one to address questions regarding coordination that are often treated in an ad hoc fashion across many different authors or even different literatures.

The first three chapters of the book will introduce the question of coordination, while treating its preconditions and implications in more depth than more formal approaches to the question tend to allow. Chapter 1 will provide a basic introduction to coordination questions for non-specialists, as well as exploring some implications of the coordination framework that even specialists may find of interest. Chapter 2 will take up a neglected precondition for coordination problems' existing in the first place: the actors involved must share a common interest in coordinating their actions that outweighs whatever interest they have (e.g., in the personal power they might have under anarchy) in not coordinating them. This condition is often taken for granted but is in the real world not trivial. The chapter will explore how Hume's approach to coordination avowedly requires seeking out innovative sources of common interest that might not at first appear. Chapter 3 will treat some neglected implications of viewing political power in terms of coordination. In particular, it will stress how essential (though difficult) it is, on a coordination view, to regard governmental authority and citizen allegiance not as two different things but as two different ways of viewing the same thing.

The next two chapters will discuss what one might call the main theme of Hume's *History*: fundamental or constitutive conventions, the broad norms of constitutional government that make lesser conventions possible. If a specifically political reading of Hume involves treating conventions of authority as in some sense prior to those of justice, a dynamic and historical reading of Hume's politics requires treating conventions of authority as something achieved rather than given, and taking seriously Hume's conviction that time is the crucial variable in establishing them. Chapter 4 will explore what I take to be the most crucial conventions in England as Hume portrays them: hereditary monarchy (with clear and unquestioned rules of succession) on the one hand, and Magna Charta[62] on the other. Chapter 5 will take up questions of political change—or viewed in normative language, political ethics—from the perspective of such conventions. The prospects for achieving such change peacefully and, loosely speaking, consensually will track the statesman's ability to manage or manipulate fundamental conventions when there is more than one competing view of what they rightly entail.

The last two substantive chapters will address the problem that real-world coordination problems are typically "impure" or "biased," such that any possible solution will benefit all participants to some degree but some much more than others. One can speak of two kinds of bias or inequality: vertical, in which those who hold positions of authority in some scheme can use their authority to reward their particular associates and dominate others, and horizontal, in which particular coordination solutions systematically advantage some social groups over others (either from the outset or else over time as society changes and governing conventions do not). Hume's political theory contains an explicit solution to vertical inequality and an inchoate but suggestive solution to the horizontal kind. Vertical inequality can be addressed by institutionalizing a challenge to the exercise of governing authority that does not question the necessary existence of that authority. Readers of Hume will recognize this as the question of authority and liberty, or prerogative and privilege. For Hume, the source of executive authority in England has been a hereditary monarch commanding the army, and the site of salutary challenges to that authority has been an ever-more confident parliament[63] wielding the power of supply. Hume's story of how England's parliament over time came to wield the supply power in opposition to tyranny, and in support of liberty, is explored in chapter 6. That chapter will claim that Hume's theory contains a justification for a neglected constitutional tradition that seeks to both strengthen government power so that it can enforce justice against vested interests, and check that power to prevent tyranny and self-dealing.

As for horizontal inequality, Hume said less about it (and, it must be admitted, cared less). That said, there is again a parliamentary story to be drawn from his slight suggestions: an ever-more inclusive system of representation provides an institutionalized mechanism for challenging and renegotiating the inequalities inherent in any scheme of authority. How in the famous phrase, "what touches all" might come to be decided by all, and how this might allay some of our concerns about coordination, is the subject of chapter 7. While acknowledging that Hume himself was no great egalitarian, that chapter will argue that Hume's scheme, which posits political representation rather than ideal deliberation as the mechanism by which new social claims can be accommodated, contains a potentially robust check on the tendency of authority structures to reproduce existing inequalities. The chapter will also break new ground, as far as I know, by conceptualizing the separation of powers as an attempt to achieve both the benefits of uncontested authority and a standing capability to mount popular challenges to the distributions of power that uncontested authority would otherwise have free reign to impose. Both the sixth and the seventh chapters, by stressing paths to liberty and equality that make no use of the neo-Kantian categories of autonomy, mutual justification, and practical reason, will also suggest how a Humean form of liberalism is both possible and arguably superior to the Kantian version that prevails among political theorists.

The conclusion will explore the larger implications of the Humean account of politics generally and authority in particular, and will explore the consequences for political theory of a set of Humean theses that cross the boundary between political theory and political science. First, it will continue the suggestion that Humean liberalism may be superior to the Kantian kind (as well as to less liberal alternatives, whether communitarian or multicultural). It is empirically superior as describing how human beings actually act, but also morally superior in attempting to further all human endeavors and projects, as opposed to arbitrarily elevating one—the desire for dignity or recognition—above all others. Second, Hume's conventional approach to virtue and authority has the crucial advantage of letting political theory and ethics change as political possibilities change. Increasing knowledge of politics should make us wiser in our political judgments. On the other hand, huge empirical variation in the circumstances political actors face will mean that no canned or a priori "ethics" that makes no reference to the strategic situation will be appropriate in all cases. Finally, what might be called Hume's ethics of charm—showing people what political institutions can do for their interests, rather than preaching that they should not expect political institutions to further their interests at all—can be seen as a way of engaging common energies so as to overwhelm concerns about foundations.

This work aspires to build bridges. It aims to engage deeply with history, doing due justice to the strangeness of the past, without abandoning the old-fashioned aim of drawing political lessons. It hopes not only to speak both to political theorists and to empirical political scientists, but to address both simultaneously. Above all, it adopts the practical perspective that used to be the common property of students of politics: it not only describes the things that Humean political theory shows to be possible but unabashedly welcomes the fact that they are possible. At its root, dynamic coordination is the science of making everyone's projects further, as much as possible, everyone else's—and of continuing to pull this off as those projects change. It can safely be neglected by those who do not care whether human beings become more likely over time to get more of what they most value out of life. Hume's *History* is for everyone else.

Chapter 1

Coordination and Convention

Edgar . . . like a true politician, concurred with the prevailing party.
—Hume, *History*, 1.99

Human beings have certain interests in common (we can for now ignore what they are). But since the social and political institutions that we have an interest in supporting are advantageous not individually but collectively, which institutions deserve our support depends on which institutions all other people believe, or can be brought to believe, deserve *their* support. Many great problems of high politics can thus be seen as problems of coordination. When the status quo or "social norm" solution is doubtful or contested, they become problems of authority, since only authority can adjudicate the norm. When the convention of authority itself is doubtful or contested, they are problems of coordinating on authority.

This chapter outlines briefly the problem of coordination and the solution to it—convention—that is most relevant in the context of large-scale politics and government. The goal is not to add to a huge literature on coordination and convention but to sketch for non-specialists what these concepts mean and why they matter, so as to explain why we should care about Hume's profound contribution to their study. Here I endorse Russell Hardin's claim that Hume has been neglected partly because he was so far ahead of his time: the problems he was addressing were not generally recognized as problems until two centuries later.[1] For that very reason, theorists schooled in the modern "canon" of great works in political theory but not in recent economics and positive political theory may not be familiar with coordination, or may assume (as indeed formal modelers often encourage us to assume) that coordination need only interest those who think that technical or mathematical models are the best method for treating all political questions.

Coordination theory, that is, divides political theorists into those who assume that no intelligent theorist can fail to know the literature on it and those who are very intelligent but have never seen the point of learning the first thing about it. This chapter will attempt to explain coordination in a way that will be clear and interesting to the second group: those inclined to doubt that mathematics can make sense of politics, or at least wonder whether whatever sense it might make is worth one paragraph of Montesquieu. Conversely, even specialists may benefit from (as well as perhaps disagreeing with) this chapter's suggestion that a qualitative, narrative account is likely to be more useful than formal models in understanding and explaining the kind of coordination relevant to the fundamentals of political authority. And they may also benefit from considering some unfamiliar political implications of coordination that Hume noted but we often forget. Though coordination problems are often seen as a subset of formal theory, the crucial contribution of Hume's political theory is to explain, and help solve, coordination problems on scales, and in situations, that the usual tools of formal theory do not address (as well as aspects of those problems, including normative ones, on which formal theory as such is deliberately silent). Though game theorists' contributions to coordination theory are of course indispensible, the contribution of Hume's *History* begins where those of most contemporary formal theory leave off.

The Problem of Coordination

The modern inventor of coordination theory was Thomas Schelling. I cannot improve on his classic examples. Here is the first one.

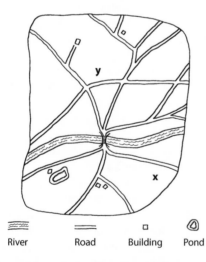

Figure 1. Map and following quotation by Thomas Schelling. Redrawn from *The Strategy of Conflict* by Thomas Schelling, Harvard University Press 1960, reprint 1980.pg. 54.

River   Road   Building   Pond

Two people parachute unexpectedly into the area shown, each with a map and knowing the other has one, but neither knowing where the other has dropped nor able to communicate directly. They must get together quickly to be rescued. Can they study their maps and 'coordinate' their behavior? Does the map suggest some particular meeting place so unambiguously that each will be confident that the other reads the same suggestion with confidence?

Among the students to whom Schelling posed the question, almost all chose the bridge. In my own more recent trials, almost all still do. The bridge jumps out for its prominence but even more for its uniqueness. A crossroads might be a natural meeting point, but the map has many of those and only one bridge.[2] Two more quick examples, among many that Schelling uses:[3]

> You are to meet somebody in New York City. You have not been instructed where to meet; you have no prior understanding with the person on where to meet; and you cannot communicate with each other. You are simply told that you will have to guess where to meet and that he [sic] is being told the same thing and that you will just have to try to make your guesses coincide.[4]

A majority of Schelling's initial sample, of students in Connecticut in 1960, chose to meet at the information booth in Grand Central Station. In a variant of the problem that asked people to guess a meeting time as well as a place, almost everyone settled, and still settles, on twelve noon. Another example:

> Write some positive number. If you all write the same number, you win.

Most in Schelling's sample, on reflection, picked the number one; the rest almost all picked powers of ten. One more example: In March 2010, I asked a group of prospective Public Policy students to name any living human being; each student would "win" if he or she picked the choice most popular with the rest. My prediction that almost everyone would pick Barack Obama was not difficult and not falsified.

The bridge on the map, Grand Central Station, Barack Obama, and the number 1 are examples of what Schelling called "focal points": each provides a "clue for coordinating behavior, some focal point for each person's expectation of what the other expects him to expect to be expected to do." While there have been many attempts to formalize focal points in game theory, Schelling resisted them on principled grounds. He argued that the payoffs one writes in a cell will matter for decision-making purposes only to the extent that they are prominent or salient. We might say, to put it differently, that "maximum payoff" or "Nash equilibrium" is no more or less a source of prominence than "highest building" or "only bridge"; that being the case, we might as well study prominence or salience directly. And discerning prominence or salience often involves intuition, guessing, or even whimsy more than logic and calculation. If this is game theory, it might be called game theory for romantics. In Schelling's words, "Poets may do better than logicians" and the game is "more like 'puns and anagrams' than like chess."[5]

While Schelling does not purport to justify or derive focal points, he does describe some qualities that tend to make something focal: uniqueness; the state of being the status quo or the status quo ante; the suggestion of a mediator; fact-finding (which fills a "vacuum of indeterminacy"); physical prominence; conventional priority ("heads or tails" gives a certain priority to heads); and analogy to a case recently brought to mind.[6] The status quo criterion threatens to collapse the coordination game altogether—we have no coordination problem if everyone carries on as usual—though Schelling brings up interesting examples of when there is a problem and "status quo" by some description solves it. The other criteria are crude in the sense of being somewhat desperate, the kind of thing we grasp at for want of a more rational or efficient standard for agreement. As Schelling puts it, we resort to focal points when we seek an "excuse" that will let us come together rather than a "reason" for doing so in a particular way.[7] Desperate people who (wrongly but not unreasonably) suppose things can get no worse than the lack of a monarch might pick an absolute monarch on the basis of height alone.[8]

Coordination problems have become the subject of a comprehensive literature and one which has further explored and specifies what the problem consists in. Robert Goodin's definition stands out in scope and clarity: "A 'coordination problem' is defined as existing whenever it is rational for *all* agents involved to prefer joint to independent decision-making." Such problems obtain when two things hold. The first is "mutual involvement" of actors (so that each actor's welfare is affected by others' decisions, giving each an incentive to coordinate his or her decision with the rest). The second is that "independent decision-making must involve risks of disagreeable outcomes for everyone involved." This condition is not trivial: "[s]ometimes [actors] gain from the confusion accompanying independent decision-making and would prefer to keep the independent decisional processes."[9] (In the next chapter we shall see how this looks: literally, medieval.) When no common interest in joint decision making exists, no coordination problem exists: a group might then be coerced into common action, but no agent will seek it spontaneously. One should add that when such interests exist but are not perceived, a coordination problem may objectively exist but will not be addressed, much less solved.

When coordination problems do exist and are known to the actors, their hallmark is this obvious and mutual interest in common decision. In so-called cooperation games (prisoner's dilemmas and their like; whether to pay one's taxes is the most accessible example), a selfish actor has an interest in doing something different from the others: i.e., my first choice is that others cooperate while I defect.[10] In coordination games, that is not the case. I have no interest in fooling everyone into driving on the right while I drive on the left, nor in persuading those around me to speak a language different from mine. On the contrary, the motto of coordination is (as Goodin points out)

"the more, the merrier" (corollary: "when in Rome, do as the Romans do")[11]—
also a theme of the next chapter.

Circumstances of Authority and Qualitative Coordination

Most literature on coordination is technical. It posits payoff matrices, de-
duces optimal strategies, and turns coordination problems into "games." For
current purposes, such precision is not just unnecessary but misleading.
The cases covered in this book, which involve solving political coordination
problems through long-term and large-scale conventions, violate the technical assumptions of the game theorists not slightly or incidentally but deeply
and essentially. Humean conventions are relevant, or most relevant, precisely
where the simplifying assumptions of game theory, fully justifiable in many
other circumstances, are deeply and essentially misleading.

Those who know a little bit about game theory typically think of it as involving agents who are choosing strategies as a means to achieving the largest
possible payoff expressed in points (or units of happiness or utility), given
that other players are trying to do the same. This picture involves two assumptions more stringent than strictly necessary: cardinal utility and instrumental rationality. Cardinal utility is fiercely controversial, for reasons too
complex to cover here, except in a longish note.[12] For now, I shall merely say
that it is of little relevance for current purposes. Hume himself never used a
cardinal terminology (which was arguably invented by Bentham, who also
coined the word "maximize"). When he spoke of utility it was in the sense of
something's being, broadly speaking, to everyone's advantage.[13] And on substance, the circumstances of high constitutional politics do not lend themselves to cardinal precision. While the distributional consequences of authority conventions are crucially important, they are best captured as debates over
political principles (as in chapter 7) rather than calculations over precisely
known expected outcomes.[14]

As for instrumental rationality, the assumption that agents' choices are
causally related to a future state that they prefer, both history and Hume's
History reveal that this assumption is sometimes violated, whenever agents'
motives are intrinsic, expressive, or categorical. (As mentioned earlier, the
ideal-typical assumption that agents are instrumentally rational is explicitly
intended by Weber—and implicitly practiced by Hume—as a method for fully
discerning and understanding the instances in which they are not.) Though
Hume for the most part hoped for the triumph of instrumental rationality,
he admitted that the mixture of religion with faction often brought about
"unaccountable" events in which "effects correspond less to their known
causes than is found in any other circumstance of government" (H 5.67;
compare 1.380, 3.206–7, 435–6; 4.18, 221; 5.342, 380, 493, 514; 6.3–4, 113, 120,
128–9). More rarely, fierce non-religious passions such as those for money,

sex, revenge, honor, and power cause the most strategic actors to act non-instrumentally as well (see, e.g., H 2.153, 371, 385, 390, 2.433, 449, 463ff., 2.489; 3.128, 227, 242, 261, 321, 462, 478; 5.509; 6.275, 287 [note m]). In fact "a man wholly interested is as rare as one entirely endowed with the opposite quality" (H 2.489),[15] though fortunately the strongest anti-instrumental passions tend to decay over time, whereas "the sense of interest maintains a permanent influence and authority" (H 2.411).

The most ecumenical definitions of game theory, however, those meant to appeal to those skeptical of its relevance, do not posit cardinality and instrumentality and speak merely of preferences over states of affairs. In Eerik Lagerspetz's formulation, game theory assumes only three components and two irreducible assumptions. The components are "(i) a specified set of n players; (ii) n sets of strategies, one for every player; (iii) n sets of rational preference orderings one for every player." The assumptions are *rationality* ("players make their choice according to their preference orderings") and *full information* (both the components [i–iii] and the rationality assumption are "common knowledge," that is, all the players know who the players are, what they want, and that they are rational; and each knows that others know, and that the others know that they know that others know, and so on).[16]

But even these specifications and assumptions—often eminently reasonable when the actors are buyers and sellers bargaining in a market—may be questioned when it comes to the fundamental issues of political order and authority central to Hume's *History*. Agents may have little idea who the relevant players are or what they might want, and in fact who the players turn out to be may be endogenous to the game's outcome. That is, which authority conventions each agent comes to live by will determine which other agents will be politically relevant in the future: the polity could expand or contract; foreigners might intervene or refugees leave, and the choices made in a game of authority could greatly affect, through the choice of political and social institutions, the number of players who are born, or survive, to play future rounds of the game.[17] And agents' preferences may not be stable over time or predictable to themselves. In fact one way political conventions might work, as noted in chapter 2, is by reshaping some actors' preferences so that future adherence to conventions becomes easier for them (or their descendants).[18] The advantages of conventions of authority take the form of peace, which puts out of business whole orders of society whose business is war; the partial privatization of religious belief, which undermines the claims to universal moral and political authority that all clerical factions once regarded as beyond question; and long-term economic growth, which is guaranteed to transform existing mores, outlooks, and aspirations beyond recognition, and to make possible achievements in art and science that cannot possibly be anticipated before they happen.[19] Under such circumstances, a model that posits determinate actors with fixed preferences over outcomes may remain technically possible but is unlikely to illuminate the historical dynamic. The founders of states are chasing dim visions—"commerce," "fraternity," the "general welfare," the "blessings of liberty"—not choosing (or even aiming at) well-specified outcomes. Their conservative opponents, however they flatter themselves to the contrary, are doing the same. They cannot know that an aristocrat or cleric or general in two centuries will look the same as he (more rarely, she) does now, or will aspire to achieve much the same things. In fact, the smart money would bet against it.

All that aside, Lagerspetz's (avowedly Humean) correction to game theory focuses more specifically on the last two assumptions, rationality and full information. Against rationality in the game-theoretical sense, Lagerspetz gives logical and epistemological reasons for doubting that people's preference orderings can be transparent to themselves, let alone to one another. (Lagerspetz's arguments are a priori, but of course the best reason for skepticism is empirical: in the real world it is very unlikely that I know everything about what you want from a situation, let alone that I know what you know about me.) Moreover, given that in coordination games there are almost always multiple "equilibria"—multiple points of common advantage in the sense that no single actor has an interest in departing from them once they are attained—rationality alone cannot reach a solution. We have an interest in reducing this ambiguity, but reason alone provides no mechanism for achieving this interest. Lagerspetz concludes that solving coordination problems requires departing from normal game theory in the direction Schelling suggested. He proposes instead a "Humean notion": "Uncertainty is an all-pervasive problem; it is custom, rather than reason, which provides a solution, but custom is not blind."[20] As mentioned in the introduction, would-be rational agents and those who sympathize with them therefore have excellent reasons for studying and understanding the historical and customary knowledge that real agents must use to solve their political problems.

Economic theory has outstanding reasons for regarding consumers as ciphers with preferences. In the market (to a first approximation), nobody cares about one's history, only one's effective demand. In politics, the reverse is almost always the case. We care deeply about who our fellow players are, and are so determined that they share a common history with us that we continually invent new national histories when migrations or cultural changes disrupt existing ones. The substance of peaceful politics being a matter of common opinions and habits, a "positive" political theory that ignores common opinions, common stories, and common habits, and studies only preference rankings, formal strategies, and payoffs, will miss not the details but the core of how political consensus arises, degenerates, and re-forms. This is true even if we posit that politics is driven by individuals' instrumental and partial interests (indeed, even if we make the very non-Humean assumptions that they pursue crude self-interest and that self-interest can be cashed out as wealth and/or power). The instrumental justification for respecting the past is that it provides a template for agreement in the future. Collective decision making under massive uncertainty only functions at all in the presence of common customs.[21]

For all these reasons, problems of political authority are less amenable to formal treatment than to Schelling's assumption of a "lumpy, discrete world that is better able to recognize qualitative than quantitative differences, that is embarrassed by the multiplicity of choices, and that forces both sides to accept some dictation from the elements themselves."[22] The cells of payoff matrices omit the very factors that in the real world are most likely to solve the problem: proper names; prominent sights, sounds, or places; prior knowledge of how particular difficulties have been overcome in the past that might serve as models or precedents for how we might reach a similar solution again.[23]

Thus, a well-known formal representation of coordination like "battle of the sexes," in which a husband and wife would both like to go on a date together but differ in their preference of where to go (opera or football game)[24] is not particularly relevant to the great questions of governmental or constitutional authority: who rightly holds governing power over whom, what procedures define the exercise of that authority, over what kinds of questions that authority holds sway, and what its limits are. And in general, the aspiration to mathematical precision requires that we treat only cases in which most of politics' biggest questions—who the players are, which political institutions they regard themselves as living under, which choices will be considered plausible or thinkable, how much (or at least in what order of preference) one stands to benefit from agreement or lose from non-agreement—have *already been solved*, and what remains is the relatively tractable question of how to distribute known benefits among several parties. That question is not trivial. Later chapters shall discuss Hume's political solution to it. (It involves legislative bargaining, and one should grant that formal theory captures many aspects of such bargaining extremely well.) But the fundamental questions of political authority are both more qualitative and more potentially vertiginous. They concern the few clues, guidelines, or common memories we can draw on to head in more or less the same direction when absolutely everything would otherwise be up for grabs.

Solving Coordination Problems: The Triumph of Convention

According to Michael Chwe, the literature on coordination problems—including his own work—proposes three basic ways of solving them: common knowledge, evolution, and focal points.[25] One might add leadership,[26] though this may be a verbal dispute, since leadership (as argued in a later chapter) may amount to either a crude focal point or a form of constitutional authorization, depending on whether the leader is self-styled and contested, or designated by institutional processes and generally recognized. Finally, Russell Hardin has explored in great detail the ways in which constitutions are sources of coordination. Constitutional government, roughly speaking, means falling in step behind—without necessarily endorsing in an ethical sense—a method of decision making and a procedure for choosing public officials, rather than the substance of a course of action.[27] Most recently, Hardin has argued that both formal and informal conventions are the central theme of Hume's thought, and that Hume's account of convention represents a systematic alternative to Hobbesian sovereignty (and the Rawlsian sense of justice) in explaining how social order may arise and persist.[28]

It must be stressed that fundamental conventions—which in politics are called *constitutional*, whether the constitution is written or bound together only by norms—are the *only* kind of solution to coordination problems that is likely to be durable across generations, agreed on across social groups and classes, impervious to short-term technological change, and likely to provide the level of certainty that enables long-term public and private planning and the prosperity that goes with them. The alternatives fare less well.

Focal points are likely to be both ad hoc and specific to subcultures. What seems obvious or salient to me may not be so to you; when it comes to focal points, a gain in speed and reliability is likely to involve a loss of generality (and vice versa). A later chapter will make this more concrete: when each of several claimants to a throne can claim some but not all of the characteristics that might make his or her rule a common rallying point, the result is not agreement but civil war. When focal points are the only source of political authority, the result not just in theory but in practice is a continued *state* of civil war; the death of one monarch results in subjects' having to cast about for another. A durable monarchy is one that is constitutionalized, with strongly conventional rules of succession. Finally, focal points are subject to manipulation: a clever cartographer who anticipated the condition of the parachutists in Schelling's example could make them meet at very inconvenient points, or those that benefited the cartographer, simply by drawing only one bridge on the map and leaving out many others. The parachutists would be forced by focal reasoning to choose the drawn bridge over better or closer ones.[29]

Leadership, once one inquires after its origin, tends to collapse either into focal points—the common cavalryman who, in the midst of a rout, grabs the standard and rallies his side by yelling "to me, to me"—or, if the leadership stems from constitutional rules, into convention. If the first, it is subject to the same problems just mentioned: multiple and conflicting attempts to play leader are as likely to multiply coordination problems as to prevent them. When it comes to coordination, partial coordination is often worse than none: it turns atomistic insecurity into pitched battle.

Common knowledge—my ability to act on a message because I know that others received the same message, and know that they know that they did, and I know that they know that I know, and so on—is an extremely effective and potentially durable coordination device in an age where means of mass communication exist and access to them is ubiquitous.[30] When (or where) this is not the case, however, the rituals involved must be face-to-face; the relevant knowledge will be common only on a local scale. Creating new common knowledge in such circumstances where it does not currently exist (and that dynamic problem is the one that interests us) in effect means submission to a charismatic leader or a mob; this fact lies at the core of Hume's argument for why we should fear, rather than welcoming, government by "common consent."[31] Premodern common knowledge might be called "natural common knowledge," and is a crude coordination solution. Reliance on it predictably led to conflict between those who had access to the common message and those who didn't. Modern common knowledge might be called "communicative": based on an intellectualized and abstract convention that can cover unforeseen circumstances, rather than on a form of coordination that requires common physical presence.[32] That kind of common knowledge (which again has the abstract character of a constitution, or at least an inchoate, practically effective sense of common allegiance and of the limits beyond which exercises of authority will not be obeyed) can usefully anchor a coordination solution on the level of a country, or even further. The kind of common knowledge that is limited to a crowd in visual range, or even earshot, cannot.

Finally, evolutionary solutions to coordination games, in addition to having rather grim implications in politics (cultures that fail to coordinate will be wiped out by those that succeed) are not durable in politics, as they often are in economics and natural history, given the ubiquity and success rates of deliberate attempts to disrupt them. As discussed in chapter 4, fundamental or constitutive conventions persist because of conscious and repeated acts of reasserting them in the face of such disruptions. Evolution alone, unless backed by purposive reinforcement, can work in economics or natural selection, but not in politics, because there the rewards that powerful agents can gain by purposely blowing up a convention are too great and too obvious.

Thus conventions, which in their formal and political form are called constitutional conventions, are the winner by default. This does not mean that they will always arise (there is no shortage of examples to the contrary), but does mean that when they do arise they are more durable than other solutions to coordination problems, larger in scale, and able to do things that other solutions cannot do. Hume himself does not present a negative account, like the preceding, of why conventions are the preferred way of solving coordination problems. But the fact that he considers no other way is itself significant. Conventions are the solutions that most palpably and fundamentally define our lives, and in particular our political lives.

The rest of this book is essentially about conventions of authority: their origins, their nature, and above all both the normative and empirical implications of how they change. Although it takes as crucial points of departure coordination theory in general, and Hardin's treatment of Hume in particular, its main concern is aspects of political conventions that positive or formal political theory does not typically address: change and disruption, accidental or deliberate; the intricate interplay between political forms and social interests; the role of language and formal names in shaping political outcomes, and the distinctive role of statesmanship (by whatever name). An inquiry that focuses on such things is typically called political theory, in its traditional sense, rather than formal theory. At the level of ultimate foundations or assumptions, formal theorists and Humean political theorists may be studying the same world and applying to it the same assumptions (especially if formal theorists are willing to use their analysis to illuminate normative questions, as there is no reason they should not as long as they make their purposes clear). But given their differences on what counts as a manageable question, a clear answer, an observable phenomenon, and a serious theory, the things that each group of scholars sees in the world tend to be very different.

Three Kinds of Convention

Hume discusses three kinds of conventions that are superficially and formally very similar, but very different in their consequences. While there is no space here for exhaustive analysis, a quick summary is crucial, especially since failure to distinguish among the three kinds leads to great confusion about what Hume is doing. In particular, differences among radical, moderate, and conservative readings of Hume (to multiply useful anachronisms) can be seen to arise from effacing the differences among these three sorts of convention. Hume is a dynamic moderate with respect to what I shall call ordinary conventions, an understated radical with respect to pseudo-conventions, and some sort of conservative with respect to fundamental conventions.

Most of the conventions that Hume discusses in the *Treatise*, and that are familiar to scholars, might be called "ordinary" conventions.[33] These ordinary conventions include property, promising, justice, allegiance to government, chastity (not virginity but approved sexual behavior), and good manners. On the basis of non-*Treatise* works one might add a few others, such as toleration and money.[34] Such conventions are rendered necessary by the limitations of human nature, especially partiality and short-sightedness. On these matters every society must not only cultivate and promulgate some form of the artificial virtues, except for allegiance to government, which is sometimes dispensable in simple societies with few goods to steal (more on this later).[35] These conventions solve coordination problems in the classic way: each of many might work adequately well, but they only work if all acquiesce in the same one (acquiesce, to use Russell Hardin's felicitous borrowing from Hume, not "choose": conventions arise over time and persist because they prove useful, and are almost never chosen in an explicit, collective, and conscious act).[36]

At this point interpreters differ not on what Hume says, but on what it means. A few things about Hume's ordinary conventions seem uncontroversial. First, all ordinary conventions are necessary—"laws of nature" in Hume's new and anti-providentialist sense—because they respond to problems of partiality and short-sightedness that are everywhere and always present in human nature, whatever else is present. Thus any convention is better than none. Second, such conventions are *indeterminate* in a double sense: they are *accidental* in origin, rooted in repeated custom and experience rather than a priori reason, and they are all *adequate* as solutions to the problems they address.[37] Third, while any convention is better than none, some might be better than others—more efficient in furthering the purposes for which they exist, or equally efficient but better in other ways. For instance, all legitimate governments provide basic security, but some more than others allow for personal liberty and promote commerce. Hume uses scientific and Enlightenment standards of observation and comparison in reaching these judgments. To the extent that he adopts a conservative fear of change, his reasons are only pragmatic or "precautionary," appealing to the actual anticipated costs of change rather than the metaphysical terrors of betraying one's ancestors.[38] Fourth, given the hazards of transition between one state and another, during which there will likely be a period in which some hold to the old convention, some to the new, and the benefits of uniform convention are endangered, it is often wise to stick with an imperfect convention than to try to change it. To put all this together: each of many conventions greatly benefits all who live under them in comparison to having none; any existing ordinary convention is therefore worth following in the usual case in which easy change is out of reach; conventions can still be judged in the abstract as better or worse than alternatives; these judgments may be used to guide action in the rare cases in which a transition to a new convention that is likely to command quick and overwhelming acquiescence is available.

"Conservative" and "liberal" readings of Hume differ not on these substantive points but on the weight applied to them and the circumstances one envisions. Those eager to stress Hume's liberalism focus on his explicit judgment that contemporary conventions regarding property and government are better than older ones, and that even better schemes can be imagined in the rare cases in which conventions may be established anew (e.g., in founding new societies or rebuilding an old one after a total dissolution).[39] Those eager to stress his conservatism focus on his portrayal of conventions as fragile as well as imperfect.[40]

Fundamental conventions are a different matter. These conventions are few, and consist of those ways of living together that provide such basic political and social goods that any challenge to them is likely to be both fruitless and immoral. To set oneself up against a fundamental convention is to propose, in effect, tearing one's existing society or polity up by the roots and beginning another—which typically involves, at the very least, fighting a generations-long war against those who quite liked the old plant.[41] When it comes to any convention, taking the kind of action that *would* be best if the convention were not present is usually pointless—since the whole point of conventions is that they are normative and self-enforcing such that people will act to re-store them to equilibrium if they are disturbed—and potentially very harm-ful. The actor who aims to overthrow or undermine an *ordinary* convention will succeed empirically only if she knows how hard this will be. She will be justified ethically only if she has reason to believe that she can successfully replace it with a new one (or has strong warrant for the proposition that none is needed, i.e., that it is what I am about to call a pseudo-convention). With respect to fundamental conventions, however, even vague plans to aim at possible alternatives can seem either eccentric or politically disloyal, because these conventions define the preconditions for political and social actions as a whole. (Think of a U.S. citizen who proposed establishing a monarchy.) As argued in a later chapter, such conventions only work if people think of the conventions' maintenance as a generations-long project from which no tem-porary departure can be legitimate. And given that people think of them that way, they are almost never worth trying to tear down, though we may gut the interior of the structure while keeping the walls standing.

It is with respect to *constitutional* conventions, and in particular those in-herited and adhered to by Queen Elizabeth, that Hume famously says:

> In the *particular exertions* of power, the question ought never to be for-gotten, *What is best?* But in the general distribution of power among the several members of a constitution, there can seldom be admitted any other question, than *What is established?*[42]

This is not a matter of valorizing ordinary conventions or of making political morality relative to "what is fixed at that moment in the culture" generally.[43] In the passage cited, Hume is referring very specifically to constitutional conventions: the word "constitution," not particularly frequent in the *History* (appearing about 200 times in 3,000 pages), occurs seven times in that para-graph alone.

As this discussion and the use of the word "fundamental" suggest, the most important kind of fundamental convention is *constitutional*.[44] By set-tling both peaceful procedures for choosing political officers and the legiti-mate bounds of political power, constitutional conventions protect us against the risks of civil war on the one hand and the excesses of arbitrary power on the other. Fundamental conventions serve ends that are so basic that secur-ing them is the prerequisite for furthering all other purposes. These funda-mental ends are few: peaceful and legitimate authority, as opposed to the law of the strongest, and personal security, as opposed to arbitrary power. Almost nothing could justify challenging these conventions, for two sepa-rate reasons. First, because their effects are largely formal, serving to limit power rather than defining it affirmatively. Thus there is little to be gained by changing their content: one can accomplish almost any end within their constraints, and very few new ends when they are gone.[45] Second, because attempts to make fundamental changes express the principle—are often explicitly *intended* to express the principle—that no political structure is, nor ought to be, immune from challenge by the current configuration of power. Once that principle is established, rebuilding the kind of barriers to momentary shifts in power that enable security in our personal and social projects will be all but impossible.

Yet a third kind of convention might be called *pseudo-convention*. Hume calls such conventions "local and temporary" or simply "prevailing." He applies these labels to variants of religious or theological belief in general, and Christianity in particular.[46] Hume similarly considers political factions durable but harmful: like weeds, they propagate for centuries, and tend to survive as long as the governments in whose soil they grow, but are as pernicious as law and government are salutary: "Factions subvert government, render laws impotent, and beget the fiercest animosities among men of the same nation, who ought to give mutual assistance and protection to each other" (E: PG, 55). Both religion and faction set people at odds with one another. Religion works on a perverse kind of sympathy that makes it unpleasant to be around others whose beliefs cross ours; faction gives partisans a perverse incentive to harm people attached to a contrary faction, since their own faction will praise them for doing so.[47]

The hallmark of pseudo-conventions is that they serve no real purpose, hence the name. (What I shall call in chapter 2 "negative" conventions may or may not be pseudo-conventions. Negative conventions prevent conventions that are more advantageous or operate on a larger scale, but may produce real advantages on a smaller or narrower scale.) Pseudo-conventions are subjectively serious. People are very attached to them, strongly resist change, and punish violators. But they are objectively unnecessary—or even harmful, as Hume thought of religion and faction and Gerry Mackie has noted with respect to the horrific but stable conventions of foot-binding and female genital mutilation.[48] That people hold fast to them, and feel more at home with those who hold to the same conventions they do, is undeniable. Writers must avoid offending them (as Hume, blackballed from a chair at Edinburgh for relative unbelief and insufficient zeal for Christian ethics, found to his peril) and politicians must carefully manage them. Even absolute princes often find that their power ends where religion begins (E: OG, 40). In particular, the transition from religious uniformity—an obvious solution to matters of religious convention—to religious toleration, a solution counterintuitive at first and obviously useful only once already established, is a tricky task and one perhaps never fully completed.[49]

But religion and faction, unlike language or constitutions, are not actually *worth* preserving on Hume's account. They do not actually further any useful human end (except in theory "to inculcate morality," which Hume with some ambiguity portrays as the clergy's only possibly useful function but one that modern Christianity, when institutionalized and factionalized, almost never fulfills[50]). Hume stresses that ordinary conventions are "obvious and absolutely necessary" to achieve crucial social ends. In this sense, "[t]ho' the rules of justice be *artificial*, they are not *arbitrary*" (T 3.2.1.19, SBN 484). He never says this about religion or faction. Faction is a special case for Hume since he is at a loss to suggest how a free government can prevent it. But religion exemplifies pseudo-convention in pure form.

Religious conventions, which make it difficult for agents to depart from common worship, are not necessary. In their modern, exclusive, and intolerant forms, they are not a universal human invention but a modern one and a step backward (E: PG, 62–3). While different religions have different effects—Catholicism and Anglicanism have an elective affinity with monarchy; Calvinist or dissenting "enthusiasm," with republics—and some are on balance less harmful than others, we could with little substantive loss easily switch from one local convention on these matters to another, or to none (E: SE, 73–9; PS, 506). Hume's usual preference in these matters is for the policy of Bishop Tunstal (which he spells "Tonstal") during the reigns of Henry VIII, Mary, and Elizabeth: switching conventions whenever political authority or other prevailing social powers require it. Annette Baier has noted that this required Tunstal to persecute people who had recently been his co-religionists.[51] The Humean reply would presumably have been that ordinary worshippers should have avoided this fate by matching Tunstal's flexibility and adapting their prayers to their princes.[52] And while rapid shifts in constitutional structure are, as a later chapter will argue, very dangerous because they weaken respect for constitutional structures generally and run the risk of legitimizing government by force or unstable accidents, rapid shifts in religion might be a good thing for exactly the same reason: they discredit religion generally. Thus, respect for religious convention is temporarily necessary but ultimately unstable. Such conventions, unlike constitutional and linguistic ones, are important only as long as most people think them important. Hume's ultimate hope, though he thought it unlikely for the next couple of centuries, was to have "the churches shut up, the clergy sent about their business."[53]

Those who see in Hume potential support for "reform, even of a radical kind," and in support of this view stress, as they commonly do, Hume's views on religion,[54] must recognize that Hume regards the risk of radical religious reform as (sometimes) worth running only because he doubts religion counts as a useful convention. Only pseudo-conventions can be treated so cavalierly. On the other hand, those who fear that a theory based on convention must be conservative on social and cultural matters should realize that much of what cultural conservatives want to treasure and reinforce may belong in *this* category of convention, not the others. One should often observe, or feign, proper behavior for as long as it remains proper, to get along with others. But there is nothing to be said against subtly or satirically undermining local or prevailing pseudo-conventions where possible. And once they have disappeared or dwindled in power, they will, by definition, not be missed.

Consequences of Convention

This work will focus, as political theory should, on politics rather than theory. It will aim primarily to improve our judgments regarding politics, not the theoretical language in which we choose to express them. But some of the implications for theory are also important, and deserve a brief mention.

Coordination and Power

Randall Calvert, author of a key work on leadership as a solution to coordination problems, has noted one implication of his theory: leadership authority does not come from social power, but the other way around.

> Because the leader produces group benefits that are degraded when leaders are overthrown or weakened, and because the realization of those benefits requires responsiveness on the part of followers, the leader does indeed have power. But as this model shows, power need not precede leadership at all. Leadership is based on the group's need for solution of social dilemmas; the focalization of the leader confers power.[55]

Calvert's insight is deep but must be generalized. Access to *any* of the ways of solving coordination problems, including focal points and common knowledge, confers power. This is the case whether the coordination involved has to do with communication or transportation. Rebel movements barricade the main highways for the same reason that they storm the main television stations: to prevent the counterrevolution from coordinating.

Access to the power that comes with leadership and its coordination role is arbitrary and fluid, a matter of assertion and counter-assertion, only in situations of rebellion and social anarchy. (Even then, it will not be truly random, but will track the rallying points that seem "natural," i.e., focal, in a particular place and time and among a particular group.) In times of stable, constitutional order, power may come from leadership, but the first claim to leadership comes from office: a governing role, and the legitimate path to claiming it, are *constitutionally* defined. (Hume notes that the members of parliament leading up to the English Civil War, "though an immense body, and possessed of the greater part of national property," would have been "naturally somewhat defenceless . . . because of their personal equality and their want of leaders" had Charles I not been stupid enough to prosecute some of his critics. His doing so "pointed out leaders" who would not otherwise have existed [H 5.216].) This prevents to a certain degree the rent-seeking behavior to which Calvert claims leaders have natural access. Leaders can easily exploit their followers if the latter have no alternative to their leadership except non-coordination (very costly) or putting forth a new leader (also costly, and uncertain of success—besides holding the potential to undermine the future gains from coordination by making the status of all leaders uncertain).[56] But constitutional government allows for challenges to leaders that do not incur these costs, for if one leader is toppled, there are guaranteed channels for producing another. Regular authority mitigates arbitrary power.[57]

No doubt an inchoate knowledge that this is true is one thing that makes established or constitutional authority so attractive—except to those who stand a greater chance of becoming leaders via political chaos than of being selected as leaders through constitutions. Where constitutional power tracks social hierarchies, especially ascriptive ones, the latter may be a very large class, and the actions of its members may be far from stupid in the short term. But since the fact that everyone knows this will, in the long run, discredit such hierarchical schemes, wise elites will plan a transition to more equitable ones.

Causes and Signals: When Decisions Become Constraints

Adam Przeworski, writing on democratic transition, has noted that the causes of big events are often better analyzed as signals. What he calls a "Schelling-like analysis" stresses that successful democratic revolutions require not just widespread discontent with the existing regime but a "coherent alternative . . . politically organized." In such situations, the accidental appearance or disappearance of rallying points—leaders who die, fall ill, or are assassinated, anniversaries of past demonstrations or the death of past opposition leaders, evidence of even momentary wavering in the regime's determination to enforce order by force—can be "causes" of large political changes even when the underlying social and economic conditions do not change.[58] In the terms used in this work, science (2), the study of individual-level explanations, takes over some of the functions of science (1), the study of large-scale social science laws.

The distinction between choice and constraints may collapse in such cases, or even reverse. In normal cases, certain options that an agent might desire will not even be in the choice set unless prior social and economic conditions obtain. But in situations of what might be called coordination monopoly, when an existing regime forecloses all alternative rallying points, "social causes," i.e., systematic changes in the conditions that give rise to social and economic grievances, will have no effect on the feasible political agenda unless the "micro" conditions that enable a collective choice of alternative coordination schemes are present. If they suddenly arise, regime change can be very swift, and can reveal in retrospect that the "right social conditions" for revolution were there all along without causing any change.

Cromwells and Constitutions

Regarding certain conventions as universally necessary will change the way we look at the possibilities of political and social change. If we want to overthrow an old convention, we must either be willing to live without a convention in spite of the costs of disagreement (think of conventions of property, or promising), or identify a form of coordination that will both replace the old conventions temporarily and enable a more permanent solution in the future. Again, our choices are limited. We can take direction from force; momentary prominence; common knowledge (whoever controls the TV stations); historical models and precedents, where these are still familiar and loved; or, most likely, charismatic leadership. Accurate evaluation of political alternatives will require comparing not an existing convention with the one we would like but an existing convention *with the alternative coordination point that alone can challenge it.* This is why Hume judged that when the mixed government of Great Britain yielded to another (as he thought it would), the least bad successor state would be a modern, law-governed monarchy even though "a popular government [might] be imagined more perfect than absolute monarchy, or even than our present constitution." For it was not a question of whether that government—one characterized by checks and balances—was imaginable but of whether it was *reachable*, and it was not. The Commons were such a powerful focal point for extra-constitutional as well as constitutional political action that the only alternative to a republic absolutely dominated by the Commons was one created by a charismatic dictator:

> If any single person acquire power enough to take our constitution to pieces, and put it up a-new, he is really an absolute monarch; and we have already had an instance of this kind, sufficient to convince us, that such a person will never resign his power, or establish any free government. Matters, therefore, must be trusted to their natural progress and operation; and the house of commons, according to its present constitution, must be the only legislature in such a popular government. The inconveniences attending such a situation of affairs, present themselves by thousands.[59]

All this explains why charismatic leaders, while not unknown in constitutional regimes, are universal among radical movements that oppose such regimes. The reason that rebels are more romantic than magistrates is that rebellions cannot act in concert without a charismatic leader—while governments can.[60] Leadership among rebels is therefore predictable rather than exceptional, a matter of the "situational charisma" whereby people in critical situations turn "as a source and means of salvation from distress" to whichever leader is at hand.[61] This is also why the romance of rebellion is short-lived: charismatic leadership can destroy a constitutional convention but cannot create one.[62] As discussed at the end of this book, however, the conclusion that all revolutions throw up Cromwells can be mitigated by something Hume could not foresee: the existence of mass media that spread knowledge of alternative conventions of authority and that in at least one specific case (Europe) make them common normative knowledge.

Political Scale versus Private Morality

The ethics of political action cannot be derived from the ethics of personal interactions. The reason is convention. In personal life, among friends and family, I have substantial control over the conventions under which I shall live. Occasionally, I can directly negotiate with my personal circle a new set of arrangements that departs from current standards in the direction of (what seems to us) greater fairness, equality, or efficiency, as with utopian communities or feminist marriage agreements that flouted sexist norms.[63] More commonly, I can and do choose friends who roughly share my values—the "homophily" that is universally found by sociologists and that alone makes their work possible (no homiphily, no "groups"). Or I can ostracize those who flout a norm that I live by and they mock. Such choices over private norms give me a strong feeling of control and responsibility when I practice them, a feeling often fulfilling enough to outweigh the feeling of rejection and exclusion that results from others' asserting, and moralizing, norms that *I* reject. While those outside my normative circle may far outnumber those inside it, the former's sentiments may be kept at a distance while the latter's reassure by their closeness. This is what makes private life so potentially rewarding: there, we can choose our preferred conventions, defining what counts as promising, sharing, sexual propriety, good manners, and if we like, religion, and can choose our friends according to which conventions they favor.

On the scale of society or politics, however, no individual controls or chooses his or her conventions. (That "we" choose them in common is, depending on what we mean, either irrelevant or false. While it is true that conventions are of human creation, no definable "we" got together to choose them, nor does any agent have reason to believe that what she does will bring about acceptance of the conventions she would favor.) This is, to anticipate, the devastating force of Hume's critique of social contract theory. The assumption that each consents to society's rules is false, since exit is normally possible only at appalling cost. The assumption that all choose a new constitution collectively, even under revolutionary conditions, is also false: coordination problems are severe, and most citizens must passively acquiesce in the choice reached by a few powerful actors, often the strongest. To plead "ideal" contracts misses the whole point, namely that all of politics consists of the conditions that violate the ideal. "It is in vain to say, that all governments are or should be, at first, founded on popular consent, as much as the necessity of human affairs will admit. This favours entirely my pretension. I maintain, that human affairs will never admit of this consent; seldom of the appearance of it" (E: OC, 465–87; quotation at 473).

Social science can derive from this a doctrine of indeterminacy. I cannot know what is "rational" in pursuit of my ends unless I have reason to expect a certain predictability in what others will do. (Such predictability often requires norms that will limit my own choice of actions.) As Hardin puts it,

I choose, in a sense, a strategy, not an outcome. Then I get an outcome
that is the result of the strategy choices of others in interaction with my
choice.

... We have reasons for taking our actions, but our reasons may not
finally be reflected in the results of our actions even if hope for specific
results is our reason for our choice of actions.[64]

On the level of ethics, the implication is that ordinary political actors cannot
normally control the outcome of a political action thoroughly enough to be
held responsible for it; nor can a refusal of such responsibility normally be
faulted. The fact that "going along with [a] bad cooperative scheme" is a bad
idea, often a moral failing, in a marriage does not in any way imply that individuals bear a similar responsibility for the results of collective decisions in
a polity.[65] As Jeremy Waldron has put it, "social problems and opportunities
confront us in our millions, not in the twos and threes that moral philosophers are comfortable with."[66] Our lesser sense of collective responsibility in
the polity-wide case is justified. It results not from a culpable egoism or lack
of virtue but from the ability to recognize the truth about large-scale collective action. Failure to question the conventions of private life often reflects a
failure to consider and evaluate the available choices and to take responsibility for the status quo as something chosen. (This failure can be called "false
consciousness" or "bad faith.") Failure to question those of public life, which
are fundamental or something close to it, reflects the knowledge that on that
scale, an individual on his or her own does not and cannot choose outcomes
at all.

But the loss of "control" and "responsibility" that large-scale political conventions entail cuts both ways. I cannot change our conventions of authority
for precisely the same reason that the powerful cannot flout them. In both cases,
conventions—at least in the short term and the typical case—frustrate an
agent's desire to exert substantial control over social outcomes. One should
not assume that conventions always serve the powerful. They embody authority rather than power, and potentially against power: they enable those
who are willing to accept a convention to repel attempts by the powerful to
dictate their own chosen terms of association.

When Hume describes, and largely endorses, people's attachment to their
"ancient government" (in "Of The First Principles of Government," one of
Hume's most disconcerting essays, which grounds all government in opinion
alone) he is making a different point from what first appears.

Right is of two kinds, right to POWER and right to PROPERTY. What
prevalence opinion of the first kind has over mankind, may easily be
understood, by observing the attachment which all nations have to
their ancient government, and even to those names, which have had
the sanction of antiquity. Antiquity always begets the opinion of right;
and whatever disadvantageous sentiments we may entertain of man-

kind, they are always found to be prodigal both of blood and treasure in the maintenance of *public justice*. . . . When men act in a faction, they are apt, without shame or remorse, to neglect all the ties of honour and morality, in order to serve their party; and yet, when a faction is formed upon a point of right or principle, there is no occasion, where men discover a greater obstinacy, and a more determined sense of justice and equity. The same *social disposition of mankind* is the cause of these contradictory appearances. (E: FPG, 33; emphases added)

Political conventions represent a social alchemy whereby the "social disposition of mankind," so often a source of partiality and strife, is harnessed in the service of "public justice." This operates not just as an ideal but as a norm that actually governs, actually enlists the unthinking aid of people who might, if reflecting on their own interests, leave power unchallenged. The transition from private advantage to public justice, from power to authority, requires such conventions.

The goal of reforming conventions to make them more equal. The use of power, within limits, in the service of that goal, may be laudable. But distrust of political conventions as such implies "empowerment" of those who have greater power—at the cost of the equality and security that only conventions that stand apart from present power can provide.

Conclusion

Coordination problems are simple in concept but complex and paradoxical in practice. Their solutions tend to be both self-fulfilling (they work if people think they work) and unstable (they stop working if people stop thinking they will work). The need to solve them gives us an interest in thinking about common reference points rather than obsessing about our own ideal outcome, and to prefer intuition to reasoning from first principles (because reason in a larger sense teaches that intuitions help us coordinate). Some solutions to coordination problems give phenomenal power to self-appointed leaders; others—especially conventions of authority—are among the only known mechanisms for defanging such leaders and thwarting their attempts to gain power. Finally, though problems of coordination are often and persistently confused with problems of cooperation (often even by experts who ought to be the ones drawing technical distinctions), in principle the two are completely distinct and in a rough sense even opposites. Coordination problems exist when all actors have an interest in doing the same thing amidst uncertainty or disagreement over what that will be. Cooperation problems exist when no individual actor has an interest in contributing to a common effort even though everyone knows what that effort would have to consist in. Cooperation problems by whatever name and with whatever variation in form—prisoner's dilemmas, public good contribution games—are often considered synonymous with "collective action" problems generally. They are not. Coordination problems represent a case in which parties who may have no acute conflicts of interest still face acute difficulties in acting together.

The politics of coordination is not automatically more equal, just, or friendly than the politics of cooperation. Again and again, Hume stresses that getting coordination solutions started requires determined action— often even tyranny or force—in the face of opposition; that powerful actors often have, at least at the start, short-term interests in sacrificing coordination for the sake of anarchic power; that disagreement over which coordination solution is appropriate occasions substantial strife to the point of civil war. But coordination problems do allow for a kind of progress that cooperation problems lack. Once we have a convention in place—driving on the right or left, taking turns in conversation, living under a constitution that defines procedures for gaining office and for limiting government's legitimate power, participating in a system of property and exchange with fixed laws of contract, using dollars or euros or the English language, agreeing to disagree over religion rather than using force to determine who among us will get to call the others heretics—we need not invent it again. A certain class of problems has been adequately solved. One reason why cooperation problems receive so much attention is that so many large coordination problems—those involving ultimate authority, the basics of market exchange, communication, toleration, even transportation and the sharing of space—*have* been solved provisionally (until the next constitutional crisis, which may never come or may come much sooner than expected). One of Hume's aims, and a central aspect of his continued relevance, is to help us to understand that they are still latent or potential problems. The solutions we take for granted are stable under perturbations only if we still accept and (in the rare cases in which they are challenged or endangered) appreciate them.

On a Humean view, the most important political questions do not involve "who gets what, when, how."[67] Disputes over the distribution of social goods and tasks, however important—and Hume implies solutions to those too— are in one sense the easy part of politics. For us to argue over distribution, taxation, or the enforced assessment of burdens, we must first agree on who "we" are; we must have a surplus over subsistence; we must know in common what counts as money; we must accept a common authority (whose proper functions, limits, and obligations can then be argued out). Before it can even think about becoming a fair scheme of social cooperation, society must acquiesce in conventions that establish several complex, difficult schemes of social coordination.

Chapter 2

Coordinating Interests

The Liberalism of Enlargement

But government extends farther its beneficial influence; and not contented to protect men in those conventions they make for their mutual interest, it often obliges them to make such conventions, and forces them to seek their own advantage, by a concurrence in some common end or purpose.

—Hume, T 3.2.7.8, SBN 538

[W]hen men's industry encreases, and their views enlarge, it is found, that the most remote parts of the state can assist each other as well as the more contiguous, and that this intercourse of good offices may be carried on to the greatest extent and intricacy.

—Hume, E: I, 299–300

My Notion is, that the uncultivated Nations are not only inferior to civiliz'd in Government, civil, military, and ecclesiastical; but also in Morals.

—Hume, NL 198 [1773]

Before turning to Hume's theory of how political coordination problems are solved—through conventions of authority—we must turn to his account of how these problems come to be politically relevant and practically soluble in the first place. My claim is that Hume's history of conventions of authority also contains a prehistory. Before constitutions can get going, actors who at first recognize no common interests with their perceived inferiors, and no reason to abandon local fiefdoms that let them flaunt their power, must be brought to prefer the advantages of peace, prosperity, and an expanded scope for potential projects and achievements to the squalid but independent authority they enjoyed in their castles and cathedrals. Analytically, the matter is simple: the relevant actors must restructure their preferences (one reason why classic game theory, which assumes fixed preferences or at least fixed preference orderings, is of limited use describing the process). Historically, the process involved great bloodshed, multiple reversals, and lots of politics: a mix of strategy, seduction, rhetoric, and above all a "great mixture of accident, which commonly concurs with a small ingredient of wisdom and foresight, in erecting the complicated fabric of the most perfect government" (H 2.525).

In order to cement their nascent authority, clever political actors—above all, monarchs—had to be alert to opportunities for forging common interests among as many other actors as possible (as long as the new alliance might include these political entrepreneurs themselves, which is not always easy to foresee). In order for us to understand this prehistory, we must retrospectively be alert to such opportunities: must understand what it took for authority to be seen as a coordination problem and how amazing that outcome sometimes was. Both standpoints, the prospective one of the agent and the retrospective one of the scholar, require what Hume called an "enlarged" point of view, which we may summarize as one that seeks out potential gains from coordination and ways of solving coordination problems when neither is necessarily obvious. Much of Hume's political theory addresses the complex, chicken-and-egg quality of this point of view. It thrives in whole societies, among social conditions that make the gains from coordinating with others obvious, but in order to establish such conditions, a few must have enlarged views before others. For salutary schemes of coordination to triumph over a stubborn and excessive attachment to individual or small-group decision making, certain barriers to instrumental reasoning must fall or be overcome. And coordination schemes must be imagined and set up that can accommodate, and when possible further, the greatest possible variety of human purposes, so as to maximize the gains of joint decision and minimize the costs of lost independence. The enlarged projects and conventions that seem to Hume such a mark of modernity are also a mark of a certain kind of liberalism: one that embraces the diversity of human aspirations and seeks ways to promote as many as possible.

Preconditions of Coordination: Negative Conventions and Enlarged Responses

The previous chapter cited Goodin's definition of coordination problems as existing "whenever it is rational for *all* agents involved to prefer joint to independent decision-making." A political treatment of coordination requires an extra proviso: agents' interest in joint decision making must not only be rational but effective. If enough politically relevant actors persistently fail to act instrumentally or to recognize their strategic interests, coordination problems will be theoretically or "objectively" present but will lack practical relevance.

These conditions are not trivial. They obtain only in certain political conditions and suggest a daunting set of political tasks. The politically relevant agents must be prone to act rationally. They must not be in states of frenzy or mass hysteria that distract them from their interests, and must not be subject to psychological pressures to believe false things about the world to their detriment. Beyond this, the gains of coordination must palpably outweigh its costs. This means that the gains must be as the kind that relevant agents can identify and approve of; and they must be quite substantial given the inevitable frustrations (instrumental and intrinsic) of forswearing independent action. The first condition entails the absence of obstacles that I shall call "negative conventions": durable human associations that make coordination schemes on a wider scale than the association seem either impossible or actively undesirable. (As already stressed, negative conventions are not the same as what the last chapter called pseudo-conventions. A religious convention, for instance, may in theory serve no necessary human purpose, but for that very reason its effect on larger political allegiances can run the range from catastrophic to negligible, and in specific cases can even be salutary. Allegiance to small political units, on the other hand, is typically palpably and strongly beneficial on that scale but a substantial impediment to forging larger allegiances;[1] religion becomes a negative convention to the extent that it plays *that* role, one of undermining larger authority conventions.) The second condition brings up Hume's account of how modern society is in effect a maximum winning coalition. Once modern conventions have been established, all kinds of people have (sometimes unexpectedly) a huge stake in them as widening their scope of achievement and activity without limiting more than necessary their freedom of action.

Negative Conventions: The Problem of Koinophobia

If political conventions rest on strategic behavior by individuals, they will fail to take root if political actors fail to act strategically, or else systematically act on subjective group identities to the detriment of their interests as individuals.[2] In Hume's view, various passions, like revenge, do one of these things episodically.[3] Religion and faction do so systematically.

RELIGION

Sometimes Hume claims that religious motives, especially under conditions of acute and collective religious frenzy, represent an "unaccountable" force that determines behavior in ways that largely efface any link between effects and their usual causes.[4] But perhaps because he thinks that acute religious passion is fleeting (H 5.572, note AA), and perhaps because he thinks milder and more intermittent forms are, unfortunately, so durable, Hume does not dwell systematically on how religion might frustrate instrumentally rational politics in his own time. Doing so, after all, might suggest a counsel of complacency in a completely and durably secular age, and despair in all other cases. Instead, and more practically, Hume traces several specific and distinct mechanisms through which religion might undermine salutary conventions, and suggests antidotes.

Hume certainly thinks that many religious actions are strategic. Like many of his time and place he portrays the medieval Catholic Church as often caring more about its temporal interests in power and wealth than about saving souls.[5] Even the perverse and immoral effects Hume attributes to most religions of his time might be instrumental in a deeper sense: religious people define their duty in terms of ceremony rather than moral duty because the former reliably signals a distinction between them and unbelievers as the latter does not.[6] Still, whatever the merits of this perversely "instrumentalist" psychopathology (Hume, as often noted, tries on early versions of arguments later pursued by Nietzsche), the results are anti-instrumental in a larger sense. The logic of Hume's argument (which in contemporary social science terms involves signaling) leads people to value actions that bless them in their own eyes, and in the eyes of others who through interest or belief will endorse the idea of such blessings, over actions that embody true virtue by generally promoting something agreeable or useful to oneself or others. Hume's claim is famously that "monkish" virtues are not just irrational but counter-rational. Those attached to such virtues value an act *more* highly to the extent that what they do for God or a Church is painful, harmful, or ugly.[7] This leads to errors of both omission and commission. People neglect their actual moral duties for the sake of pursuing prayer and self-mortification. But they are also widely excused from violating their duties if they say a great many prayers, give privileges to a church, or endow a monastery.[8] (The Crusades were the ultimate example of this: "The greatest criminals were forward in a service, which they regarded as a propitiation for all crimes" [H 1.238].) In fact, the higher the palpable costs of an action done in the name of religion, the more it may be prized. In the Saxon era in particular,

> Monastic observances were esteemed more meritorious than the active virtues: The knowledge of natural causes was neglected from the universal belief of miraculous interpositions and judgments: Bounty to the church atoned for every violence against society: And the remorses for cruelty, murder, treachery, assassination, and the more robust vices, were appeased, not by amendment of life, but by pennances, servility to the monks, and an abject and illiberal devotion. (H 1.51)

Ceremonial and hierarchical religions like the Catholic or high Anglican, what Hume calls superstition, teach these anti-instrumentalist virtues directly, systematically, and on the individual level (since collective moral endeavors are supposed to be the province of the hierarchy). Fervent religion in the Protestant or Jansenist style, which Hume calls "enthusiasm," undercuts convention more indirectly through undermining collective action. Enthusiasm encourages a perverse individualism. The enthusiast is confident that God favors those who follow personalized moral intuitions—which the individual knows to be godly because they're *not* widely shared—over those who respect social norms. Enthusiasm "inspire[s] the deluded fanatic with the opinion of divine illuminations, and with a contempt for the common rules of reason, morality, and prudence." And if mere "enthusiasm" leads mostly to immoderate anticlericalism, the "fanaticism" of more thoroughly antinomian movements (like the Independent strain in English Civil War-era Protestantism, first led and then tamed by Cromwell) leads the believer, "indulging the fervors of zeal, and guided by the illapses of the spirit," to "resig[n] himself to an inward and superior direction . . . consecrated, in a manner, by an immediate intercourse and communication with heaven" (E: SE, 77; H 5.442).[9]

Such attitudes, Hume admits, were accidentally useful in the period leading up to the English Civil War. Irrational belief that God took their side led the opponents of Charles to brave dangers that in the event led to a more perfect constitution (H 5.556-9, note "J," and passim). But in theory and in general, a distrust of conventions, which might be called koinophobia, prevents coordination problems from being acknowledged, let alone addressed.[10] In fact, koinophobia threatens to explode existing conventions in favor of reliance on an inner light.

In a more superstitious variant of koinophobia, hierarchical but nonestablished churches are tempted to engage in "usurpations" whereby the pseudo-convention of piety and religious deference is held to override, or invalidate, earthly laws, customs, and treaties (see, e.g., H 1.265, 282, 321, 430; H 2.111, 144). Provided that they act in the name of otherworldly loyalties, those who cause systematic harm by undermining conventions of authority in this way are even likely to win praise and names like "saint." Regarding Thomas à Becket, whom he regards as a usurper for the ages, Hume bitterly calls it

> a mortifying reflection to those who are actuated by the love of fame, so justly denominated the last infirmity of noble minds, that the wisest legislator and most exalted genius, that ever reformed or enlightened the world, can never expect such tributes of praise, as are lavished on the memory of pretended saints, whose whole conduct was probably, to the last degree, odious or contemptible, and whose industry was entirely directed to the pursuit of objects pernicious to mankind. It is only a conqueror, a personage no less intitled to our hatred, who can pretend to the attainment of equal renown and glory. (H 1.337)[11]

FACTION

Hume's philosophical works treat religion much more extensively than faction and portray it as a more systematic threat to moral and social life as a whole. In the *Essays* and *History*, which are as centrally concerned with politics and policy as the *Treatise* is with jurisprudence and the *Dialogues* with theology, faction comes to play a much larger role. It is because of faction that political actors are even less noble than economic ones. Far from pursuing self-interest in ways that potentially benefit everyone, political actors devoted to factions pursue harm toward their political enemies in a mode that is inevitably zero-sum (at best).

When treating human life as a whole, Hume writes extensively and derisively against systems that would reduce all benevolent and public-spirited affections to self-love (see especially EPM.App.2, SBN 295ff.). But the thesis that "every man must be supposed a knave," i.e., *worse* than self-interested, actively prone to harm others and traduce moral norms, was (Hume thought) though "false in fact," "true in politics." This was precisely the fault of faction. The check of honor, so important to moral behavior, is under factional conditions not just removed but reversed in direction. Shameful acts are applauded by all who matter—that is, one's own party—if the harm they cause accrues to the factional enemy (E: IP, 42–3, emphases removed).[12] "It is no wonder that faction is so productive of vices of all kinds: For, besides that it inflames all the passions, it tends much to remove those great restraints, honour and shame; when men find, that no iniquity can lose them the applause of their own party, and no innocence secure them against the calumnies of the opposite" (H 6.438; compare H 3.228).

One might say that faction keeps conventions from being self-enforcing. In fact, if I violate a norm in harming a factional enemy, e.g., by lying or breaking a promise, my own partisans will take the enemy's protests as signs that the attack has hit home. The louder the protests, the more favorable the assessment. When magistrates become partisans, or at least have to please parties to stay in office, the effect is particularly egregious. "[G]overnors and rulers" who are "indifferent persons" with respect to most social interests have "no interest, or but a remote one, in any act of injustice" and on the contrary an "immediate interest in every execution of justice" (T 3.2.7.6, SBN 537). But magistrates who are partisan, or fear for their lives and office unless they please partisans, are slaves of partisan conspiracy theories: when parties imagine plots by public enemies, the fact that no plot in fact exists becomes a reason for framing the innocent rather than freeing them.[13]

The category of zero-sum behavior, of course our category rather than Hume's, may be called the hallmark of Humean faction.[14] This is most obviously true across parties, as partisans come to give the other party's happiness a value not positive or zero, but negative: "[T]he misery of adversaries, according to the usual maxims of party, [are] regarded . . . as [one's] own prosperity and triumph" (H 3.266).[15] And of course, extreme partisan differences may render very difficult otherwise beneficial interactions like economic exchange and intermarriage. By the end of the English Civil Wars, the Roundheads and Cavaliers spurned such interactions to such a degree that they resembled not just separate nationalities but hostile ones (H 6.141).

But the zero-sum effects can occur within parties as well. At some point the need for markers of party loyalty may lead partisans to adopt artificial behaviors that do not reflect their private preferences. Since the Roundheads practiced an austere morality, "the character of a man of pleasure was affected" among the Cavaliers "as a sure pledge of attachment to the church and monarchy." Cavaliers spent money they did not have so as to be able to say proudly, "We laugh while they tremble" (H 6.141).[16] Religion's "unaccountable" quality, its ability to divorce moral motivation from worldly consequences, sometimes by accident has positive consequences and even more frequently brings about actions that waste time and resources but otherwise cause little harm. Faction, however, is inherently a matter of enmity. I can only demonstrate zeal for my own party by acting zealously to harm yours. Conflicts of "imaginary interest" are required for factions' existence. Where homophily does not provide them, "spite and opposition to persons whose sentiments are different from [one's] own" will step in (E: PG, 63).

Treating Koinophobia: Extensive Sympathy versus Enlarged Interests

It is crucial to note the kind of operation taking place in these instances and the mental habits that make it possible. In one place, Hume suggests that superstition can actually be cured. Since its cause is the terror of unknown causes for our misfortunes, "philosophy" (which in this case presumably means both the theoretical study of cause and effect and the study of actual causes, which we now call science) is the only "sovereign antidote" (E: OS, 577; compare E: SE, 75). But as Jennifer Herdt points out, Hume never assumed that this antidote would work for more than a few: skepticism was an elite taste.[17] For the most part, Hume suggests treatments for the symptoms of religion and faction rather than cures for its causes. Those treatments fall into two broad categories.

EXTENSIVE SYMPATHY

The first might be called "extensive sympathy": shorthand for a larger project of reshaping and correcting our sentiments. In this approach, social communication—through rhetoric, modes of education that enlist the passions, moral and political approval and disapproval, and so on—is to be employed, persistently and deliberately, to "correct" our moral judgment. It is hoped in particular that these methods will weaken the barriers that limit each person's sympathies to her own religion, sect, or party. In place of a limited sympathy that merely takes in others' emotions (which can result in a negative feeling: we shun or despise others' misery or even, in factional or competitive contexts, welcome it), we are to cultivate in ourselves and others an "extensive" sympathy. Extensive sympathy renders vivid not only the fact of others' misfortunes but their subjective distress in the face of them: their desire to gain happiness, and avoid unhappiness. Through extensive sympathy we come to care about the personal desires and social circumstances of others, which may be unfamiliar to us but matter greatly to those they concern. This is the central theme of Jennifer Herdt's study of religion and faction in Hume, and of the general course of treatment she sees Hume as proposing. She interprets Hume's own work (especially the *History* and what she calls his other "popular" writings) as trying to extend our sympathies through a variety of emotional and rhetorical methods—partly by painting others' suffering more brightly, partly by deflating (through irony, gentle criticism, or bitter satire) the false beliefs that make religious and factional divisions seem more warranted than they are. Recent political theorists who have drawn on Hume have likewise attempted to make sympathy safe for politics by making it more extensive in this sense: by extending or correcting sympathy's objects to make them less partial and sectarian, and less prone to replicate existing social divisions.[18]

This set of treatments is by no means implausible and by no means without textual warrant in Hume (though not always in this context; the project involves applying to political and social questions reflections and criteria that Hume developed most fully in discussing esthetics [E: ST: 226–49]). Hume does think that good judgment involves stepping outside our own concerns, learning to praise qualities that further others' projects even if they do not touch our own. While he doubts that we will sacrifice our own *interests* for the sake of such projects, that does not necessarily harm the case, since overcoming religion and faction requires only that we not actively spurn conventions that taken as a whole *further* our interests as well as those of others.[19] Finally, while taking preferences to be exogenous, outside the scope of analysis, reflects disciplinary conventions in economics and so-called positive political theory that are sound and enable a productive division of labor, there seems no reason why history—or a political theory informed by both strategic analysis and history—should follow suit. In fact there may be excellent reasons why it shouldn't, given the clear historical evidence that prevailing preferences chance over time and have systematic effects. Certainly Hume's political theory on a historical scale takes for granted that sentiments change over time, in ways that matter greatly for politics, and that some particularly visionary government policies are calculated to hurry along such changes.[20]

The problems with the extensive sympathy remedy are neither interpretive nor a priori but practical and moral. First, it tends to beg the question. It is not clear how we can be expected to get virulent partisans to read books that debunk or ironize their prejudices; bigoted religionists to read accounts of how infidels are very nice people (or vice versa, depending on how one wields the adjective "bigot"); or demagogues with a stake in current configurations of power to endorse modes of deliberation or education that are explicitly aimed at undercutting their power. In fact, actual partisans and orthodox religious figures hated Hume (as he lamented). His very secularism and nonpartisanship—related, since the parties of Hume's time had stronger religious commitments than Hume acknowledged—severely limited his impact.[21] Second, there is a problem of specification. It is not clear exactly which norms or practices, in concrete terms, a society is supposed to institutionalize in order to make extensive sympathy more common. Portraits of extensive sympathy tend to be adverbial: they prescribe a spirit in which one should act, not a set of actions that can be performed (or their lack noted, according to clear criteria). Third, and related to the first two, the sentimental remedies slight problems of coordination. In order to work, the educational, cultural, religious, and political reforms that are called for must be all but unanimous. If they are not, the practices of extending or correcting others' sympathies will become a hobby for liberal souls whose sympathies least need correcting, since those most prone to bigoted religion and uncompromising faction will spurn these practices as both optional and (by definition) uncomfortable. But because the actions involved are not well specified, it is hard to imagine a non-coercive convention that would embody them, and whose violations would be subject to quick, informal sanctions. Thus the practice of extending our own and others' sympathies is unlikely to expand from a minority taste to a society-wide convention. Fourth, there is a problem of self-effacingness. While it is certainly possible to read Hume's philosophy primarily as an attempt not to describe political passions but to change them, the relevance of such a reading may be questioned in an age when philosophy lacks much social role. It is unlikely that reading Hume, or his interpreters—including me—will enlarge the public's sympathies with one thousandth the efficacy that a single movie or TV show could apply to that purpose (or the opposite one).

Finally, there is a fundamental and non-contingent problem of feasibility. The aspiration to "concord" (Herdt) or "common ground" (Sharon Krause) implies that we should cultivate extensive or corrected sympathy with respect to everyone's situations, desires, or projects at once, and they with ours. Leaving aside the time and effort that would be required to do this with respect to every member of a society (though this objection seems non-trivial), this aspiration seems literally impossible to the extent that societal outcomes that pain one person are required for the happiness of another. While a liberal society can *tolerate* both conservatives and progressives, both religious traditionalists and sexual libertines, none of its members can coherently feel *sympathy* with the projects of all these groups at once. There seem only two ways of answering this objection. One could say that a corrected or extensive perspective will reveal many members of society's projects to be narrow, partial, or distorted, not worthy of the kind of sympathy worth having. Taking the usual analogy with taste: a cultivated taste might be one that appreciates a deft portrayal of a philistine in a work of fiction, and perhaps even the philistine character as a whole for qualities other than his esthetic taste, while rejecting for the same reason the substance of what he likes.[22] But in the moral and political case, this standpoint becomes much less coherent. To sympathize with someone while regarding a huge number of their *moral* aspirations and judgments as invalid, in fact reprehensible and destructive, seems impossible (and Hume directly suggested as much).[23] Alternatively, we could claim to sympathize with others on a very formal level. We might aim at a society in which everyone as much as possible can be happy by his or her own lights, while conceding that this will not produce harmony, since not everyone's happiness is compatible with everyone else's. But to think this way is to abandon the aspiration to substantive concord or common ground that distinguishes the extensive sympathy view from the project of enlarged interests defended here.

The most fundamental objection, however, is on the level of values. Advocates of enlarged sympathy assume that our society, and our liberalism, should be based on a common aspiration to respect one another's wishes and ends. But the great attraction of Hume—and generally, of resting order on convention rather than normative agreement—is that he does *not* require this: he decouples social order from normative consensus.[24] The conventions of property and contract protect equally the purchase of *Left Behind* and that of *The Dialectic of Sex*; the conventions of authority further the activities of the police officer and tax collector whose jobs enable both transactions. If one's political theory aspires to let people make their own moral choices without asking for (nor demanding) the approval of others, there is no improving on such results. Provided that others allow me to live as I please and, through their actions (e.g., the work and exchange and political allegiance that enable economic growth and public goods) encourage the preconditions for my living better—as I define that, of course—their attitudes toward how I live are no more my business than the substance of how I live is theirs. If the political order that protects me depended on their actual approval, this would be a weakness, not a strength.

Enlarged Interests

An approach that stresses "enlarged interests" rather than "extensive sympathy" preserves this normative diversity and avoids the problems just discussed. The Humean system's respect for normative diversity and its immunity to those problems are related. Because Hume works with the grain of our diverse passions and interests rather than engaging in the systematic moral critique that normative theorists typically fault him for slighting (or else praise him for secretly advocating), there is no mystery to the question of why people would go along with his scheme (they have an interest in doing so), no problem of specification or normative coordination (since what's at stake is a limited set of actions, not an unlimited aspiration to harmony of judgment), and no problem of contradiction in a call to sympathize simultaneously with contradictory projects (since sympathy with their substance is optional, perhaps not desirable).

That said, however, one attractive quality that is sometimes attributed to mutual advantage theories—non-judgmentalism toward preferences—can fairly be attributed only to theories that assume that people's preferences fail to clash in radical ways and that their institutions are already adequately good. Hume's theory is not like this. He is not shy to judge some social aspirations and the social types who typically feel them as destructive or anti-social, because neither his historical nor his programmatic work assume that the hard problems of social order have been definitively (as opposed to imperfectly and provisionally) solved. Hume aims to explain how various projects and desires that in their early form *were* incompatible with another could be re-defined or transformed so as to be safe for one another. In doing so he can explain how counter-intuitive social institutions were able to arise for the first time, and may continue to arise in the future, in spite of their contributions to mutual advantage initially not being clear.

Hume's doctrine of justice is famous for assuming a redirection, rather than a negation, of self-interest. Against moralists like Hutcheson who inveighed against self-interest and extolled justice as a purely moral motivation, Hume wrote that "whether the passion of self-interest be esteemed vicious or virtuous, 'tis all a case, since itself alone restrains it: So that if it be virtuous, men become social by their virtue; if vicious, their vice has the same effect" (T 3.2.2.13, SBN 492). But this redirection can only work once people have invented, and now respect, rules of justice that "seek their end [self-interest] *in an oblique and indirect manner*" (T 3.2.2.21, SBN 497; emphasis added). In terms of sociology and moral psychology, the transformation is profound. The same desire to benefit oneself and one's dear ones that once motivated violent clan warfare is wrenched into a learned attachment to peaceful acquisition and exchange that is so deep as to seem natural.

I shall claim that Hume's solution to other passions and projects that seem at cross-purposes is similar. In each case we must find ways of flattering the passion, and enabling the project, by gradually ending the customary modes in which the passion was expressed and the project pursued—and establishing new ones. Philosophic interpreters who focus only on the *Treatise* (which focuses on conventions of self-property and exchange) have tended to portray Hume, as he in that work to some extent portrayed himself, as concerned with civilizing the single passion of "love of gain."[25] Closer to the mark are those intellectual historians who see the Scottish Enlightenment generally (and sometimes, though not always, Hume particularly) as valorizing a plural society that encouraged the diverse pleasures of "civil" life and "the proliferation and diversification of personality under the conditions of commercial growth." In contrast to civic humanism and civic republicanism, which called for all citizens to practice an identical civic virtue for intrinsic or instrumental reasons, the new ideal, which might be called "civil pluralism," justifies political institutions as the method for furthering diverse projects (of which politics is only one, and a specialized one).[26]

In his first work Hume said of the love of gain, "[T]here is no passion, therefore, capable of controlling the interested affection, but the very affection itself, by an alteration of its direction." The rest of this chapter will argue that Hume came to believe this of other potentially antisocial passions as well:

factional loyalty, the love of power, the love of status and social distinction, the desire for glory in battle, even (more equivocally) religious enthusiasm. Negative conventions are to be addressed by redirecting the ends they pursue rather than moralizing against them or seeking to bend them toward forms of altruism. Exclusive attachments to religion and faction are undermined not by convincing people that exclusivity is wrong but by showing them that inclusivity works—in the specific sense of doing better at promoting the objects of religion and faction *largely intact*. Similarly, modern conventions can be found that give a new kind of nobility what nobles always want (status, power, and the prospect of telling weaker people what to do); a new kind of government official what rulers always want (power, and an extensive sphere of action in which to use it); and a new kind of general what generals always want (glory, won through excellence in battle).

Keeping societal conventions going in the face of religion and faction, and other negative conventions and aspirations to be discussed, does require a certain kind of mental adjustment or development. But the development or adjustment required takes place mostly on the level of institutional ingenuity, not moral psychology. An "enlarged" outlook does not guiltily, annoyingly, or moralistically (depending on whether the first, second, or third person is asking) question the moral worth of our own aspirations and those of our fellow citizens. Rather it seeks out, and in retrospect appreciates, new accounts of how those aspirations may, could, or should be embodied in the future so as to harmonize with those of others.

Hume uses "enlarged" very frequently and in many different senses but with a shared core meaning. Most generally, enlarged means something like "inclined, and able, to think and act with a view to enduring interests of as many people as possible, rather than one's own beliefs, interests, or prejudices or those of one's time and place." "Enlarged reflections" lead us to realize that the enemy general is serving his country just as our general is serving ours (EPM 9.8n57, SBN 274–5).[27] "Large" views are instrumental and future-directed rather than conservative and wedded to precedents that may no longer serve the common interest; in contrast, "narrow prejudices" are the enemy of "cool foresight and deliberation" and "pernicious to national interest" (H 5.42, 160; H 6.109). In domestic politics, the "natural progress of human sentiments" is characterized by "gradual enlargement of our regards to justice," as we come to see that a convention that is beneficial among a small circle would be equally beneficial if extended (no greater appreciation of the *substance* of others' projects is implied [EPM 3.1.21, SBN 192]).[28] On the international level, similarly, an enlarged view puts aside not national feeling as a whole but the "narrow and malignant" assumption that one country's benefit must be another's loss, as opposed to all being mutual beneficiaries from trade (or, more rarely, diplomacy [E: JT, 328]).[29] A narrow perspective regards the triumph of one's own religion as a public good—mistakes pseudo-conventions for conventions—while an enlarged one takes account of the "general happiness of society" or its "civil interests" (H 5.458, 544; compare 3.399, 447; 4.54; 5.264). On one occasion to "enlarge" one's view seems equivalent to adopting a proto-Millian sense of fallibilism. By deliberately reminding ourselves that our past reasoning has sometimes seemed impeccable but has in the event been proven false, we can "check or controul" our first-order belief that our reason provides certainty now (T 1.4.1.1, SBN 180). And in general, to enlarge one's views is to abandon the view that others should trim their lives to fit one's own inclinations. An enlarged mind realizes that one's own dominant passion is just that: one's own, not that of others. Life is made "agreeable" by the "variety or . . . judicious mixture" of such passions, not uniformity (E: SC, 160).[30]

Treating Negative Conventions: Public Zeal versus Party Prejudice, Mission over Domination

Enlarged treatments (not cures) of religion and faction build on such insights. Typically, Hume proposes more than one treatment in hopes that each will help a little, so that combined they might prevent the pseudo-convention's worst effects.

Faction

The case of faction is the easier of the two: two kinds of enlargement are to work in concert.[31] First, enlarged fallibilism is to be applied to show both parties, with respect to both their principles and their historical myths, that they are not "so fully supported by reason as they endeavour to flatter themselves" (E: CP, 494). Hume's vaunted "moderation," it has been suggested, refers to this process. Hume aims not to vindicate the median opinion for its own sake, but to calm factional passions by replacing unwarranted certainty regarding theoretical and factual propositions with a proper (mild) level of belief, combined with the recognition that partisans on the other side have some, though to one's own mind inadequate, warrant for contrary beliefs.[32] (Crucially, it is clashes of party *principle* that can be accommodated in this way—*not* those of "interest" or office seeking, which are inherently zero-sum and continued to induce different factions to fight fiercely during and after Hume's time. The goal is to prevent "all *unreasonable* insult and triumph of the one party over the other" and to encourage "moderate *opinions*" [E: CP, 494; emphases added]: that is, to reduce the zero-sum game to no more than a game, with jobs at stake, not an existential struggle.[33])

Second, the scope of partisan attachment is to be enlarged so as to redirect the pleasure of partisan fellowship toward the "party of human kind"—just as justice, by redirecting the love of gain away from clan warfare to peaceful economic competition, induces a kind of indirect and institutionalized cooperation among former enemies. A person immune to partisan feeling would

be, Hume judges, "more or less than man" (probably less). But when we socialize with others—presumably across party lines, though not necessarily
deliberately so—we systematically receive "blame and approbation" from
other people in proportion to whether we practice or oppose "vice and disorder, [human kind's] common enemy." As we gain acquaintance with more
and more people of different standpoints and opinions, our benevolent sentiments come to be reinforced through the same mechanisms that would otherwise give rise to sectarian attachments. When our attachment to humankind is "roused from . . . lethargy" through social approval and disapproval,
the partisan passions can be "overpowered" by what in effect is *partisan feeling for the whole*. The sentiments that produce the good of society "form,
in a manner, the *party* of human kind against vice or disorder, its common
enemy" (EPM 9.9; SBN 275).[34] When Hume asserts reasons for maintaining
"with the utmost ZEAL, in every free state, those forms and institutions, by
which liberty is secured, the public good consulted, and the avarice or ambition of particular men restrained and punished," or says that "the surest way
of producing moderation in every party is to *increase our zeal for the public*"
(emphasis added), or takes for granted that there exists a civic passion called
"disinterested zeal"(E: PRS, 26, 27; H 5.380),[35] he is not proposing something
magic or ineffable (nor merely exhorting us, as some have argued, in ways
that are in tension with his larger strategic scheme[36]) but merely applying
to conventions of authority the same logic that applies to those of justice. In
both cases, social teaching is meant to reinforce the truth that our passions
are more durably satisfied when applied to an enlarged sphere than when
limited to a narrow one, because only in the former case do everyone's passions accord with one another's rather than clashing in zero-sum fashion.[37] As
Forbes has pointed out, Hume himself held a "passionate attachment to the
constitution" over and above any particular party or minister.[38]

To be sure, Hume's story of how factions come together with common
purpose seems more vivid when there is a common enemy more concrete
and palpable than mere "vice and disorder." For instance, the Glorious Revolution coalition united Whig and Tory against a king who proposed to impose his religion through tyranny and foreign invasion, and against the will
of 99 percent of the public. In another instance, Scotland was "united as in a
national cause, which indeed it has become, in some measure," by the "virulence" of John Wilkes' movement, whose anti-Scottish libels struck fear into a
whole nation and have been rightly compared to modern anti-Semitism.[39] In
contrast, Hume's call for a Coalition of Parties seemed to lack urgency when
he wrote it (well before Wilkes). But there is no reason to doubt that Hume's
method works more generally, and plenty of evidence that it does work. It is
not only possible for zeal toward public institutions to exceed and counterbalance zeal for party; in stable constitutional regimes, it already does so, per-
vasively and constantly. That is: almost nobody attached to one party would
countenance political assassination of a leader attached to another, or even

theft of an election. Partisans in fact unite passionately and fervently to de-
nounce any of their number whose zeal is thus misplaced. And if it is a matter
of the degree of the "industry . . . with which every individual is bound to
pursue the good of his country" (as opposed to the "passion" that Hume also
calls for),[40] a great many more people, of greater and more diverse talents,
work for any modern government than for any modern faction—and the
coercive taxation that everyone endorses as a means to fund government is
only occasionally and controversially used to fund parties. In this way Hume's
hope for political institutions has been fulfilled. Constitutional "checks and
controuls" make it "the interest, even of bad men, to *act for* the public good"
(E: PRS, 15–16; emphasis added), that is, to act positively, to work hard to
benefit the public, not merely to abstain from harm. Political passions are to
be channeled, not destroyed.[41]

Religion

Of these two techniques of enlargement—psychic detachment and redirection of passion—only the second can easily be applied to religion. John Immerwahr claims that Hume's *Dialogues Concerning Natural Religion* (and the
dialogue form in general, common in Hume and borrowed more from Cicero
than Plato) was meant to provide a sense of fallibilism, to "sap the violence
from *any* religious position."[42] This is valid to a point but question-begging.
Hume's skeptical, detached approach to religion was not likely to appeal to
those who needed it most. It was in fact guaranteed to enrage anyone with a
strong Christian faith, let alone a fanatical form of it (as Hume knew: he did
not dare publish the *Dialogues* during his lifetime).

Redirecting religious passion might in principle be easier than turning it
skeptical. I have argued that toleration is to sectarian and intolerant religious
feeling what justice and property are to the love of gain: the former of each
pair, an artificial virtue, is as good for society as the latter, more like a natural
passion, is harmful.[43] Unlike peaceful acquisition of money, toleration is hard
to see as the object of passionate attachment—but it is such an object, invis-
ibly. Our zeal for toleration shows itself in the fact that in tolerant societies
almost everyone instantly condemns violence based on religion, and cooper-
ates with the police who investigate it. (Even nonviolent vituperation of those
who do not share one's religion is generally looked down on, and in some
countries outlawed.)

One might also imagine, especially on the part of clergy and lay zealots,
a redirection of religious passion from positional to absolute objects. Rather
than wanting to have more adherents *than others*, or to capture the State to
force that, the leaders of a religion might come to aspire to win more adherents *overall*. And the spread of conventions of toleration might hold out
greater prospects of that than persecution does, especially given the typical
religion's belief that one or more gods providentially ensure its own triumph

rather than that of its competitors. Missionary zeal is not the same as a zeal for persecution, and might be a strong substitute for it.

None of this was, to be sure, Hume's own explicit argument. No doubt because he feared the intellectual effects of religion as much as the political ones, he concentrated on the hope that religion itself would lose intensity. Superstition would be eroded through science and the experience of corrupt religious establishments. (Such experience "opens [men's] eyes.")[44] Enthusiasm would abate on its own, since frenzies of religious energy are hard to sustain and tend to settle down to more orderly passions. (As Hume notes, the Quakers, once fanatical and radical opponents of social convention, were by his time not only harmless in their behavior but nearly Deist in their theology [E: SE, 78].) But from a purely politic perspective, toleration and missionary zeal are a sufficient solution and an effective one—and more consistent, perhaps, than Hume's own anti-Christianism with the enlarged principle of allowing others' passionate attachments to flourish if they do not cross ours.

The rest of this chapter will show how this account of Hume's project—which Hume spells out most explicitly with respect to religion and faction, the main threats to conventions of authority remaining in his time—plays out with respect to social groups in a history which was in Hume's past. In each case, as seen in Hume's work, a given group once had a characteristic object (driven by a passion) that was anti-social, that could be fulfilled only if the passions of others were thwarted. In each case, Hume in omniscient mode engages in a bit of skepticism that appeals to the elite, knowing reader. But on a more practical level, setting enlightened elites aside, he also describes the workings of a more practical, political project—the kind that was able to work in a less-civilized past as well as on narrow characters in Hume's present—whereby the group's passion could be channeled in a peaceful and pro-social direction. Hume often seems to be criticizing whole ways of life. But he can be seen on a larger view to be criticizing, and welcoming the historical decline of, obsolete ways of *pursuing* ways of life. Though few human ends are inherently contemptible, in the state of society that Hume variously calls rude, crude, barbaric, or ancient, almost all human aspirations end in failure. In a "civilized" society with a "regular" government, almost all of them are more likely to succeed.

According to Hume, for "a civilized nation, like the English," "[a]n acquaintance with the ancient periods of their government is chiefly *useful* by instructing them to cherish their present constitution, from a comparison or contrast with the condition of those distant times" (H 2.525 [emphasis in original]). The comparison or contrast is to be taken seriously and systematically: we moderns can learn from history not just that modern conventions succeed but why. Ancient and medieval history is not a mere catalog of miseries but a vivid reminder of the formidable barriers to overcoming misery—and of how they were torn down. The medieval social orders were as pluralist as Maitland thought they were but without the benign effects he painted: they roughly embodied not merely different interests but different aspirations or ways of life between which coexistence was difficult and productive coordination more or less impossible (and this was reflected in an incoherent constitution: each order was subject to its own set of rules (H 2.284; compare H 2.108 and H 2.529 [note "E" to H 2.109]). The triumph of law and uniform rights over this motley constitution certainly required royal force. But royal force—resting, as always, on opinion—in turn required a redirection of the old orders' energies, one by one and through continual effort. The reason why Hume's "establishment" thesis in support of the Glorious Revolution compromise seems so unchallenging and conservative to some is that they ignore how it was built.[45] The centuries-long coalition that made England one society was not obvious at all. It required that glory-seeking military commanders become professional soldiers, barons become gentlemen, meddlesome priests become pampered bishops with an interest in indolence, and violent kings bent on conquest become politic statesmen who realized that they would gain more power over more people by protecting commerce and taxing it than by throwing one primitive army against another.

Military Glory: Ancient Courage and Modern Professionalism

Hume did not doubt that military glory was dazzling and that people tended to praise it. The courage and "disdain of fortune" that it involved were "immediately agreeable" and made up a large part of "the sublime": the kind of greatness of character that we praise in speeches (even regarding our enemies) and seek in epic poetry or other narrations (EPM 7.4–16, SBN 252–6).[46]

But the love of military glory that characterized the "generality of mankind" was an unfortunate social force. Hume also sought to undermine the attractiveness of such glory through satire for the masses and reflection for the few. He mocked military conquerors as puffed-up, foolish, and more likely to ruin themselves than to win undying fame; to this extent he was part of the Enlightenment project of the "demolition of the hero."[47] On the collective level, Hume stressed "how little reason kingdoms have to value themselves on their victories, or to be humbled by their defeats; which in reality ought to be ascribed chiefly to the good or bad conduct of their rulers, and are of little moment towards determining national characters and manners" (H 2.262). But he did not exaggerate how much this kind of demolition could accomplish. Reflective thinkers could "oppose the popular notions on this head" by painting in concrete terms "[t]he infinite confusions and disorder, which it [military glory] has caus'd in the world." But Hume admitted that the personal qualities of conquerers remained attractive regardless of the success of any attempt to reveal the results of their actions as harmful.[48]

Hume's most consistent project, therefore, was not to destroy military glory but to modernize it. His attitude in the *History* toward military commanders is often one of sincere praise, provided that the commanders display strategy and discipline rather than wild courage; refrain from harming noncombatants (or else fight on the sea, where the laws of war are famously easy to observe because no noncombatants are present); defend their country's settled and palpable interests rather than aiming at violent glory or religious conversion; fight defensively against foreign enemies or else reluctantly in civil wars; and take pride in retreating to fight another day rather than perishing gloriously but uselessly.[49]

But most systematically, Hume spends huge swaths of the *History* undermining the ancient preference for personal valor over efficient military organization. He aims to show the reader that military achievements are more praiseworthy, more worth the attention of both practitioners and admirers, to the extent that they take place under modern conditions: discipline, organization, and military science worth the name.

Hume was one of the first to systematically trace—and support—the implications of what is now called state-building. In the military realm, boring, professional modern armies, funded by taxation, disciplined by full-time drill and field experience, and backed by military science, always defeat romantic, disordered bands of feudal retainers or citizen-soldiers that rely on personal valor. "[N]othing, in military actions, can supply the place of discipline and experience" (not even the "fumes of enthusiasm" that one might think would provide an inspired substitute [H 6.30]). Cromwell's rise to power was the result primarily of his skill in raising and disciplining a small force that grew to a large one, and his shrewdness in allocating commissions by merit rather than birth (H 5.429; 6.30, 57; and contrast 2.100). More specifically: the great Montrose's loyalty and courage, however "sublime, elegant, or noble," was no match for a "disciplined" army sustained by "domestic peace" (H 6.24, 6.21). England's victory over the Spanish Armada stemmed not from God's grace but from superior English shipbuilding and naval training; the English, knowing their advantage, "beheld without dismay [the Armada's] tremendous appearance" (H 4.268–9).[50] Dutch naval commanders' "skill and bravery" in 1653 could not sink an English fleet whose ships, because of ship money, were bigger than everyone else's; thirteen years later, the English navy was on the wrong side of this calculation and "found, that the greatest valour cannot compensate the superiority of numbers, against an enemy who is well conducted, and who is not defective in courage" ("not defective": courage is now a baseline requirement for battle, not something that on its own can win it [H 6.50, 6.202]).[51] In general, good discipline, equipment, and logistics consistently triumph over either greater numbers or more superficially impressive forces (e.g., mounted rather than on foot). Crucially, this can be expressed in personal and evaluative terms that make us proud of generals who embody the result: "[P]olicy and prudence" are as important as "ambition and courage"; "[P]olicy, foresight, and judgment" have the advantage over "rash and precipitate valour" (H 1.11, 16, 148; 2.134, 183–5, 225–6, 246–7, 314,

488; 3.95, 101; 4.28, 261, 263, 264, 378; 5.437, 468–70; quotations on H 2.488, 2.262).[52] With the coming of "politeness and refinement," courage may draw less force from "anger" but gains in its place "a sense of honour, which is a stronger, more constant and more governable principle"—and more expressive of "genius"(E: RA, 274). Without discipline, greater numbers only mean a greater propensity to maneuver badly or even to panic (H 2.111–12, 192, 208). Those inclined to lament the death of ancient bravery should realize, Hume notes, that all the "barbarians" in England were no match for one Roman legion (H 1.12).[53]

Scholars are right to note that Hume thought standing armies a danger to liberty and favored militias where it was possible to sustain them (as it often wasn't); he was to that extent an old-style "republican."[54] But we should also note that he preferred *disciplined* militias subject to lengthy training under executive command (a "regular militia," as he once calls it) to the undisciplined, ad hoc forces favored by skittish parliamentarians, and thought the former preferable on the grounds of liberty as well as efficiency.[55] Hume blesses the attributes of a professional army—"officers and soldiers, . . . discipline and arms"—with the highest compliment he can give a modern and productive institution: "regular" (H 1.344, 4.315). The development of such armies from the brigands hired by Henry II by means of scutage to their modern, professional versions is a great theme of the *History*.[56] In an early version of Weber's iron cage argument (though Weber's phrase was really closer to "steel box"), Hume notes that under Charles II, England had no choice, "from motives both of honour and security," but to follow the "princes of Europe" in "perpetually augmenting their military force, and consequently their expence." England had to "adapt its revenue to the new system of politics"—above all, a system of raising formidable militaries. The commons neglected this necessity at national peril. Conversely, an able statesman like Louis XIV showed his shrewdness by learning the modern prerequisites of military victory: Dutch shipbuilding and English naval tactics (H 6.159, 6.234, 6.299).

But all this became possible only once "commerce and industry" developed. Before then, regular armies being impossible, conquered territories could be held only by settling new inhabitants on them and dispossessing the natives. (Hume reminds us that there are things worse than military occupation—for instance, civilian occupation [H 1.344; compare 2.238, 269].) In fact, money and military capacity are mutually reinforcing: kings need money for professional armies, and once they have such armies, can enforce the order required to collect taxes. Once Henry II fielded his first scutage-funded armies,

> The armies were less numerous, but more useful, than when composed of all the military vassals of the crown: The feudal institutions began to relax: The kings became rapacious for money, on which all their power depended: The barons, seeing no end of exactions, sought to defend their property: And as the same causes had nearly the same effects, in the dif-

ferent countries of Europe, the several crowns either lost or acquired authority, according to their different success in the contest. (H 1.374)

To sum up the argument, "one good county in England is able to make, at least to support, a greater effort than the whole kingdom was capable of in the reign of Harry V. . . . Such are the effects of liberty, industry, and good government" (H 4.379, Appendix III). So much for the glories of Agincourt, which young men ought to forget.

If the virtues of state-building, the benefits of "civilized" life, constitute Hume's first lesson, his second is more subtle and ingenious. Hume not only demonstrates that a modern military and society lead to victory. He suggests that only after the triumph of military science do the actions of a commander justify taking *credit* for victory. The same "anyone might win" characteristic that makes some ancient and medieval battles seem romantic because they turn on personal valor should rather, in Hume's portrayal, make them seem ridiculous because they turn on accident. Even as late as the English Civil War era in the seventeenth century, war was "but a headlong impetuous conduct; each party hurrying to a battle, where valour and fortune chiefly determined the success" (H 5.469; compare 2.341). By pairing "valor and fortune" as equally arbitrary or senseless, Hume signals a sweeping disdain toward the pre-civilized set of values that directed the whole education of a nobleman, or a polity, toward the former. Only when two serious military forces that know what they are doing (and have the discipline to do it) meet each other does the superior skill or strategy of an officer mean something substantial and merit praise.

When armies consisted of retainers, sent home to agricultural work after the battle, battles were often won and lost through sheer surprise—a guarantee of capricious political as well as military outcomes (H 1.43, 2.163). Absent the resources for a "regular and steady effort," "all the projected ends were commonly disappointed" (H 2.256). The sign of a "miserable state of military discipline" is that battles ended in routs—partly because neither side could easily calculate its chance of victory, so that both were prone to chance it, partly because without discipline there was no coordination, no "order in great armies," so that retreats turned quickly to panics. When armies are disciplined and military science in place—and, crucially, after the invention of gunpowder—armies can anticipate such outcomes reliably and the weaker side will not take the field when defeat is predictable.

> Conquests have become less frequent and rapid: Success in war has been reduced nearly to be a matter of calculation: And any nation, overmatched by its enemies, either yields to their demands, or secures itself by alliances against their violence and invasion.[57]

As often, Hume is using social science in praise of the second-best. It would be better if wars never occurred. Since they must occur, it is better that they be predictable in advance, so that countries can, through diplomacy or balancing power, prevent unexpected or catastrophic defeats.

Hume intends not only to trace the end of a medieval way of life but to cement it by dispelling any lingering nostalgia that might divert us from modern paths. The barons were "wretched soldiers" (H 2.9, with a vivid example) whose exclusive devotion to war made them objectively inferior to, that is, less deserving of praise than, their civilized equivalents who benefitted from a modern economy, military science, and the division of labor. "[T]he military force of those ages, . . . being ignorant of every other art, had not properly cultivated the art of war itself, the sole object of general attention" (H 2.225–6). The "impetuous valour" of the feudal nobility made them eager to fight in impossible situations rather than saving their courage for tenable ones (H 2.365; compare H 2.388, 395–6; 5.472). (On a rare occasion in which feudal battles involved female leaders, a macho determination to fight a woman who commanded superior forces, rather than waiting for reinforcements, was equally self-destructive.[58]) Poor discipline fed on itself, as civil wars decided by "hasty battles" did not allow for the systematic learning and experience that allowed for improvements in military discipline. Thus the medieval English during the Wars of the Roses could be constantly fighting yet "ignorant of the improvements, which the military art was beginning to receive upon the continent" (H 2.485).

Military rule, on Hume's portrayal, undercuts the civil progress that those who care about military professionalism have reason to treasure. Upon the collapse of the Roman emperors' effective rule,

> The military government, which soon succeeded, rendered even the lives and properties of men insecure and precarious; and proved destructive to those vulgar and more necessary arts of agriculture, manufactures, and commerce; *and in the end, to the military art and genius itself, by which alone the immense fabric of the empire could be supported.* (H 2.519; emphasis added)

But to the extent (in Hume's view a great extent) that feudalism was a species of warlordism, the feudal system as a whole is subject to the same critique. A system that valorized martial glory was, for systematic reasons, fatal to success in both peace *and* war:

> Though nothing could be worse calculated for cultivating the arts of peace or maintaining peace itself, than the long subordination of vassalage from the king to the meanest gentleman, and the consequent slavery of the lower people, evils inseparable from the feudal system; that system was never able to fix the state in a proper warlike posture, or give it the full exertion of its power for defence, and still less for offence, against a public enemy. The military tenants, unacquainted with obedience, unexperienced in war, held a rank in the troops by their birth, not

by their merits or services; composed a disorderly and consequently a feeble army; and during the few days, which they were obliged by their tenures to remain in the field, were often more formidable to their own prince than to foreign powers, against whom they were assembled. The sovereigns came gradually to disuse this cumbersome and dangerous machine, so apt to recoil upon the hand which held it; and exchanging the military service for pecuniary supplies, inlisted forces by means of a contract with particular officers, (such as those the Italians denominate *Condottieri*) whom they dismissed at the end of the war. (H 2.99)

Mercenary armies were not a full or stable solution either, since "[t]he poverty of all the European princes, and the small resources of their kingdoms," meant that advantages gained after a battle were often necessarily wasted, for lack of money to pay soldiers, rather than pursued (H 2.367; compare 2.269, 415). A lesson regarding modern state-building is often drawn from these passages, and rightly so. But we might also note a more personalized lesson: a soldier eager to be "formidable . . . to foreign powers" is hereby being taught to value modern conventions rather than longing for knights in rusty armor.

True "charismatic" leadership—in Weber's original sense of a leader perceived to have special powers and divine favor—presents a special problem. The problem is that it works: Joan of Arc, Hume's clearest example, really did reverse the course of English conquests in 1429 by serving as a rallying point and self-fulfilling source of morale. Hume is faithful to his theory here. Since leadership and discipline, like politics, depend on opinion, the opinion of divine favor may work just as well as the real thing (especially since in Hume's view there is no real thing). Hume's response is to suggest, with irony toward Joan and honest praise of military commanders of real skill like Dunois, Suffolk, and Bedford, that Joan's *faux* generalship was, in retrospect still is, less honorable, less to be sought, than the real thing. Joan rallied the French because she was chosen by God, and only as long as they believed that; she was a strong focal point but an unstable one (H 2.397ff., esp. 401–2). As soon as she recanted (under great duress) her claim to have a divine mission, this was "[e]nough . . . to convince both the French and the English, that the opinion of divine influence, which had so much encouraged the one and daunted the other, was entirely without foundation" (H 2.409). Joan's charisma might be compared to the fleeting "zeal and courage, which the notion of an attack inspires," or to the momentary gains to one side's morale, and loss to the other's, when an ally counted on by one side suddenly defects to the other (H 2.480, 517).

The hallmark of modern, systematic leadership, in contrast, is troops flocking to follow a commander with a well-earned reputation for good strategy. As usual Hume makes the point against the Maid of Orleans with irony: before one battle, Joan

displayed in her hands a consecrated banner; where the Supreme Being was represented, grasping the globe of earth, and surrounded with flower de luces. And she insisted, in right of her prophetic mission, that the convoy should enter Orleans, by the direct road from the side of Beausse: *But the count of Dunois, unwilling to submit the rules of the military art to her inspirations*, ordered it to approach by the other side of the river, where, he knew, the weakest part of the English army was stationed. (H 2.400, emphasis added)

True honor in a modern commander, Hume is suggesting, requires that the "military art" rely on its own virtues rather than superstitious supports. Joan was only pretending to have the military expertise that the commanders actually had—the expertise suited to "a profession, which requires more genius and capacity, than any other active scene of life" (H 2.403–4). Hume's praise of generals who display the modern virtues appropriate to that profession (especially pre-modern generals who did so before their time) is continuous and sincere. He aims to show that military glory, properly understood—the rational pursuit of national defense when conflict is inevitable—is an end best served by modern conventions, not ancient ones. In fact, he shows it so well that one scholar quite reasonably worries not that Hume is a pacifist but that he justifies a certain kind of modern militarist, one who avoids civil war in civilized nations but acquires glory through "civilizing" barbarous ones.[59] Hume himself strongly tended to the peace party. He thought the Seven Years' War unnecessary and thought the American colonies should be let go rather than retained at great cost.[60] And while Great Britain in his time spent the vast majority of its income on war, Hume's own list of public goods lists mostly peaceful ends: draining marshes, building bridges, opening harbors, building walls, cutting canals (T 3.2.7.8, SBN 538–9). But there remains an essential tension in Hume's work, affecting both his historical and his programmatic judgments: reconciling the militarily ambitious to a peaceful order required—and still requires—reassuring them that such an order need not choke the paths of glory.

Barons: From Independent Sovereigns to Honorable Gentlemen

The last chapter mentioned Robert Goodin's observation about coordination games: "Sometimes men gain from the confusion accompanying independent decision-making and would prefer to keep the independent decisional processes."[61] This basically summarizes Hume's account of England's barons. In the feudal era, they did not support the rule of law because in its absence they themselves were law. Civilization was a matter of bringing the barons, through a mix of force and bribery, to believe that great wealth and status among fellow subjects, under equal laws, was more desirable than a lawless and miserable domination over slaves. This was eventually a change in identity: barons became gentlemen. But Hume does not engage in a complacent apples-to-swords comparison that would merely assert that consumption is more fun than violence. (Such arguments usually leave the violent unpersuaded.) He strives to show that modern gentlemen were better off than barons with respect to most things that the barons themselves used to value. Barons loved hospitality, but modern nobles can practice much more of that. They loved the security that came with command of their own forces, but the security provided by national armies is far greater. They loved war, but a modern eighteenth-century gentleman who buys a commission can, if competent, accomplish much more in war than any baron could. They loved honor, but peace provides new and more durable forms of that. The life of an eighteenth-century "polite" gentleman is, on Hume's portrayal, not only better than that of a medieval baron; it is better in ways that the latter would have recognized.

That the barons are the chief villains of Hume's *History* is no secret.[62] The mechanisms by which England's monarchs substituted their own authority for that of barons—and were eventually limited in that authority themselves by Commons-dominated parliaments—will be covered in later chapters. But that dynamic story of transition must be supplemented by a static account of what a new equilibrium could be based on: the great barons had, and came very slowly to realize that they had, a durable interest in giving up their "right to oppress and tyrannize" (H 1.463).[63]

"Rustic Hospitality" versus Civilized Luxury

For Hume, the history of all hitherto existing societies is largely the history of elites' consumption patterns. It matters greatly not just how the great acquired their property but how they intended to spend it. Barons spent their wealth on private armies; gentlemen spend it on luxuries. When barons used their money to maintain men-at-arms at their own board, they guaranteed the loyalty of private armies that cemented each baron's local domination at the cost of preventing economic growth and political peace. When they came instead to value the status that came with luxury over the personal domination that came with poor but loyal retainers, the aristocrats lost their personal military power. When they became able to exert only the limited power of the large consumer, they promoted political peace by omission.

For Hume, barons before the Tudor era were concerned above all with "rustic plenty and hospitality." Such hospitality, in an era when the barons were the strongest political power, was not simply a matter of private consumption but a "political institution" of its own. This de facto institution both siphoned off the economic surplus that might otherwise have stimulated inventions and trade and allowed the barons to over-awe any economic actors who, by gaining wealth, might have threatened their own rule:

> The languishing state of commerce kept the inhabitants poor and contemptible; and the political institutions were calculated to render that poverty perpetual. The barons and gentry, living in rustic plenty and

hospitality, gave no encouragement to the arts, and had no demand for any of the more elaborate manufactures: Every profession was held in contempt but that of arms: And if any merchant or manufacturer rose by industry and frugality to a degree of opulence, he found himself but the more exposed to injuries, from the envy and avidity of the military nobles. (H 1.463–4)

"[R]ustic hospitality" (Hume essentially repeats the phrase) was the source of the barons' political power. Because "[a] great number of idle retainers, ready for any disorder of mischief, were maintained by him," a baron had no need for law courts but "sought redress by open force and violence."⁶⁴ England under such circumstances was less a state than an anarchic state system: the barons were "a kind of independent potentates, who, if they submitted to any regulations at all, were less governed by the municipal law, than by a rude species of the law of nations" (H 2.179; compare 1.353). An economic form of the security dilemma cemented this equilibrium; each baron was "obliged" to spend his agricultural surplus on men-at-arms, rather than employing servants or investing in manufactures, because the others did (H 2.523). (Among the many benefits of royal authority, discussed in the next two chapters, is that it overcame this dilemma.)

What disrupted this equilibrium were one technological change and the development of two new conventions. The technological change was that "agriculture improved" (H 2.523; compare H 5.134–5).⁶⁵ The conventions were (by implication) printing, which gave the moderately wealthy something to spend time on besides war, drink, and hunting; and money, whose "encreas[e]" made the further development of commerce possible.⁶⁶ The chance to increase agricultural profits and convert them into money was particularly hard to resist—so much so that it ended slavery:

> In proportion as agriculture improved, and money encreased, it was found, that these [in-person] services, though extremely burdensome to the villain, were of little advantage to the master; and that the produce of a large estate could be much more conveniently disposed of by the peasants themselves, who raised it, than by the landlord or his bailiff, who were formerly accustomed to receive it. A commutation was therefore made of rents for services, and of money-rents for those in kind; and as men, in a subsequent age, discovered, that farms were better cultivated where the farmer enjoyed a security in his possession, the practice of granting leases to the peasant began to prevail, which entirely broke the bonds of servitude, already much relaxed from the former practices. After this manner, villenage [sic] went gradually into disuse throughout the more civilized parts of Europe: The interest of the master, as well as that of the slave, concurred in this alteration. (H 2.523–4)

That the end of slavery benefited both master and slave is key to the story. Economically speaking, rustic hospitality involved great deadweight losses.⁶⁷

But it is crucial to the logic of Hume's account that barons had no initial reason *to* think economically. Money is not automatically more attractive than power. In the initial stages, for barons to convert their lands and retainers into wealth for consumption was illegal; in later stages, it seemed dishonorable. Changing both these facts required deliberate political strategies that exploited non-economic passions to pave the way for economic ones.

When Hume says that Henry VII's "system of policy" was to "depress the nobles and exalt the people" (3.80), he intends a compliment not only to Henry's intentions but also to his prudence. The "most important" of the laws Henry enacted was the one allowing ancient families to break their feudal entails and sell off their lands. As John Danford points out,[68] Hume attributes economic motives to Henry elsewhere, but not here. Henry's goals in this case were *political*. He aimed to change the relative power of the kingdom's orders, and succeeded:

> It is probable [Hume writes], that Henry foresaw and intended this consequence, because the constant scheme of his policy consisted in depressing the great, and exalting churchmen, lawyers, and men of new families, who were more dependant [*sic*] on him. (H 3.77)

Eventually, the nobles' immoderate taste for luxury and new license to sell land meant that land—and with it, power—passed from them to a new class of gentlemen who had as much money as the old nobles, or more (H 5.134–5). One might add that the nobles' own descendants could and did also keep their land, or even expand it, on the condition that they were better than their ancestors (as a class) were at economic management. In contrast, Edward I, who shared Henry VII's "salutary purpose" of "keeping these tyrants [the great barons] in awe, and restraining their illegal practices," lacked Henry's strategic nous. It was he who assented to the first law that *allowed* the barons to entail their estates, a law that "made it impracticable to diminish the property of the great families, and left them every means of encrease and acquisition" (H 2.143).

PUTTING NOBLES ON THE HONORS SYSTEM

Political strategy not only made it possible for the barons to move resources from power to wealth but also deliberately changed the object of *honor* from the first to the second. Medieval barons gloried in how many armed men they fed at their table and the courage with which they could butcher one another. Their modern successors came not only to enjoy something better but to *pride* themselves on it:

> The nobility, instead of vying with each other, in the number and boldness of their retainers, acquired by degrees a *more civilized species of emulation*, and *endeavoured to excel* in the splendour and elegance of their equipage, houses, and tables. The common people, no lon-

ger maintained in vicious idleness by their superiors, were obliged to learn some calling or industry, and became useful both to themselves and to others. And it must be acknowledged, in spite of those who declaim so violently against refinement in the arts, or what they are pleased to call luxury, that, as much as an industrious tradesman is both a *better man and a better citizen* than one of those idle retainers, who formerly depended on the great families; so much is the life of a modern nobleman *more laudable* than that of an ancient baron. (H 3.76–7; emphases added)

The old virtues of a baron—hospitality toward subordinate lieutenants and courage in the pursuit of conspiracy to commit mass murder—are now limited to criminals. Just as gangsters still call themselves lords and their men soldiers, Hume calls the barons' men "robbers" and, as collectives, "gangs."[69]

And just as Henry VII's policy hurried this process along without being responsible for starting it, Hume's rhetoric aims to cement a result that is solidly built but in danger of cracking under a gothic vogue for medievalism: the "humour of blaming the present, and admiring the past" that is "strongly rooted in human nature" (E: PAN, 464). Those who command armed robbers are not admirable and certainly not romantic: they are beneath contempt. Gentlemen and gentlewomen distinguish themselves by wealth and taste, not solely because they prefer comfort to violence (though by now they do) but because there is more *honor* in wealth, peacefully acquired through work and service, than in robbery. As a by-product—not that would-be nobles will much care—these new forms of emulation promote the peace and prosperity of others. The new aristocrats are the kind of people whose desire to think themselves superior to the rest of us leads them to support general conventions rather than oppose them.

Honor, if we are not careful, can trump wealth. Where titles and offices are more honorable than trade, traders who make some money will not reinvest it but use it to buy a title.[70] If Hume thought that economic self-interest automatically ruled the world, he would presumably have said that only the love of wealth can overcome honor, and that honor would automatically decline in civilized times. He in fact said the opposite on both scores.[71] Hume cites repeated examples in which pre-modern nobles deliberately sabotaged economic progress so as to preserve the military virtues and "independent" tyranny that they valued more than wealth.[72] Hume's claim that in the medieval age "[e]very profession was held in contempt but that of arms" is a statement not of impersonal fact but of intention: "political institutions were *calculated* to render [the inhabitants'] poverty perpetual," and merchants who gained wealth were deliberately despoiled, by barons, out of envy (H 1.463–4 [emphasis added]).[73] At the twilight of the medieval age this was already starting to change. The key event "favourable to justice and to liberty" is that "civil employments and occupations soon became *honourable* among the English" (emphasis added). The study of law furthered the "science of government," but society was only ripe for that science because, of the two thousand law students at the time, "most" were "of honourable birth" (H 2.522). Noble sons—their fathers perhaps wearied by the Wars of the Roses—were no longer required to study war.

Instead they began to compete with respect to public service. The foundational year was 1349. Edward III had already started the process of sublimating ambition: his foreign conquests "excited a strong emulation and a military genius among the English nobility; and these turbulent barons, over-awed by the crown, gave now a more useful direction to their ambition, and attached themselves to a prince who led them to the acquisition of riches and of glory." But Edward then had the genius to institutionalize this. "That he might farther promote the spirit of emulation and obedience," he founded the order of the garter, modeled on European honor systems but new to England (H 2.242). We might note, though Hume leaves it implicit,[74] that he thereby began the English honours system. This system, which still operates throughout the Commonwealth and is, to Americans' astonishment, taken remarkably seriously, is at the same time "aristocratic" in the sense of inegalitarian; unrelated to feudal status or birth; and consistent with any desired degree of equality in realms other than honor (law, politics, economics). It is often thought that modernity renders honor obsolete in favor of dignity.[75] Hume disagrees. A modern society preserves honor—for those few who believe in it, and think having it makes them better than others—but renders its pursuit useful, or at least mostly harmless, to others.

DURABLE SECURITY

Whether or not one believes that honor regularly trumps wealth, it is clear that security often does. And on this dimension as well, Hume claims that modern government exceeds pre-modern anarchy in the baron's own coin. The barons hoped, through their private armies, to protect themselves against both the king and one another. But though they could only appreciate it retrospectively, the rule of law promised to protect them better on both counts.

Barons versus Monarchs

Along one dimension, only law-based government gave the great security against their own monarch. Some of this was a matter of formal, legal authority. While barons who held their land as feudal tenants were on one level "protected both by law, and by the great privilege of carrying arms," the monarchs retained all kinds of vestigial rights that under specific, often quirky circumstances gave them more or less arbitrary power over things about which the barons cared deeply: their goods, their freedom of movement, their daughters' marriages (H 1.476ff.). Legal progress, most obviously Magna Charta, did much to change this over time (and will be covered in a later chapter).

But on a more basic level the barons' insecurity was a matter of structural incentives: the barons' practice of irregular violence gave monarchs an incentive to practice the same.

> They [the barons] had indeed arms in their hands, which prevented the establishment of a total despotism, and left their posterity sufficient power, whenever they should attain a sufficient degree of reason, to assume true liberty: But their turbulent disposition frequently prompted them to make such use of their arms, that they were more fitted to obstruct the execution of justice, than to stop the career of violence and oppression. The prince, finding that greater opposition was often made to him when he enforced the laws, than when he violated them, was apt to render his own will and pleasure the sole rule of government; and on every emergence to consider more the power of the persons whom he might offend, than the rights of those whom he might injure. (H 1.254)

An alternative equilibrium based on establishing crude conventions of law and improving and solidifying them over time is obvious to us—but could not have been comprehended by the barons. Hume here, as usual, attributes the pre-Tudor barons' customary violence not to vice but to ignorance. They lacked their descendants' knowledge of what could be achieved through conventions that they had not yet experienced: "true or regular liberty . . . requires such improvement in knowledge and morals, as can only be the result of reflection and experience, and must grow to perfection during several ages of settled and established government" (H 1.254). This analysis suggests that a medieval virtue, based as it was on simple ignorance of anything better, is not a suitable object for veneration or nostalgia. It also suggests that we cannot go back; while politics may not embody a one-way ratchet of progress, political knowledge almost certainly does. (As Hume puts it, the rule of law, "when it has once taken root, is a hardy plant"; being "profitable to every mortal," it is much less likely to be forgotten than achievements in the liberal arts, which only a few know and value [E: RPAS, 124].) The condition that the barons experienced as feudal law, with necessary imperfections, would seem to us a privative state of lawlessness compared to how civilized polities work. While peaceful and prosperous countries sometimes fall back into rule by warlords, they do not easily recognize that rule as normal, nor as law.

Barons versus Barons

Again using something like economists' language of deadweight loss, Hume says that feudalism made the barons' vassals insecure without making the barons secure:

> Even the gentry themselves were subjected to a long train of subordination under the greater barons or chief vassals of the crown; who, though seemingly placed in a high state of splendor, yet, having but a slender

protection from law, were exposed to every tempest of the state, and by the precarious condition in which they lived, paid dearly for the power of oppressing and tyrannizing over their inferiors. (H 2.522)

Elsewhere Hume is more specific about the price: the barons possessed "independence" at the cost of "true liberty" under law. This is not a matter of metaphysics or Rousseauian autonomy, but one of security, and Hume explains the link between liberty and security very simply. In the absence of security, a baron could not live as he wanted to, because anyone with power could "influence his conduct" and leave him only a single option: submission or war. Hume's metaphor implies that a pre-modern baron had no more liberty than a shipwreck (another agent who can boast of having no formal authority set over him): "the current of a faction might overwhelm him."[76] The barons, "disorderly and licentious tyrants, who were equally averse from peace and from freedom," systematically prevented security not only for others but for themselves (H 2.525).[77]

In passing we may note that what Hume thinks is true of barons with respect to one another was also true with respect to baronial attempts to unseat the king. Once again the liberty involved was illusory, really only "licentiousness." In subverting the principle of loyalty or allegiance, the barons only undermined their own privileges by giving license to raw force (H 2.319–20).[78] Here Hume's judgment of barons' self-interest is exclusively retrospective. Hume's entire discussion of baronial government is set in 1399, when the barons, by unseating Richard II and placing Henry Bolingbroke, Duke of Lancaster, on the throne, are about to begin the dynastic struggle (later called the War of the Roses) that would render most of their houses extinct and guarantee royal ascendancy (H 2.322–32). If the barons had had more "enlarged" views, Hume may be suggesting, they might have preserved their role in the polity, peacefully adapting to an increasingly regular and royalist order on the lines of their counterparts in France. As it was, an ancient equilibrium—part security dilemma, part point of honor, part a lack of acquaintance with the legal principles that made equal rather than feudal justice comprehensible—made the nobles fight fiercely for their ancient, anarchic power. But the nobles themselves, once law was established, eventually discovered that they lacked the slightest interest in looking back.

Statesmen: Power through Service

Frederick Whelan has noted that statecraft or statesmanship is central to Hume's *History* (though Hume avoids those words, preferring the language of "politic" measures or "policy"). Hume's statesmanship, however, downplays empty or esthetic hero worship in favor of pragmatic standards. Humean leaders are to be praised if they know how to bring about a desired outcome in unexpected circumstances, and are to operate within conventions of law,

justice, transparency, and accountability whenever possible. The latter criterion, notes Whelan, is what makes Hume not just a realist but a realist who is
also a kind of liberal.[79]

Again, the question is how statesmanship can be made safe for liberal conventions, given that power politics, whether domestic or international, seems
so clearly a zero-sum game. As in other cases, Hume answers it partly by
noting that modernity gives statesmen more of what they want and partly
by noting a transformation of the mode in which they want it. Statesmen
who prize their long-term interest over superficial glory are more likely to
succeed in gaining territory and will do so at a lower cost. Beyond this, the
long-term interest of rulers lies, Hume stresses, in founding and buttress-
ing conventions—especially legal orders—rather than in pursuing conquests.
A continuing interest in power and rule will, at the end of this process, be
fulfilled through public service. Hume makes this point both negatively and
positively, by mocking conquerors and praising lawgivers.

Magnificence versus Prudence

Whelan has argued that Hume's assessments of statesmen in the *History*,
which draw on the categories "expedience," "policy," and "necessity," show the
presence there of a realist sensibility not completely unlike Machiavelli's.[80]
Though that may be true, realism cuts (at least) two ways: it stands in equal
opposition to crimes and to blunders. That is, it counsels departures both
from textbook Christian—later Kantian—ethics and from outmoded forms
of ceremony and chivalry that do not effectively bring about the ends that
statesmen seek. Hume *qua* realist repeatedly criticizes, or mocks, flamboyant
acts of violence or betrayal not for being un-Christian but for undermining
military and diplomatic success.[81]

The key opposition is that between "glory" and "interest." While the
schemes of rulers may be motivated by either, Hume favors—and is pleased
to note in history—a shift from the first to the second. In the language of
modern international relations theory, Hume is a normative rather than an
empirical realist. He thinks balance-of-power policies a very good thing. He
is not afraid to use evaluative language, and goes so far as to call maintaining
the balance "the aim of modern politics" (by which he means the proper aim,
not the one always pursued). But he doubts that most statesmen of his day
actually practice power politics consistently or well (see E: BP, 337–8). The
History is therefore partly a teaching exercise aimed at demonstrating that
rulers bent on war have succeeded more often and more fully to the extent
that they think instrumentally and place interest over glory.

Hume often simply lays out the difference between good strategic planning
and mere bombast, leaving the reader to judge by results. He is not above the
occasional moralistic label: the "glory of conquests" is "vain and criminal" (H
5.49). But for the most part his teaching is not direct or pedantic but charac-

teristically ironic. To create room for the argument that prudent statesmen will see their true interests as lying more in conventions than in conquests, Hume argues that those bent on glory who do *not* calculate consequences (and there will obviously be some "generous natures" who are like this) will not only "destroy their own peace, and that of the rest of mankind" (5.51) but, more importantly from their perspective, will fail to win what *they* are looking for: not money or security (obviously) but glory, or fame.

Once again, Hume does not assume that everyone has economic motives, nor that they can be bought off with economic rewards. He writes of "power, which of all acquisitions, is the most coveted, and in comparison of which even reputation and pleasure and riches are slighted" (E: CP, 498). But the fact that many will sacrifice comfort and safety for power can be turned toward the public good if we are able to make keeping power conditional on enforcing justice rather than flouting it:

> The love of dominion is so strong in the breast of man, that many, not only submit to, but court all the dangers, and fatigues, and cares of government; and men, once raised to that station, though often led astray by private passions, find, in ordinary cases, a visible interest in the impartial administration of justice. (E: OG, 39)

This interest becomes clearer when we remember that "justice" for Hume is a system of pro-social avarice. A ruler who works with the grain of people's "natural" projects will have an easier time and reap greater gains than one who pursues the militarized virtue of a Sparta:

> [T]he less natural any set of principles are, which support a particular society, the more difficulty will a legislator meet with in raising and cultivating them. It is his best policy to comply with the common bent of mankind, and give it all the improvements of which it is susceptible. Now, according to the most natural course of things, industry and arts and trade encrease the power of the sovereign as well as the happiness of the subjects; and that policy is violent, which aggrandizes the public by the poverty of individuals. (E: C, 260)[82]

Thus the common people were not the only ones "affected . . . both in their personal *and civil* capacities" by the "introduction and progress of freedom" (H 2.522; emphasis added). The rulers were affected even more. Though government enforces impartiality and enables the pursuit of wealth, its specialized personnel are motivated neither by impartiality nor by greed; they want power.[83] The genius of modern society is that it makes the governing elites' power track not military victory but elections and civil service exams; it grants power on the condition that these elites observe and enforce, rather than subverting, legal conventions.

Hume's ironic undermining of government-sponsored military glory works on three levels, each less direct than the next. Sometimes Hume merely mocks those who engage in vainglorious military adventures; sometimes he mocks those silly enough to praise them; sometimes, and with the deepest irony, he merely notes the arbitrage opportunities accruing to statesmen too smart to fall into one of these first two categories.

In the first mode, Hume makes fun of those whose love of glory leads them to act foolishly. (For Hume to make this argument was not easy or safe. Many of the figures Hume names were English national heroes; some still are.) Because the special "lustre" of military glory attaches to persons, inducing us to praise their courage and greatness of mind even if we deplore the results of what they do (EPM 7.11–15, SBN 254–5; compare T 3.3.2.14–15, SBN 600), Hume's irony also attaches not just to acts but to actors. Hume leads us backward through the steps from the results of adventurers' actions to the way we properly should—but often don't—assess the character of the adventurers. He reveals their personal qualities to be superficially pleasing but actually harmful. To this end Hume uses direct assertion and contrast, especially blunt and shocking contrasts: Edward IV was "more splendid and showy, than either prudent or virtuous; brave, though cruel" (H 2.493).[84] As in that sentence, Hume's irony relies on some favorite adjectives; attractive but dangerous adornments are contrasted to modern, instrumental virtues.[85] The adjectives "magnificent," "splendid," "noisy," or "showy," or the noun "spectacle," might have been used in Christian writing to connote lack of humility. In Hume, who considers humility a vice, they often describe actions or states that look pleasing in themselves but are *causally unrelated to good outcomes*. The suggestion is that intelligent readers (Hume's so-called men of sense) who, rightly, judge by results or, better, by the results that could reasonably have been expected, should regard such gaudy qualities skeptically.[86] Thus Essex, Elizabeth's consort and self-appointed leader of an invasion of Ireland, is described not as someone heedless of bloodshed and dangerous to England's constitutional order (though both descriptions would have been fair) but as a ship flying with "sails, which were already too much expanded," who needed only the encouragement of his enemies to "push him upon dangers, of which he seemed to make such small account." After Essex's expedition failed miserably, he blamed everyone but himself, wrote letters to Elizabeth filled with "peevish and impatient expressions," and generally displayed his own idiocy (H 4.317ff.; quotations on 318, 321). His career ended in intrigue, arrest, trial, and execution. Being "ambitious of fame" (H 4.317) did not make him either happy or successful.

A second mode of irony appeals to what was likely the ruling passion of many of Hume's readers: snobbery. To value military conquest in a leader was to adopt the values of "the vulgar"; while the vulgar judge by appearances, the kind of people who read the *History* ought to judge by results. This theme is present from Hume's earliest work; even there Hume's elitism takes the form not of slighting the common people's interests but of lamenting the people's short-sightedness in praising a supposed virtue that subverts that interest.

While "the generality of mankind" considers military glory "the most sublime kind of merit,"

> [m]en of cool reflexion are not so sanguine in their praises of it. The infinite confusions and disorder, which it has caus'd in the world, diminish much of its merit in their eyes. When they wou'd oppose the popular notions on this head, they always paint out the evils, which this suppos'd virtue has produc'd in human society; the subversion of empires, the devastation of provinces, the sack of cities. (T 3.3.2.15, 600–601)

That is from the *Treatise*. But Hume in the *History* sharpens the contrast between the popular notions of most people and the well-founded praise granted by the reflective, and gives it a special edge on this particular point. When Henry VIII ascended the throne at age eighteen, even "men of sense" had hopes of his future abilities but "the people" were enchanted right away; they are "always enchanted with novelty, youth and royal dignity" (and Hume goes on to describe in detail Henry's appearance and bearing [H 3.83]). Hume's final assessment of Henry is that his "exterior qualities were advantageous, and fit to captivate the multitude: His magnificence and personal bravery rendered him illustrious in vulgar eyes." But this only shows the debased character of the public opinion that was judging him:

> the English in that age were so thoroughly subdued, that, like eastern slaves, they were inclined to admire those acts of violence and tyranny, which were exercised over themselves, and at their own expence. (H 3.322)

In particular, Hume accuses popular opinion of loving war for its own sake, and of taking an eagerness to fight wars for the touchstone of good leadership. Richard II, admirably peace-loving in Hume's view, was discredited and dethroned on that account. The Duke of Glocester played on "all the vulgar prejudices, which prevailed on this subject; "[t]he populace" readily followed "[t]he military men" on this score; and "all men" soon came out for Glocester and his war policy as "the true support of English honour" (H 2.306). Henry V, the hero of Agincourt, "possessed many eminent virtues; and if we give indulgence to ambition in a monarch, or rank it, as the vulgar are inclined to do, among his virtues, they were unstained by any considerable blemish"(H 2.378). As for Richard Lionheart, he was "much beloved" because military talents make great impression on the people—but a more sober assessment of his reign would have found it "very oppressive," with both high and arbitrary taxes, and his character on balance bad for the polity:

> open, frank, generous, sincere, and brave; he [Richard] was revengeful, domineering, ambitious, haughty, and cruel; and was thus better calculated to dazzle men by the splendor of his enterprizes, than either

to promote their happiness or his own grandeur, by a sound and well regulated policy. (H 1.403)

Public opinion matters, and the truthful or accurate historian will never forget that military virtues of youth, vigor, and courage are attractive to most people. The sensible observer, however, will note this bias without sharing it. The implications of Hume's snobbery are, as usual, complex. In an aristocratic age, the fact that Hume looked down on "the vulgar" did not necessarily mean Hume was more snobbish than his readers; in proposing to extend the privileges of politeness to those in "the middle station of life," he was often less so.[87] And in this case, disdain for showy militarism necessarily extends upward as well as downward; it casts discredit on both the vulgar multitude and the kings they tend to favor.

Most deliciously, Hume in several places *literally* sells glory short. He nonchalantly relates how prudent actors who noted vainglory in their opponents were able to profit from it. The vainglorious were encouraged to overestimate their own chances and take on foolish ventures, while the prudent coolly calculated the odds, betting against those ventures' success. When he needed money from parliament in 1491, Henry II, through a series of "magnificent vaunts," proposed a grand invasion of France that "all men of penetration" could have seen through. (England's allies were dodgy and France was well prepared.) Parliament, however, "seized with a desire of military glory . . . credulously swallowed all the boasts of the king," dreaming of the gates of Paris and a French crown for their king. Not only did "the nobility" vote a huge war tax; "many of them borrowed large sums, or sold off manors, that they might appear in the field with greater splendour." Henry fared nicely out of the scheme: he feinted with a small invasion, spent little, and quickly struck a treaty with France for "wholly pecuniary" terms (a huge immediate payment plus a large, perpetual, French annuity for all English kings). He thus "made profits upon his subjects for the war; and upon his enemies for the peace" (H 3.38–41).[88] Conversely, when Henry VIII, "more bent on glory than on interest," planned in earnest another grand invasion in 1513, Maximilian, the Holy Roman Emperor, seized his chance. Having promised 8,000 men to assist Henry, Maximilian naturally reneged on that but instead enlisted in Henry's army as a captain. This cost nothing except a vain show and provided both profit and power: "while he exhibited this extraordinary spectacle, of an emperor of Germany serving under a king of England, he was treated with the highest respect by Henry, and really directed all the operations of the English army" (H 3.102–3). Finally, Hume takes particular pleasure in noting how crusaders, intent on "glory" and "salvation," got their just rewards. As they were selling their property to finance trips to the holy land, the wise princes who took the other side of that deal acquired two goods at once: cheap land, and fewer foolish and troublemaking barons (H 1.239).[89]

As with Hume's argument for modern military virtue, there is a potential tension here. It is true (and an argument often used by normative realists) that a focus on interest over glory prevents something that all may agree is bad: wars fought and lost over trifles, at no gain to the country fighting them. That said, a statesman who has the prudence and self-control to place interest over glory will be a more effective conqueror—which is not necessarily good for his or her own subjects, let alone those of the foreign country (H 2.272). Hume heaps scorn on the mistaken view that kings should be judged by their military successes. But as he knows this mistake to be very common, even in his own no doubt civilized time, scorn is not enough.[90] For modern statesmanship to further the public interest, it must do more than embody the intelligent pursuit of conquest. Hume hopes instead to redirect the reader's judgment of statesmen away from their success as conquerors toward more "durable" achievements, and more peaceful ones.

Durable Success

If a modern military reputation is grounded on science, a well-earned reputation for strategic and logistic planning, and the resources of a sound modern state, a modern statesman's reputation for virtuosity in geopolitics has similar prerequisites. A modern prince, even if bent on war, must study economics.[91] The more general lesson Hume drew famously blurred, or rather denied, the distinction between civic, martial, and commercial virtue and the alleged tradeoffs among them. Hume not only contested the "republican" thesis that economic growth sapped martial virtue, but reversed it. The "greatness of the sovereign and the happiness of the state are, in a great measure, united with regard to trade and manufactures." The economic surplus provided by free labor and commerce not only is a benefit in peacetime but can be quickly diverted in war to "the public service" (through either conscription or taxation) to a degree that no poor but martial republic, where few hands can be spared from subsistence, can match (E: C, 261–2).[92]

This is an argument about luxury, but also about statesmen. The phrase "greatness of the sovereign" should be taken seriously, and the essay is pervaded with the language of grandeur. Commerce is praised for promoting "[t]he greatness of a state" (more than once), the state's "dominions" and "fame," "the power of the public," "the ambition of the sovereign," "the riches and strength in any state," "the power of the state" (E: C, 255 [and 257], 256, 262, 263, 265 [emphasis omitted in the last]). Hume is selling the advantages of commercial society to statesmen less interested in wealth than in power and glory. He has to remind statesmen that the "common bent of mankind" is to prize avarice over glory, because they themselves are the other way around. The relationship between rulers and ordinary citizens that Hume recommends (and thinks most likely to succeed) is one of mutual advantage, not common feeling.

Hume here is subtly and by stages luring us away from war and toward peace. In "Of Commerce," the greatest military capacity accrues to the state that holds it in reserve—reinvesting profits, as we would now say—rather than using it up in constant fighting. In "Of Public Credit," Hume argues with some heat that Britain's practice of financing wars on credit is unsustainable: however sound the practice is for meeting emergencies, it is ruinous when made a way of national life. Hume here actually uses the same language for excessive deficit spending that he uses for excessive militarism: deficit spending lets a minister "make a great figure," allowing for expenditure without taxation, but its ultimate results are "unnatural," an exercise in turning human endeavors away from honest work toward speculation (E: PC, 352, 357).

But the greatest point to be made against conquest, from the view of the statesman, is that it does not last. If thought about what is enlarged encourages those who practice any art to make their peace with modernity and its large-scale institutions, thought about what is "durable," "lasting," or "solid" is even more philosophical. It promotes Hume's beloved "cool reflection" regarding which human pursuits are worth the struggle in the first place—and the answer is the establishment of voluntary conventions. When Charles V retired from the slaughtering business to pursue philosophy and clock-making,

> [t]he *cool reflections* of age now discovered to him the emptiness of his former pursuits; and he found, that the vain schemes of extending his empire, had been the source of endless opposition and disappointment, and kept himself, his neighbours, and his subjects, in perpetual inquietude, and had frustrated the sole end of government, the felicity of the nations committed to his care; an object which *meets with less opposition, and which, if steadily pursued, can alone convey a lasting and solid satisfaction.* (H 3.446; emphases added)

In modern language, war is zero-sum (or, more likely, negative-sum). Peaceful government "meets with less opposition." It is a coordination problem, and a characteristic of successful solutions is that everyone welcomes their continuation; they are self-enforcing.[93]

Thus Hume's praise of moderation and prudence, which might seem a residue of ancient ethics, is in fact part of a theory of convention. A statesman who conquers foreign countries may expect them to spend all their efforts trying to conquer them back. But one who establishes and buttresses conventions may expect to see them further strengthened by future generations of subjects who find them useful. When Edward III was planning (again) to invade France, the Duke of Lancaster, on Hume's invented account, counseled instead that he make peace and seek "the praise of moderation . . . an honour so much the greater, as it was durable, was united with that of prudence, and might be attended with the most real advantages" (H 2.259). Edward did not long take that advice. Drawing too many lessons from "splendid, though imprudent" military successes, and wrongly believing that the French nobles whom he had conquered somehow enjoyed paying him high taxes, he overreached, made enemies, and lost not only his French possessions but much of his authority in England. "Splendid and noisy scenes" of his early life were replaced by "mortifications," and Edward "experienced, from the sharpness of some parliamentary remonstrances, the great inconstancy of the people, and the influence of present fortune over all their judgments" (H 2.270). On Hume's view, while Edward III deserves praise for "prudence and vigour" in his domestic administration, his foreign wars are admirable only to the extent that they gave barons an outlet for their aggression; they were "in other respects, neither founded in justice, nor directed to any salutary purpose" (H 2.271–2). Similarly, Louis XIV in trying to be both a conqueror and a persecutor ignored the advantages of the convention of toleration: those who want foreign influence will be more likely to get it through toleration, which adds friends abroad, than persecution, which unites enemies (H 6.498–9).

The "cosmic irony" that John Valdimir Price has seen as a hallmark of Hume's work—the humanistic counterpart, we might note, of the game theorist's distinction between individuals' choosing outcomes in private life and their choosing strategies in collective life—may indirectly support this point.[94] To the extent that rulers cannot expect to achieve the particular ends they aim at, they might be persuaded to turn to *non*-particular ends: to the establishment and support of conventions that make human enterprises of all kinds more likely to prosper. They will do better if they cut with, rather than against, the grain of conventions likely to win public support.

"LEGISLATORS and founders of states" deserve "the first place of honour" among all human beings because "peace and security" are second-order or general goods that make possible all others. The happiness accruing to economic growth is a matter of what we hold securely, not what may be taken from us, and "wise laws and institutions" educate us better than abstract philosophy or strict religions can (E: PG, 54–5). While England has no founders as such, its constitution being a gradual accretion, one can identify the founders of particular elements in it, and Hume singles them out for praise: Alfred the Great for inventing the jury and encouraging trade, industry, and learning; Edward I for repressing the barons, enforcing equal laws, and (more or less) supporting Magna Charta (H 1.77–81, H 2.75).[95] Hume thinks the latter deserves his common epithet "the English Justinian" because of the scope of his legal reforms *and their endurance*:

> the chief advantage, which the people of England reaped, and still continue to reap, from the reign of this great prince, was the correction, extension, amendment, and establishment of the laws, which Edward maintained in great vigour, and left much improved to posterity: For

the acts of a wise legislator commonly remain; while the acquisitions of a conqueror often perish with him. (H 2.141)

It is unlikely that a thousand people living in England can name three French provinces that Edward conquered. Certainly none benefits from the conquest. They might not be able to name Edward's legal reforms either, but they benefit from them: clear jurisdictional boundaries among courts; the office of the justice of the peace; an independent judiciary with which the privy council would not interfere; improvement of contract law. "Instead of their former associations for robbery and violence, men entered into formal combinations to support each other in law-suits" (an abuse that parliament in turn addressed [2.142]). This, Hume suggests, is the hallmark of true greatness.

Hume here is attempting a self-fulfilling prophecy. By praising those who write laws as earning more durable fame than those who conquer territory, Hume is hoping to cement the fame of lawmakers and undermine that of conquerors. There is plenty of scope for statesmen to win praise by wielding power. But Hume means to seduce us toward a standard of judgment and of public opinion that will grant them that praise only if they broadly support the institutions that benefit others too.

Moral Heroism and Common Life

The attempt to tame heroism by redirecting it may seem self-defeating. As previously discussed, Hume thinks religious devotion tends in the moral realm to take forms that are either absurd or actively harmful (to oneself or others). Those seeking "distinguished marks of devotion" that merit "divine favor" must latch onto something that ordinary human attachments and concerns would *not* motivate and might counsel against. Acts performed out of prudence, justice, or benevolence seem not distinctly pious but merely moral, human rather than superhuman.[96] By the same logic, efforts to socialize or pacify noble or magnanimous acts, or to give them forms that harmonize with the interests of those with no taste for such things, might undermine their status as heroic.[97] For all his attempts to explain "greatness and elevation of mind" as mere confidence or self-esteem (Hume's word), Hume must admit that

> an excessive courage and magnanimity, especially when it displays itself under the frowns of fortune, contributes, in a great measure, to the character of a hero, and will render a person the admiration of posterity; at the same time, that it ruins his affairs, and leads him into dangers and difficulties, with which otherwise he wou'd never have been acquainted. (T 3.3.2.14, SBN 600)

We might note that peaceful courage or magnanimity, which harm only their bearer, is perfectly consistent with a peaceful equilibrium. The artist who dies sick and impoverished, seeking the rewards of art itself and its appreciation by posterity, proves her own purity of devotion by *not* following the usual norms of prudence and good citizenship. But her doing so in no way prevents others from observing those norms. Similarly, intellectual heroes (whose importance to Hume John Siebert has noted) may certainly be courageous in the inquiries they pursue without therefore harming the public peace, provided they observe the basic conventions of allegiance and justice.[98]

But military glory is different. When the sack of cities is seen as glorious, citizens cannot be safe. And yet such glory, attractive because it risks death, will only be military glory if it also deals death. Hume addresses this problem by describing a limited-purpose chivalry—without ever calling it that—that redefines heroism as peaceful civic sacrifice on the one hand or the proper treatment of prisoners on the other.[99]

Hume effects this redefinition by describing the siege of Calais in 1347. Hume calls this the "age of chivalry and gallantry," but he is being ironic; he is about to show us what medieval chivalry amounted to (H 2.236).[100] Calais resisted Edward III's siege for almost a year; finally, reduced to starvation, it sued for peace on the condition that Edward spare the defending soldiers' lives. Edward was at first so affronted at the resistance that he demanded unconditional surrender with a view to slaughtering the townsmen. He was persuaded to compromise: he would spare the townsmen provided

> that six of the most considerable citizens should be sent to him to be disposed of as he thought proper; that they should come to his camp carrying the keys of the city in their hands, bareheaded and barefooted, with ropes about their necks. (H 2.237)

The citizens of Calais were understandably upset at this Sophie's choice; having to choose six of their number to die was "more severe" than dying as a body. Hume here has a double opportunity: to undermine Edward III's reputation as a conqueror (excessive praise in Hume's eyes, as just noted) and to put forth a new standard of heroism.

Eustace de St. Pierre, "whose name [Hume judges] deserves to be recorded," volunteered to be one of the six.

> Another, animated by his example, made a like *generous* offer: A third and a fourth presented themselves to the same fate; and the whole number was soon completed. These *six heroic burgesses* appeared before Edward in the guise of malefactors, laid at his feet the keys of their city, and were ordered to be led to execution. It is surprising, that so *generous* a prince should ever have entertained such a *barbarous* purpose against such men; and still more that he should seriously persist in the resolution of executing it. But the entreaties of his queen saved his memory from that infamy: She threw herself on her knees before him, and with tears in her eyes begged the lives of these citizens. Having ob-

tained her request, she carried them into her tent, ordered a repast to be set before them, and after making them a present of money and clothes, dismissed them in safety (emphases added).[101]

While Edward professed the "generous" and "heroic" principles of chivalry, the burgesses practiced them—without harming a soul. Here is a suitably self-sacrificing and superogatory heroism for modern, civilized times (H 2.238).[102]

Hume emphasizes the contrast by comparing Edward's actions toward the Calais burghers with how Edward treated a French knight who met him in pitched battle: Edward showered the knight with praise, gave him a gift of pearls, freed him from captivity, and while doing so stressed the danger that he (Edward) had braved by fighting him. "Nothing," writes Hume,

> proves more evidently the vast superiority assumed by the nobility and gentry above all the other orders of men during those ages, than the extreme difference which Edward made in his treatment of these French knights, and that of the six citizens of Calais, who had exerted more signal bravery in a cause more justifiable *and more honourable.* (H 2.241; emphasis added)[103]

The purpose of telling the two stories is to civilize heroism, to describe a kind of heroism that does not require feudal "superiority" and does not divorce the hero's passions from others' interests.

What Eustace did for courage, Edward Prince of Wales (the "Black Prince" of legend) did, in Hume's view, for magnanimity: made it civilized, polite, and potentially cooperative, a matter of vindicating one's own reputation without dragging down that of others. After describing the Battle of Poictiers— vividly; Hume likes a tale of good strategy—Hume spends almost as much time relating what happened to the captive King of France (Jean II) after the English won that battle. Again, the default outcome did little credit to medieval chivalry; each of two bands of soldiers on the English side were threatening to kill the king rather than yield such a rich captive to the other. But in Hume's view,

> [h]ere commences the *real and truly admirable heroism* of Edward: For *victories are vulgar things in comparison of that moderation and humanity* displayed by a young prince of twenty-seven years of age, not yet cooled from the fury of battle, and elated by as extraordinary and as unexpected success as had ever crowned the arms of any commander. He came forth to meet the captive king with all the marks of regard and sympathy; administered comfort to him amidst his misfortunes; paid him the tribute of praise due to his valour; ... Edward ordered a repast to be prepared in his tent for the prisoner; and he himself served at the royal captive's table, as if he had been one of his retinue: He stood at the king's back during the meal; constantly refused to take a place at table;

and declared, that, being a subject, he was too well acquainted with the distance between his own rank, and that of royal majesty, to assume such freedom. All his father's pretensions to the crown of France were now buried in oblivion: John in captivity received the honours of a king, which were refused him when seated on the throne: His misfortunes, not his title, were respected; and the French prisoners, conquered by this *elevation of mind*, more than by their late discomfiture, burst into tears of admiration; which were only checked by the reflection, that such *genuine and unaltered heroism* in an enemy must certainly in the issue prove but the more dangerous to their native country. (H 2.251–2; emphases added)[104]

Elevation of mind is here quietly but unmistakably redefined. The dignity of a monarch is now shown by "moderation and humanity"—qualities that can be, and were in this case, practiced by ordinary soldiers in emulation of their leader.

Battle victories in comparison are not immoral but *vulgar*. The observation "his misfortunes, not his title, were respected" is radically anti-feudal. When the Black Prince led Jean II in a London parade in which "[t]he prisoner was clad in royal apparel, and mounted on a white steed, distinguished by its size and beauty, and by the richness of its furniture," while "[t]he conqueror rode by his side in a meaner attire, and carried by a black palfry," Hume calls the situation "more glorious than all the insolent parade of a Roman triumph" (H 2.253). Anticipating Nietzsche, Hume urges us to think that one in power displays true power not by mistreating captives but by having enough confidence that he or she does not need to. More prosaically, such diplomatic treatment can help cement terms of peace when these would be more advantageous than war. On Hume's portrayal the Anglo-French Peace of Bretigni (1362) was severe on the French but observed by Jean, to the extent that he could, in recognition of his good treatment at English hands (H 2.261–2).[105]

This is not a single instance but the consistent mark of civilization. When Hume writes of barbarism, he sometimes intends to describe a whole style of life (as in the four-stage theories popularized by his Scottish Enlightenment contemporaries). But he just as often intends a narrower, moral meaning. To be barbarous is to engage in wanton cruelty not justified by any threat to be defended against. Even more specifically, the mark of barbarism is to mistreat prisoners.[106] When Hume writes, referring to the Black Prince's example, that "the otherwise whimsical principles of chivalry . . . [in this case] gave men, in those rude times, some superiority even over people of a more cultivated age and nation" (H 2.253), he may intend this distinction. A prosperous, scientific society may be "cultivated" rather than "rude," but the test of being civilized rather than barbarous is moral, not technological (though over time and on a society-wide scale it usually tracks technology). "Civilized" in this sense is often contrasted by Hume with its opposite, "inhuman."

Conclusion

Coordination problems in game theory, and the recent political science built around them, begin with the assumption that the parties' interests are at least partially congruent or common. Hume's *History* gently suggests that this assumes too much. The success of modern conventions requires that social groups whose projects are utterly incompatible with those of others in society have those projects redefined or transformed even as the passions that animate them largely remain. Hume believes that history has largely accomplished this in the few lucky places that are his main concern. Hume's *History* both explains how this happened and seeks to make the reader appreciate and support the good outcomes that result from its having happened. (That the *Essays* largely do the latter without the former helps explain why they tend to seem period pieces, celebrating a complacent time without making clear the contrast that makes it worth celebrating.)

Jeremy Waldron has claimed that partial coordination problems (the kind in which a distributional component is mixed with a strong element of common interest) define the "circumstances of politics": "the felt need among the members of a certain group for a common framework or decision or course of action on some matter, even in the face of disagreement about what that framework, decision or action should be."[107] His claim is that authoritative political institutions solve such problems, and legislatures solve them in particularly attractive ways. Hume in the *History* is concerned not only with addressing the circumstances of politics but also with explaining how they arise out of other circumstances. The "felt need . . . for a common framework or decision or course of action" was an achievement, not a starting point. Focusing on this prehistory of coordination helps explain several aspects of Hume's politics that otherwise resist systematic treatment, as well as illuminating several political problems whose importance might not otherwise be clear.

Modernity for Romantics

Hume's unabashed preference for modern commercial civilization over its predecessors can make him seem a fanatical defender of commerce and of the modern societies that have commerce as their basis. Duncan Forbes claims, on the strength of the *Essays* (especially "Of Refinement in the Arts"), that Hume's modernism showed him

> at his least sceptical: he had none of the doubts and misgivings which Adam Smith and all the other leading thinkers of the Scottish Enlightenment had about the all-round benefits of commercial civilization. The progress of civilization is improvement on all fronts.[108]

This is more or less true. But it is crucial to look at the kind of progress that occurs and the logic that drives it. In that Essay, Hume writes,

Another advantage of industry and of refinements in the mechanical arts, is, that they commonly produce some refinements in the liberal; nor can one be carried to perfection, without being accompanied, in some degree, with the other. The same age, which produces *great philosophers and politicians, renowned generals and poets*, usually abounds with skilful weavers, and ship-carpenters.[109]

The liberal arts thus include generalship and poetry, as well as politics and philosophy—not a medieval list, but hardly that of the counting-house either.[110] The Humean defense of work invokes multiple and complex motivations to pursue different kinds of work, including work that might not pay well in money.[111] This is modernism for romantics, at least for mitigated romantics who want to live glorious lives within society rather than attempting to dominate society and injure their inferiors with impunity. Nor is the only standard that of utility. Generals and poets seek "renown," and on the enlarged stage of modern life are much more likely to get it than they would have in an age of regional scribes and monkish chroniclers.

Hume faulted Machiavelli's conclusions (though not his mind, which in Hume's opinion displayed "genius") for drawing lessons from "little disorderly principalities" that later experience of larger, more stable governments has "entirely refuted" (E: CL, 88).[112] Current political theory, much of which continues to bludgeon the ancient and early-modern question of whether the best city-state should be commercial or civic, is subject to the same criticism: the beauty of a modern state lies in not having to choose. Modern societies provide unprecedented scope for *non*-economic goods that in a barbarous age could only be snatched by very few, in fleeting moments, amidst a life devoted to survival and subsistence. A much larger proportion of society can now pursue those goods, on a much more massive scale. (One meaning of "enlarged" is the literal one. Not only is an audience made up of ever more people from different backgrounds the best judge of good artistic work [E: ST, 233], but that judgment must presumably be, on account of both its quantity and its quality, more pleasing to the artist.) The American actor of moderate talent who appears in regional or stock theater at low wages still lives better than any actor in Hume's Edinburgh, will live to act in more and better plays, and quite possibly plays in the course of a year to larger audiences. The would-be scholar who can afford the cheapest apartment in a dying American city can now use a library with 250 times as many books as the (private) Advocates' Library, the grandest in Scotland, access to which Hume considered a stroke of great luck (E: MOL, xxxvi).[113] Though the matter is of course more complex, even moralists who prefer the simple virtues to grand achievements should, in Hume's view, prefer modern life to ancient, since

[v]irtue, which is nothing but a more enlarged and more cultivated reason, never flourishes to any degree, nor is founded on steady principles

of honour, except where a good education becomes general; and where men are taught the pernicious consequences of vice, treachery, and immorality. (H 1.179)[114]

Hume's mutual advantage theory is thus more capacious than most. While Hume agreed with the commercial thesis that political institutions should partially indulge and partly channel human passions, all toward socially beneficial ends, he had a wider idea than the passions-and-interests thesis normally assumes of *which* passions should be indulged and channeled. When it came to some passions that might seem anti-modern—for military distinction, for power, for the fame of great political deeds—Hume sought to modernize them, not eliminate them. This is partly because he doubted that elimination, or subsumption under commerce, was possible. Whether one welcomes the fact or not (and Hume is often acutely ambivalent), not every mode of life has a price. People will enable the goods of political conventions if they find the fruits of observing them sweeter than the alternative in terms of whatever it is *they* most prize—which may not be money. Fortunately, Hume thinks this can be accomplished; his evidence is that in England it largely has been accomplished. The skillful politician pays off threats to conventions of authority in the threateners' own coin, not his own. Even granting that such politic bargains often fail to persuade in real time, we can now at least persuade would-be disruptive figures that the new settlement gives them more of what they prize than the imagined glories of the past would have, even if actors at the time could not have known that.

Hume often deals in unintended consequences. In this case, too, mutual gains in opportunity do not require either that the person receiving the opportunity appreciate the institutions that enable it or that the supporters of those institutions understand and value the fact that they also further the projects of those who mock them. It might be better for social coordination if I regard the enlargement of opportunities in general terms, not thinking too hard about the fact that they further simultaneously both projects I value and those I hate. Those who seek to broaden liberal horizons often argue that liberal individualism requires extra-liberal supports.[115] Hume's claim to enlarging our understanding rests on the converse claim: *both liberal and nonliberal projects* rest most solidly on liberal foundations. The conventions that make possible peace and prosperity under law provide unimaginable benefits not only to those who explicitly endorse the primacy of those ends but to those who think they reject the primacy of peace and prosperity. Hume chronicles a neglected great transformation. The heirs to ways of life whose adherents would once have been reactionary, in complete rebellion against modern ways of living, over time become mildly alienated and nostalgic, dreaming of their forbears' former glories but quietly unwilling to risk current opportunities. If critiques of the Enlightenment specialize in genealogy, the Enlightenment itself triumphs through irony.

The Liberalism of Enlargement

Arguably, enlarged thinking is the central aspiration of Hume's political thought. Enlarged in Hume's time was—as "liberal" was not, yet—the standard adjective for "free from narrowness," broad-minded.[116] If we substitute "liberal" in many of the passages where Hume uses "enlarged," we can see how important Hume is, or should be, to the tradition of thought that seeks to transcend sectarian passions—though his preferred mode of transcendence is not the one we're used to.

Hume believes that enlarged thinking is a minority taste. It is the ideal *legislator* who has "enlarged sentiments and cool reflections," who deliberately seeks to extend the benefits of inventive and innovative conventions to those who do not share that taste. And it is the ideal philosopher who shares this propensity to seek general and non-intuitive rules.[117] (Put differently, institutions in the broadest sense, conventions personified, are almost by their nature more enlarged than individuals, because the latter are typically passionately devoted to particular ends while the former are not.[118]) An enlarged approach to liberal society is willing to take most people as they are, that is, passionate and partial. And it is willing to grant that the political philosopher's job's description, "not to do any thing, but to observe every thing, . . . [thereby] combining together the powers of the most distant and dissimilar objects" (Adam Smith),[119] is a specialized vocation, not a civic duty. Enlarged liberalism redirects our projects through the workings of institutions. It turns us away from a desire to dominate others by directing us toward the instrumental and intrinsic pleasures of diverse sorts of work.[120] It spurns the kind of allegedly liberal moralism that allows people to choose any project they want as long as it's altruism, or even the kind that requires everyone to redefine their projects so that they consciously affirm everyone else's.

Commerce and industry play a particular role here. While it might not spur the kind of reflection required for extensive sympathy, a progressive, commercial society is perfect for enlarging sentiments by spurring energy and new thought. "The mind acquires new vigour; enlarges its powers and faculties; and by an assiduity in honest industry, both satisfies its natural appetites, and prevents the growth of unnatural ones . . ." (E: RA, 270). The active, inventive energies released carry over into all spheres:

> We cannot reasonably expect, that a piece of woollen cloth will be wrought to perfection in a nation, which is ignorant of astronomy, or where ethics are neglected. The spirit of the age affects all the arts; and the minds of men, being once roused from their lethargy, and put into a fermentation, turn themselves on all sides, and carry improvements into every art and science. Profound ignorance is totally banished, and men enjoy the privilege of rational creatures, to think as well as to act, to cultivate the pleasures of the mind as well as those of the body. (E: RA, 270–71)

For Hume, the "privilege of rational creatures" is the enhancement and cultivation of our projects—not the pursuit of an alleged autonomy that would give us an identity independent of our projects. His liberalism, as Annette Baier has noted, embraces all our passions and encourages us to apply reason to perfecting what we do with them.

Humean liberalism is in principle cosmopolitan as well as cultivated. Students of coordination games have noted their "more the merrier" aspect; "the bigger a coordination coalition the better it is."[121] A Humean liberal is someone who is more attached to expanding the membership of conventions, so as to gain increasing returns to scale, than to preserving the purity of conventions that operate on a smaller scale (and whose narrow scope may make them seem natural).[122] But once again, Humean liberalism need not be conscious. It does not matter whether we affirm it as long as we live by the conventions it describes and (via moments of conscious statesmanship) aims to bring about.

Hardin says the Humean liberal will follow Adam Smith's maxim *pas trop gouverner* (do not govern too much).[123] In the case of commerce, Hardin's context, that may be largely true of Hume's thought. In the wider scheme of things, it is incomplete. The Humean liberal may seek a great deal of government when necessary to keep negative conventions—or a simple bullheaded independence that spurns the conventions everyone else observes—from disturbing social peace and cooperative enterprises. (Even French laicism, aggressive opposition to religion in the public sphere, could conceivably be defended on Humean grounds, though I would not do so.) And he or she might be very ambitious in using government to enlarge the sphere of cooperation in the international realm, seeking trade-based alliances rather than war-governed enmities. The right motto would be, instead, "do not confuse joint interests for common values" in a double sense. Religious or factional groups must not expect that social conventions or governmental authority can be founded on the basis of everyone in society coming to endorse their own, sectarian moral views. For its part, government must not think that because it's allowed wide scope to enforce conventions that benefit all, it's authorized to dictate substantive ends to individuals (though it may well have the raw power, in the short term and at potential cost to its durable authority, to insist on such).

Hobbes' first law of nature is "seek peace, and follow it." If Hume had more of an affinity for natural-law talk (instead, he radicalizes Hobbes' program of re-expressing laws of nature in terms of moral virtues that have a prudential basis)[124]—his first law of nature might be "seek opportunities for gains from coordination, and follow the conventions that provide them." Modernity has room for many lives. But every good modern subject or citizen must have one tacit quality: a propensity for alliance, a rejection of the fanatic's determination to live for the sake of his enemies instead of his friends.

Chapter 3

Convention and Allegiance

There are things which exist and facts which hold only if the
relevant individuals believe that they exist or hold and act
according to these beliefs. . . . [I]nstitutions and institutional facts
fall under this description.
—Eerik Lagerspetz (1995: 6, emphasis omitted)

You don't hold elected office in this town. You run it because people
think you do. They stop thinking it, you stop running it.
—*Miller's Crossing* (1990)

I am reading Hume's *History* as a book about conventions of authority—and
the artificial virtue, namely allegiance, that describes adherence to that convention. The *History* treats authority's characteristics or qualities, its operation, its preconditions, its effects, and the circumstances responsible for crisis
and change in authority and allegiance. There is no logical difference between
describing the *History* this way and describing it the more usual way, as a story
of the development of the English constitution.[1] But there is a psychological
difference: the language of authority and allegiance reminds us that constitutions and institutions are simply other ways of describing conventions that
human beings have found to be advantageous. Since all government rests on
opinion, the units of political governance have no existence apart from the
opinions and habits of those who live under them.

Of Hume's three best-known artificial virtues—fidelity to promises, justice, and allegiance[2]—the last has received the least attention. This is true
even of those concerned with Hume's political theory. Many causes contribute to this: the obsession of political theory with questions not of politics but
of social policy, so that property comes to seem much more interesting than
allegiance; a tendency to take Hume's political ideas from the *Treatise*, which
contains fourteen mentions of allegiance, rather than the *History*, which has
almost seven times that amount; the fact that those who do study the *History*
tend to be either historians who do not seek general lessons or conservatives
who distrust them (or both); and the political context of Anglo-American

thought, in which allegiance to stable constitutional conventions can be taken for granted. Hume's casual claim that "the principal object of government is to constrain men to observe the laws of nature" (T 3.2.8.5, SBN 543) surely plays some role as well in effacing the importance of allegiance, even though it blatantly contradicts Hume's own account, a few pages earlier, of how allegiance to government—and only that—not only defines and enforces the rules of property but produces all public goods, from bridges, harbors, and canals to fleets and armies (T 3.2.7.8, SBN 538–9). For whatever reason, the processes by which government, "one of the finest and most subtle inventions imaginable" (ibid.), arises from its component parts, namely partial and short-sighted individual human beings, is often regarded as far less important than the question of what government should do once it gets started.

This chapter aims to give allegiance the attention it deserves, with a view to explaining not conceptual or logical issues but the problems of political stability and change. In fact, even the conceptual questions require an account of stability and change. Since the main title to allegiance is "long possession," what counts as possession, and what counts as long, bear not just on allegiance's effects but on its content, its definition. Hume tells us that these questions defy "sound reason and philosophy": they depend on "general opinion" (or when that is divided, "the swords of the soldiery," "war and violence" [T 3.2.10.15, SBN 562; E: OC, 483, 486]). Since government is "an invention of men," and "the origin of most governments is known in history" (T 3.2.8.4, SBN 542), the substantive content and actual development of Humean allegiance are likewise a matter not of logical deduction but of politics and experience.

This chapter will proceed in five parts. First, it shall stress the implications of taking seriously the status of allegiance as purely an artificial virtue, and authority as purely a convention. Reifying governmental institutions, as if they had an existence apart from our belief in them, is a tenacious mental habit, but Hume's treatment reminds us of its incoherence. Seeing government as effectively a mutual aid society has several good effects. It undermines the view that there is something exceptional about magistrates that makes them proof against universal human short-sightedness and partiality. It makes explicit the fact that no government is "legitimate" and no citizen "law-abiding" in a vacuum, but that all authority and allegiance bind particular citizens to particular governments. And it makes clear that authority and allegiance name dynamic phenomena that exist and change in historical time. Second, this chapter will explain why Hume's theory of justice stresses security of property and largely leaves out immunity from bodily injury: the convention that prevents wanton personal violence is not property (the impersonal counterpart of justice) but authority (the counterpart of allegiance). Third, it will discuss how the mutual dependence or mirror-image quality of allegiance and authority helps explain Hume's theory of legitimate rebellion and legitimate emergency powers. Both will turn out to have very similar foundations as exceptions to the general rule that conventions of allegiance promote the public good. Fourth, it will explain how Hume's theory of authority in the *History* illuminates his dissatisfaction with contract theory in its historical form. While private contracts in actual history were deals that powerful social actors struck to safeguard their ability to dominate others without check, modern authority is a kind of non-consent-based public bargain whereby all citizens lend a certain support to the government in return for all obtaining certain benefits. Fifth, it will explore the radical case in which authority is forfeited altogether: the so-called egregious tyranny that Hume alludes to in the *Treatise* but illustrates only in the *History*. In conclusion, it will discuss both the general theoretical implications of Hume's theory and the advantages of viewing authority as a matter of convention rather than adopting headier alternatives.

Authority and Allegiance: Two Names, One Thing

For Hume, allegiance to government is an artificial virtue. The corresponding convention, authority, is likewise stable because of human artifice (though not, except occasionally and partially, design). We value allegiance because we have experienced its past advantages and make a habit of reminding each other of its likely future ones. Allegiance is "invented," not by philosophers' thinking about it but, like other technologies, through a mixture of experience, judgment, and luck (and, eventually, conscious understanding and deliberate reform, on which more later). Our "political duties" rest on "human conventions" (T 3.2.8.5, 3.2.8.4, SBN 543, 542).

Much mischief has resulted from a bit of hypothetical or conjectural history in the *Treatise*: there, Hume posits that primitive societies with no possessions beyond subsistence might exist without government, since the rules of justice are clearly advantageous without the need for magistrates to define or even to enforce them. Hume neither considered this a historical claim nor asserted its relevance to any history we might read. His conjectural condition of justice-cum-anarchy applied only to a subsistence society of hunters and fishers—Hume mentions American Indians, and may also be thinking of the Golden Age societies of ancient philosophy—with no "considerable goods" and no foreign wars (T 3.2.8.1–3, SBN 539–41).[3] Only a "small, uncultivated society" could do without government. Given any "encrease of riches and possessions," people would immediately leave this anarchic state. In "large and polish'd societies" justice is "impossible" without government: "[t]hrow any considerable goods among men, they instantly fall a quarreling (T 3.2.8.4, SBN 542; 3.2.8.2, SBN 540; 3.2.8.5, SBN 543; 3.2.8.1, SBN 539). Without our "civil duties, or obedience to the magistrate," "no government cou'd subsist, nor any peace or order be maintain'd in large societies, where there are so many possessions on the one hand, and so many wants, real or imaginary, on the other" (T 3.2.8.6, SBN 544).[4] Any modern and prosperous order of property relations is not, pace Hayek, a spontaneous one.[5] Hume writes that government is "in some circumstances absolutely essential to mankind" (T 3.2.8.1, SBN 539). Those circumstances are, essentially, those in which the disposable income of at least one member of society exceeds zero.

So while Hume does not rule out small bands in which leadership rests on force, love, or charisma, "civil government" as we know it is no older than "allegiance." Both the institution and the virtue have the same origin: our mutual interest in preventing our short-sighted tendency to act unjustly (T 3.2.7.6–7, 3.2.8.5; SBN 537, 543). Without the convention of allegiance, there can be random human beings who carry weapons and make speeches, but no government: "[C]ivil magistrates, kings and their ministers, our governors or rules," are those whom "we call such": we "immediately interest [them] in the execution of justice." Government is a mutual aid society. Those who run it enforce the same rules that they observe, and share the ordinary citizen's[6] interest in their being observed.

> Men are not able radically to cure, either in themselves or others, that narrowness of soul, which makes them prefer the present to the remote. They cannot change their natures. All they can do is to change their situation, and render the observance of justice the immediate interest of some particular persons, and its violation their more remote. These persons, then, are *not only induc'd to observe those rules in their own conduct*, but also to constrain others to *a like regularity*, and inforce the dictates of equity thro' the whole society. And if it be necessary, they may also interest others more immediately in the execution of justice, and create a number of officers, civil and military, to assist them in their government. (T 3.2.7.6, SBN 537; emphasis added)

If the language is less moralistic than, say, Locke's, the consequence is the same as Locke's: "force without right" is no government but merely crime or aggressive warfare, injustice that happens to be performed by those tasked with enforcing justice.[7] Annette Baier has pointed out how radical this seemed in Hume's time, in which the egalitarian contract theories of Hobbes and Locke had by no means erased older notions that social hierarchies were natural and that deference was always owed upward (the doctrines of Filmer, but even Hutcheson, who considered Hume's doctrine a poor support for virtue). For Hume, "authority" or "allegiance" meant *only* the duty to obey magistrates, not social deference and obedience generally.[8] John Stewart, in a similar vein, has described Hume's state as "bare and exposed, stripped of grandeur and mystery."[9]

Not only Hume's arguments but his language reflects his determination to humanize government. Hume's reliance on the language of virtue, sometimes seen as a throwback to ancient or religious forms of reasoning, can in fact be seen as integral to his hyper-modern theory of convention: government is constituted by ordinary citizens' allegiance, by an observed tendency to take direction from certain people called magistrates (later officials) combined with an internalized norm of doing so. Authority and allegiance, which appear within one hundred words of each other twenty-five times in Hume's work, are counterparts or mirror-images of each other.[10] Hume repeatedly portrays a high level of one as going with a high level of the other; a government that governs by authority is one that has earned allegiance, and vice versa. While Hume already suggests this link in a famous essay,[11] the fact that authority and allegiance are a matter of degree, things that can rise or fall or be gained and lost, is most fully apparent in the *History*, a book about change.

Magna Charta, as will be seen in the next chapter, instituted a combination of "limited . . . authority" and "conditional allegiance" (H 2.6–7). But a specific proviso of limitations, while politically very important, is not conceptually essential: allegiance and authority are *always* limited. There are failures of authority that correspond to partial withdrawals of allegiance. "The government couldn't get people to cooperate with its officials when it ordered X" (limited authority) is equivalent to "the people chose not to cooperate with their magistrates when the magistrates tried to order X" (conditional allegiance). Government exists to serve certain ends and loses its rationale when it fails to do so. Even despotic government, which arguably does not even rule by authority in its proper sense, faces implied, traditional limits. The Turkish sultan may not levy taxes; the people's religion is frequently "intractable"; "and other principles or prejudices frequently resist all the authority of the civil magistrate; whose power, being founded on opinion, can never subvert other opinions, equally rooted with that of his title to dominion" (E: OG, 40). Though Hume rarely speaks of rights, we can if we like restate his position in terms of rights. If we see allegiance as a virtue, a "civil right" is merely a name for a generally observed and recognized practice of not obeying the government when it attempts to command certain things. And a violation of rights is an attempt by government to do those things (through immediate threats of force, since the governed have no intention of acknowledging its authority to do so). Since such an attempt would, in a settled and constitutional government, probably fail—landing the government officials who made the attempt in prison—it will probably not be made.[12]

Hume sometimes uses the concept of obligation (or the verb oblige) more or less interchangeably with allegiance, and "obedience" or "duty of obedience" interchangeably with both, especially in pre-modern, feudal contexts (see E: OG 38; H 1.432, 435; 2.89, 412). Yet allegiance, Hume's usual word, better captures Hume's intended meaning: what ties us to government is something partly subjective, largely concrete, and dependent on historical path. Allegiance connotes something between loyalty and obligation, between a felt sentiment that may not be rational and an imputed moral responsibility that may not be felt. Allegiance always involves a feeling, though one that can be critiqued, corrected, or changed in mode or intensity, as with our sentiments of taste.[13] Allegiance also involves not a conviction that one ought to "obey the State," but a feeling of "attachment" to a *particular* form of government— usually the "ancient" one (E: FPG, 32; compare E: IPC, 512). When Hume writes, "I must confess, that I shall always incline to their side, who *draw the bond of allegiance very close*" (E: PO, 490), he is endorsing not an insistence that we "obey the law" in the abstract, nor that we render our obedience conditional on whether government is observing or transgressing some allegedly objective (or rational) normative principle, but a shared habit of attachment and understood actions that involves particular citizens and particular sets of governors. Examining an abstract duty would be beside the point in a world of convention, since what we ought to do depends on what we can suppose others will durably do—and there is no reason to suppose that what they will durably do includes seeking out rational justifications of things. On the contrary, what others will durably do, with important exceptions in crises, is live by the conventions to which they are accustomed.

Thus allegiance is path-dependent not for mystical reasons involving ancestor-worship but for very prosaic ones. When it comes to government, unlike other manufactured goods, comfort matters far more than performance:

> It is not with forms of government, as with other artificial contrivances; where an old engine may be rejected, if we can discover another more accurate and commodious, or where trials may safely be made, even though the success be doubtful. An established government has an infinite advantage, by that very circumstance of its being established; the bulk of mankind being governed by authority, not reason, and *never attributing authority to any thing that has not the recommendation of antiquity.* To tamper, therefore, in this affair, or try experiments merely upon the credit of supposed argument and philosophy, can never be the part of a wise magistrate, who will bear a reverence to what carries the marks of age; and though he may attempt some improvements for the public good, yet will he adjust his innovations, as much as possible, to the ancient *fabric,* and preserve entire the chief pillars and supports of the constitution. (E: IPC, 512–13, emphases added)

That is, institutional reforms, however important in substance, should observe old forms so as to take advantage of existing authority conventions. Modernizing Hume's mechanical metaphor, if one asks what the best steering, acceleration, and braking mechanism for a new car is, the answer is one that uses a wheel and two pedals. A car that lacked these features, however technically brilliant, would find few customers because operating it would require relearning how to drive. For the same reason, few existing drivers would want to share the road with that car.

The *History* deepens our understanding of how authority and allegiance are connected. It illuminates in particular allegiance's dynamic, narrative structure, whereby authority is built, and allegiance won, only in stages. "Government and allegiance" are assumed to have the same "lawful foundation," which foundation possesses "mighty authority" (E: OC, 472). The Tory and Whig parties during the Glorious Revolution argued over whether James II's abdication gave "authority" to his legal heir or whether, on the contrary, "the great security for allegiance being merely opinion, any scheme of settlement should be adopted, in which, it was most probable, the people would acquiesce and persevere" (H 6.527).[14] But they were arguing opposite sides of the same question: what kind of government would command authority *and* allegiance.

The Common People: Security through Allegiance

That authority is universally useful in complex societies does not guarantee that its full benefits will be automatically present. Like all conventions, authority is not a natural state but an artificial practice developed the hard way: through experience of the severe harms that come from lacking it.

Hume's theory of justice is essentially a theory of the benefits that result from secure property rights (culminating in a claim that justice needs no other explanation than approval of those benefits and reluctance to lose them). As such, it is often said to slight the interests of those without property. Under Humean property conventions, each is given (and historically, Hume thinks, was given) secure possession, and exchange rights, in what he or she initially had when the scheme came into play. Those who started out poor in this initial state, or are descended from those who did, gain (some say) little from such conventions as opposed to conventions that would either distribute property more fairly, under a reformed scheme, or protect personal liberty and safety more stringently than property, or both.[15] These criticisms are commonly and not unreasonably based on the *Treatise*, as containing Hume's fullest account of justice. Various possible responses might base themselves solely on that work as well. First, the objection focuses too much on one of the advantages Hume attributes to property—"security" in being able to hold what one has—while neglecting the other two: "ability," opportunities to divide and specialize labor; and "force," the opportunities for combined labor whose products far exceed the sum of what individuals could do (T 3.2.2.3, SBN 485). In current terms, justice may benefit bankers more than tailors, but only justice enables the planning, long-term investment, and overall growth that makes it possible for there to *be* bankers and tailors (where once were only warlords, priests, and peasant-slaves). Even thieves are much better off in modern societies than in savage ones: the pickings are much better and the prisons not always fatal. Second, one should view conventions in dynamic terms: even if the initial content of conventions gives the worst-off relatively little, their form—their stability *as* conventions—provides a framework in which future advantages may be pursued and those advantages may be leveraged toward later demands for more perfect conventions (see chapter 7).[16]

Still, both these defenses seem to slight the interest that everyone, and those with little property in particular, have in bodily security, protection from personal violence. In Hume's defense, some have argued that Hume regarded security as important but sufficiently safeguarded by natural sentiments like benevolence without the need for conventions;[17] others might note that Hume did not think people had any rational incentive to murder or assault independent of theft (since your physical injury does not improve my welfare [T 3.2.2.7, SBN 487]). But these possible Humean responses seem obtuse in the face of known facts. Whatever general aversion to murder humans may have can demonstrably be overcome by other passions. And motives of honor, revenge, or status—to which Hume was very alert in other contexts, especially in the *History*—can just as reliably motivate the practice of murder as avarice motivates the practice of theft.

A thorough look at the *History*, as opposed to the *Treatise*, suggests a different answer. From the *History* it is clear that Hume cares deeply about personal security. The plight of those who lack it is one of his central and most harrowing themes. Hume's theory of justice does not address personal security because *the convention that ensures security is not property but authority, and the virtue undergirding that convention is not justice but allegiance*.[18] Commoners gain security only to the extent that a baronial system of legalized theft and extortion is replaced by one law for all: initially monarchical and absolute, later—through slow changes and a few violent ones—limited, parliamentary, and increasingly democratic and egalitarian. The second part of the story will be the subject of later chapters. Here we can examine Hume's account of the first leap from force into allegiance and authority. The previous chapter described how Hume proposes channeling or redescribing clashing, antisocial passions into forms that make coordination possible. But allegiance and authority are, and have been, most directly appealing to actors who have no such problems among themselves. The common interests of ordinary people (for Hume "the people," "the populace," or, when their interests are more general still, "all orders of men") were clear enough, their security interests congruent in obvious ways, to give them every reason to seek a rallying point for coordinating their common efforts against their enemies. And the relevant rallying point was salient enough: monarchy. The monarch had an obvious and direct interest in supporting a scheme by which all gained. That is, his authority was to be acknowledged and strengthened in return for—and constituted by—the common people's allegiance. Both parties would be motivated by their common interest in reducing the power of the barons.

The Historical State of Nature: Personal Violence

As already noted, the "state of nature" that Hume discusses in the *Treatise* is explicitly conjectural and names a condition without *justice*.[19] Avoidance of the "wretched and savage condition, which is commonly represented as the *state of nature*," is linked with the "interest, which all men have in the upholding of society, and the observation of the rules of justice": justice and society are near-synonyms (T 3.2.7.1, SBN 534).[20] To illustrate his theory of conventions and artificial virtues, Hume should logically posit a state of nature that lacks all of those virtues and conventions (T 3.2.2.28, SBN 501). Yet in the passages directly describing this conjectural state of nature, Hume speaks only of the absence of justice, using it by synecdoche (or mere confusion) to stand for all the conventions, including promising and authority. This has helped give rise to the understandable view that property is the only convention Hume really cares about.

In the *History* Hume does not explicitly depart from the *Treatise* account of convention but radically changes his emphasis. In conditions that Hume describes as close to or resembling a state of nature, the greatest lack people feel is not justice but authority. And the result of their lacking it is not unstable property but physical danger, personal insecurity. "Men must *guard themselves at any price against insults and injuries*; and where they receive not protection from the laws and magistrate, they will seek it by submission to superiors, and by herding in some private confederacy, which acts under the direction of a powerful leader"(H 1.169; emphasis added). Until the discovery of civil law, "men, not protected by law *in their lives and properties*, sought shelter, by their personal servitude and attachments under some powerful chieftain, or by voluntary combinations" (H 2.521–2; emphasis added).

> If we consider the ancient state of Europe, we shall find, that the far greater part of the society were every where bereaved of their *personal liberty* [Hume's emphasis], and lived entirely at the will of their masters. Every one, that was not noble, was slave: The peasants were sold along with the land. (H 2.522)

"[T]he ancient Germans were little removed from the original state of nature" because their social union was "more martial than civil" and protected them more against public enemies than "fellow-citizens" (H 1.174).

Without abandoning his view that complex societies with a lot of possessions necessarily need authority, Hume here illustrates that many simple societies with very few possessions also need it. While all rich societies need civil governments, not all societies that need civil government are rich. The Anglo-Saxons' possessions were so few that theft posed few problems, but society was not therefore peaceful: people united into "particular confederacies" for defense; assaults were very common and settled by escalating vendettas; and "endless disorders" resulted—without there being much property (H 1.174).[21] A little later in history, society was "very little advanced beyond the rude state of nature" because it was a state where justice for *personal* injuries involved "absurdities":

> where stated prices were fixed for men's lives and members; where private revenges were authorized for all injuries, where the use of the or-

deal, corsnet, and afterwards of the duel, was the received method of proof. (H 2.521)[22]

And the remedy, or lack thereof, to this violence, was authority: "The pretended liberty of the times, was only an incapacity of submitting to government" (ibid.). When Hume describes the twelfth-century Irish as being in "the most rude state of society . . . distinguished by those vices alone, to which human nature, not tamed by education or restrained by laws, is for ever subject," his list of those vices or social ills is a set of synonyms for assault or worse: "rapine," "violence," "convulsions," "murder" (as well as, to be sure, lack of agriculture). "[C]ourage and force, though exercised in the commission of crimes, were more honoured than any pacific virtues" (H 1.339–40).

But the period that most resembled the "wild state of nature" took place in fourteenth-century France. Again, a lack of security was produced by "a dissolution, almost total, of civil authority" (the king was England's prisoner and civil war among the French had left authority disputed). The result was "confusions, the most horrible and destructive that had ever been experienced in any age or in any nation." The former sources of authority became agents of savage and total violence. Troops, unpaid, mustered their own armies by enlisting criminals; their plunder and sieges starved out even walled cities. "The peasants, formerly oppressed, and now left unprotected, by their masters, became desperate from their present misery." Deriving no benefit from those who vainly asserted their own authority, the peasants observed no restraints in attacking these non-authorities:

> The gentry, hated for their tyranny, were every where exposed to the violence of popular rage; and instead of meeting with the regard due to their past dignity, became only, on that account, the object of more wanton insult to the mutinous peasants. They were hunted like wild beasts, and put to the sword without mercy: Their castles were consumed with fire, and levelled to the ground: Their wives and daughters were first ravished, then murdered: The savages proceeded so far as to impale some gentlemen, and roast them alive before a slow fire.

The extremes of violence followed on an extreme lack of authority, even the partial and partisan authority of pseudo-conventions:

> In other civil wars, the opposite factions, falling under the government of their several leaders, commonly preserve still the vestige of some rule and order: But here the wild state of nature seemed to be renewed: Every man was thrown loose and independant of his fellows. (H 2.253–5)

For whatever reason—and one might credit Hume's reading of medieval chronicles, which often amount to a catalog of who killed whom in what order—Hume came to place personal violence, not insecurity of possessions, at the center of his story of government. History had made him more of a Hobbist. The common people's immediate and short-term interest in government was not that it protected property (at the time regular government arose, as Hume is the first to acknowledge, more English subjects were property than owned it) but that it prevented wanton violence, an interest universally shared.[23] Whoever protested against "acts of violence and of arbitrary power" was vindicating the interests of "all orders of men" (H 2.117–18).

Barons: Rivals to the Crown, Oppressors of the People

Hume's *Treatise* account of government, by which we correct for our short-sightedness and partiality by empowering a class of magistrates with an "immediate interest in every execution of justice" (T 3.2.7.6, SBN 537), is often considered abstract and unrealistic. The *History* makes it practical and vivid. Government arises, as Hume writes in a later and more practical Essay, out of "experience" of "order in society," and magistrates have an "interest in the impartial administration of government" that is not only immediate but "visible" (E: OG, 38–9). In England, the magistrate who first had such a palpable interest was the monarch. A king or queen's only hope of defying England's barons was to align his or her own interest in power with the common people's interest in security. In the previous chapter the barons appeared as uncooperative elements who threatened to frustrate coordination; here they appear as common enemies that, from the perspective of the king and commoners, provided an occasion for coordination (against them). The people (compared even to the lesser gentry famed in English historical development)

> had still a stronger interest to desire the grandeur of the sovereign; and the king, being the legal magistrate, who suffered by every internal convulsion or oppression, and who regarded the great nobles as his immediate rivals, assumed the salutary office of general guardian or protector of the commons (H 1.464).

Hume in that passage is summarizing in general terms a policy that Edward I made concrete. He was the first to combine the perennial royal yearning for more power and less troublesome barons with the sharp insight that expanding his power and putting down the barons required an alliance with those whom royal law would protect:

> He considered the great barons both as the immediate rivals of the crown, and oppressors of the people; and he purposed, by an exact distribution of justice, and a rigid execution of the laws, to give at once protection to the inferior orders of the state, and to diminish the arbitrary power of the great, on which their dangerous authority was chiefly founded. . . . he made the crown be regarded by all the gentry and com-

monalty of the kingdom, as the fountain of justice, and the general asylum against oppression. (H 2.75)

Hume calls this policy—or rather "the plan of his policy," a systematic
program— "equally generous and prudent," that is, both in the public interest and strategically clever (H 2.75).[24] The deal that was struck constituted
a change so great that it amounted to a "re-establishment" or re-founding
(H 2.75). The "conditional allegiance" discussed in a later chapter was contingent on the monarch's tangibly providing the common benefit of equal laws.

The breadth of the potential coalition was staggering, and sometimes neglected in summaries of Hume's history that stick too close to the surface of his
narrative. While Hume favors the language of liberty (for polemical reasons,
to dispute the Whig thesis that English liberty was ancient in origin), his account is less Mill than Montesquieu: the meaning of liberty that most interests
him is not individual fulfillment, perhaps an elite taste, but security under
law.[25] And while Hume's narrative, for excitement's sake, stresses the battle between the king and the barons, his asides and appendices note whose interests
were at stake in it: essentially, everyone's. It was not only "the people" whose
interest led them to support the "grandeur of the sovereign." The weaker barons also had an interest in replacing feudalism with "general and equal laws,"
since "the annihilation of royal authority left them exposed without protection
to the insults and injuries of more potent neighbours" (H 1.464).[26]

Thus, under feudalism, anyone who was not either a great baron or (to
some extent) a clergyman had to choose between utter submission to a baron,
in return for rough protection, or independence, which denoted a state in
which the agent of one's violent death was up for grabs. In this situation kings
had to choose between abandoning their people to such subordination—the
normal outcome except under the most vigorous monarchs (and to a great
extent even then)—and consolidating their own power in as absolute a form
as possible, for the public good. As of the reign of Richard II, who was deposed by a baronial alliance,

> The laws had been so feebly executed, even during the long, active,
> and vigilant reign of Edward III.[,] that no subject could trust to their
> protection. Men openly associated themselves, under the patronage of
> some great baron, for their mutual defence. They wore public badges,
> by which their confederacy was distinguished. They supported each
> other in all quarrels, iniquities, extortions, murders, robberies, and
> other crimes. Their chief was more their sovereign than the king him-
> self; and their own band was more connected with them than their
> country. Hence the perpetual turbulence, disorders, factions, and civil
> wars of those times: Hence the small regard paid to a character or the
> opinion of the public: Hence the large discretionary prerogatives of the
> crown, and the danger which might have ensued from the too great
> limitation of them. If the king had possessed no arbitrary powers, while

all the nobles assumed and exercised them, there must have ensued an absolute anarchy in the state. (H 2.331)

As noted, Hume thinks the barons both acted as criminals in their own confederacies (against the formal law of the realm, such as it was) and protected and abetted common criminals. Even when there was no civil war, there was no stable peace (H 2.11, 279). When unwisely granted the right to build castles, barons pursued private struggles that left England "a scene of uninterrupted violence and devastation"—both directly, through a kind of cold civil war, and indirectly, since the support of private armies required "unbounded rapine" (H 1.285).[27] The remedy again was authority:

> It required the authority almost absolute of the sovereigns, which took place in the subsequent [Tudor] period, to pull down those disorderly and licentious tyrants, who were equally averse from peace and from freedom, and to establish that regular execution of the laws, which, in a following age [the Stuart] enabled the people to erect a regular and equitable plan of liberty. (H 2.525)

Crucially, the barons benefitted not just from lack of authority but from lack of country-wide and uniform allegiance. They thrived during times when the ties of allegiance were weak. Their power was not just private but political. That is, they did not challenge political authority but rather arrogated it: they "were a kind of independant potentates, who, if they submitted to any regulations at all, were less governed by the municipal law, than by a rude species of the law of nations" (H 2.179). During the civil war between King Stephen and the Empress Mathilda (a.k.a. Queen Maude), powerful nobles purchased immunity in their own domains in return for their loyalty. During the War of the Roses, the Earl of Warwic famously became known as the Kingmaker, and the effect of his changes of allegiance justified the name. "His numerous retainers were more devoted to his will, than to the prince or to the laws: And he was the greatest, as well as the last, of those mighty barons, who formerly overawed the crown, and rendered the people incapable of any regular system of civil government" (H 1.285, 2.428).

While Hume's account of the formal feudal constitution is critical enough, he thinks it even more important to stress

> another power still more important than either the judicial or legislative; to wit, the power of injuring or serving by immediate force and violence, for which it is difficult to obtain redress in courts of justice. In all extensive governments, where the execution of the laws is feeble, this power naturally falls into the hands of the principal nobility; and the degree of it which prevails, cannot be determined so much by the public statutes, as by small incidents in history, by particular customs, and sometimes by the reason and nature of things. The Highlands of Scotland have long been entitled by law to every privilege of British

subjects; but it was not till very lately that the common people could in fact enjoy these privileges. (H 1.173–4; compare 1.253, 1.168–9)

As Hume put it in a late essay, mocking dogmatic Whigs who still imagined liberty under the "ancient constitution,"

> The people had no authority, and even little or no liberty; till the crown, by suppressing these factious tyrants, enforced the execution of the laws, and obliged all the subjects equally to respect each others rights, privileges, and properties. If we must return to the ancient barbarous and feudal constitution; let those gentlemen, who now behave themselves with so much insolence to their sovereign, set the first example. Let them make court to be admitted as retainers to a neighbouring baron; and by submitting to slavery under him, acquire some protection to themselves; together with the power of exercising rapine and oppression over their inferior slaves and villains. This was the condition of the commons among their remote ancestors. (E: CP, 497)

(Note that authority is here lumped with liberty as something the people "have"—it is their possession, and to their advantage.) The monarchy was "regarded by all the gentry and commonality of the kingdom as the fountain of justice, and the general asylum against oppression" because it provided "protection to the inferior orders of the state, and [diminished] the arbitrary power of the great, on which their dangerous authority was chiefly founded" (H 2.75).

Rebellion and Prerogative

Though space allows only a short treatment here, the mirror-image quality of authority and allegiance can help illuminate the much-discussed question of when Hume considers rebellion legitimate or justified, and in particular complicate the common accusation that Hume judges popular rebellions too harshly. The basic story is that both the people's habit of allegiance and magistrates' practice of authority have as their purpose the maintenance of security and order. Constitutional laws not being perfect, neither allegiance nor authority can preserve security and order in all cases. The people can become seditious mobs; the magistrates, egregious tyrants. In such cases of "urgency" or "necessity," both popular resistance to their regular government *and* governmental disregard for regular constitutional rules will occur. And both will be "justified," if one likes, in the sense of being instrumentally rational in pursuit of the same purposes that limited government normally (but not in the current instance) serves. However, since both prerogative and rebellion are dangerous and tend to excess, we should welcome constitutional innovations that prevent the abuses of both popular allegiance and governmental authority before they become serious. Conventions of authority that can do this are predictably and durably better than the pre-constitutional method of using rebellion and prerogative to check each other.

For Hume, rebellion makes sense when government tyranny is so "egregious" (or similar words) that it no longer serves our interest in promoting justice. In such exceptional cases, government has essentially become a greater threat to justice than private actors would be. But citizens' rebellions have a governmental counterpart: claims of "necessity" by a ruler, the kind of claims once called "prerogative,"[28] *also* reflect the view that the interests of the people are not served by existing constitutional arrangements, which must therefore be set aside temporarily with a view to re-establishing them later. Prerogative is rightly seen as an ad hoc solution that is justified when regular government fails. It rightly fades into insignificance once "regular" or constitutional government comes to be better and better established and its advantages more fully recognized. Prerogative is not, writes Hume sarcastically, "like those eternal essences of the schools, which no time or force could alter."[29]

Hume's goal is to reduce the need for both prerogative and rebellion. In more "barbarous" times, when rules were few or controversial, necessity or emergency was the usual appeal in both governmental and popular decisions (H 1.161). Under civilized or regular government, such claims come to seem exceptional or illegal—and cease to be "convenient," that is, conducive to public good, to the extent that they discredit the general rule. Hume desperately wants to avoid the state of affairs before the English Civil War, when the excesses of prerogative and rebelliousness sadly justified each other. Then, an unclear and "fluctuating" constitution rendered Charles I's "exorbitant" conception of royal prerogative excusable—but "public liberty" was "so precarious under this exorbitant prerogative, as to render an opposition not only excuseable, but laudable, in the people" (H 5.236).[30]

Because Hume thinks that the results of such political exceptions are likely to be destructive, he is famously suspicious of departures from allegiance and authority (drawing "the bond of allegiance very close" [E: PO, 490]). Less famous is the fact that he extends his suspicion to *both* government and governed. (When Michael Walzer wrote that the problem of "dirty hands" in governance paralleled the problem of civil disobedience by citizens, the comparison had a longer pedigree than he knew.[31]) Popular claims to rightful resistance are justified, if at all, by government's abuse of its constitutional discretion. The reverse is also true: government claims of necessity are justified, if at all, by popular rejection of ordered government in favor of factional dictatorship. In both cases, one may act to restore the primary purpose of government: to protect us against social actors who would otherwise tend to bring about injustice and personal violence.

Given the polemical context of Hume's time, which opposed the Tory doctrine that government should never be violently resisted against the Whig doctrine that it should be (at least in the past; Whigs were more equivocal once in power themselves), Hume's treatment of rebellion plays a much greater role in his philosophical work than his treatment of prerogative and has become much better known:

> When men submit to the authority of others, 'tis to procure themselves some security against the wickedness and injustice of men, who are perpetually carried, by their unruly passions, and by their present and immediate interest, to the violation of all the laws of society. But as this imperfection is inherent in human nature, we know that it must attend men in all their states and conditions; and that those, whom we choose for rulers, do not immediately become of a superior nature to the rest of mankind, upon account of their superior power and authority. What we expect from them depends not on a change of their nature but of their situation, when they acquire a more immediate interest in the preservation of order and the execution of justice. But besides that this interest is only more immediate in the execution of justice among their subjects; besides this, I say, we may often expect, from the irregularity of human nature, that they will neglect even this immediate interest, and be transported by their passions into all the excesses of cruelty and ambition. Our general knowledge of human nature, our observation of the past history of mankind, our experience of present times; all these causes must induce us to open the door to exceptions, and must make us conclude, that we may resist the more violent effects of supreme power, without any crime or injustice. (T 3.2.9.3, SBN 551–2)

Here it is the governors who break the constitutional rules and the people who are therefore freed from their bonds (as well as having an interest in restoring firmer and better rules). In general, one good departure from fundamental laws deserves another. "As interest, therefore, is the immediate sanction of government, the one can have no longer being than the other; and whenever the civil magistrate carries his oppression so far as to render his authority perfectly intolerable, we are no longer bound to submit to it. The cause ceases; the effect must cease also" (T 3.2.9.2, SBN 551).[32] Contrariwise, when the danger of a ruler's misconduct does not rise to the "great, urgent, inevitable" level that "dissolves all law and levels all limitations," extralegal action by a people or its representatives is not justified.[33] The general argument is that, the end of government being "security and protection,"[34] ensuring that end may require suspending some of the rules that ordinarily promote security and protection but have failed in specific cases.

Especially in the *History*, however, this argument applies not just to the people vis-à-vis magistrates but also to magistrates vis-à-vis the people. Just as the "general practice and principle of mankind" never condemns rebels against egregious tyrants like Nero or Philip II, (T 3.2.9.4, SBN 552; compare E: PO, 489–90), "impartial reasoners" will admit that Charles I had good arguments for suspending—though not abolishing—Magna Charta in order to ensure security and protection:

> Where a general and rigid law is enacted against arbitrary imprison-
> ment, it would appear, that government cannot, in times of sedition
> and faction, be conducted but by temporary suspensions of the law;
> and such an expedient was never thought of during the age of Charles.
> The meetings of parliament were too precarious, and their determina-
> tions might be too dilatory, to serve in cases of urgent necessity. Nor
> was it then conceived, that the king did not possess of himself sufficient
> power *for the security and protection of his people,* or that the authority
> of these popular assemblies was ever to become so absolute, that the
> prince must always conform himself to it, and could never have any
> occasion to guard *against their practices, as well as against those of his
> other subjects.* (H 5.195; emphases added)[35]

Magistrates are not exempt from human partiality and short-sightedness, but
neither are citizens or members of parliament. In both cases, the remedies are
dangerous but justified in the absence of something better.

"Necessity" in these contexts is not a rhetorical claim but appeals to a consistent standard: public advantage. Necessity justifies departures from legality by subjects *or* by princes, illegal rebellion as well as illegal prerogative.
The claim with respect to prerogative that "[i]n every government, necessity,
when real, supersedes all laws, and levels all limitations" is directly parallel
to Hume's claim that "Resistance, therefore, being admitted in extraordinary
emergencies, the question can only be among good reasoners, with regard
to the degree of necessity, which can justify resistance, and render it lawful or commendable" (H 5.128; E: PO, 490; see also H 6.173). Hume, putting
arguments into a party's mouth without citation and without rebuttal (a sure
sign that he is hiding theory behind narration) insists on the precise parallel: "necessity" or "extreme distress" justifies extralegality by *both* princes and
citizens—and, when present, will be "palpable" and obvious to both.[36] This
standard is not relative to governing institutions, though its application is.
Which institutions have authority in a given place and time determines how
often claims of necessity will be valid and which ones. (The more unsettled
or pre-constitutional the regime, the more need for both prerogative and rebellion.) But it does not alter the standard itself. "What is established?" is a
question bearing on the minor premises of such claims, not the major one.

Hume regards the Glorious Revolution settlement as having made conventions of authority and allegiance so solid that departures are almost never
considered. As Duncan Forbes has put it, the "new plan of liberty" after the
English Civil War era was not so much a new constitution as a "new attitude
to law and government in general, as 'rigid', systematic, and uniform."[37] This
new attitude, the result of the English civil wars, required betting on Englanders' ability to make the virtue of allegiance and the conventions of authority ever stronger. Hume thinks this bet worth taking in hindsight, though
dangerous at the time, for two basic reasons. First, an extra-constitutional,

under-institutionalized balance of fear between populace and ruler tends to be self-fulfilling. Though "enormous tyranny . . . may justly provoke rebellion," rulers' fear of tyrannicide often leads to tyranny, and popular fear of tyranny often leads to excesses in rebellion.[38] Second, actions taken from asserted necessity cannot (unlike institutions) reliably benefit from learned insights about the virtues of general rules as correctives for human partiality and panic. "[A] present necessity often forces states into measures, which are, strictly speaking, against their interest" (E: PC, 364). But whether it is safer to render both unconstitutional rebellion and unconstitutional governance taboo or rather to use one to check the other is fundamentally an *empirical* question. Parliament's abolition of arbitrary tribunals established the "noble, though dangerous principle" (or "maxim") of "adhering strictly to law." But for parliament to trust in that principle was at the time, given parliament's lack of evidence that it would work, "rash and adventurous" (H 5.329).[39]

When Hume counsels philosophers and politicians not to say too much about the exceptions to allegiance and authority lest people draw over-broad lessons (E: PO, 490–91),[40] he is not being an elitist who distrusts the people so much as a modern believer in the uniform flaws of human nature. He sees the biased and short-sighted actions by the people *and the governors* that existed before regular, legal conventions of authority and allegiance were sufficiently strong; and he fears that such actions might again become necessary and common if those conventions were weakened. The "simplicity" of constitutional laws—their ability, as we might put it, to draw bright lines around conventions and provide clear rallying points for those who want to act for the common good—is "best calculated to prevent the extremes on either side" (H 6.293). An inquiry that obsessively dwells on the artificial and contingent character of those lines and rallying points runs the danger, in Hume's view, of promoting those extremes, partly because abstract reflection would reveal that any number of governmental institutions are adequate, rather than letting us know what particular constitution others will rally to. "Examples and precedents, uniform and ancient" are the keys to settling "the nature of any constitution, and the *limits* of any form of government": there is "indeed no other principle by which those *land-marks or boundaries* can be settled" (H 5.583; emphases added). Many are prone to blame Hume's theory of authority because they think his goal is to tame Lockean rebellion. They might think better of him if they saw him as applying the same standards to prerogative as to rebellion—and as having less faith than Locke did that an Appeal to Heaven, which means to bloodshed, is an attractive way of limiting the scope of either one.

The Costs of Consent: From Private Deals to Public Service

In origin and motivation, Hume's treatment of consent theory was largely political. Since consent theory (sometimes, though by no means always or even predominantly, derived from Locke) was one element of Whig party cant, discrediting consent would further Hume's goal of moving beyong partisan myths about how the constitution came to be and forging a bipartisan consensus based on all Britons' present and future interest in maintaining that constitution.[41] But in the course of carrying out this political task, Hume developed a treatment of consent that is more complex (and even more biting) than often realized, and that contains claims about the ties between citizens and government that have never been fully explored.

General Consent: An Oligarchy of Leaders

Hume's explicit argument against consent theory in the *Essays* and *Treatise* takes aim at what might be called general or collective consent doctrine: the claim that the only legitimate governments are those that the governed as a body have agreed to. Hume demolishes this elaborate hypothetical as a myth (not to say sham), while endorsing the conclusion drawn from it, that resistance to tyranny is sometimes justified (T 3.2.9, SBN 549–553; E: OC, 465–87). In his rebuttal, he pursues several lines of argument that have become familiar. According to Hume, all existing governments have their origins in conquest or guile and owe their later authority to their long duration. In peaceful times, few subjects can be said to "consent" to government; during crisis times, when "military force or political craft" is decisive, the inclinations of ordinary citizens or subjects have even less force. Nor does tacit consent solve the problem, since a poor subject with no savings and no foreign language skills hardly has the realistic possibility of leaving. Finally, everyone (including they themselves) regards a country's nationals as having political obligations independent of their consent, and general opinion is the decisive standard in moral matters.[42]

None of this rules out the possibility that some government could arise from consent, as Hume in one passage concedes may have happened in the past, and in another imagines might happen in the future.[43] But Hume's distrust of consent theory more generally draws not just on a priori moral notions but on the practical—and to Hume's mind insoluble—problems of large numbers. His basic point is that consent on a large scale requires coordination, and in the absence of institutions this will give huge power to first movers or powerful private forces.[44] In every alleged act of mass consent, "the people" will not consent as a whole or even through a spontaneous majority. Those who really set the agenda and determine the terms of consent will be either old elites or spokespersons arising on a truly random basis.

> [W]here no force interposes, and election takes place; what is this election so highly vaunted? It is either the combination of a few great men, who decide for the whole, and will allow of no opposition: Or it is the fury of a multitude, *that follow a seditious ringleader, who is not known,*

perhaps, to a dozen among them, and who owes his advancement merely to his own impudence, or to the momentary caprice of his fellows.

. . .

In reality, there is not a more terrible event, than a total dissolution of government, which gives liberty to the multitude, and makes the determination or choice of a new establishment depend upon a number, which nearly approaches to that of the body of the people: *For it never comes entirely to the whole body of them.* Every wise man, then, wishes to see, at the head of a powerful and obedient army, a general, who may speedily seize the prize, and give to the people a master, which they are so unfit to chuse for themselves. So little correspondent is fact and reality to those philosophical notions. (E: OC, 472, emphases added)

Hume's distrust of elections by "multitudes" can be seen as impugning not ordinary subjects' capacity but their necessary dependence on arbitrary leaders to coordinate: the people cannot "chuse for themselves" because there is no such thing as social choice independent of some method of ordering it. Hume could have called tumultuous elections of new governing authorities "ignorant" (and he certainly calls them that often enough; the poor's situation gives them no leisure to think). But here that is not his argument. He calls these elections "*disorderly*" (ibid.).[45] His objection in the *History* to "those, who maintain an original contract between the magistrate and people," is

that great revolutions of government, and new settlements of civil constitutions, are commonly conducted with such violence, tumult, and disorder, *that the public voice can scarcely ever be heard; and the opinions of the citizens are at that time less attended to* than even in the common course of administration. (H 6.528)

Again, the *History* puts flesh on the skeletal theory. During the Civil War, when parliament declared itself the source of all sovereign power, and then tried and executed the king, Cromwell engineered the whole affair, acting as "master of the parliament" through agenda-setting as much as raw force. (Cromwell previously made sure to eradicate the egalitarian tendencies in the army that he had encouraged during his rise as favorable to his power [H 5.513ff.].) "*That the people are the origin of all just power*" was a doctrine that Hume calls "specious [i.e., plausible], but . . . belied by all history and experience"; in the current instance it was belied by the fact that the Commons undertook to speak for the people—and Cromwell dictated to the Commons (H 5.533). In another example, when the New Model Army took Scotland, it conquered first and then asked nicely for "voluntary consent." Finally, when Cromwell asked an English parliament to ratify a new constitution, his deference to the "confidence of the public" was limited; he placed guards at the doors of parliament to exact loyalty oaths to him in advance, and when parliament still argued about provisions of his constitution, he

dissolved it (H 6.44, 69–71).[46] After James II's abdication and the "temporary dissolution of government, the populace were masters"; they took the
opportunity not to establish a new government but to slaughter Catholics
(H 6.517).

Only the Glorious Revolution represents a "singular exception" of a government settled without force and by a fairly representative body. But what
accounts for this is largely the historically unique availability of an alternative
leader who was both trusted by all parties and moderate in his methods—
William of Orange (H 6.528).[47] And even in that case, Hume never abandons
his observation that in the Revolution "the majority of seven hundred determined that change for near ten millions" who acquiesced in the decision but
had no active "choice" (E: OC, 472).

Special Consent: Bargains by Barons

But the *History* illuminates this coordination problem in more than one way.
It not only says that alleged mass consent is in fact directed by first movers
and self-chosen leaders; it also points out that the only actors who actually
and historically governed by consent were not free citizens but feudal barons. The logic of coordinated action guarantees in practice that when governmental authority is primitive or lacking, the only parties capable of stating
their consent in one voice will be those with enough concentrated force not
to need coordination and enough resources to realistically threaten non-
consent. Consent, that is, was and had to be reactionary: powerful actors used
private compacts to freeze governmental arrangements in place, in defiance
of the present and future public interest. And in the absence of a government
capable of enforcing contracts, these compacts could only hope to overcome
present interest by invoking moral (usually religious) guarantees for fidelity that allowed moral and religious entrepreneurs to undermine what little
security partial consent might otherwise ensure. Ironically for those who
think social contracts are the antidote to hierarchy, the only actually existing
government by consent has been based on agreements extorted by warlords
(a.k.a. barons), guaranteed very tenuously by moral hostages placed in the
hands of churchmen.

Hume denies that existing governments are based on fidelity to promises.
But feudal government was another matter. Feudalism was an actually existing social contract: a politics of personal pledges secured solely by honor.
"The great independance [*sic*] of men made personal honour and fidelity
the chief tie among them; and rendered it the capital virtue of every true
knight, or genuine professor of chivalry" (H 1.487).[48] Powerful actors constituted a government by consent; they drew up explicit agreements for divid-
ing amongst themselves the political goods they prized, namely particular
exemptions from justice and the privilege of dominating particular sets of
commoners.

The hallmark of this "independence," under which barons acknowledged no political obligation not founded on consent, was precisely the triumph of private contracts and pledges over public authority. When the rebellious earl of Glocester returned to royal allegiance under Henry III, he

> escaped with total impunity. He was only obliged to enter into a bond of 20,000 marks, that he should never again be guilty of rebellion: A strange method of enforcing the laws, and a proof of the dangerous independance of the barons in those ages! These potent nobles were, from the danger of the precedent, averse to the execution of the laws of forfeiture and felony against any of their fellows; though they could not with a good grace refuse to concur in obliging them to fulfil any voluntary contract and engagement, into which they had entered. (H 2.63)

Even money, before modern institutions of allegiance, was not only a pledge for promises but a substitute for justice. In the feudal era, justice might be proclaimed as universal but in practice was "avowedly bought and sold": barons paid the king money in return for promises of fair dealing (H 1.479ff.). That they bought not a pardon but fair dealing shows that there was a convention of justice but not the institutional mechanisms for enforcing it. Lacking was what Hume calls the "*distribution* of justice,"—or, as above, "execution" of the laws—which requires settled government (H 1.488; emphasis added).[49] Not until the establishment of Magna Charta did royal violence against persons begin to be considered "as public injuries" and threats to "general security" as opposed to being "injurious to individuals . . . hazardous chiefly in proportion to the number, power, and dignity of the persons affected by them" (H 1.488).

Through the age of the War of the Roses, allegiance involved an explicit contract. In the feudal contract's familiar, stylized formulation, the vassal offers obedience and service in return for the liege's protection and a grant of land.[50] But Hume's narrative suggests that feudal allegiance rarely took this scripted, traditional form. Barons in fact struck particular, individual agreements regarding allegiance as if those agreements were modern contracts— and as modern contract theory would suggest, they regarded themselves as free from obligation if the terms of contract were violated. When Mathilda (the monarch fighting a war of succession with Stephen) wanted the papal legate's endorsement of her title, she "promised upon oath" that in return for his "allegiance" she would let him dispose of various church offices; he agreed on the "express condition" that she fulfill those promises (H 1.289). While the feudal tie was in theory deeply personal, that made it less public-spirited without being less mercantile or power-based. Feudal contracts, we might say, combined the psychological risks of marriage with the unenforceability of treaties. When Charles VII of France in 1435 needed military help from the Duke of Burgundy, "the vassal was in a situation to give law to his superior" and "exacted conditions" by which the King gave up land without the Duke doing homage or swearing fealty. "Such were the conditions, upon which France *purchased* the friendship of the duke of Burgundy" (H 2.412; emphasis added). Like all contracts that supposedly create authority, these lacked an enforcement mechanism, so they were easily disavowed on the claim that they had been extorted, or else required the most primitive commitment strategy (exchanges of hostages) to be credible (H 1.89, 430, 435). That the contract allegedly created a personal tie merely created occasions for undermining it through alienation of affections: through cajolery or, especially, religious rhetoric, a lord's allegiance could be "debauched" or "seduced" (H 1.390; 2.430; 4.54).

This points toward another fundamental weakness of allegiance as private promise: outside parties could undermine such allegiance by undermining the motive that bound people to promises, namely, religion. Popes in particular, with baronial or royal allies, for centuries played the Lockean game of asserting that only those with certain ghostly credentials could be parties to social contracts. Henry II's negotiations with Becket were constrained by his fear that excommunication would make his subjects "renounce their allegiance." When King John was excommunicated and his kingdom laid under interdict, the Pope explicitly freed subjects from allegiance (and went so far as to declare John a spiritual pariah: all who talked with John were also excommunicated); subjects became once again bound by their oaths only after John knelt (H 1.329–30, 430).

As always, the undermining of allegiance endangered ordinary subjects more than their rulers (who could sometimes escape to live in exile). When Pope Paul III objected to Henry VIII's execution of a bishop, he summoned the King to account for his crimes. Failing that, he proposed to hand over Henry's subjects to death, destitution, or slavery:

> [H]e excommunicated them [Henry and "his adherents"]; deprived the king of his crown; layed the kingdom under an interdict; declared his issue by Anne Boleyn illegitimate; dissolved all leagues which any catholic princes had made with him; gave his kingdom to any invader; commanded the nobility to take arms against him; freed his subjects from all oaths of allegiance; cut off their commerce with foreign states; and declared it lawful for any one to seize them, to make slaves of their persons, and to convert their effects to his own use. (H 3.223)

These strikes against allegiance, not content with placing all Englanders' bodies in mortal danger, also threatened their souls with mortal sin. Those who persisted in their allegiance felt not only endangered but *guilty*, having internalized a pseudo-virtue (religious obedience) rather than the true one (allegiance). Under the interdict against King John just mentioned,

> though many of the clergy, from the fear of punishment, obeyed the orders of John, and celebrated divine service, they complied with the ut-

most reluctance, and *were regarded, both by themselves and the people, as men who betrayed their principles, and sacrificed their conscience* to temporal regards and interests. (H 1.427, emphasis added)

If medieval government by consent consisted of corrupt bargains by the powerful, and relied on religious guarantees that could easily be corrupted in turn, modern allegiance can improve on consent in both respects. It allows each member of society to affect governmental authority by giving or withdrawing resources from it; and ensures that governmental forms will be independent of religious differences and religious manipulation. While modern allegiance may in theory be an alternative to general consent (and may suffer in theoretical comparison with the alleged liberty involved in the latter), in actual history it replaced *private* deals between powerful barons and weak central governments, guaranteeing the former's immunity from the latter. The *History* brings out the consequences of founding government on private pledges between vassal and liege, and quietly notes the advantages accruing to a more modern—and mercantile—model. Mutual advantage is the worst justification of political society except for all the others, which involve those with social power bargaining over personal rights to oppress everyone else.

From Private Consent to Public Bargaining

A crucial turning point occurred under Elizabeth. Before the invasion of the Spanish Armada, Pope Sixtus V[51] issued a new bull excommunicating her, absolving her subjects from oaths of allegiance, offering indulgences to Spanish invaders, and so on and so forth, *and it did not matter*. Elizabeth, who had persecuted Catholic political conspirators while turning a blind eye to (technically illegal) ordinary Catholics,

> would not believe, that all her catholic subjects could be so blinded, as to sacrifice to bigotry their duty to their sovereign, and the liberty and independence of their native country. She rejected all violent counsels, by which she was urged to seek pretences for dispatching the leaders of that party [*sic*]: She would not even confine any considerable number of them: And *the catholics, sensible of this good usage, generally expressed great zeal for the public service.* Some gentlemen of that sect, conscious that they could not justly expect any trust or authority, entered themselves as volunteers in the fleet or army. (H 4.265–6 [emphasis added])[52]

Hume skips past what made this revolutionary: Elizabeth could trust that the subjective allegiance of her subjects had nothing to do with the Pope's opinion of their allegiance. A decisive shift had occurred. Though the Pope did not know it, allegiance had started to be a matter of advantage—something owed, in return for services rendered—rather than a pledge, guaranteed by one's favorite conception of God (or, in practice, by someone claiming to be a mortal deputy thereof). Oaths eventually came to be exclusively a tool of religious factions—who extorted them to prop up force-based governments that served only their own sects—rather than the basis of civil allegiance to established regimes.[53]

This in turn allowed a sort of political pricing system, by which subjects granted less allegiance to the extent that their governments did their job less well. While Hume never gives an explicit account of how this works, several points in the narrative suggest such a trend. Already, toward the end of the War of the Roses, Hume portrays the English people as "satisfied with the present government" (that of Edward IV); their "sense of allegiance" was based not on their theoretical attachment to York or Lancaster but on their fear of reliving "past calamities" (H 2.483). When France's King Henry III assassinated the Duke of Guise (head of the Catholic faction), the populace "renounced allegiance to him" to the degree that "the most powerful cities and most opulent provinces appeared to combine in a resolution, either of renouncing monarchy, or of changing their monarch." Hume's telling description of this is that "Henry, finding slender *resources* among his catholic subjects, was constrained to enter into a confederacy with the Hugonots" (H 4.280 [emphasis added]). By the time of the Civil War era in Scotland (1645), a politician could believe with confidence that the "allegiance of the kingdom" could (absent military defeats preventing it) be settled, "through peaceful means," through the majority vote of a parliament (H 5.463). The transition was beginning from a politics that turned on duels between interdicts and Star Chambers to a politics that turned on the counting of votes and the size of demographic groups.

In the last chapter I mentioned Hume's account of scutage: once barons were required to provide money rather than men for national defense, the result was better armies as well as far-reaching constitutional changes. Advantage-based allegiance might be called *political* scutage. Its effects were just as far-reaching (and unintended) as those of scutage but in this case evolved from below rather than being invented from above. As with scutage, which replaced a military arrangement that "was extremely burdensome to the subject, yet rendered very little service to the sovereign" (H 1.373–4), allegiance avoids the deadweight loss involved in basing government on contracts that no authority can enforce and that criminals with a priest on the payroll (or vice versa) can easily undermine. While defenders of contract theory often assume it to be radical, Hume portrays it as excessively traditional. Contract theories of government demand that we rest authority on what the prevailing moral theory asserts to be honorable, rather than on what experience demonstrates to be serviceable.

Government by advantage is well served by mercantile metaphors.[54] Modern politics begins when allegiance ceases to be a personal promise and starts to become a collective resource granted, in aggregate, by the people in return for magistrates' adequate performance of their task. The feudal deal whereby kings granted barons political authority in return for military service has been reversed. Now it is, in practice, though not in oath, the people who allow the government authority—provided that, and only so long as, it serves us.[55]

Egregious Tyranny and Disallegiance

Tyranny, for Hume, is a relative term. When institutions are underdeveloped, and foreign powers or domestic (especially religious) factions threaten international or civil war, forms of enlightened arbitrary rule—Hume does not shrink from the word "despotism"[56]—may be the least bad way of giving subjects the rudiments of security and justice. Thus Hume defends, indeed lavishly praises, Alfred I ("the Great") not only for introducing juries and rough methods of holding magistrates accountable, but for instituting systems of mutual surveillance that required subjects of various kinds to systematically observe and vouch for one another's behavior. Such surveillance would be "destructive of liberty and commerce in a polished state" but was, at a time when the people were not "enured to obedience and justice," necessary, and "well calculated to reduce that fierce and licentious people under the salutary restraint of law and government" (H 1.77).[57] And Hume repeatedly excuses—without quite justifying—Henry VIII's tyrannical methods toward religious factions as representing possibly the least bad way of managing a remarkably peaceful transition, all things considered, from a uniformly Catholic society to one mostly Protestant.[58]

But there are some acts of tyranny that no circumstances can excuse. Hume in his systematic works never defines the kind of "egregious," "flagrant," "grievous" tyranny (or "tyranny and oppression") that he claims justifies citizen resistance.[59] But in the History he gives examples that illuminate what such allegiance-destroying tyranny looks like. Speaking broadly, it describes a state in which conventions of authority that would serve all citizens' interests are available—perhaps have been enjoyed in recent memory—but the governing powers spurn them in favor of acting against all citizens (or, more commonly, a minority subgroup) in predatory ways that leave them less secure than they would be without government.[60] The Scots under Charles II, a monarch who used furious measures to suppress presbyterian Covenanters in that country, suffered a "long train of violence and oppression" or a "continued train of oppression." Faced with the kind of "tyranny, from which no man could deem himself safe," they considered moving to the Carolina colony. "Any condition seemed preferable to the living in their native country, which, by the prevalence of persecution and violence, was become as insecure to them as a den of robbers" (H 6.416–17, 467). The Irish suffered a similar condition for hundreds of years. In 1315 the "horrible and absurd oppressions" they suffered under their normal overlords, the English, "made them . . . fly to the standard of the Scots, whom they regarded as their deliverers," and Hume does not blame them (H 2.159). The state of Ireland as of 1599 was no better, lacking not merely authority but even humanity, and therefore sapping allegiance:

> [T]he English carried farther their ill-judged tyranny. Instead of inviting the Irish to adopt the more civilized customs of their conquerors, they even refused, though earnestly solicited, to communicate to them the privilege of their laws, and every where marked them out as aliens and as enemies. Thrown out of the protection of justice, the natives could find no security but in force; and flying the neighbourhood of cities, which they could not approach with safety, they sheltered themselves in their marshes and forests from the insolence of their inhuman masters. Being treated like wild beasts, they became such; and joining the ardor of revenge to their yet untamed barbarity, they grew every day more intractable and more dangerous. (H 4.311)[61]

These are cases of foreign domination, in which weak ties of sympathy often yield despotic rule (and "authority" only over the colonists, not the natives [see E: PRS, 18]). On the Continent, though Hume treats the case less explicitly, Peter the Cruel of Castile seems to represent a rare case of allegiance being totally dissolved in a purely domestic case. Due to the "ferocity" of Peter's rule—he was a "tyrant," "abandoned to all sense of virtue and honor," prone to exact "barbarities" on his people—he came to rule by "present terror alone" and "incurred the universal hatred of his subjects." Those subjects welcomed a foreign conqueror, and switched their allegiance to a new dynasty without the slightest regret (H 2.263–7). (The barons of Normandy in 1103–6 represent a similar case.[62])

In England, there are a few cases of tyranny that Hume seems to think nothing can excuse (and he brings out his favorite adjectives to emphasize this). The institution of pursuivants, agents of Elizabeth's council or high commission who carried off and imprisoned without trial anyone who dared filed a lawsuit against their masters, amounted to "egregious . . . tyranny"; Hume calls the pursuivants "a kind of harpies" (H 4.365). Similarly, Hume labels as "grievous and incredible oppressions" the practice of purveyors under Elizabeth, who could in effect take any goods from any subject for paltry compensation, and terrorize would-be political opponents through the threat of doing so (H 4.406, note "BB"). In general, egregious tyranny is compared to an animal condition: again in a mirrored relationship, both the agents of government and the sufferers reach a kind of subhuman state. (The former are "harpies" or practice "ferocity," from Latin *ferox* "wild beast"; the latter are reduced to the state of wild beasts.)

But the clearest victims of egregious tyranny in a purely domestic case (though in a sense they were rendered foreigners as a result) were the Jews, subject in medieval England to "the most barefaced acts of tyranny and oppression." Jews "were entirely out of the protection of law" as well as "extremely odious from the bigotry of the people . . . abandoned to the immeasurable rapacity of the king and his ministers" (H 1.483, Appendix II). In concrete terms, Jews were subject to officially sanctioned kidnapping (they were put in jail and kept there until they paid ransom [1.483]) and massacres supported by leading citizens of London (H 1.379). They were *de facto* outside the protection of both property and authority conventions. When King Edward Longshanks finally expelled the Jews *en masse*, he made matters *de jure*. He made sure to confiscate all the Jews' property as they left: a sign, in Hume's eyes, of "egregious tyranny." Hume freely says the Jews were "robbed," Edward being their "plunderer" (H 2.77–8). It would be hard to describe England's Jews as owing allegiance, as opposed to submission out of necessity, to a government that refused them all protection.

Finally, government by military force alone achieves the status of egregious tyranny or justified disallegiance by a kind of omission. Such governments do not lose authority, since they never had it in the first place; when the immediate threat of violence dissipates, so does their sway. Hume uses "terror" (when used to name a policy) in the contemporary sense, a practice of exacting obedience through the fear of death unalloyed with claims to authority or sentiments of allegiance (see, e.g., H 1.140, 2.350; 5.291, 365, 372). Cromwell, in Hume's view, was a particularly expert practitioner; he brought to mass terror something like Machiavelli's sense of "spectacle." In Cromwell's hands terror was a public performance, and those submitting to terror felt not allegiance but rather "awe."[63] Authority requires something more. In essence, a government seeking authority must prove it is not the public's enemy but, roughly put, its ally—a minimal standard, but many governments manage to fall short of it.

Conclusions

Plural Personation

Hobbes viewed the sovereign as an entity that "personates" or represents us. Here as in many things, Hume gestures in the same direction as Hobbes but sees further. On the level of origins, Hardin has shown that Hume's account of social coordination through convention is more credible than Hobbes' insistence that all is chaos absent sovereign command.[64] On the conceptual level, Hume's theory of authority and allegiance can be seen as an improved version of Hobbes' famous portrayal (in the frontispiece of *Leviathan*) of a sovereign composed of the bodies of his subjects. Government, according to Hume's portrait, does not speak for its subjects or citizens but acts through them. A government's authority is dependent on and contingent on subjects' opinion that its authority tracks their interest. And unlike the individual limbs of a body, we as subjects or citizens can refuse to do as the would-be commander proposes. We do not need to attack the head in order to flout its commands; we need only weaken our propensity to cooperate with those commands in order for them to stop being commands.

But Hume's most useful theoretical technology involves the substance of personation or representation, not its form. The parliamentary solution to the biases of coordination described in chapters 6 and 7 could be seen as a plural- ist and egalitarian correction to Hobbes' one-sided, "take it or leave it" (and one had better take it) portrait of sovereignty. The mechanisms discussed in those chapters accord with what Monica Brito Vieira and David Runciman have proposed as an alternative path to democratic theory: rather than tak- ing Athenian democracy as a normative paradigm and then asking (a little quixotically) how its values can be preserved under conditions of mass poli- tics, one can take representation and state-building as the central and non- optional building blocks of modern mass politics and then explore how they have been democratized and might be further improved.[65]

Bright Lines and Civilized Governments

I have argued that Humean authority, as it develops, is continuous rather than discrete. Politicians may command more or less authority, and different ones, different amounts; citizens, correspondingly, may display more or less alle- giance. This would seem, however, to contradict Hume's own statement about artificial virtues: that they *do* correspond to bright lines. While the natural virtues "run insensibly into each other," "rights, and obligations, and prop- erty, admit of no such insensible gradation . . . a man either has a full and perfect property, or none at all; and is either entirely oblig'd to perform any action, or lies under no manner of obligation." That, Hume submits, is how we know that contracts and property are artificial constructs, and promising and justice artificial virtues: bright lines are unnatural but characteristic of conventions, whose utility requires that obligations be definite and assignable (T 3.2.6.7, SBN 529).

The apparent contradiction is easily resolved. Authority and allegiance are continuous only in "barbaric" societies, where the convention is not yet solid and the object of the virtue not yet agreed on. Their operation becomes much closer to a bright line in civilized societies, which more or less by definition have a principle of authority that is uncontroversial and an object of alle- giance that is generally observed. (This need not be a ratchet. Hume's wor- ries that England late in his life was tending toward "barbarism" may reflect his judgment that the Wilkes and Liberty movement was producing a casual attitude toward allegiance. The Wilkesites spurned parliament's rulings yet proposed no alternative, let alone a viable one.[66]) As authority becomes more settled, the question "how much, how many?" that is commonly asked by politicians, businesspeople, labor leaders, and economists yields over time to the question of lawyers: "guilty or not"? That said, authority will never be quite as solidly drawn as property, and will always tend to admit of marginal cases. After all, bright lines are always more common when tribunals settle an issue, whereas "[h]alf rights and obligations" seem natural when matters are left up to common opinion (as must be the case when matters of authority are themselves at issue; see T 3.2.6.8, SBN 531). Treason now has quite a clear definition, no fuzzier than that of theft. "Unlawful enemy combatant" is a different matter.

The Paradox of Particular Allegiance

Constitutions are often explained as devices of precommitment. Alternatively, they can be described as ways of solving cooperation problems by reducing them to coordination problems: we acquiesce to a common power that can then tax and adjudicate the level of public goods.[67] Neither account fully explains the mode in which we are committed to constitutions, which is both *deep* and *particular*. One hallmark of stable constitutional regimes is that the people who live under them are deeply attached to *their own* fundamental institutions, not others. Constitutional monarchies and constitutional republics are both perfectly decent governments to live under, but those who live under one would not be willing to swap their form of government to the other, or back again, even once per generation. Nor are the subjects of monarchies indifferent with respect to which royal family rules, nor the citizens of the most stable republics (e.g., the United States and Switzerland) indifferent as to which of several plausible constitutions will be theirs. Authority in this respect is very different from property. As Hume recognized and approved of, people neither know nor care which of several property conventions governs them as long as the convention does an adequate job. (Most Americans who buy something online from France, or Louisiana, probably have only the faintest understanding of who Napoleon was, let alone of his Code.)

The deep and particular quality of authority, and of its agent-centered brother allegiance, arises, I submit, from the fact that authority chooses magistrates with proper names and gives them a role that others do not share.[68] All citizens may benefit equally from authority, but not all can share equally in the power defined by authority. Those who hold office have more power than the rest; and political order, which requires abiding by magistrates' decisions, is not compatible with that power being distributed equally. Even Athens, though nominally a direct democracy with no permanent political class, elected its generals—some of whom, like Pericles, thereby became leading "politicians."

I do not care if I am trading under a convention alien to me because I need not have any personal relationship with the trader. (That's the point of a market economy.) I do care if I am governed by a convention I am not accustomed to, because politics is inherently somewhat personal—and ever more personal, incidentally, as one moves down the educational chain from those who think about politics and policies in the abstract to those who merely rely on them.[69] I am attached to my form of government because I want to have some personal attachment to, some identification with, the process that selects my governors. Another country's magistrates could be very good at what they do without my being willing to let them do it to me. How we decide *who* settles controversies over property and other things is more consequential to citizens than how we decide the details of what property is. Though a political scientist who analyzes politics from outside can aspire to replace the proper names of political and social unities with variables, so as to draw generalizable causal conclusions,[70] the perspective of a citizen does not generally allow this.

But this suggests a further problem: the holders of authority must be accepted as such by an overwhelming majority of citizens regardless of whether their particular qualities or political programs are those the citizens would ideally prefer. This will be easiest to the extent that the object of allegiance is a constitution. Allegiance in such cases does not require endorsement of the officials in charge, merely acquiescence in the mode of choosing them—whether elective or hereditary. If hereditary, however, the institutions should be more formal than substantive, so that attachment to the regime does not require attachment to a permanent and ascriptive ruling class. Otherwise the constitution will win the assent only of those who do not mind permanent dependence (a significant minority of human beings, but never a stable and overwhelming majority). Finally, the regime should include modes of adjusting to shifts in economic and political power and in prevailing political opinions. The substance of policy should ideally not be all, or even a substantial part, of the object of allegiance, lest every instance of dissent over policy motivate disallegiance.

This is to say that all citizens (or subjects) benefit, and know they benefit, from there being fundamental conventions that are both deep and particular without defining the substance of policy. Such conventions will constitute a political society without permanently determining the choices made by the members of that society, individually or collectively. Hume thought that England was blessed with such conventions. The next chapter will explore what they are and how they arose.

Chapter 4

Crown and Charter

Fundamental Conventions as Principles of Authority

Nor is the rule concerning the stability of possession the less
derived from human conventions, that it arises gradually,
and acquires force by a slow progression, and by our repeated
experience of the inconveniences of transgressing it. On the
contrary, this experience assures us still more, that the sense of
interest has become common to all our fellows, and gives us a
confidence of the future regularity of their conduct: And 'tis only
on the expectation of this, that our moderation and abstinence are
founded.

—Hume (T 3.2.2.10, SBN 490)

Nor is it sufficient to say, that example and precedent can never
authorize vices: Examples and precedents, *uniform and ancient*, can
surely fix the nature of any constitution, and the limits of any form
of government. There is indeed no other principle by which those
land-marks or boundaries can be settled.

—Hume (H 5.583, note KK; emphasis added)

[T]acit conventions are sometimes harder to destroy than explicit
ones, existing in potentially recalcitrant minds rather than on
destructible paper.

—Thomas Schelling[1]

This chapter will discuss Hume's theory of fundamental conventions, of how
"examples and precedents" come to count as "uniform and ancient." Few
deny that Hume regards both private and public law as matters of convention; Hume repeatedly uses the word himself. But few have recognized that
he regards certain conventions as *fundamental*: immune to alteration (except
in the extremely long term, at least generations and more likely centuries) by
the usual methods of political power and social change. The claim that Hume

does believe in fundamental conventions, that he rests a distinctive form of constitutionalism on the foundations of custom and mutual advantage, is unusual. It finds little support in Hume's philosophical works, only in the less familiar *History*. Justifying it will require more detailed citation of the *History* than in other parts of this work.

Part of the problem is that Hume for deliberate and political reasons avoids saying what counts as fundamental and how it becomes so. As always, he refuses to bring to matters of authority the level of theoretical clarity that might force disagreement on first principles and thereby risk civil strife. One of the only times he uses the phrase "fundamental laws" is in a passage asserting their existence but *denying* that we can know what they are with sufficient certainty "to set bounds to the legislative power, and determine how far it may innovate in the principle of government" (T 3.2.10.14, SBN 561).

But the part of the phrase "fundamental law" that causes Hume to worry—because it might lead to crises of authority that he dreads, and might justify the kind of revolutions he thinks are almost never worth it—is "law," not "fundamental." The development of fundamental *conventions*, in contrast, could be seen as the central story of the *History of England*. These conventions are both below and above ordinary laws. Below, because their fundamental status can never be codified as such. Above, because they limit, at least arguably, the authority of the lawmaking body, whose own right to enact positive law itself derives from fundamental conventions.[2] This may explain Hume's tendency to refer to fundamental laws as anything but laws. He describes them as "rules," and a constitutional government is "regular," from the adjective form of rule. In particularly strong cases they are "foundations" or "fundamentals" (the latter used as a noun in the singular). The norm of observing such fundamentals is a "maxim"; subjective or conscious attachment to it is a "principle," a motive for action; the whole constitutional scheme, when not called simply the "constitution," is a "plan," "system," or "fabric."[3]

Once one looks, it is not hard to determine what Hume regards as England's constitutional fundamentals: on the one hand, the codified and universally recognized rules of succession that constitute a "regular" monarchy; on the other, Magna Charta with its various accretions (*habeas corpus*, the Bill of Rights). To abolish monarchy or Magna Charta are almost certainly beyond the authority of either parliament or rogue monarchs. I would claim—though there is no space here to pursue the claim—that these conventions implicate not only authority but identity. If England ceased to be a monarchy, or formally abolished its liberties, it would fundamentally cease to be the same country (politically speaking), the same polity. It would be a new polity, ripped up at its political roots—just as the United States would be a new country if it disavowed its Declaration of Independence and Constitution, or France if it never again appealed to liberty, equality, and fraternity (a slogan that the Vichy regime temporarily shelved, proving the point). Crown and charter are not just fundamental conventions but constitutive ones.[4]

Perhaps all fundamental conventions are constitutive. They can only become fundamental by being seen as immune to popular will or other forms of power; and they can only win such immunity by being seen as matters that go deeper than choice and burrow into identity. This represents a rational basis for what might seem like irrational political attachments. In return for not having the option of changing our formal institutions of government or abandoning their historically determined rights—the former a dubious privilege, the latter not even that—the citizens of polities that have fundamental conventions gain assurances of peace, personal security, and legitimate authority that are tremendously useful and almost impossible to dislodge.

Fundamental conventions develop, like all conventions, through long custom and practice—a custom and practice that become accepted because they are useful in the widest sense. The best ground for government's claim to authority, as for private persons' claim to property, is long possession. But fundamental conventions command a force that goes beyond long possession—a force that might be called *cumulative*. Fundamental conventions, and they alone, have been asserted and reasserted for a very long time—for centuries. They have triumphed not only against occasional violations of their terms but against repeated and durable violations that would normally be enough to erode, through new custom and prescription, any claim that the old conventions are still in force. As we will see in the case of both monarchy and Magna Charta, the claim that *no* amount of violations can serve as a precedent is key to their fundamental character. Hume states and documents this no-precedent rule most explicitly with respect to Magna Charta, but the story he tells of monarchy is remarkably similar: the rules of ordered monarchy become fundamental through repeated restoration after departures, and through assertions that not the departures but the restoration represent the proper state of things. As we will see in the next chapter, one of the hallmarks of statesmanship is to make ambiguous situations seem like restorations, so that de facto possession of government will coincide with constitutive or fundamental authority, rather than being threatened by it. This is not mere manipulation because there are severe limits to what such statesmanship can bring about: rights and governing power are not, as Hobbes wanted them to be, matters of sovereign will alone. The proposals of statesmen will accord with the public's opinion of "right to power" (E: FPG, 33), and will persist in stable fashion, only to the extent that they can plausibly claim to track fundamental conventions.

If my argument here is correct, Hume can escape the alternative posed in *Federalist* No. 1 that political constitutions must depend either on "accident and force" or on "reflection and choice."[5] Fundamental conventions are distinct from both. They are made possible by Hume's persistent determination to decouple authority from founding: a governing convention's origin has literally nothing to do with its continuing force or validity. Some accidental political events—and force, we shall see, is just another kind of accident—have no effect beyond the moment. Those that do, have continuing effect in virtue of something other than accident: they become customs because they prove useful. They sometimes become more than customs, namely fundamental conventions, because they have been continuously asserted and reasserted as being so basic to a polity's background assumptions of governing that to abandon them would be to court normless anarchy (and a loss of identity) or civil war. Fundamental conventions begin as accident, persist through being recognized as useful, and become entrenched by becoming so necessary for political coordination that they are useful in a larger sense even if their current operation seems inconvenient. They have traveled so far from accident that they seem immemorial and inalterable, the kind of things that can render an existing practice illegitimate no matter how long (at least up to a few generations) it has persisted. Because they are inalterable and immemorial, however, fundamental conventions are also all but immune from "reflection and choice." "Civilized" has two antonyms: "barbaric" and "spontaneous."

Barbaric Coordination: Focal Points and Common Knowledge

In previous chapters I have described Hume's attempt to show that every individual, to some extent and in some spheres, has an interest in coordination. When the projects, desires, or customs characteristic of one significant group in society conflict with those of others to an extent that threatens society's ability to coordinate, all have an interest in re-directing their own and others' conflictual projects so that they become compatible with the projects others are likely to pursue.

This does not determine *what* people will coordinate around, the form or nature of that which can bring them to common action. Hume, I have claimed, regarded constitutional orders as the best and most stable coordination solutions. But that does not mean he regarded them as "natural" in the sense of intuitively obvious. On the contrary, other methods of coordination—mutual surveillance, focal points, personal leadership—are much easier to discover and follow though much less useful; they are obvious at the cost of being fleeting and small-scale. This is fine if we are talking about a brand name, but disastrous if we are talking about political institutions. If we rely on mutual surveillance, focal points, or personal leadership, we will be at the mercy of short-term, largely esthetic factors ("prominence," "charisma"), and will be able to coordinate only within the range of sight or hearing—therefore only within small groups that cohere within themselves but remain at odds with one another.

The progress from barbarism to civilization (which for Hume are, as noted in the previous chapter, political and legal categories, not socioeconomic ones)—can be glossed as progress from crude forms of coordination to systematic and impersonal ones. Barbaric or crude coordination based on location, leadership qualities, vague family ties, personal friendships, or bat-tlefield speeches yields to civilized coordination in which the basis of conven-tion is impersonal and potentially country-wide: constitutional rules defining the proper holders of authority, and constitutional principles delimiting that authority. "Civil" or "regular" government began when crude focal points began to be disregarded in favor of more regular and abstract ones, when the Saxon rule that "princes governed more by example than by authority" began to be reversed (H 1.15). It was completed when crude focal points were *always* disregarded, when those with no legal or constitutional claim to rule were consistently regarded as having no claim at all.

"In matter of Government," says a character in one of Hobbes' dialogues, "when nothing else is turn'd up, Clubs are Trump."[6] Hume, as usual, assumes Hobbesian extremes as his implicit background: Hobbes describes what hap-pens when conventions fail. But where Hobbes relies on aphorisms and a pri-ori definitions, Hume, through history, discovers a more complex story. There is always a trump suit, but it is not always clubs. In times of chaos—and the death of a king without a clear succession rule is always such a time—a vari-ety of crude indicators, not just the capacity for physical violence, could serve as focal points. The conclusion is potentially more pessimistic than Hobbes'. Because we do *not* automatically "bandwagon" to the side of the strongest warlord, we will not rally behind a single leader but will fight until we reach an overall consensus. The problem with natural rallying points is not that they do not work but that there are too many of them. Constitutional devel-opment is the story of needing such rallying points less and less. It involves an empirical story of changes, clashes, and evolutions in coordination solutions, matters that defy deductive treatment. The Hobbesian maxim "seek Peace, and follow it"[7] is for Hume not wrong but irrelevant. In seeking peace, the usual problem is that we do not know where to look. From a Humean per-spective, Hobbes is not sufficiently serious about civil war and political order. Hobbes feared the former and praised the latter. Hume exhaustively studied both, and all conditions in between.

In chapter 1, I mentioned the classic methods of solving coordination problems: common knowledge, leadership, conventions, and focal points, evolution or natural selection, and convention. Constitutional government effectively relies on the last two. It means, roughly speaking, falling in step behind, without necessarily approving of in a moral sense, a method of deci-sion making and a procedure for choosing political authorities, rather than the substance of a course of action—or even the second-order substance of a ruler or leader, empowered to make first-order decisions, who is trusted by oneself but has not been chosen according to constitutional rules.[8]

Put in these terms, Hume's civilized or regular governments are those that coordinate through constitution or evolution—which Hume claims are the same thing in practice, though not in concept—rather than through focal points or common knowledge. One way of defining a constitution is a fundamental convention of ignoring first-order focal points. (As Hume puts it in criticizing Machiavelli's political science, the "treacherous, deceitful, and inconsistent system of politics" practiced by Italians in the great Florentine's day was "ill calculated to support [the Italians'] states" [H 3.51].) The constitutionalist makes a norm out of the empirical observation first derived from church politics: "the race is not to the swift, nor the battle to the strong, neither yet bread to the wise."[9] Fortunately, authority is not a matter of arbitrary "time [i.e., timing] and chance" either. Conventions persist and have patterns, and the methods of improving conventions have patterns as well.

Chapter 1 discussed focal points, which one might summarize as *immediately prominent features of a situation that allow parties to coordinate absent prior agreement or knowledge by each party of what others intend to do.* The characteristics of focal points include, to recap: uniqueness; the state of being the status quo or the status quo ante; the suggestion of a mediator; fact-finding; physical prominence; conventional priority (heads over tails); and analogy to a case recently brought to mind. In a premodern context, when instantaneous communication was not possible and images of unexpected situations could not be transmitted in real time, focal points—absent suppositious cases involving maps but no prearrangements—will be limited to what can be seen or heard by all participants in a particular place. They will have to be directly perceptible and local. Leadership, when it is in doubt and not preordained, will be similar: the only way to become recognized as a leader will be to assert oneself in a local area, since the fact of one's leadership outside that area could not be either recognized or communicated.

The local quality of premodern focal points and leadership stems from the local quality of premodern common knowledge. Premodern common knowledge might be called "natural common knowledge," and is a crude coordination solution; focal points and leadership solutions that can win only local attention are likewise crude in this way. Reliance on any of these methods predictably leads to conflict between those who cannot possibly have access to the common message and those who do. As noted in chapter 1, the only sort of common knowledge that can operate on a national level is "communicative": the product of memory and abstract norms, not the senses.

Most of human history is the story of crude coordination solutions. Using such solutions as the basis of allegiance was what made English politics before the Tudor era a story of "many barbarous ages" in which no durable order persisted (H 2.518). (Once again, science (1), which traces social causes, presupposes the things explained by science (2), which explains individual choices. No mass coordination solutions, no civilization—and no chance for complex social forces to develop.) The interesting story within that barbarism is how the germs of durable conventions—constitutions, principles—began to grow *before* mass communications let them propagate through quick transmission of nationwide common knowledge. That early growth involves at least two dimensions. One follows from Hume's psychological science; the other is convention all the way down. Universally and according to the science of man, the source of steady, durable political authority is always and everywhere, given the grounding of our positive and normative beliefs in experience and mental habits, "long possession." Conventionally, the content of that authority varies according to *which* "principle[s] of authority" (H 1.464, and see below) have been long in our possession.

In the contemporary United States, allegiance is owed to a *constitution* from which even presidents derive their authority (and which they swear an oath to preserve). In Britain, the oath is sworn to the monarch, but Hume suggests that it would be misleading to think that the monarch *as a person* is owed allegiance. Britons implicitly swear to the *monarchy*, that is, to a rule of royal succession. And the first constitutional principle learned in England was the principle that monarchs succeed one another not by force or ability but through consistent, defined rules of hereditary succession. The second principle, which defined what government was rather than who held it, was given by Magna Charta. Hume calls the Charter the "most sacred foundation of the laws and constitution," "never . . . formally disputed" since 1297 and, in spite of all departures from it, consistently from that time "regarded as the basis of English government, and the sure rule by which the authority of every custom was to be tried and canvassed" (first quotation on H 5.178, the last two on 2.123).

Crude Monarchy: Accident and Force

Hume considers the passing of political power from a parent to a child to be natural in a rough sense, but a sense too rough to ground political order. When a parent dies and the property must be given to someone, the children "naturally present themselves to the mind" (T 3.2.3.11, SBN 512). Yet in the political realm, where the good to be allocated is not property but allegiance, this mental pattern plays little role. The sources of political allegiance are long possession, present possession, conquest, succession, and positive laws—in that order of precedence and strength.[10] "When neither long possession, nor present possession, nor conquest take place," as when a monarchy's founder dies, "the right of *succession* naturally prevails in their stead." The reasons include the father's [*sic*] presumed consent, the "imitation of the succession to private families" and "the interest, which the state has in chusing the person, who is most powerful, and has the most numerous followers" (T 3.2.10.9, SBN 559).[11] Leaving aside the first criterion, which seems inapt (since hereditary considerations demonstrably operate even in opposition to consent), and the second, which seems circular (it works in public only if the convention has previously been accepted in private), we are left with the third. That is, we have an "interest" in agreeing on a ruler, and family ties work as a coordination point *absent anyone else* who is currently in charge, historically in charge, or in command of military force. When there is more than one child, or the rules of inheritance seem complicated (does an illegitimate child succeed? An adopted one? A girl in a patriarchal society? The dead king's grandson rather than his brother?), this coordination point will fail. It is no accident that Hume then thinks some positive law, eventually a constitutional law, will have to settle the matter. Until it does, succession will not define unique heirs and will not solve coordination problems.

In fact, Hume thinks the best example of allegiance by succession is *elective* monarchy. Succession, we might say, explains not Queen Elizabeth II but Kim Jong Un and George W. Bush. "[T]his case of succession is not the same with that of hereditary monarchies, *where custom has fix'd the right of succession. These depend upon the principle of long possession above explain'd*" (T 3.2.10.9n82, SBN 559n2; emphasis added). This claim, in a footnote, suggests two crucial points. First, it describes a shift in our mental attitudes toward allegiance, away from the holder of office toward the rule by which he or she holds it.[12] Once succession is established, a new monarch can command the authority of an old family. The new king or queen has only current possession, but the possession of the dynasty as a whole is long and customary, therefore secure. Second, it proposes as all-important—but unexplained— how the original "custom" that fixes the right of succession might originate and which conventions, in contrast, it must replace. Not until the *History* would Hume ask and answer that question.[13]

Because "natural" coordination solutions are both plural and crude, they often produce as much conflict as they prevent. There are too many figures around whom one might rally. Family ties are persuasive to a point (H 1.161–2) but do not determine unique successors; in any case, they are often subordinate to present possession or conquest (i.e., military force). Thus in early monarchical systems, the death of a king predictably resulted in struggles over which royal, or occasionally a non-royal, would succeed. These struggles divided not radicals from conservatives but one faction of would-be peaceful subjects from another. Even those seeking to obey the "true king"—no doubt most people, out of an interest in survival—could not be certain who that was.

This is Hume's story of the seven Anglo-Saxon kingdoms (or Heptarchy). Each time a king died, succession was determined by a witches' brew of crude focal points: proximity to the seat of power, military ability or the allegiance of large armies, personal cleverness, powerful friends, current possession, and "the will of [a royal] father, a circumstance which had great authority with the Anglo-Saxons" (H 1.64). These, not an agreed rule of blood descent, is what determined succession—or, since they frequently crossed each other, failed to determine succession and produced endless wars. It was a party question in Hume's time whether Anglo-Saxon kings were hereditary (the Tory view) or elective (as the Whigs maintained).[14] Hume, as usual, gave an ironic answer that crossed both parties: they were *not*, in any thoroughgoing sense, hereditary—but that was the problem.

Hume's explanation is that the use of "general principles" in fixing a "regular succession" required more cultivation and a greater gift for abstraction than the Anglo-Saxons were capable of:

> It is easy to imagine, that an independant [*sic*] people, so little restrained by law, and cultivated by science, would not be very strict in maintaining a regular succession of their princes. Though they paid great regard to the royal family, and ascribed to it an undisputed superiority, they either had no rule, or none that was steadily observed, in filling the vacant throne; and present convenience, in that emergency, was more attended to than general principles. (H 1.161)

This macro (or science (1)) explanation is only contingently true and in a sense completely optional. Whether or not we accept Hume's link between cultivation of arts and sciences and the ability to fix the rules of succession, the consequences of a monarchy that lacks the latter are clear enough from Hume's historical account (artfully drafted to make this point) of the Anglo-Saxon Heptarchy.[15]

In the Kentish kingdom, Escus was the legitimate heir of his father Hengist, but as he lacked "military genius," warlords seeking land and glory threw the kingdom to Aella, king of Sussex (H 1.25). Another Kentish king, Egbert, killed two cousins to ensure the succession of his own son Edric—unsuccessfully, for Egbert neglected to kill his own brother Lothaire, who upon Egbert's death held the throne for a while until Edric enlisted foreign aid and killed his uncle. All Kentish royals proceeded to kill one another until the whole line was dead and the King of Wessex took over in 723 (H 1.34). In Northumbria, Adelfrid took power through a combination of force and marriage to the king's daughter, expelling the king's infant son, Edwin. But Edwin took refuge with the King of East Anglia and with the help of that King retook his throne (H 1.36). While Edwin's rule was long and stable, on his death the kingdom broke in two; a younger son took one half of the kingdom through force and forced the true heir to flee (H 1.37–8). King Oswald in 634 reunited Northumbria. After his death in battle his brother Oswy succeeded, and killed the legitimate heir to (at least) half the kingdom. Oswy was succeeded by a son who, dying childless, was in turn succeeded by a bastard brother, Alfred. When Alfred died, his son and heir was only eight years old and was killed by a relative, who was himself killed within a year. A few years later there were other assassinations, especially after one king became a monk and abdicated. A non-royal (Mollo) then held the throne briefly but was killed by a prince of the blood (Ailred), who was in turn soon "expelled by his subjects." Ethelred, Mollo's son, succeeded but "underwent a like fate." Then a brother of Ailred was "deposed and slain by the people"; his nephew Osred succeeded for a year, followed by Ethelbert, "another son of Mollo, whose death was equally tragical with that of almost all his predecessors." After that there was "universal anarchy" until the people, "having, by so many

fatal revolutions, lost all attachment to their government and princes," suc-
cumbed to conquest by Wessex. That assassinations and vendettas have fatal
effects on early, fragile rules of succession is a constant theme of Hume's early
volumes (see, e.g., H 1.34).

Without the need for further names, the pattern is clear. Hume makes it
explicit: history is pointless when allegiance is so unstable. Hume famously
disposes of the Kingdom of East Anglia in one paragraph, explaining:

> It is almost impossible, and quite needless to be more particular in relat-
> ing the transactions of the East-Angles. What instruction or entertain-
> ment can it give the reader to hear a long bead-roll of barbarous names,
> Egric, Annas, Ethelbert, Ethelwald, Aldulf, Elfwald, Beorne, Ethelred,
> Ethelbert, who successively murdered, expelled, or inherited from each
> other, and obscurely filled the throne of that kingdom. (H 1.39–40)

Because "an exact rule of succession was either unknown or not strictly
observed," a king who took power "was continually agitated with jealousy
against all the princes of the blood, whom he still considered as rivals, and
whose death alone could give him entire security in his possession of the
throne." That death was often arranged—with the result that whole royal lines
tended to become extinct (H 1.49).[16]

This tradition of intra-dynastic murder, founded on the perverse incentives of a system that valued royal blood but did not settle crowns on a specific line, guaranteed at best a fragile order. "[C]ivilized monarchy, possessed
of tranquillity within itself, and secure against foreign invasion" (H 1.50), became thinkable only with the accession in 827 of Egbert, who united the Heptarchy into one kingdom, more or less modern England. Egbert, crucially,
faced no pretenders—though his own positive title still rested on the crude
grounds of conquest and personal merit:

> as the race of the ancient kings was totally extinct in all the subjected
> states, the people readily transferred their allegiance to a prince, who
> seemed to merit it, by the splendor of his victories, the vigour of his
> administration, and the superior nobility of his birth. (H 1.55)

Until Egbert ended the Heptarchy and its practice of ambiguous succession,
political chaos had prevented legal and social progress: "The Saxons, though
they had been so long [almost 400 years] settled in the island, seem not as
yet to have been much improved beyond their German ancestors, either in
arts, civility, knowledge, humanity, justice, or obedience to the laws" (H 1.50).

Hume admits (at H 1.25) that there are inadequate historical records for
these events; the causes of breaks in succession are often a matter of conjecture (though the fact that Hume arranges his conjectures as he does is
evidence regarding what his theory is, as opposed to whether history supports it). But later events are clearer, as are patterns that prove the absence
of regular, settled, succession rules. In 1041, the English were under Dan-

ish rule when king Hardicanute died. As Hardicanute's Danish heir was out of the country and no other close relatives were alive—distant relatives did not count in the absence of detailed rules setting priority among them—the Danes were at a loss. The Anglo-Saxons at the same moment actually faced exactly the same problem; but by pure luck, they happened to find one member of their old royal family, Edward, at home.

> [T]hough the descendants of Edmond Ironside were the true heirs of the Saxon family, yet their absence in so remote a country as Hungary, appeared a sufficient reason for their exclusion, to a people like the English, so little accustomed to observe a regular order in the succession of their monarchs. *All delays might be dangerous; and the present occasion must hastily be embraced; while the Danes, without concert, without a leader, astonished at the present incident,* and anxious only for their personal safety, durst not oppose the united voice of the nation. (H 1.130, emphasis added)

Edward's only potential opposition was Godwin, a powerful lord with no blood tie to the royal family but "whose power, alliances, and abilities gave him a great influence at all times, especially amidst those sudden opportunities, which always attend a revolution of government, and which, either seized or neglected, commonly prove decisive." But when Godwin decided to settle for a promise that Edward would marry Godwin's daughter, King Edward was crowned with little opposition. (The English now call him "The Confessor.")

By 1051, Edward won support among the English for his "humanity, justice, and piety" even though they doubted his "vigour and capacity" (H 1.135). But the ability of a king without military vigor to hold the throne was unusual. As late as the twelfth-century reign of Henry II, kings did not dare to delegate even "frivolous" military commands to generals: their "feeble authority" would not have survived this signal of personal weakness (H 1.302). One sign of this "rude and barbarous" policy of succession, or rather lack of a policy, is that a people who followed it could not tolerate female heirs, since such were deemed incapable of vindicating their rule on the battlefield (H 2.197).[17] Another is that it was safe, though insulting, to leave a pretender to the throne alive provided that his personal qualities were lacking. The pretender had no chance of taking the throne if he had a legitimate title but no charisma, nor military skill (see H 1.260–61 on Edgar Atheling).

Before the rules for succession were established, the game of thrones was something between a scavenger hunt and a game of Australian-rules football: whoever rushed most quickly to attain the most primitive focal points became the monarch. In 1087, William Rufus managed to beat out his older brother Robert for succession, in spite of the latter's better claim under primogeniture, because William "trusted entirely for success to his own celerity" and managed to lay his hands on several useful chits: a dubious will from his father, some key fortresses; the royal treasure; and the favor of the primate and several other bishops (H 1.228–9). Similarly, in 1100, Henry I became king by beating his older brother, Robert, to the punch. On the death of the previous king (a yet elder brother), Robert was honeymooning in Italy on the way back from a Crusade and an impulsive marriage. Henry seized his chance: he hurried to the royal treasure at Winchester; took possession of it by threatening to kill its in-dignant keeper with his own sword; "hastened with the money to London"; and "having assembled some noblemen and prelates, whom his address, or abili-ties, or presents, gained to his side, he was suddenly elected, or rather saluted king; and immediately proceeded to the exercise of royal authority." "[C]ourage and celerity" won the day; "[p]resent possession supplied the apparent defects in Henry's title, which was indeed founded on plain usurpation." Henry was crowned before his brother had been dead three days (H 1.251–2).

The First Constitutional Regime: Hereditary Monarchy

One of Hume's contributions as a theorist is to point out the constitutional logic of apparently random events and practices.[18] If all government rests on opinion and all acts should be judged by their utility and agreeableness, whether a political action counts as constitutional and whether it makes the constitution better are functions of how it is perceived and what it accom-plishes, not whether it is formally reckoned as having constitutional status. Measures that seem to affect private persons can be crucial parts of public law. In his essay "Of Some Remarkable Customs," Hume takes up the Athe-nian practice of the γραφή παρνόμων, "indictment of illegality," under which a citizen who introduced a new law, passed by the assembly, could later be criminally accused if the assembly later thought the law unjust or unwise. This practice seems contrary to "undisputable" maxims of good government (Hume even calls them "axioms"). But in fact, it was the least-bad accommo-dation to the problems of an unchecked direct democracy.

> The ATHENIAN Democracy was such a tumultuous government as we can scarcely form a notion of in the present age of the world. The whole collective body of the people voted in every law, without any limitation of property, without any distinction of rank, without controul from any magistracy or senate; and consequently without regard to order, justice, or prudence. The ATHENIANS soon became sensible of the mischiefs attending this constitution: But being averse to checking themselves by any rule or restriction, they resolved, at least, to check their dema-gogues or counsellors, by the fear of future punishment and enquiry. (E: SRC, 368–9)

The indictment for illegality was therefore, we might say, a *constitutional* measure. It was an apparently private law, and a bad private law at that, with crucial and indeed constitutive public functions. It was "esteemed so essential to their form of government, that AESCHINES insists on it as a known truth, that, were it abolished or neglected, it were impossible for the Democracy to subsist" (ibid·).[19]

The rules of monarchical succession now—though not in Hume's time, when their importance was obvious—have the same character of seeming less fundamental and constitutional than they are. Primogeniture and the succession rule known as representation, which places grandsons in the elder line ahead of sons in the younger,[20] have the characteristics of Humean conventional rules. It is very useful to have such rules; the natural structure of our minds provides certain patterns that any convention must roughly track in order to be stable, but a variety of conventional rules are consistent with those mental patterns; the choice between such rules is therefore arbitrary and the potential source of disagreement; convention solves the problem of disagreement but is hard to establish. "The interest of a nation requires, that the succession to the crown shou'd be fix'd one way or other, but 'tis the same thing to its interest in what way it be fix'd" (T 3.2.10.13, SBN 560). What makes primogenture and representation constitutional rather than merely legal conventions is the fact that they involve allegiance, rather than property or social norms like chastity and good manners.[21] In effect, some conventions of authority need to be fundamental in order for controversies over allegiance to be settled by some standard other than "the swords of the soldiery" (T 3.2.10.15, SBN 562); there need be no fundamental laws regarding property or contracts because disputes over those can be peacefully settled by authority. That is why the establishment of what may seem fairly rudimentary conventions—the succession of kings to the kind of fairly absolute monarchy that we wouldn't much value today—is so important. An "exact rule of succession" (H 1.48) is fundamental to the authority of government as such, though such rules may seem trivial when compared to authority's perfection under settled rules of liberty and parliamentary government.

When Hume first takes up the principle of succession in the *Treatise*, he treats it in personal or dynastic terms. Long possession gets a set of subjects used to a "set of men" (Hume's phrase, with unintentional gender bias)[22] as their monarchs. It is this "set of men" that is analogous to what republican citizens would call a "form of commonwealth," what we would call in general a constitution or regime:

> we shall find, that there scarce is any race of kings, or form of a commonwealth, that is not primarily founded on usurpation and rebellion, and whose title is not at first worse than doubtful and uncertain. Time alone gives solidity to their right; and operating gradually on the minds of men, reconciles them to any authority, and makes it seem just and reasonable. Nothing causes any sentiment to have a greater influence upon us than custom, or turns our imagination more strongly to any object. When we have been long accustom'd to obey any set of men, that

general instinct or tendency, which we have to suppose a moral obligation attending loyalty, takes easily this direction, and chuses that set of
men for its objects. (T 3.2.10.4 [SBN 556])[23]

This account as it stands seems inadequate. If it takes so long to give a set of
monarchs legitimacy, the first links of the chain seem impossible to forge. It
seems that the second or third in a line would have to succeed without controversy in order to pave the way, through the workings of "custom," for later
descendants. Yet so early in the line, such peaceful succession seems unlikely.
It would take great luck for so many lineal descendants to succeed without
bloodshed or controversy. But unless they did, the rule of succession would
neither remain obvious nor be able to prove its utility—and would therefore
not establish itself. Also, the idea of a "set of men" is question-begging. An
unambiguous set presupposes that *one line* of the royal family be taken for
granted as having title to rule—yet the many ambiguous cases named earlier
once again makes this seem unlikely.

Whether Hume recognized these problems when writing the *Treatise* cannot be known. It is clear that by the time he wrote the *History* he settled on
a solution to both of them: not a named set of monarchs but the *rule of succession* is what becomes established by long possession. It is that rule that
has proven its utility through long experience. And the rule can be applied
(though not without controversy) to a new dynasty because, being abstract,
it can continue and solidify a principle that subjects have learned to observe
through the experience of an old dynasty. Once settled as a convention, the
rule determines who counts as the next royal in line. The rule of hereditary
succession, refined and specified over time, becomes a *"principle of authority"* (H 1.464; emphasis added): whether explicitly labeled such or not, a *constitutional* rule. Cromwell's "military usurpation" rendered "the principle of
loyalty to [one's] sovereign" the same as "the more enlarged and more enlightened affection towards a legal constitution"; the principle and the affection
united to motivate a yearning for Restoration (H 6.38).[24] But when there is
a king on the throne, one can distinguish the two. The more "enlarged"—
governed by abstract and impartial rules—a constitutional order is, the more
citizens' allegiance is owed to the constitutional rule, not the current king. It
is common to say that Hume thought the present possessor of the crown had
the best prima facie title to it.[25] This is true in only a perverse sense. Present
possession is indeed a claim in the absence of anything better. But it is so
inferior to a regular rule of monarchical succession that two volumes of the
History are devoted to revealing how dangerous and anarchic the present-
possession standard was, and to describing the process by which civilized
subjects left it behind forever.[26] Not present possession but a rule of succession established by long experience provides constitutional title to rule. That
is what gives safety to established governments and guarantees failure to rebels (except where egregious tyranny is involved).[27]

A principle that arises by long possession might seem to entail a boring, repetitive story. Such a principle becomes solid by being asserted over and over again and associated with good outcomes, meaning chiefly peace (though compared to a baron-dominated political system, stable monarchy meant liberty and justice as well; see below). That said, there is a certain excitement in following the settled rules of succession as they replace one crude focal point after another. We can watch the rules gain strength gradually in the face of setbacks and in defiance of violations that come over time to be increasingly resented and more immediately resisted.

In the first stages, hereditary succession, not yet precisely defined in difficult cases, at least triumphed over the focal point of crude force. In the Anglo-Saxon era, a king facing a pretender could remove the threat by blinding or mutilating his rival (H 1.43). The implication is that nobody who could not fight would be considered fit to rule (and mutilation was an even more effective strategy than murder, because it made competent heirs to the pretender wait their turn). In later times, imprisonment (or secret murder) replaced mutilation as a strategy, in a sign that a blind or one-handed monarch was no longer unimaginable. Another sign of this shift is that women or boys began to be able to succeed their parents in spite of their not being expected to lead in battle. Normandy rather than England led the way in 1001 when William I was succeeded by his son, though a minor: this was "[a] sure proof, that the Normans were already somewhat advanced in civility, and that their government could now rest secure on its laws and civil institutions, and was not wholly sustained by the abilities of the Sovereign" (H 1.115; compare 1.225). In 1135, the Empress Matilda, though a woman, overcame feudal assumptions that a king was primarily a (male) warrior and succeeded in claiming allegiance in many quarters in spite of her sex—though a pretender (Stephen), by combining various crude focal points (family ties, wealth, amiability, and a quick seizure of the ritual anointment and later the royal treasure), challenged the title and began a civil war that ended in stalemate (H 1.279ff.).[28] Henry II's accession in 1154 as the first Plantagenet monarch was mostly a matter of legitimate succession (Matilda was his mother), learned through bitter experience with civil war. But it required large dollops of crude focal points—powerful friends, land, ability compared to his rival—to cement it (H 1.300). The first European monarch not to command his own armies was Charles V of France, in 1365 (H 1.302, 2.262). Even as late as 1488, Scotland "had not yet attained that state, which distinguishes a civilized monarchy, and which enables the government, by the force of its laws and institutions alone, without any extraordinary capacity in the sovereign, to maintain itself in order and tranquillity" (H 3.24).

Consistent with Hume's defense of free trade, the settled rules of English succession were foreign, Norman imports that became established only gradually. Hume notably writes of primogeniture and representation as technological inventions, matters of political science for which earlier ages would have had a clear use but of which they were ignorant:

These innovations arose from the feudal law; which, first introducing the right of primogeniture, made such a distinction between the families of the elder and younger brothers, that the son of the former was thought entitled to succeed to his grandfather, preferably to his uncles, though nearer allied to the deceased monarch. But though this progress of ideas was natural, it was gradual. In the age of which we treat, the practice of representation was indeed introduced, but not thoroughly established; and the minds of men fluctuated between opposite principles. (H 1.407–8)[29]

Hume shows that the principle was not "established" by following this passage with a description of King John's accession in 1199. John was *not* the legitimate heir according to the rule of representation. But he managed to mount the throne in place of the legitimate heir, Arthur, through baronial friendships, quick action, and an understanding with the Archbishop of Canterbury: crude focal points again (H 1.408–9).[30] After John's death, his son Henry III—a boy at the time—might not have held the succession if William, Earl of Pembroke, the marshal of England at the time, had not made sure to have him crowned, anointed, and approved by the Pope very quickly (H 2.5). Still, representation appears to have made rapid progress; it was observed in odd ways even when fragile. In 1272, physical proximity was still in danger of trumping legitimate succession. The late Henry III's King's council, knowing that the "the English were as yet so little enured to obedience under a regular government, that the death of almost every king, since the conquest, had been attended with disorders," made sure to guard against the worrying fact that the legitimate heir, Edward I ("Longshanks," not the pre-Norman "Confessor": the numbering starts over in 1066), was out of the country crusading. The council hurriedly proclaimed Edward heir and got the parliament explicitly to ratify that choice. That said, civilized rules had by then gained enough ground that Edward's title was from then on in no danger, even though he took a year's vacation in France before returning to reign (H 2.73–4). In 1291, representation was still not secure in Scotland, with grave consequences: to forestall a civil war between the partisans of the king's grandson and those of his younger son, the Scots appealed as an arbiter to Edward of England, who demanded as the price of arbitration that both claimants acknowledge Scotland's feudal subordination to England. (To be sure, when it came to the substance of the decision, Edward consulted European lawyers—who told him to use the rule of representation, as he did [H 2.85–93].)

By 1376 the convention of representation was almost secure—but not quite. As Edward III and the Prince of Wales were both dying, people were so afraid that the rule of representation would be ignored—that Edward's younger son John of Gaunt would challenge the succession of Edward's grandson in an elder line (Richard II)—that Edward felt a need to reaffirm very publicly in parliament Richard's right to succeed (H 2.271, 2.320). Later, Richard II's own character endangered, and finally cost him, his rule, in spite of his clear title and the established state of regular monarchy. But monarchical government by a hereditary ruler was by then England's "natural state," customary and constitutional in spite of intermittent experiences of baronial factions usurping it (H 2.305–6; quotation on 304).

Any reader of Shakespeare knows the story of Richard's deposition in favor of Henry Bolingbroke, the controverted Duke of Lancaster (later Henry IV), but Hume's observations and the arguments he praises are more important than his narrative. The bishop of Carlisle, defending king Richard in parliament against the charges that led to his deposition, argued that a title rooted in representation and reaffirmed in Edward's speech had become fundamental, that attempts to obliterate it through parliamentary action would fail and only spur future civil wars. The rightful succession of the elder son's line, "however it might be overpowered by present force and faction, could never be obliterated from the minds of the people"; the new government would "stand on no principle; and would scarcely retain any pretence, by which it could challenge the obedience of men of sense and virtue" (H 2.319–21).[31] But these words were prophetic rather than popular; the parliament had Carlisle arrested and deposed Richard anyway. The baldness of this shows, says Hume, the contrast between 1688,[32] which saw

> a great and civilized nation, deliberately vindicating its established privileges, and a turbulent and barbarous aristocracy, plunging headlong from the extremes of one faction into those of another. (H 2.321)[33]

The standard reading of this, not incorrect, would be that Hume is stressing the barbarism of pre-Tudor times so as to vindicate his thesis that the English constitution of his time has modern, not ancient, origins. But the *History* is not just a pamphlet, and the details of Hume's narrative display a subtler message (though consistent with the other): primogeniture and representation were by this time constitutional fundamentals. They could be violated, but these violations were considered illegitimate. Neither power nor positive law could durably justify them.

Despite Carlisle's personal defeat, the deposition of Richard II was still a turning point because Carlisle, though scorned, was right. Bolingbroke/Lancaster, by deposing Richard and becoming King Henry IV, was seen as having violated fundamental principle, and was still so seen by half the country two generations later. The principles of due succession were not yet strong enough that no one dared violate them. But they were strong enough to prevent violators from enjoying the peace that comes with the opinion of *legitimate* (in Hume's time one said "lawful") authority or allegiance. Lancaster had present possession, power, and parliamentary whim on his side, but these could no longer overbalance constitutional fundamentals. He did not even dare to have himself proclaimed the choice of the people, since this basis lacked popular legitimacy:

The English had so long been familiarized to the hereditary succession of their monarchs, the instances of departure from it had always born such strong symptoms of injustice and violence, and so little of a national choice or election, and the returns to the true line had ever been deemed such fortunate incidents in their history, that Henry was afraid, lest, *in resting his title on the consent of the people, he should build on a foundation, to which the people themselves were not accustomed*, and whose solidity they would with difficulty be brought to recognize. (H 2.333, emphasis added; see also 2.317)

In the end, Lancaster made the best of his only claim to rule—present or de facto possession of the crown. He had no choice but to rule through Machiavellian, pre-constitutional methods: force and guile (as well as *fortuna*: Henry IV was lucky that his various opponents never attacked him all at once [H 2.342]). His "policy," "valour, prudence and address," secured his own person and even the succession of his son, but he ruled by terror rather than principle:

The great popularity, which Henry enjoyed before he attained the crown, and which had so much aided him in the acquisition of it, was entirely lost many years before the end of his reign; and he governed his people more by terror than by affection, *more by his own policy than by their sense of duty or allegiance.* (H 2.350; emphasis added)[34]

Lancaster's "bad title" guaranteed that his reign would be consumed with putting down rebellions; he was left little time for foreign policy or domestic achievements (H 2.349). Allegiance, by this time, could only track constitutional fundamentals: the rule of succession. Hume places in the mouth of Yorkists a sentiment that places such rules on the same level as the principles of political order generally:

the deposition of Richard II. and the advancement of Henry IV. were not deliberate national acts; but the result of the levity and violence of the people, and proceeded from those very defects in human nature, which the *establishment of political society, and of an order in succession,* was calculated to prevent. (H 2.438; emphasis added)[35]

The Wars of the Roses reflected the fact that even Bolingbroke/Lancaster's grandson Henry VI could only equivocally be judged as belonging among the "set of men" to whom allegiance was owed.[36] By the time of an attempted compromise of the war in 1460, "visible marks of a higher regard to law . . . than has appeared in any former period of English history" included not merely procedural deference to parliament, as the logical body to mediate a succession dispute, but the substance of the mediated solution: Henry VI was to keep the throne during his lifetime, with the inheritance of it to pass on his death to the ancient, established line (that of York [H 2.447–8]). This was an agreement grounded in principle, and when it fell apart, the resulting war was fought over principle.

Weak monarchy was by this time the tribute that illegitimate rule paid to principles of authority. By the time of the Lancaster kings in the 1400s, a weak king with a strong title dared to do more than a strong king with a weak one. Henry IV and Henry V, "though men of great spirit and abilities, abstained from such exertions of prerogative, as even weak princes, whose title was undisputed, were tempted to think they might venture upon with impunity" (H 2.382). Another tribute paid by usurpation to constitutional fundamentals was that usurpation started to seem simply a crime. Richard III's seizure of the throne at the cost of the true heirs' lives would have been the usual course of affairs in the Saxon era. By the late fifteenth century, Hume feels free to call it "vice and murder, exalted on the throne" (H 2.518)—not only murder, at which we feel natural revulsion, but *another* vice: the artificial vice of usurpation, the seizure of power in defiance of fundamental convention.

By the end of the middle ages, even before Henry VII's accession in 1485 united the two disputed royal lines (more or less: see the next chapter), only exceptional circumstances could counterbalance allegiance to hereditary monarchy under the rules of succession. When a king was incapacitated but still living, so that his command was uncertain, his authority became the plaything of faction (though the authority as such was unchallenged; mentally weak kings could be sidelined, but not deposed).[37] Or in the "hurry of passion" of a total military mobilization, calculated to "allow men no leisure for reason or reflection," a king (in this case Henry V) could make people forget about the fact that his title was usurped—a temporary expedient, ceasing with the foreign war. Again the story is familiar from Shakespeare: the War of the Roses broke out after Henry V died and his young son's regent could not keep the father's foreign conquests (H 2.373–4, 2.426).

By the time of the accession of James I the process was complete. United in welcoming James as the uncontested heir to the throne (according to both the Catholic and Protestant ideologies that had caused such division between the partisans of Elizabeth and those of Mary Queen of Scots), the people of England

> considered, that, though the title, derived from blood, had been frequently violated since the Norman conquest, such licences had proceeded more from force or intrigue, than from any deliberate maxims of government. The lineal heir had still in the end prevailed; and both his exclusion and restoration had been commonly attended with such convulsions, as were sufficient to warn all prudent men not lightly to give way to such irregularities. (H 5.3–4)

The fact that hereditary monarchy is a constitutional regime, and the principles of succession counterintuitive and hard-won conventions, helps us both to understand Hume's theory of allegiance and to appreciate its substantive importance.

First, it explains how the rule of law begins: as a sort of meta-convention. When the kings themselves ruled by name, prominence, and personal courage, they were living symbols of lawlessness. A "legal and regular" monarchy, with rules of primogeniture and representation (or some equally arbitrary but precisely defined alternative [H 1.407]), establishes the first principled limits on monarchical power. From then on, there are two things no monarch may do: crown himself (if not the legitimate heir) and choose his successor. Hume in the *Treatise* mentions the French Salic law, which forbids succession through the female line, as an example of the "*fundamental* laws" (Hume's italics) that are "suppos'd to be inalterable by the will of the sovereign" (and even that of the legislature absent "evident," i.e., absolutely clear, reason to set it aside for the "public good" [T 3.2.10.14, SBN 561]).[38] When Henry IV (a.k.a. Bolingbroke, a.k.a. Lancaster) tried to adopt the Salic law as a surreptitious way of delegitimizing the line of Mortimer (later York), the House of Commons was "apprehensive that they had *overturned the foundations of the English government.*" Though parliament passed the law Henry requested, it soon demanded, and passed, a reversal.

> During the long contests with France, the injustice of the Salic law had been so much exclaimed against by the nation, that a contrary principle had taken *deep root in the minds of men; and it was now become impossible to eradicate it.* (H 2.347–8; emphases added)

Hume in the *History* spends no little time establishing how the Salic law came to be taken as inviolable in France—but had no force at all in England (H 2.196–8). This arbitrariness is the classic sign of a convention. That it operates as a limitation on the sovereign is also the sign of a *fundamental* or constitutional convention. Henry IV, even when parliament's power was still very slight and Magna Charta was irregularly observed, was in this respect already more bound by law than was any hypothetical sovereign imagined by Hobbes.[39]

Second, understanding hereditary monarchy as a constitutional regime-makes clear that change of dynasty is a *regime* change, a violation of constitutional principle. If it is hard for us to imagine why wars of royal succession were so endless and bloody (even when they involved no foreign interests, as the ones Hume describes often did not), it may help us to compare them to the French Revolution and its aftermath. The wars between York and Lancaster were not merely personal. The two sides were fighting over *constitutional principle.* These wars, no less than the quarrels between republicans, monarchists, and imperialists through nineteenth-century France, concerned the legitimate form of the regime—albeit a regime (hereditary monarchy) toward which we no longer feel much affection.

Third, this explains why Hume was so leery of elected executives. An elected monarch would be chosen not by merit—whatever that is, and Hume is generally skeptical of objective standards—but by the kind of riotous battles over crude focal points that have proven so disruptive in history:

a crown is too high a reward ever to be given to merit alone, and will always induce the candidates to employ force, or money, or intrigue, to procure the votes of the electors: So that such an election will give no better chance for superior merit in the prince, than if the state had trusted to birth alone for determining their sovereign. (E: PRS, 18)

If our current elections do not look like this, it is not because "popular sovereignty" is likely to result in anything but civil war, but because settled constitutions establish procedures for choosing executives by orderly means. Only popular loyalty to a constitution, written or unwritten, keeps elections from being the free-for-alls of the Anglo-Saxon world.

If the House of Commons ever became the sole governing power in Britain, Hume feared, England would have a "civil war every election," presumably for similar reasons. Hume cannot understand why we would throw out a secure constitutional rule for a predictable raw struggle over power. This worry made perfect sense in Hume's time, and only seems obtuse now because of later discoveries in political science (e.g., caretaker or "lame-duck" governments, electoral commissions, very strong formal or conventional constitutional rules mandating maximum terms in office, and in most countries heads of state who do not rule and therefore may be entrusted with presiding over elections). Hume fears a future that will resemble the foundings of the past:

When an artful and bold man is placed at the head of an army or faction, it is often easy for him, by employing, sometimes violence, sometimes false pretences, to establish his dominion over a people a hundred times more numerous than his partizans. He allows no such open communication, that his enemies can know, with certainty, their number or force. He gives them no leisure to assemble together in a body to oppose him. Even all those, who are the instruments of his usurpation, may wish his fall; but their ignorance of each other's intention keeps them in awe, and is the sole cause of his security. By such arts as these, many governments have been established; and this is all the *original contract*, which they have to boast of. (E: OC, 471; italics in original; underlining added)

Hume's general point, restated, is that the alternative to political conventions is government by crude focal points—in this case a monopoly over common knowledge, which will be enough to secure a tyrant in office and even to gain him the future reputation of consent.

All this serves to deepen the lesson, discussed in the last chapter, that constitutionalism is counterintuitive. Its presence represents the triumph of bitter experience and long custom over what seems to be common sense, the triumph of an unexciting and bloodless process over apparent merit and charisma. A constitution lets a new and possibly short-lived holder of political office command the allegiance that comes with long possession. Even an absolute and arbitrary monarchy, with settled rules of succession, is an epochal advance over Anglo-Saxon primitive charisma.

Magna Charta: Conditional Allegiance and Limited Authority

Magna Charta plays a central role in Hume's story of "regular" and legitimate government. But it is very hard to tell just what that role is. The "ancient constitution" doctrine of Old Whigs and common lawyers (and later, with different and more sophisticated theoretical backing, of Burke) had said that Magna Charta had immemorial origins in the shadows of time and should be venerated for its hoary antiquity. Deliberately spurning that tradition, Hume argued that Magna Charta when first signed was both ineffective and mostly a charter of rights for barons; that Magna Charta did represent a relatively ancient tradition of personal or legal liberties but that parliamentary privilege played no part in it; and that many praiseworthy parts of English law had foreign origins.[40] Beyond that, Hume seems to fluctuate among a variety of incompatible beliefs: Magna Charta was an original contract; its legitimacy lay (and lies) in custom; it had been ignored in practice for hundreds of years at the time that parliament pleaded its validity against Charles I in the 1620s; it was, nevertheless, binding as customary law and parliament was right to vindicate it; the Petition of Right was unprecedented and revolutionary on the one hand and merely a restatement of Magna Charta on the other.

These positions can be reconciled and explained through a theory of convention. Magna Charta, along with regular monarchy, is a fundamental convention, congruent with natural justice but not derived from it. It is the basis for judging both ordinary and constitutional laws. Contrary to the old-Whig claim that ancient rights were once unquestioned but had since decayed, Magna Charta was initially weak and became stronger with repeated assertion. Rights, like dynasties and squatter's rights (and for similar reasons), become secure through custom and long possession. Magna Charta in fact has become so solid that no departure from it, however long-standing, can erode its validity. Most strikingly, the Charter—but no other law or provision in England besides hereditary monarchy—has armored itself against erosion through a meta-convention whereby departures from its provisions may not be counted as precedent. And that is how the Charter could be, in the early seventeenth century, both disused for generations and binding *qua* fundamental—whether the Stuarts knew it or not.

In all these ways, Magna Charta comes close to being both unique in England and unique to England. No other country will have a fundamental charter of rights and authority quite like this one. Many will have no charter (whether written or mythic) that has such force. But historical uniqueness does not track methodological uniqueness. The Charter is a convention that follows the same social and psychological rules as other conventions. The differences in kind with respect to its authority derive from differences in degree with respect to its origins. The same forces that cemented Magna Charta could cement other conventions. They just happen in the case of England to have cemented this one and only one other (i.e., regular monarchy).

Like other conventions, Magna Charta began with accident and force. Rebellious barons, triumphant in the field, demanded that King John "submit at discretion." Operating as "open enemies" to the king, the barons dictated Magna Charta on their terms—in plain words, "extorted" it (H 1.442, 446). The Charter's later establishment or settlement under Edward Longshanks was likewise "extorted" by barons through slightly less violent means, as their condition for granting funds: Hume uses the word twice, as a compliment (H 2.121–2, and also see chapter 7). While the violent origins of this and more or less all other old laws may now seem obvious, Hume's stress upon it mocked the old Whig theorists by omission. They had insisted that Magna Charta reaffirmed rights of more ancient origin. Hume clearly *does not care* whether or not this is true. Magna Charta "*either granted or secured* very important liberties and privileges to every order of men in the kingdom" (H 1.442–3; emphasis added); Hume does not think it relevant to ask which were granted, which secured, and which to whom. Of another code attributed to Henry I, Hume writes that it was both forged and, if it indeed showed the legal customs of Henry I's time, no credit to those (it endorsed private revenge [H 1.278]).[41]

Whether Magna Charta appealed backwards to old rights is not important. Those rights became secure at Runnymede ("Runnemede" to Hume) because it was there that they were codified and made famous. Unlike dimly remembered ancient traditions, the Charter was "memorable" (H 1.144), and we should take the adjective seriously. (It here is likely to mean "easy to remember" rather than "worth remembering."[42]) Magna Charta could serve as a rallying point, as a source of principled appeal against royal power—and eventually baronial power as well. The Charter's initial force lay not in its practical effect (it had little) but in the principles of public right that it created:

> Acts of violence and iniquity in the crown, which before were only deemed injurious to individuals, and were hazardous chiefly in proportion to the number, power, and dignity of the persons affected by them, were now regarded, in some degree, as public injuries, and as infringements of a charter, calculated for general security. (H 1.488)

The Charter was thus "a kind of epoch in the constitution." It was of central constitutional importance, Hume notes, "without seeming anywise to innovate in the distribution of political power" (which still lay largely in the barons [H 1.488]). To be clearer, we might say that the Charter's constitutional importance comes from the fact that its statements of right did *not* depend on royal power. The Charter, like the settled rules of royal succession, embodied political principles that were vivid to the imagination and did not track current distributions of the command over violence. A convention of authority, however imperfect and fragile, had begun to trump force.[43]

The Charter was only a turning point in retrospect. It became fundamental after, and as the result of, repeated rallies to its standard and appeals to its principles. Hume stresses repeatedly how it was more important to keep the Charter salient than to observe its provisions scrupulously. When John's successor Henry III

> at any time was checked in his illegal practices, and when the authority of the Great Charter was objected to him, he was wont to reply; "Why should I observe this charter, which is neglected by all my grandees, both prelates and nobility?" It was very reasonably said to him: "You ought, sir, to set them the example." (H 2.18)[44]

Once the Charter was in force, battles between the king and barons were, crucially, *legal* or constitutional battles. In these battles each side had an interest in reaffirming Magna Charta against the other because the Charter's principles, especially those against arbitrary imprisonment, potentially limited all political actors (or from a different point of view benefited them all). As a result, both sides' tactical assertions of Magna Charta resulted in a strengthening of its status as a convention—with the eventual effect of limiting *both* sides, even though each had only intended to use it for advantage against the other.

When Edward I "Longshanks" had the upper hand over the barons (i.e., most of the time; he was a strong king), he set a usual though intermittent example of supporting the charter. But he also strengthened it immeasurably by applying its provisions against the barons as well as the king. This is how he "made the crown be regarded by all the gentry and commonalty of the kingdom, as the fountain of justice, and the general asylum against oppression" (H 2.75). When the barons had the upper hand, they insisted that the king not only give up some money or troops but also reaffirm Magna Charta— thus repairing the gaps in the convention of Magna Charta that Edward's own violations had opened. When Edward I acceded to one such demand in 1297, Hume refers to this as the "settlement of the charters" (H 2.120). But words mattered. At first Edward signed and sealed the charters with a signing statement asserting his "royal dignity or prerogative, which in effect enervated the whole force of the charters." The barons wisely forced the king, a little later, "to grant to the people, without any subterfuge, a pure and absolute confirmation of those laws, which were so much the object of their passionate affection" (H 2.121).

Magna Charta only became solid through repeated *and public* reaffirmations.

> It is computed, that above thirty confirmations of the charter were at different times required of several kings, and granted by them, in full parliament; a precaution, which, while it discovers [i.e., reveals] some

ignorance of the true nature of law and government, proves a laudable jealousy of national privileges in the people, and an extreme anxiety, lest contrary precedents should ever be pleaded as an authority for infringing them. (H 2.122–3)[45]

"Accordingly," i.e., *as a result* of the anxiety and the demand for reaffirmation it provoked,

we find, that, though arbitrary practices often prevailed, and were even able to establish themselves into settled customs, the validity of the Great Charter was never afterwards formally disputed; and that grant was still regarded as the basis of English government, and the sure rule by which the authority of every custom was to be tried and canvassed. (H 2.123)

Again, as with all conventions, appearances and words matter. What "formally" holds, is "regarded" as fundamental, does not determine what is done in every case. But it determines whether what is done in every case will become a durable practice or will be seen as a regrettable, perhaps outrageous, departure from the rule. This must be worked out over time. There is no *ex ante* standard for fundamental law, any more than there is for "family heirloom": even an object slightly imperfect (within reason: something must merit many years' attachment) triumphs through stubborn affection. Hume's account of the French Salic law, the only example in the *Treatise* of a "fundamental" law, is very similar: it "acquired equal authority with the most express and positive law" by being "old and established opinion," "supported by ancient precedent" and by many reaffirmations made "unanimously" and "without dispute or controversy," "confirmed by recent instances, solemnly and deliberately decided" (H 2.196–8).

The determination not to let violations become precedents resulted over time in a unique convention (or meta-convention) regarding the Charter, and one that flouts Hume's normal respect for precedent as a criterion that safeguards peace and order.[46] *Only* when regarding the charter did—and does, Hume would say—past practice not create a precedent. Fundamental law survives regardless of the quantity and duration of political practices that violate it:

The jurisdiction of the Star-chamber, martial law, imprisonment by warrants from the privy-council, and other practices of a like nature, though established for several centuries, were scarcely ever allowed by the English to be *parts of their constitution*: The affection of the nation for liberty still *prevailed over all precedent*, and even all political reasoning." (H 2.123, emphases added)

Hume insists on this point again and again. Edward III's repeated reaffirmations of the Charter made sense on the assumption that though his violations were frequent, the nobles were steadily determined to deauthorize them:

If the maxims of Edward's reign had not been in general somewhat arbitrary, and if the Great Charter had not been frequently violated, the parliament would never have applied for these frequent confirmations, which could add no force to a deed regularly observed, and which could serve to no other purpose, than to *prevent the contrary precedents from turning into a rule, and acquiring authority.* (H 2.274; emphasis added)

It is precisely because custom is the only rule of political legitimacy (outside cases of egregious tyranny) that continual resistance to all violations of right is necessary to prevent their de facto existence from becoming de jure.

By the same right that one prerogative is assumed without law, another may also be claimed, and another, with still greater facility; while the first usurpations both serve as precedents to the following, and give force to maintain them. . . . [H]ence the care of all ENGLISH patriots, to guard against the first encroachments of the crown; and *hence alone* the existence, at this day, of ENGLISH liberty. (E: SRC, 374 [emphasis added])[47]

Note Hume's emphases on the national qualifier. Each country has its own fundamental conventions. England's (Hume mentions the ban on taxation without consent of parliament, which is a Charter provision, §14) are particularly its own.

Though this is a matter of guarding rights by preventing a custom, repeating such prevention establishes an overarching custom of its own. A meta-custom of reaffirming a principle in the breach can be extremely effective at creating mental habits and fixing the salient equilibria, preventing contrary practices from becoming "established." Thus Hume says that Edward III's reign was "extremely arbitrary," giving a page of examples, but adds that

These facts can only show the *practice* of the times: For as to the *right*, the continual remonstrances of the commons may seem to prove that it rather lay on their side: At least, these remonstrances served to prevent the arbitrary practices of the court from becoming an established part of the constitution. (H 2.277)

Of Magna Charta and an allied charter concerning public forestry rights, he writes:

Though often violated, they were still claimed by the nobility and people; and as no precedents were supposed valid, that infringed them, they rather acquired, than lost authority, from the frequent attempts, made against them in several ages, by regal and arbitrary power. (H 2.7)[48]

This same meta-convention was cited by the Commons in support of the Petition of Right. Though the Charter had been violated for as long as anyone could remember, this did not matter:

Privileges in particular, which are founded on the GREAT CHAR-
TER, must always remain in force, because derived from a source of
never-failing authority; regarded in all ages, as the most sacred contract
between king and people. Such attention was paid to this charter by
our generous ancestors, that they got the confirmation of it re-iterated
thirty several times; and even <u>secured it by a rule, which, though vul-</u>
<u>garly received, seems in the execution impracticable. They have estab-</u>
<u>lished it as a maxim,</u> *That even a statute, which should be enacted in con-*
tradiction to any article of that charter, cannot have force or validity. But
with regard to that important article, which secures personal liberty; so
far from attempting, at any time, any legal infringement of it, they have
corroborated it by six statutes, and put it out of all doubt and controversy. If in practice it has often been violated, abuses can never come in
the place of rules; nor can any rights or legal powers be derived from
injury and injustice. (H 5.192–3; italics in original; underlining added)

Hume explicitly denies Court arguments to the effect that Magna Charta had
faded through disuse. Charles can on Hume's view be acquitted of many alleged crimes, but some were real, "transgressions of a plain limit, which was
marked out to royal authority" (H 5.570, note "W").[49]

In the debates over Magna Charta during Charles I's reign, which pitted
the Crown against the Commons, the House of Lords (whose position Hume
more or less endorses, saying that it "acted, in the main, a reasonable and
a moderate part" [H 5:195]), proposed reaffirming Magna Charta and "the
tenor of the ancient customs and laws of the realm," while allowing some
limited, circumscribed, and extra-legal exceptions in cases of necessity, in the
name of royal prerogative (H 5.195). In effect, the Lords endorsed the no-
precedent rule once again—as does Hume. Charles I himself acknowledged
its force when, during his period of ruling without parliament, he grounded
his assertions of royal authority on "necessity" rather than "right" (H 5.209).
And though Hume does not say so, the Petition of Right recapitulated the
old convention of reassertion. It was insisted on by the Commons and signed
by Charles (whose consent was, again, "extorted" [H 5.200]); it was called a
"petition" rather than a bill because the Commons claimed that it contained
no new liberties, only reasserting old ones (H 5.192). The no-precedent rule is
explicitly said (by Hume, speaking in parliament's voice) to trump the usual
rule of "prescription" or long possession: "As the rights of mankind are for
ever to be deemed sacred, *no prescription* of tyranny or arbitrary power can
have authority sufficient to abolish them" (E: CP, 494).[50] Again, Hume does
not say so—perhaps thinking the fact familiar—but the Petition itself explicitly reasserted the "no precedent" convention.[51] Hume is so fond of the
meta-convention "violations constitute no precedent" that when he mentions
exceptions to his own laws of political science he not only pleads the unavoidable role of "fortune and accident" but jokes that such exceptions "are not to

be drawn into precedent" (E: OC, 476).[52] Hume repeatedly and conspicuously stresses that political crimes and assassinations constitute no precedent (H 2.317, 452); he vilifies Richard III for a usurpation that might have served as a very dangerous precedent (H 2.517–18); he even (when speaking through the person of a historical figure) uses the word "false" (as well as "danger-ous") to describe a precedent wrongly drawn from "successful violence" (H 2.319–20).[53] When a rule is openly violated, it normally weakens. But when such violations are noted, condemned, and coupled with a solemn statement of the rule's validity and of the fact that the violation *was* a violation, the rule grows stronger. To condemn repeatedly the violations of a rule is to reaffirm the rule. If this practice of condemnation and reaffirmation can become en-trenched, acts that resemble previous violations will seem—and therefore will be—unprecedented.

Seeing Magna Charta this way solves several interpretive puzzles and, more important, several political ones (some covered in a later chapter).

First, it explains the otherwise odd fact that Hume refers to Magna Charta as a "kind of original contract" (H 2.7)—in spite of his famous refusal to ground political authority in any such thing. One place in which Hume calls the Charter a contract is easily explained as ironic mockery. Hume puts into the mouths of parliamentarians under Charles I the argument that the Char-ter is "a source of never-failing authority, regarded in all ages, as the most sacred contract between king and people," and then the further argument that it had to be "re-iterated thirty several times." Thought through, this is ri-diculous. If Magna Charta existed for "all ages," without an identifiable start-ing point, it cannot be much of a contract; and if its sanctity were so obvi-ous, "never-failing," and bred in English bones, it would not have required reiteration (H 5.193).[54] But another passage, in Hume's own voice, is harder to dismiss. In a passage cited in the last chapter, Hume says Magna Charta and the forestry charter

> were, during many generations, the peculiar favourites of the English nation, and esteemed the most sacred rampart to national liberty and independance. As they secured the rights of all orders of men, they were anxiously defended by all, and became the basis, in a manner, of the English monarchy, and a kind of original contract, which both lim-ited the authority of the king, and ensured the conditional allegiance of his subjects. (H 2.6–7)

The first thing to note seems pedantic but is not: a comma followed by "which" was used in Hume's time for both restrictive and nonrestrictive clauses.[55] The passage makes perfect sense if we take it here as restrictive. Magna Charta became the *kind of original contract that* both limited the authority of the king and ensured the conditional allegiance of his subjects—not the other kind, the alleged kind whereby the citizens as a body can at any time threaten to re-model the government if they differ with its measures. Given that Hume's biggest objections to original contracts include the fact that they do not involve most subjects and enable astute leaders to seize absolute power by manipulating mass assemblies, Hume may be saying that this kind of contract is not the kind that his usual arguments against social contracts aim to discredit—perhaps because its status is based on its solemn reaffirmation over very long periods of time rather than on the wills of those who happen to be prominent in any given instance, and perhaps because tussles over its application have turned something that was once a typically corrupt and unenforceable feudal contract into something that really does benefit all. Similarly and more substantively, this is not the "total dissolution of government" whose effects Hume most fears. To appeal to Magna Charta in particular as *the* original contract is to imply the illegitimacy of making a new one. Finally, we may note that the language of ramparts and defense seems at least as relevant to an accepted convention as to an actual promise: Magna Charta seems more like a line on a map than like a provision in a deed. "As they secured the rights of all orders of men, they were anxiously defended by all" perfectly describes an arrangement for mutual advantage that is not grounded on an actual promise. It describes a convention, not the kind of contract whose terms are explicitly spelled out and signed off on.

The second question is whether Hume's praise of Magna Charta constitutes praise for "natural rights" and a universal standard for liberty. In the key passage, Hume writes that the legal rights established by Magna Charta

> involve all the chief outlines of a legal government, and provide for the equal distribution of justice, and free enjoyment of property; the great objects for which political society was at first founded by men, which the people have a perpetual and unalienable right to recal [sic], and which no time, nor precedent, nor statute, nor positive institution, ought to deter them from keeping ever uppermost in their thoughts and attention. (H 1.445)

Neil McArthur says that Hume here "seems to refer to a doctrine of natural rights." The rights were granted by the king but their legitimacy does not rest on that grant: "Hume seems to say just the opposite—that people's awareness of their rights is not to be deterred by the acts of positive institutions, be it the courts ('precedent') or the legislative power ('statute')."[56] Donald Livingston, admitting that this passage presents problems for his conservative and particularistic theory of rights, and of politics generally, claims that Hume regards Magna Charta rights as at the time of their creation rooted in feudal order, and as retrospectively defining a "new type of political order," though not a universalistic or egalitarian one. In a self-described Nietzschean mode, Livingston glosses Hume as saying that "rights are what can be negotiated between spirited characters."[57]

Both of these arguments are inventive and in their way very Humean. Hume indeed thinks that Magna Charta trumps *ordinary* or non-fundamental conventions. And he indeed tends to be both elitist in his politics and prone to praise greatness of mind. But the reading above suggests an alternative to both views. Hume is telling a story about how rights can have their origin in a political act but become ever more *immune from politics from then on*. That Charter rights are immune to time, precedent, statute, and "positive institution" does not imply that they rest on nature. Their durability comes from the process of settled convention just discussed: repetition, and the meta-convention of non-precedence. Because this convention occurred once, in the past, and binds subjects as well as government, it is not a matter of current choice. Rights are "unalienable" to the extent that they are grounded in a fundamental convention. On the contrary, a right that is (allegedly) natural is fragile because any contrary opinion about nature—and we can count on there being one—can potentially efface it, and do so both quickly and thoroughly.

"Perpetual" is a striking word as well. It means, particularly in law, not something eternal in both past and present, but something established from a certain point on, *irrevocable*.[58] The crucial passage, after all, does not even use natural rights language: it speaks of the "objects of government," and uses historical language. Rights are something we "recall," not something that we hold as self-evident. Claims that Hume in this passage lays out "his view of the proper civil liberties," or that it should be read as agreeing with *Treatise* claims that certain "laws of nature" track what is useful in all societies, may be fair.[59] But they do not establish the stronger claim that Hume is appealing to natural rights in the usual sense of rights deriving their *authority* from nature. The authority of Magna Charta rights is a product of history. An "epoch of the constitution" is an occurrence in time, not an eternal truth. On the other hand, Livingston's heady claim that "those who cannot make their resentment felt" are rightly left out of the post-Magna Charta scheme seems likewise to go a bit far. The barons extorted Magna Charta, but later reaffirmations were more legal and less violent. More to the point, Charter rights came to apply to "all orders of men," not just the barons, and Hume expressly states that they would not be valuable were this not the case. Livingston's claim that conventions cannot survive unless some have enough greatness of mind to "make their resentment felt" in reasserting the conventions that ground rights,[60] is valid but speaks solely to political actors' unequal political importance, largely stemming from unequal ability to claim salience as a leader under a constitutional scheme. It does not entail inequality with respect to the political and legal rights that result from the relevant assertions. In civilized times it is in fact rare, and unpersuasive, for groups to assert their own rights without at least in principle affirming others' rights as well, universally.

The third puzzle, already alluded to, is why, if "prescription" or "repeated experience" is, for Hume, the basis of all legitimacy,[61] Magna Charta continued to be the basic or fundamental law of England in the realm of James I and Charles I. After all, by the time of the disputes with parliament that culminated in the English Civil War, experience of what life under an actually operating Great Charter would look like—a monarch constrained by its provisions, parliaments and subjects secure under its protection—had been absent for more than a century; the Tudors had been absolute, not to say despotic. The short answer (with more in the next chapter) is that a fundamental convention, protected by the meta-convention of non-precedence, can survive a long break in customary continuity. Put differently, an experience repeated long enough, and with enough insistence that departures from it entail no precedent, can create a convention so solid that departures from it will be customary but not legitimate.[62]

One sign of this unique durability is the distinction between Tudor "prerogative" and James I's explicitly advocated absolutism. Prerogative is an assertion of standing necessity and of the monarch's right to judge that necessity. Hume believes that in practice a government that continually asserts prerogative is absolute and arbitrary—"tyranny," or even Eastern despotism.[63] The crucial difference is that Tudor governance involved tyranny in practice, but not as a matter of formal convention. Prerogative involved a decades-long claim of authority to make exceptions to the law, but did not explicitly abrogate the law or the convention. Appeals to prerogative could be, and were, subjected to criticism, on the basis that claims of necessity had been extended too far and for too long. Or such appeals could be defended as justified by real emergencies. Both sides of such disputes, however, implied in making reference to prerogative the existence of a non-emergency legal order based on limited authority and conditional allegiance. But James I's "speculative system of absolute government," whereby all authority was royal and limits on it only by royal grace, was a different matter entirely. Admitting the validity of *that* would have destroyed forever the convention of limited authority and conditional allegiance (H 5.19; see also 5.91–2). Resistance to James I's claims proved that the Magna Charta convention was intact.

Conclusions

Hume's judgment that the two fundamental conventions of English politics up to his time have been hereditary monarchy and Magna Charta helps frame his account of constitutional crises. Such crises in England, given its conventions, have involved clashes *within* one of these conventions, an attempt by a rising (or falling) power to *assert* or *reassert* one or both conventions in unaccustomed ways, or (as famously in the lead-up to the English Civil War) clashes *between* the conventions. The next chapter will discuss how these have been resolved, and how political strategy affects both the possibility of resolution and the shape it takes. For now, three theoretical lessons can be drawn.

First, Hume's key, summary claim that Magna Charta both "limited the authority of the king, and ensured the conditional allegiance of his subjects" (H 2.7) illuminates historically the claim that the previous chapter made analytically. Authority and allegiance are two ways of looking at the same thing. What we call authority when describing what a government can do tracks what we call allegiance when describing what the governed will put up with. This would not be true if there were a cosmic order prescribing different duties to governors and subjects, but it becomes true if all government is based on opinion. No ruler can completely abrogate conventional limits to his authority because his title to rule is neither stronger than nor separate from those conventions. Hume's overwhelming preference for established governments tracks an empirical generalization from this general principle: the "bulk of mankind" never attributes authority "to any thing that has not the recommendation of antiquity" (E: IPC, 512–13). If authority is to exist in relative independence of power, as it must in any government but a tyranny, people must feel allegiance to it. They will not do so unless authority observes conventions that can be relied on because each can expect all others to recognize and (mostly) respect them.

Hume gives two different accounts of England's constitutional development. One describes the progression of liberty, the other the measures of power. But the two stories have their chronological divisions in more or less the same places, and Magna Charta is a turning point in both (H 4.355, note "l," and 2.524–5).[64] The parallel should not be surprising. Changes in the constitutional rights of English subjects are equivalent to changes in what it meant to govern England constitutionally. When Thomas Wentworth in the debates over forced loans and arbitrary allegiance said of King Charles' privy council that "By tearing up the roots of all property, they have taken from us every means of supplying the king, and of ingratiating ourselves by voluntary proofs of our duty and attachment towards him," he was describing the outline of all regular authority. When he added "We must vindicate: What? New things? No: Our ancient, legal, and vital liberties; by reinforcing the laws, enacted by our ancestors," he was vindicating the particular form of conditional allegiance, Magna Charta, that outlined such authority in England. In England, perhaps alone among countries in Hume's day, conventions of rights and limited government were more or less equally ancient, and established, as conventions of hereditary monarchy.[65] Hume admits that the King's partisans could find no fault in Wentworth's constitutional theory, and could only plead necessity in defense of the King's violations (H 5.191). All stable authority is limited; all stable allegiance is conditional.

Second, the most important political distinction among countries may concern not the form of their conventions but the degree to which they have become conventions.[66] Hume certainly realizes that an absolute hereditary monarchy under durable rules of succession is regular or constitutional government in a very narrow sense. (It might be better to speak of a constitutional element in a regime that is as a whole still unsettled and largely governed by force.) Hume once suggests that lack of an orderly succession rule is a sign that a country lacks "regular government" (2.73–4), but never the inverse, that orderly succession alone constitutes regular government. Hume dates England's "regular system of liberty" to a time much later than the rough limits of royal authority present in the fourteenth and fifteenth centuries: to the rise of the Commons in the early seventeenth century, and the Commons' resolve to make a "final determination" of the extent of royal power (H 5.179, 182; compare E: MOL, xxxviii). This is consistent with his definition of a free *government* as one involving both a partition of power among more than one branch and regular laws that are publicly known and operate in "the usual course of administration" (E: OG, 41). A "system of government," a synonym for constitution, involves a "certain system of laws, forms, and methods of succession" (T 3.2.10.14, SBN 561). The last of these alone is not enough. Not only was there no "regular idea of a constitution" in 1179, when "force and violence decided every thing" (H 1.362). There was also no single "syste[m] of government" that applied to all, nor settled laws or rights to bind the monarch, as late as the end of Edward III's reign in 1377 (H 1.284). The Tudor government was a "regular system of government" but a nearly despotic one, not a modern civilized monarchy on the French model (H 5.557). It was the prerequisite for a later "regular and equitable plan of liberty" but did not itself govern under such a plan (H 2.525). David Miller rightly calls feudalism in Hume's scheme a "barbarous version of limited monarchy," in which "the barons challenged the power of the king, though without reaching any formal constitutional arrangement for sharing authority," and in which there was—unlike in civilized absolute monarchies, modern limited monarchies, and free republics—no "regular enforcement of the rules of justice."[67]

Still, to denigrate regular monarchy is to miss something very important. The convention of orderly succession represented the first triumph of conventions of allegiance over accident and force. And the barons' willingness to observe this convention represents the first triumph of authority over power. Constitutional government required the progress of parliamentary self-assertion—a famous part of Hume's story, and England's—as well as "refinements" or technological improvements in the science of government. But this could only get going once the outlines of allegiance were already clear and provided the basic model for such conventions. A pattern of government, occurring partly by accident and partly through the purposeful (though necessarily fleeting) application of force, leads to a custom when the results are seen to be salutary or at least acceptable. Astute appeals to the custom, combined with at least partially successful attempts to vindicate it in the face of opposition, make the custom more durable and a possible object of subjects' allegiance: an embryonic convention. Soon attempts to use force against the convention start to require an excuse and perhaps to evoke condemnation after the fact. Eventually, those attempts will predictably fail for lack of support, since the polity's members in general, and in some cases even the usurper's own followers, would rather follow the convention than the usurper. Now we have a convention of allegiance that is more powerful than armies and castles. Civilization has no other origin. Even tyrannical governments rest on opinion, but only tyrannical governments rest on raw opinion alone.

Third, the transition from monarchs who hold authority by their own strength, courage, and talent (and birth, though as only one factor among many) to those who hold it constitutionally illuminates a pervasive but underappreciated aspect of all constitutional government: the separation of allegiance from merit. The story of constitutional government in England is partly a story of how the Anglo-Saxon monarch, whose "authority depended more on his personal qualities than on his station," gave way to modern monarchs for whom the exact opposite was the case (their contingent political *power* being another matter [H 1.161]).

That Hume's conventionalism decouples the question of who rightly holds *property* from the question of who deserves it is already well known. This separation is grounded on two reasons. First, only impersonal rules provide the security that makes property so beneficial: I can only count on holding my property, so that I can improve it or gain through exchanging it with others, if such holdings and exchanges are immune to periodic inquiries as to whether my moral character and that of my trading partners are up to the standard of our material assets.[68] Second, personal merit is never an obvious question. Even cases that do not seem intrinsically doubtful will become so due to our self-preference, our "avidity and partiality." Thus, if we want to avoid "infinite confusion," we observe an impartial rule, not a judgment of personal merit (T 3.2.6.9, SBN 531–2). Property is founded not on particular judgments but on "general rules, which must extend to the whole society, and be inflexible either by spite or favour" (T 3.2.3.3, SBN 502). It is precisely because natural human judgments are substantively fair—they "accommodate themselves to circumstances, and have no stated invariable method of operation"—that the rules of justice, which are artificial, rightly ignore such judgments (T 3.2.6.9, SBN 533). Citing such passages, Brian Barry has stressed that Hume, no less than John Rawls in our time, unequivocally separates justice from desert.[69]

Because Hume not unreasonably regards disagreement over allegiance as even more dangerous than disagreement over property (T 3.2.10.6, SBN 557), a separation between authority and political merit turns out to be as crucial to the artificial virtue of allegiance as a separation between property and personal merit is to the artificial virtue of justice. We need not only to acknowledge some political decisions as having authority even when we disagree with the substance of those decisions, but also to acknowledge accepted ways of settling on which rulers will wield authority in spite of disagreements over who is best qualified to do so. Hereditary monarchy is an institution for ensuring legitimate rulers in the absence of agreement as to the best ones (and with a view to forestalling civil war as to the best). Once again, a "principle of authority" comes to trump immediate force or Machiavellian talent. Constitutions describe how authoritative office-holders are to be selected, not which ones deserve to be selected.

This principle has costs: we can no longer pretend to guarantee that our heads of state will be particularly good at their jobs. This would be disastrous if the separation of allegiance from merit did not extend in both directions. That is, Hume notes that by his own time both absolute and limited or mixed monarchies have come to realize that actual government operations should be conducted not by the object of universal allegiance but by a person of personal (and controverted) merit: a prime minister. Hume's discussion of prime ministers (begun at E: CL, 88, as an example of how Machiavelli did not know everything, but continued through the *History*) is therefore more important than it seems. The modern office of prime minister solves a myriad of problems and reveals the benefits of institutionalized over crude coordination.

Most obviously, ministerial government makes it possible for a monarchy to be well governed regardless of the monarch. Before prime ministers were invented and as long as barons' lawless power competed with royal authority, a king could only keep his throne and enforce the laws by possessing great personal qualities, chiefly "vigour" or "abilities" or "capacity." These are Hume's equivalents to Machiavelli's *virtù*—"firmness and dexterity" (H 2.16) being Hume's counterparts to Machiavelli's roles of lion and fox—and like *virtù*, these qualities were regrettably unlikely to track private goodness.[70] Ministerial government lets settled monarchies draw on a succession of vigorous governors whose particular talents are suited to particular circumstances. (We might note that Machiavelli, who lived before prime ministers, thought this an advantage unique to republics.[71]) And they can do this so consistently that this vigor is scarcely noticed: competence is just as routinized as authority, though not in the same person. The monarch need not be personally able in order to retain authority; the prime minister need not have authority to govern ably.[72]

More subtly, the separation of allegiance and merit allows a separation between rank and power. Hume stresses to his readers inclined to chivalric nostalgia that aristocratic honor poses a fundamental problem for government. A powerful lord will refuse to obey an official of lower rank, while one of higher rank will, given the baronial penchant for usurpation, pose the Machiavellian threat of overthrowing government to exert power in his own right. England faced this problem in 1315; Scotland, as late as 1488 (H 2.160, 3.24; compare 2.295). This is the most basic reason why ministerial government marks such a crucial distinction between "barbarous" and "civilized" monarchies. Only when prime ministers can make decisions that bind those *whose social rank exceeds theirs* can it be said that authority is at least potentially binding irrespective of persons. Where rank is strong, contempt for law is "founded on the nature of things" (H 1.170). Good government, as usual, means government through strong conventions.

Robert Manzer says of Hume and the *Federalist* that "the modern science of politics was once used as a tool not only for developing new political institutions, but also for shaping opinion about a constitution."[73] Hume's *History* is often—most obviously by Duncan Forbes—seen as doing this through history. But it also does so as political theory. It provides a systematic and general story of how conventions are founded and reinforced over centuries, through "custom" in the broad sense but more specifically through deliberate political reassertion in the face of departures. If only such repeated reassertions can ground the kind of stable allegiance that makes for peace and prosperity, the case for attempting to found wholly new conventions is weakened—not just with respect to those who love a particular nation's story, but for those who wish the national story were different but have reason to accommodate themselves to the one that prevails. Just as an American who believes that it is more efficient to drive on the left side of the street would be insane to put that belief into practice, a political leader who doubts the substantive worth of her country's constitutional conventions. to the extent of *actively* attempting to act in defiance of them, at that moment ceases to be a leader who hopes to win voluntary allegiance, and to govern from something other than force. The ways in which leaders can be both creative and forward-looking in spite of this counsel is the subject of the next chapter.

Chapter 5

Leadership and Constitutional Crises

[Charles I] deserves the epithet of a good, rather than of a
great man; and was more fitted to rule in a regular established
government, than either to give way to the encroachments of a
popular assembly, or finally to subdue their pretensions. He wanted
suppleness and dexterity sufficient for the first measure: He was not
endowed with the vigour requisite for the second.

—H 5.542–3

The previous chapter discussed fundamental political conventions: those
generations-long, identity-producing customs, likely to be few in any society,
that define what political authority is, independent of who wields it, and how
that authority is limited, independent of the magistrate's personal ambitions or
stated purposes. This chapter is about what leadership can do to repair breaches
in those conventions or to maintain them in the face of new configurations of
power. It will treat cases of partial order, involving crisis but not chaos. When
there are no stable political conventions at all—or when conquest or radical
revolutions have torn existing ones up at the roots—leadership is as Machiavelli portrayed it in the *Prince*: a matter of force and guile, personal charisma
and deliberate terror, whatever will convince people that the new leader's rule
is relatively durable (and through convincing them, make it so; once again,
coordination solutions are self-fulfilling). When long experience and relative
satisfaction with the fruits of fundamental conventions have cemented the authority of an entire constitutional order, leadership takes the peaceful, bloodless form that political theorists rarely regard as the occasion of great heroism
(though that is very much our fault). The kind of leadership that seems both
unambiguously heroic and relevant to relatively stable regimes concerns the
case in between: when some political conventions defining authority and its
rightful limits are widely recognized but not to such an extent, or with sufficient agreement on applications, as to prevent civil strife.

Disagreement over which conventions are legitimate or fully constitutional, what the conventions mean or prescribe, or which should dominate
when they clash (or seem to clash) can result in conflicts that actually last lon-

ger than they would under a stylized state of pure chaos (when the Hobbesian strategy, "follow the most successful warlord," dominates—or would dominate, if there were ever a condition without focal points). At the same time, leadership under such conditions of disagreement over fundamental conventions can be at least semi-legitimate. Some leaders may command at least shaky constitutional authority. Beyond this, conditions of relative peace and imperfectly effective limitations on executive authority may allow ordinary citizens or subjects who are not mere warlords to become new leaders, to marshal a following by appealing to conventions that are partially secure.

The treatment here will synthesize two approaches to Hume that happen to yield the same result in the cases discussed. This book up to now has taken a mildly rational choice approach that stresses Hume's treatment of collective action in general and coordination in particular. This approach tends to de-emphasize the distinction among agents, portraying them all as facing a common problem of achieving as many of their goals as possible when everyone else is trying to do the same. In contrast, Frederick Whelan has portrayed Hume's *History* as (among other things) his book about leadership, reading it as a liberal, law-governed alternative to Machiavelli, but still part of the realist or reason-of-state tradition on these questions.[1] The rational choice tradition tends to stress strategic situations; the reason-of-state tradition, the ability of prudent and forceful individuals to reshape situations and overcome—to some degree—unfavorable circumstances.[2] The latter tradition seems to have grown less compelling in an age of mass, competitive politics than it was in Machiavelli's petty principalities. For competitive polities, like competitive markets, allow each agent to choose from myriad alternatives put forth by others, and in so doing to alter others' choices. It is not that there is no ship of state but that there is constant flux with regard to who pilots it and who serves as crew.

But just as there are markets in which one or a few actors are not mere "price-takers" but have market power, there are political situations in which one or a few actors are not mere choosers under uncertainty but have old-fashioned political power. These occur when leadership is not random but designated by conventions of authority. Such conditions give prominence either to one actor or a limited number who have the recognized authority to direct outcomes (or at the very least set agendas). Under such circumstances, "reason of state" describes not an arcane mystery of ruling but rationality under specialized conditions. The "rational-choice" insight that individual agents do not choose outcomes, only strategies, still applies, and statesmanship cannot work miracles. Since constitutional leaders rely on others to carry out their purposes, they can succeed to the extent that they respect, or seem to respect, the conventions from which they draw authority. Hume, as noted, was determined to avoid blaming individual agents who failed to take actions outside their feasible set, or who failed to act on information they did not have. There is no need to depart from methodological individualism and instrumentalism in order to endorse Montesquieu's famous maxim: "At societies' birth, it is the leaders of republics who make the institution; from then on it is the institution that forms the leaders of republics."[3] Constitutional authority enables and furthers some large-scale exercises of force and guile that warlords and petty princes could not even imagine, while rendering others difficult or impossible.

If for Hume "the many are governed by the few" through opinion (E: FPG, 32), any even moderately "regular" or "settled" government is founded on the wielding of existing, fundamental opinions that the mere force of leaders' will cannot quickly change. Of course, such fundamentals are willed or chosen in a different sense: Hume always stresses their agent-based, artificial character. Put in our terms, fundamental conventions are congealed choices and strategies; they arise and persist to the extent that people have found it more advantageous to acquiesce to them than to reject them. As mechanisms for durably outwitting political chaos, they represent a collective, peaceful, depersonalized version of *virtù*. Humean princes, dependent on opinion, succeed to the extent that they enlist other agents' purposes in their own, which means, for the most part, acting in accord with existing conventions rather than flouting them. Put differently, allegiance to authority is a virtue for princes as well as citizens, a requirement for anyone whose ends require collective action. The conventions that would seem like constraints to Machiavellian politicians define the prerequisites of peace, prosperity, and liberty for ordinary citizens— who therefore have good reason to maintain them and to follow only those leaders who respect them.

For Hume, settling on some legitimate ruler is more important than vindicating our partisan opinions of which ruler that should be. That said, when claims to legitimate authority "are mingled and oppos'd in different degrees, they often occasion perplexity; and are less capable of solution from the arguments of lawyers and philosophers, than from the swords of the soldiery" (T 3.2.10.15, SBN 562). As Whelan has noted,[4] this implies that Hume effectively has two theories of authority. One tells us to adhere to settled authority. The other addresses the problems that occur when we face a choice between two authorities, each of which claims to be settled (or authoritative, or legitimate). To the first-order question of which regime is best, and the (famous) second-order answer that the established one should be chosen even if not absolutely best, we must add a third-order question: which established authority, as it were, is to count as *most* established. Again, these problems are political all the way down since questions of allegiance allow no higher appeal to law or authority. Since Humean armies are governed by opinion, even force is a matter of convention: soldiers' allegiance, and not incidentally the taxation power by which they are paid, will in the long run turn on perceived political authority.

Hume's *History* answers the first question of authority: "what is established" is the standard. If philosophy suggests that civil war is very bad, history shows us just how bad. But the *History* also teaches statecraft regarding the second and third questions. Those who care about peaceful and durable settlement will study the craft of convention. Treating several historical cases will reveal the patterns. In each case, two or more durable conventions are in conflict and the dispute is finely balanced; the only question is whether the result will be settled by raw violence, whose success can be only temporary, or by authoritative violence that makes artful use of convention. If Hume aims to prove Machiavelli obsolete, he aims to do the same for Hobbes. The attempt to manufacture sovereignty from the raw materials of force and propaganda is a sign of failure and cannot be made durable. He who lives by primitive focal points will die by them (as Hobbes knew too; as noted earlier, his maxim "when nothing else is turn'd up, Clubs are Trump" is a counsel of despair when "something else"—an accepted authority—is lacking[5]). Hume's innovation is to show how unexpected conventions exist and can be wielded to create authority even when civil war is raging, or threatened. His treatment of constitutional crises aims to show that leaders are often holding strong cards in some suit other than clubs, as well as the authority to name their strong suit as trump.

Chapter 2 discussed the forging of conventions from unpromising materials: the strategic, generations-long, hit-or-miss process by which the unsocial aspirations of recalcitrant individuals and social groups are reshaped into forms more compatible with those of fellow citizens. This reshaping sometimes results from strategy (roughly speaking) but much more commonly from a process of feeling one's way, in which partial acquiescence in conventions of authority reshapes social possibilities so as to make future acquiescence by new generations more likely. This chapter treats situations in which this process is reasonably far along. Far from wanting to strike out independently and take their chances on warlordism, most social actors are seeking an authoritative solution to their problems and are merely unsure what it is. Far from operating like diplomats, who lack coercive authority and must persuade a variety of powerful actors one by one that peace is in their interest, the leaders discussed in this chapter are at least partially and contingently recognized as already having authority, provided they can shunt aside other claimants to that title or patch together a rough consensus as to how fundamental conventions properly define and limit that authority. Put analytically, the actors in this chapter know (in effect) that they face a coordination problem and that convention is the best way to solve it. They are looking to leaders to create a common opinion about *which* convention is in effect.

The kind of leadership involved is not liberal in the prevailing sense. It makes no reference to autonomy or practical reason, in which Hume does not believe. But in an alternative, realist sense it is thoroughly liberal and potentially democratic. A constitutional leader neither believes rationalist myths to the effect that reason yields political agreement (and that humans have an inherent desire to justify themselves with reasons), nor pursues naked or crude self-interest via brutal and bloody methods under the assumption that others will do the same. Hume defends a form of leadership, based on sympathy and strategy, that aims at justice, liberty, prosperity, peace, and toleration—while recognizing that the road to these goods travels not through reason or consent but through custom, skillfully wielded. In demanding that political authority be a matter of actually valued convention, that it cut along the grain of our passions and opinions rather than against it,[6] Hume could in fact be seen as more liberal than any rationalist. And his scheme, though not distinctly democratic, is open toward democracy to the extent that majority voting becomes part of an authoritative convention that defines democracy's procedures and form. That is, the scheme is open to the kind of constitutional, representative democracy that most of us recognize as authoritative as well—as opposed to the limitless, antinomian kind more likely to be demanded by political philosophers in their closets than welcomed by the *demos* itself.

Heroic Masonry: Cementing Conventions

Henry VII: Title Insurance

The first Tudor king named Henry is less famous than his son, but for our purposes more instructive. Others have noted that on Hume's account the Wars of the Roses were so virulent because two dynasties' claims were so evenly matched: the Lancastrians represented the status quo dynasty, familiar for several decades; the Yorkists, the status quo ante dynasty, out of power in most subjects' memory but with a better claim from the ancient line.[7] Henry VII, the heir to Lancaster who took the throne, in classic War-of-Roses fashion, through violence (defeating renegade Yorkist Richard III on Bosworth Field), played a subtle constitutional game to pass on his crown without violence. Hereditary succession was, as traced in the previous chapter, the prevailing constitutional convention of the time. Henry's task was to make that convention point in one direction rather than two.

When Henry VII mounted the throne, England was exhausted by war and wanted an undisputed, traditional, monarchical line. Henry did his best to manufacture one, first by marriage—he was engaged to Elizabeth, the Yorkist heir, and soon married her—and then by craft. Hume's account of the situation Henry faced is summarized ably by Whelan:

> Henry could (and did) present himself as the heir to the Lancastrian claim, but his position under the rules of hereditary succession was defective. His marriage to the heiress of York strengthened his dynasty, but for him to claim the throne through her would seriously jeopardize his personal power. A favourable act of Parliament could be procured (as Henry IV had done), but there was no doubt in that age "how superior the claim of succession by blood was to the authority of an as-

sembly." He might have invoked the right of conquest, but this would have alienated his new subjects by seeming to threaten their rights and privileges. All in all, says Hume, his best option was to claim the throne simply by virtue of his "present possession" of it, a fact which many hoped would mean the end of the long period of civil wars. If he governed with "vigour and abilities," and if he were to have capable heirs, he might hope to "secure perpetual possession of the throne" for his family. Indeed, when he died twenty-three years later after a stable reign, his son's title was "undisputed." Mere present possession had evolved into the prescriptive right of the Tudor dynasty.[8]

This reading of Henry as a Machiavellian new prince—"present possession" yields to legitimacy in one generation through able government—is masterful but incomplete. It makes Henry's machinations seem more simply Machiavellian and less convention-based than they were.

For one thing, Henry clearly acted so as to marshal any conventional source of authority that he could—birth, force, conquest, marriage, present possession—albeit in quiet ways that effaced the way that each of these conventions potentially clashed with the others. Absent Boswell, or Elizabeth, Henry would not have been in a position to act like a Machiavellian prince in the first place. No one would have followed him regardless of the Machiavellian virtues he might have displayed, or tried to display. For another, his situation was not one of having to establish a new dynasty in one generation. On the contrary, he had only to hold on to the throne *personally* for one generation so that his son, whose hereditary claim as heir to both York and Lancaster was far better than his, could inherit the crown on old-fashioned, wholly traditional grounds. Furthermore, while Henry stood on present possession, he did not exactly *assert* it as his title. The parliamentary proclamation that he dictated was delightfully ambiguous: "[t]hat the inheritance of the crown should rest, remain, and abide in the king," with no reasons or qualifications given. When Henry obtained for insurance a papal bull threatening those who denied him with excommunication, it listed *all* Henry's titles, "by succession, marriage, parliamentary choice, even conquest" (H 3.11). Henry himself could not assert some of these titles without risk or offense, but the pope could. By engineering a division of authority between parliament and pope, Henry was able to draw on conventional claims (and the primitive focal point of conquest) without asserting them.

Finally, Henry never neglected his wife's Yorkist claim. He was reluctant to proclaim it not because it was weak but because it was so strong. If his wife were to die before he did, the elder Henry (if his claim rested on hers) stood to forfeit the throne. If he were to have a son whose ambition exceeded his "filial piety," he stood to be toppled from that throne.[9] One of the first things Henry VII did during his reign is break his promises of leniency to old Yorkists—he persecuted them instead. Even a pretended claimant to the Yorkist inheritance (Perkin Warbec, who impersonated a nonexistent long-lost son) was a dangerous rallying point for opposition (H 3.42ff.). And Henry was afraid enough of the Earl of Warwic, the last male Plantagenet (and by default the last legitimate Yorkist claimant) as to maneuver to have him accused, tried, and executed on palpably ridiculous charges: a "violent act of tyranny, the great blemish of Henry's reign."[10] Whelan is right to say that Machiavellian measures of "watchful policy and steady severity," as well as the luck of facing a weak baron class that had been reduced by the Wars of the Roses and economic factors, kept Henry VII in precarious, never quite authoritative or legitimate, power (H 3.64, 80). But this situational Machiavellianism was made necessary by the constitutional background. The Yorkist pretenders were not just rival practitioners of force and guile. They represented, on one interpretation, a constitutional *principle*.

It is crucial to note that Henry's hoped-for *descendants* faced no such worries. Though his own title might rest on multiple but fragile bases, Henry VII knew that his son's claim would be utterly legitimate: unchallenged heir to Edward III.[11] When Henry VIII took the throne, "the contending titles of York and Lancaster were now at least fully united in his person" (H 3.84). One reign could never have founded a Tudor dynasty. But Henry VIII's dynasty was old, not new. The fundamental convention of royal succession was solid enough that all would acknowledge a king to whom the convention unambiguously pointed.

The fact that present possession was neither a good title nor a solid one is what accounts for what could be called historical enjambment between the War of the Roses and the Tudor age. The War ended in a sort of peace when Henry VII defeated Richard III (though various pretenders bedeviled the former's reign). But the new order was not firmly established until Henry VIII brought the dynastic dispute to an end. Hume himself places the start of the "useful, as well as the more agreeable part of modern annals" (H 3.82) at the *end* of Henry VII's reign in 1509, not the beginning, and the *History* in other ways suggests that that reign straddled the strife of the War of the Roses era and the absolute monarchy of the Tudors.[12] Hume's explicit reason is changes in technology and manners: as a result of navigation, the revival of classical learning, printing, gunpowder, and the Reformation, "a general revolution was made in human affairs" (at least in Europe [H 3.81]).

But the stability and instability of political conventions completes the story. The revolution in human affairs in England required a settled government to take root, and this came only with Henry VIII. By the time Henry VIII's teenaged son Edward VI died in 1553, the people of England, by then Protestant after a fashion (and Edward very much so), overwhelmingly preferred to proclaim a legitimate but Catholic heir (Mary) over Lady Jane Grey, who shared English subjects' religion but departed from the legitimate line, and whose claim threatened to lead to a monarch overawed by the powerful lords who promoted her. Seventy years after Richard perished on Bosworth

Field, "[t]he miseries of the ancient civil wars were not so entirely forgotten, that men were willing, by a departure from the lawful heir, to incur the danger of like bloodshed and confusion" (H 3.401). Ten years later than that, parliament's fears that Queen Elizabeth's death would leave a disputed succession led them to entreat Elizabeth to fix an heir, whoever it was, through marriage or parliamentary proclamation. They still remembered "the evils which their fathers had experienced from the contending titles of York and Lancaster" (H 4.59).

General Monk: Lemming-in-Chief

The fact that any convention of authority (above a certain threshold) is better than none, and fundamental conventions much better than none, has an unexamined corollary: that a political actor can sometimes win allegiance, especially when civil war has lessened all parties' attachment to their favored outcome, by promising to bring about one among many potentially stable outcomes without saying which one. This suggests a political strategy that we might call "naked bandwagoning": asserting vague or trivial goals until one has gathered enough support (with opponents lulled by one's seeming moderation) to insist on more specific and far-reaching ones. Hume portrays several versions of this strategy throughout the *History*.[13] But the case of General George Monk (we now spell his name "Monck"), who ended England's Civil War and restored a constitutional monarchy, displays extremes of both means and ends. Regarding means, Monk's naked bandwagon was particularly radical: his march from the North of England to London declared *no* goals whatsoever and drew partisans of both the parliament and the king. His initial appeal rested solely on personal reputation; his later appeal, solely on that plus bandwagoning. As to ends, Monk rejected the chance to set himself up as a new Cromwell and opted instead for a restoration of *all* England's fundamental conventions: the old Stuart line of monarchs, a free parliament, and Magna Charta. He was, for Humean purposes, the perfect constitutional prince.

The last days of the English Commonwealth, in which the New Model Army ruled on its own or through a puppet Committee of Safety, represent in something like pure form both the conditions and the central problems of coordination. As Hume portrays it, nearly all English subjects acknowledged their common interest in restoring a limited constitutional monarchy and a free parliament.[14] Military rule had displayed many of the characteristics of extreme or egregious tyranny; as previously noted, it only equivocally deserved the title of authority as opposed to mere compliance enforced through threat of death. The military usurpers had no claim to rule other than force and present possession; their authority was "founded on palpable injustice," was supported by "no national party," and threatened to culminate in ever-escalating "sanguinary measures" (H 6.141; see also 116). (Cromwell's so-called committee of safety could not possibly give the army greater legitimacy; Hume calls it an "ill-founded fabric," in other words, a shaky structure, and it fell apart almost immediately [H 6.127].) In the present, military rule was "oppressive and ruinous" and amounted to "slavery." In its future, precarious state it held out the prospect of "bloody massacre and extermination" for the nobility and gentry, "perpetual servitude" to "sanctified robbers" for everyone else (H 6.117, 120).

Under the circumstances, the opposing parties in the country—the moderate-parliamentary presbyterians and the royalist Anglicans—were willing to overlook the unequal benefits they were likely to gain from restoring the monarchical convention (benefits that turned out to be *very* unequal; the first Restoration parliament formally outlawed the Presbyterian religion, though only in Scotland did its persecution of Presbyterians employ extreme methods). These parties laid aside their differences and practiced "secret reconciliation" or informal coalition (H 6.117). No significant sector of society opposed the obvious coordination solution of restoring at once all of England's fundamental conventions: hereditary monarchy, a free parliament, and a set of laws, building on Magna Charta, that safeguarded subjects' rights. (On Hume's portrayal, to be accepted for argument, the only die-hard anti-monarchists left were in the army.) Having experienced the extremes of both "tyranny" and "anarchy," "every party, except the most desperate," not only wished for restoration as "the only remedy for all these fatal evils" but "ardently" wished it (H 6.129). "All men, however different in affections, expectations, and designs, united in their detestation of the long parliament" (H 6.133).[15]

But while allegiance was neither owed nor paid to the army, there were acute first-mover problems in restoring allegiance to the King. Though the army could not command allegiance, it had arms and spies; an early attempt at a royalist rising was uncovered and its leaders thrown into prisons (which soon grew very full [H 6.118–19]).[16] During the Glorious Revolution, the first-mover problem would be solved through foreign invasion by William of Orange. In the current case, the exiled King Charles (later Charles II), with no army and no allies, felt "totally desperate":

> His friends had been baffled in every attempt for his service: The scaffold had often streamed with the blood of the more active royalists: The spirits of many were broken with tedious imprisonments: The estates of all were burthened by the fines and confiscations, which had been levied upon them: No-one durst openly avow himself of that [monarchical] party: And so small did their number seem *to a superficial view*, that, even should the nation recover its liberty, which was deemed no wise probable, it was judged uncertain what form of government it would embrace. (H 6.122; emphasis added)

Potentially, England could reach an overwhelmingly popular, settled and legal solution. But in the meantime, the army's power and its desperate interest in using it threatened "all the horrors of the ancient massacres and pro-scriptions" (H 6.141).[17]

In these circumstances, General George Monk saved three kingdoms through what we might call Fabianism rampant. He marched through Eng-land and, until the last moment, said nothing. Neither of these actions was easy. Monk's standing among the army and the general population was per-sonal (what I have called primitive).[18] It stemmed not only from his power-ful army command but from his prudence, his moderation (having reduced Scotland through Cromwell's preferred method, i.e., massacring a town to terrorize a country, he had henceforth governed it well and justly [H 6.44]), and his lack of partisan fervor, which he had maintained at some risk when the New Model Army was very partisan indeed. Soldiers flocked to his stan-dard, and the population welcomed his progress, because they trusted him personally, even lacking knowledge of his program (H 6.123, 129). (Monk provided a "ray of hope" [H 6.129]: in Schelling terms, not a new "reason" for acting but an "excuse" that enables common action.[19]) Monk's dissimulation of his intentions likewise took tremendous self-discipline. He knew that if he expressed his final goal, which would alert the military enemy to his inten-tions, his army could be suppressed while still small. Monk was therefore determined to trust no one—not even his own brother (H 6.126)[20]—and he said almost nothing until he reached London, though he let everyone hope. When invited to address parliament, his speech was "prudent," ineloquent, and purposely opaque. It "still kept every one in suspence, and upheld that uncertainty, in which it seemed the general's interest to retain the public" (H 6.131).

When Monk did commit himself, he committed, though Hume does not put it this way, to bodies that could coordinate through common knowledge. By forming an alliance with the citizens of London, he gained to his side a useful mob that showed its allegiance by city-wide feasts of rump roast (a vi-sual pun on the Rump Parliament): the roasts, like all fire signals, were a pre-telegraph method for producing common knowledge, the billboards or televi-sion advertisements of their time. By inviting back, with his army's protection, the members of parliament whom the New Model Army had excluded—he had previously refused to negotiate without those members present—Monk created an instantly sympathetic, and fairly legitimate, national body: some-thing like a real parliament (H 6.132–3). Monk only invited a royal envoy to address the parliament *after* making sure the parliament was strongly in favor of considering Restoration. He had sustained a "state of suspense" until he had made sure that everyone wished what he did (H 6.138). Throughout all this, Monk refused the offer to take supreme power himself—a temptation that Hume thought barely anyone could resist (H 5.450). He consistently held out for a settled government, not a personal one (H 6.125, 133). As a result, Monk's role effaced itself. When Charles was restored, the King joked "that it must surely have been his own fault, that he had not sooner taken possession of the throne; since he found every body so zealous in promoting his happy restoration" (H 6.139).

Eugene Miller notes that "No figure in the entire *History* is praised more highly" than Monk.[21] Indeed, Hume's praise, usually moderate and balanced, is in this case phenomenal. Monk,

> by restoring the antient and legal and free government to three king-doms, plunged in the most destructive anarchy, may safely be said to be the subject, in these islands, who, since the beginning of time, ren-dered the most durable and most essential services to his native country. (H 6.247)

And Monk accomplished this with hardly any bloodshed. The greatest Briton of all time, however, succeeded not only because of his "moderation and prudence" or even his lack of ambition. He succeeded because the govern-ment he proposed *was* "ancient and legal and free": ancient and legal because grounded in constitutional conventions; free because of the content of those conventions. Because it was all these things, it was recognized by all parties. Had Monk tried to found a new republic, or to set himself up as a King, he could at best have ended up another Cromwell, a prudent tyrant whose rule ended at death. Cromwell had chosen to cut the threads of all existing con-ventions, relying for his power on charisma, force, and guile; Monk served his country by gathering up those threads and splicing them back together. Monk was not a new prince. He had the object of a peaceful constitutional-ist and used the methods of a magistrate. He "forc[ed]" others "to seek their own advantage" (T 3.2.7.8, SBN 538), to reach a new equilibrium based on freely accepted convention, by solving collective action problems that had prevented individuals from reaching that equilibrium themselves.

Rational Regicide: Queen Elizabeth and the Problem of Succession

Queen Elizabeth (I) is one of Hume's central figures, portrayed as a master of political strategy in an age in which religious strife and foreign war made politics supremely dangerous. Here one episode will be stressed: her execu-tion of Mary, Queen of Scots and the frock-and-dagger maneuvers that pre-ceded it. On a reconstruction of Hume's account, Elizabeth faced a critical situation because different religious sects drew opposite meanings from the same political convention. Under the circumstances, her own royal survival, and James I's uncontested succession, could only be established through murder—not, as in Henry VII's case, through marriage.

As stated, by Henry VIII's reign there was widespread agreement not only on the principle of hereditary succession but on the particular line whose claim to the throne was legitimate: his. However, on the question of which of his *heirs* was legitimate, opinions differed sharply—and, given Henry's spat with the Catholic Church regarding his marriages, precisely tracked religion. Henry's only legitimate son, Edward, was clearly an heir according to all parties,[22] but in an age of high mortality his line could not be counted on until he had children. (In the event, he died in his teens without issue.) With Edward gone, the only consistent theory for Catholics, who thought Henry VIII's marriage with Catherine of Aragon legitimate, its annulment and Henry's remarriage to Anne Boleyn illegitimate, was that the legitimate heir was Henry's first daughter Mary (later Queen Mary Tudor), and after her, Mary Queen of Scots. The only consistent theory for Anglicans (a useful anachronism[23]) who defended Henry's break with the Church and who therefore thought Henry's marriage with Catherine illegitimate, its annulment appropriate, and his marriage with Anne legitimate, was that the legitimate heir was Elizabeth.[24]

Faced with this logic, Henry VIII and the regency that followed him (Edward VI being only nine years old), attempted to make logic punishable by treason. They pushed through a series of parliamentary Acts whose theories of succession contradicted not only themselves, internally, but one another.[25] The wills of Henry VIII and later of Edward VI attempted to make yet different changes *without* parliamentary consent (and therefore with dubious legality). Henry's will attempted to exclude the Stuart line (Mary Queen of Scots, followed by her son James) if Edward, Mary (Tudor), and Elizabeth all died without issue. Edward's will attempted to pass over Mary Tudor right away (on pro-Protestant grounds) and settle the crown on Lady Jane Grey.[26]

None of this was a problem shortly after Edward's death in 1553. The king's will; the vague feeling that Henry's first marriage, even if (as he claimed) against church law, had been in good faith; and above all the fact that "the miseries of the ancient civil wars [i.e., those of the Roses, ended about seventy years earlier] were not so entirely forgotten" made Englanders stick with the "lawful" heir by fundamental convention, namely Mary, rather than the one that their own religious theories would strictly require, namely Elizabeth (H 3.401).[27] Similarly, Mary Tudor during her reign, as well as other Catholics, including her husband Philip, King of Spain, assumed that Elizabeth, not the Scottish line (by then represented by Mary, Queen of Scots) was the next "lawful heir"—though to be sure Queen Mary's hatred of Elizabeth made Protestants fear either an attempt to thwart this law, or else a secret murder.[28]

When Elizabeth took the throne on Mary I's death, with the next heir by blood being the Queen of Scots (henceforth so called to distinguish her from Mary Tudor), matters were different. The "situation of England" with respect to succession had become "not a little dangerous" (H 4.228). Hume's narrative suggests three key reasons why this was so.

First, half the country was subject to an external religious authority that competed strongly with England's fundamental conventions as an object of allegiance. In 1571, a papal bull excommunicated Elizabeth and absolved English subjects from their oaths of allegiance to her—as well as calling it "highly criminal" for Catholics to attend Anglican churches, as many had been quietly doing.[29] To the argument that Elizabeth had never been a legitimate heir to the crown was added the more vivid and newer claim that, whether originally heir or not, she was now "lawfully deposed" (H 4.194).[30] By using the ironic "sovereign pontiff" to refer to the Pope (H 4.189), Hume points up a crucial asymmetry. Catholics were subject to a convention, or rather pseudo-convention, of authority which, while not directly challenging the rules of royal succession, at the least claimed the right to arbitrate disputes about their application. Anglicans were not so subject: when a Catholic was on the throne, the Anglicans recognized no super-national authority that could license disallegiance, and no exact equivalent to excommunication.

Second, the Queen of Scots had let herself become a focal point for rebellion. As always in coordination games, proper names and titles matter. Mary made the fateful decision to let herself be *called* Queen of England as well as Scotland—clearly signaling her willingness to serve as a rallying point for those who would challenge Elizabeth's rule through invasion or conspiracy. (Elizabeth had never acted similarly with respect to her predecessor, Mary Tudor.) Again and again ambitious male Catholics, English as well as foreign, attempted to become England's King by killing Elizabeth and marrying the Queen of Scots. The latter did nothing to quell such schemes and sometimes encouraged them.[31] More important, the Queen of Scots made no attempt to end her symbolic status as a rallying or focal point for violent opposition to Elizabeth. In Hume's summary, even when not the "cause" of rebellion, she let herself be the "occasion" (H 4.159).

Third, England's half-settled constitution let Elizabeth sustain her own position through a policy of ambiguity—but this policy unintentionally left the Queen of Scots' prospects simultaneously tantalizing and uncertain, the most dangerous state conceivable from both her standpoint and Elizabeth's. Elizabeth was in the position, both enviable and dangerous, of inheriting an imperfect convention of authority. The rules of royal succession by specified birth order had been established before the War of the Roses and re-established through Henry VII's sleight-of-hand—but Henry VIII's divorce, and the religious struggle regarding its legality, had divided the country regarding their application. The parliamentary acts that had named both Mary and Elizabeth as legitimate had succeeded only adequately but not perfectly at defeating the more coherent religious logic that said they couldn't both be such. Many though by no means all Catholics still wanted to skip Elizabeth's succession and go straight to the next in line, the Queen of Scots. Conversely, the will of Henry VIII, which wrote out the Queen of Scots from the line of succession, was still believed in by some, though by no means most, Protestants.[32]

Under the circumstances, further action by monarch-in-parliament seemed necessary. Elizabeth was urged to name her successor—or else marry and produce one the natural way—and on the surface would have been able to wield exceptional constitutional power in settling the crown on any of several reasonable candidates. But Elizabeth, whom Hume portrays as extremely fond of the waiting game which maximized power by keeping options open, openly declared that she would *not* name a successor. When the Queen of Scots asked Elizabeth to endorse her own claim to be the legitimate successor, Elizabeth's answer was, on Hume's portrayal, surprisingly candid. Elizabeth admitted, in essence, that she would refuse to name a successor in order to avoid uniting all enemies around a rival—especially given religious divisions in the state and the fact that the Queen of Scots had questioned Elizabeth's claim and asserted her own (H 4.45–7, compare 4.81–2). To be sure, Elizabeth tried to finesse the situation, giving the Queen of Scots' partisans hope in *peaceful* succession, by saying (a) that she hoped the latter's claim "would then be found solid" after her own death, (b) that she (Elizabeth) herself would do nothing to weaken it, and (c) that if the Queen of Scots' claim was so good she should have no trouble vindicating it against rivals whose claims would be both weaker than hers and at odds with one another's (H 4.47). Still, the same religious conflict that made Elizabeth fearful must have had the same effect on the Queen of Scots, who could, absent unequivocal constitutional backing for her title, expect to inherit the crown only by winning a likely religious war.

Perhaps because she knew that the Queen of Scots' claim *was* by far the best according to the usual constitutional rules, making the naming of any other successor constitutionally and politically dangerous, Elizabeth also refused to name any other heir. Cecil, in Elizabeth's name, would in defense of this assert a more general form of the rivalship argument that Elizabeth had hurled at the Queen of Scots, speaking of the "dangerous sacrifices men were commonly disposed to make of their present duty to their future prospects" (H 4.82, meaning that would-be assassins would sharpen their knives against Elizabeth in the hope of preferment under the grateful successor). Elizabeth later induced parliament to pass a law defining as near-treason the act of mentioning any but Elizabeth's hypothetical children as her "heir or successor"—which implied, as Hume says, that Elizabeth intended *never* to name a successor (H 4.81–2, 4.146).[33]

The result of all this is that the Queen of Scots could not reliably plan on succeeding by merely waiting, as Elizabeth had succeeded Mary Tudor on the latter's natural death. This was particularly true once the Queen of Scots became very sick while Elizabeth was still alive (H 4.228).[34] But the Queen of Scots *could* hope, though without being sure, to be acclaimed as the natural successor *if Elizabeth were to be killed*. In that case, as Elizabeth's spymaster Francis Walsingham feared, she would be the "heir of blood, to whom the people in general were likely to adhere" (H 4.229). This provided an odd mixture of desperation and hope that made Mary extremely dangerous. She was the rare conspirator against a sitting monarch, under an established convention of succession, who had both incentive to try something violent and a decent chance of holding the throne if she succeeded. This was the unintended consequence of Elizabeth's chosen strategy of deliberate ambiguity.[35] But it was a strategy made possible by a particular constitutional situation: one in which an imperfectly defined rule of succession made the successor's identity very likely but far from certain.

For all these reasons, and increasingly over time, the Queen of Scots was not only Elizabeth's successor but an "heir and rival" subject to the queen's "unrelenting jealousy" (H 4.126); a "pretender" to the throne (H 4.46, 165) who harbored "dangerous designs" against Elizabeth (H 4.46); "a competitor, whom, from the beginning of her reign, [Elizabeth] had ever equally dreaded and hated." (H 4.236; compare 176). "All the enemies of Elizabeth . . . had *naturally* recourse to one policy, the supporting of the cause and pretensions of the queen of Scots" (H 4.155, emphasis added). Those enemies were a huge religious faction that had only one rallying point, just as Elizabeth had ensured that the Protestants had only one:

> [T]he general combination of the catholics to exterminate the protestants, was no longer a secret; and as the sole resource of the latter persecuted sect lay in Elizabeth, so the chief hope, which the former entertained of final success, consisted in the person, and in the title of the queen of Scots: . . . this very circumstance brought matters to extremity between these princesses[, . . .] rendering the life of one the death of the other. (H 4.243)[36]

It is crucial that this is a matter of state, not of guilt. Mary was, on Hume's view (for which he carefully marshals evidence), very much guilty of conspiracy and treason. But the logic of the situation suggests that reason of state *required* finding a way to kill her in any case, regardless of such guilt. That logic (as Hume puts it, the "circumstance")

> pointed out to Elizabeth the path, which either regard to self-preservation, or to the happiness of her people, should direct her to pursue[. . .] necessity, more powerful than policy, thus demanded of the queen that resolution, which equity would authorise, *and which duty prescribed.* (H 4.243–4; emphasis added)

History followed logic. Hume assumes that Elizabeth and her partisans *wanted* to catch Mary in treason, and finds no fault in them either for so wishing or for being glad of finding what they sought.[37]

The removal of a demonstrated, evident anti-constitutional focal point is an outstanding reason for an individual political killing—the moral equivalent to waging a just war, given that the removal of the focal point removes the standard around which the rebel army would rally. When there is no legal provision for execution, Hume clearly thinks that reason of state demands—as a matter of necessity and public good, not malice or ambition—extralegal murder. In the late Roman republic, which lacked capital punishment:

> However criminal, or, what is more, however dangerous any citizen might be, he could not regularly be punished otherwise than by ban-

ishment: And it became necessary, in the revolutions of party, to draw the sword of private vengeance; nor was it easy, when laws were once violated, to set bounds to these sanguinary proceedings. Had BRUTUS himself prevailed over the *triumvirate*, could he, in common prudence, have allowed OCTAVIUS and ANTHONY, to live, and have contented himself with banishing them to RHODES or MARSEILLES, where they might still have plotted new commotions and rebellions? His executing C. ANTONIUS, brother to the *triumvir*, shows evidently his sense of the matter. (E: PAN, 414–15 [emphasis in original, not for stress but to indicate Latin words])

After Mary's execution, perhaps better called a state killing, Elizabeth faced no serious domestic threats—and the constitutional logic would have predicted none. Those who had asserted the validity of Henry VIII's will (or more radically, Edward VI's), out of a strained desire for a Protestant successor, quieted down once the regular successor by blood, Scotland's James VI, was Protestant.[38] Catholics who had asserted the Queen of Scots' title to the throne, and believed Elizabeth to be a usurper, had a religious motive to resist James' title but no constitutional rationale, given the effort they had expended to vindicate the lawful title of his mother, Mary. As England became more Protestant, papal bulls against heretics alone could not dethrone the constitutional line—especially since Elizabeth was, all things considered, tacitly fairly tolerant of Catholics.[39]

All these are negative considerations against challenges to James I's crown, but Hume stresses the positive: James' "hereditary right remained unquestionable" (H 5.3). Departures from hereditary succession were by now considered violent departures from the valid constitutional norm: exceptions were attributed to "force or intrigue" whereas "deliberate maxims of government" demanded regular succession (H 5.3).[40] The constitutional rule had been reinforced by reversions after such irregular departures:

> The lineal heir had still in the end prevailed; and both his exclusion and restoration had been commonly attended with such convulsions, as were sufficient to warn all prudent men not lightly to give way to such irregularities. (H 5.3–4)

For current purposes, the point is not so much that James' succession was stable but that it was *predictably* stable. By killing the Queen of Scots, Elizabeth could reasonably expect to end the dynastic and religious war that her father's marital adventures had started. Because the Queen of Scots shared her gender, Elizabeth could not splice together the constitutional dispute through marriage and reproduction as Henry VII had. But by contriving a death, she did what Henry had done by contriving a marriage. The title of England's future James I was sound by multiple standards: he was, as parliament recognized upon Elizabeth's death, "lineally, justly and lawfully next and sole heir of the blood royal of this realm" (H 5.551). (If anyone wonders why Hume does not condone reason-of-state excuses for the trial and execution of Charles I, the answer is simple: Charles II.) And here, by the way, is a rare instance in Humean theory of a systematic reason to prefer republics to monarchies. In republics, the fact that no particular person serves uniquely well as a successor means that none in particular is a unique object of jealousy. Conventions not rooted in blood involve fewer occasions for shedding it.

Secret Revolutions and Parliamentary Princes

The Stuart volumes of Hume's *History* are, among other things, studies in how political strategy ought to manage inevitable constitutional change. As such, they illuminate, as clear cases of usurpation could not, the proper management of clashing constitutional conventions. On Hume's view, widely accepted since his time, the first Stuart monarchs (James I and Charles I) inherited from Queen Elizabeth a government that was in practice very near an absolute monarchy. In insisting on royal prerogatives and downplaying the constitutional role of parliament, James' and Charles' speech and actions roughly reflected prevailing customs.[41] Social and economic changes, however, had resulted in parliament's having vastly more bargaining power than it had before, as well as a different political and cultural outlook favorable to "civil liberty."[42]

By James I's time, monarchy and Magna Charta (which crucially provided, among other things, that parliament must approve all taxation) were both fundamental conventions in England. In the early seventeenth century, these conventions came into conflict. Hereditary monarchy essentially located legitimate political authority in the king. Magna Charta both limited that authority and, by requiring parliamentary assent to taxation, divided governmental authority de facto (but crucially not, or not clearly, de jure [see *inter alia* H 5.35, 170, 562]).[43]

On Hume's view, the two conventions eventually proved compatible, if uneasily so. The settlement that enshrined them both after the Glorious Revolution produced, Hume thinks, "the most *entire system* of *liberty*, that ever was known amongst mankind" (H 6.531).[44] The question is why this resolution did not occur right away. Aside from a few accidental explanations—misunderstandings leading to "peevishness" and escalating mistrust (H 5.88)[45]—the basic story is that no leader at the time united Machiavellian skill at wielding power with the more peaceful virtue of attachment to fundamental conventions. The monarchs excelled at constitutional speculation but not practical politics; parliament, the reverse; a durable settlement would have required both; the result was tragedy.

When an existing accommodation between two conventions is unsettled by social change, the kind of people who will understand how to manage that change will resemble Machiavellian politicians in a modern form. Since Hume generally agrees with Harrington that power follows property,[46] it stands to reason that the kind of politician attuned to power relations will most easily adapt to large changes in property relations. But if the resolution of these changes in property makes use *only* of raw political power, the conventions of authority that are universally accepted as beneficial to all may be jeopardized. And since those conventions grow slowly over time, there is no reason to believe that anything equally stable will take their place. In the absence of authority, force will rule temporarily, and nothing permanently. A stable constitutional settlement, after abrupt changes in society and economics, therefore requires something rarely seen: politicians determined to employ Machiavellian means toward constitutionalist ends.

Speculative Monarchs

Both James I and Charles I had more theoretical intelligence than political skill. When it came to classical learning and high political theory, James I was, Hume strikingly asserts, "at the time, one of the greatest geniuses in Europe" (H 5.34; see also 4.202, 5.155). That said, James' talent for "politics or prudence," or practical "penetration" was, frankly, "little." "His capacity was considerable; but fitter to discourse on general maxims than to conduct any intricate business" (respectively H 5.79, 99, 121; see also 5.11, 558). James' geopolitical incompetence—out of love of monarchical authority, he refused to stir up trouble among his enemies' subjects—"exposed him to the imputation of weakness and of error" (H 5.82; compare 5.8). In particular, his pride in his own intellect led him to state his personal beliefs in religion and politics in open and systematic form, under the false belief that the quality of systematic theological and philosophical arguments bore a causal relationship to good political outcomes. He trusted the "seeming evidence [i.e., seemingly obvious truth]" of his royalist views while neglecting the "force or politics" through which actual absolute monarchs on the Continent had vindicated them (H 5.18–19). His theological speculations limited his ability to maneuver on religious policy when parliament made demands on that score.[47] Most damningly, James lacked tact. That he believed in a hyper-absolutist, divine-right theory of monarchy, under which all the subjects' personal and property rights were contingent on his grace, was forgivable. That he was so "rash and indiscreet" as to say so *publicly* was not. By doing so, he "tor[e] off that sacred veil, which had hitherto covered the English constitution, and which threw an obscurity upon it, so advantageous to royal prerogative" (H 5.93; compare 5.60 5.91).[48] James' character in general was not "ambitious and enterprizing" but on the contrary lazy, weak, and peace-loving—good qualities in that he started no wars and was unable to vindicate his absolutist pretentions, but useless when it came to bargaining with parliament (H 5.7, 21, 121; compare 5.84, 105, 134; quotation on H 5.66).

Charles I, just as speculative as his father James was but little wiser, was—unfortunately for him and for his people—more courageous.[49] He openly asserted a belief in passive obedience (the doctrine that subjects could never rightly rebel on any provocation) and purported, as James had, to possess "the whole authority of the state"—thus alerting his opponents to his ultimate intentions in a form which made it very hard to disavow them later.[50] Like James, Charles considered his own political opinions self-evident; unlike James, he went so far as to consider any challenge to them evidence of bad faith and seditious intentions (H 5.161). And, like James, Charles put "principles of piety and conscience" above constitutional peace and public safety; he refused to come to a settlement with parliament at the cost of abolishing the rule of bishops in the Church (H 5.213, and even more clearly, 5.453). From the perspective of a political science that rests on human convention, both James' and Charles' belief in the pseudo-convention of divine right of kings—they thought themselves entitled by cosmic ordination to rule their people whether their people endorsed that sense of entitlement or not—is particularly culpable.[51]

Most of all, Charles was a bad bargainer. Like his father, he was prone to assert monarchical claims that he lacked the "vigour and foresight" to vindicate (H 5.221). To the "violent . . . combination of a whole kingdom" (Scotland, rebelling against the attempted imposition of a liturgy modeled on the Anglican) Charles had "nothing to oppose but a proclamation" where he pardoned past offenses and urged future obedience (H 5.257). According to Hume, Charles first learned the basic principle of geopolitics, "a just idea of national interest," in 1639, fourteen years into his reign (H 5.262). Repeatedly, Charles vacillated between vain reassertions of divine power (or allegedly self-evident authority) and excessive concessions to parliament that left him unable to defend the monarchy's distinct and proper role as an independent executive, just and vigorous in enforcing equal laws (H 5.259).[52] The King's "facility" (literally "easiness" in the face of opposition, the opposite of princely *virtù*) had cumulative effects. Each concession became "the foundation of demands still more exhorbitant." Soon Charles' "situation" rendered unavoidable the kind of concessions that his "disposition" was in any case prone to favor (H 5.373).

Charles' awkward vacillations between vain boasting and surrender revealed his most fatal political trait: extreme rigidity. He lacked not only the "vigour" to subdue parliament and establish an absolute monarchy but the "suppleness and dexterity" he would have needed to "give way to the encroachments of a popular assembly" in ways that might have preserved his life and part of his constitutional role (H 5.242–3). Charles tended to regard parliament's growing assertiveness as a sign of its insolence, not of his own weakness. The very factors that led parliament to conclude that absolute monarchy was untenable led Charles, who drew a strict line between facts and principles, to conclude it was non-negotiable (H 5.236; see also 5.278). Charles' attempts at guile and ambiguous evasions were obvious, inept, and ill-timed: he temporized when it was time to act decisively and vice versa (H 5.198). "[H]e did worse, than embrace the worst side: For, properly speaking, he embraced no side at all" (H 5.267).[53]

In sum Charles, like James, displayed private virtues unsuited to the public business of his time. Charles worried more about his friend Strafford's impeachment and execution than about a bill that forbade the king from dissolving parliament without its own consent—a bill that "rendered the power of his enemies perpetual, as it was already uncontroulable." This spoke to Charles' "integrity" and "goodness" but not his "resolution" or "penetration" (H 5.325). Hume suggests that Charles made himself loved and hated but not feared, with results that were maximally bad for the polity compared to the alternatives of universal popularity (or unpopularity) on the one hand or vigorous policy on the other.[54]

All this said, Hume thinks that Charles possessed one quality crucial to a good ruler under stable constitutional government—though fatal in a crisis—namely devotion to established constitutional order.

> Had he been born an absolute prince, his humanity and good sense had rendered his reign happy and his memory precious: Had the limitations on prerogative been, in his time, quite fixed and certain, his integrity had made him regard, as sacred, the boundaries of the constitution. Unhappily, his fate threw him into a period, when the precedents of many former reigns favoured strongly of arbitrary power, and the genius of the people ran violently towards liberty. (H 5.543)

Hume suggests (not completely convincingly, though it matters little for the point) that Charles took promises to be inviolable points of honor. Once he signed a law, he considered it binding on him not *qua* constitutional ruler but *qua* feudal prince.[55] Hume's statement that Charles "deserves the epithet of a good, rather than of a great man; and was more fitted to rule in a regular established government, than either to give way to the encroachments of a popular assembly, or finally to subdue their pretensions" (H 5.542), is sometimes taken as unequivocal criticism. One interpreter glosses Hume as saying that Charles, like all the Stuarts, was "inept."[56] But one should take literally the whole of Hume's assessment: Charles was unsuited to times of constitutional crisis, but perfectly suited to times of constitutional peace. The point becomes clearer by contrast: the leaders of the parliament were the opposite.

Politic Parliamentarians

Machiavelli wrote, "it never or rarely happens that any republic or kingdom is ordered well from the beginning or reformed *altogether anew outside its old orders* unless it is ordered by one individual" (emphasis added).[57] Hume's account does not falsify this claim. Parliament was able to act as a Prince because it was *not* acting altogether anew. On the contrary, it was able to draw on old (though disused) conventions of personal and parliamentary liberty as agreed-upon focal points:

> And though in that interval [the reign of the Tudors], after the decline of the peers and before the people had yet experienced their force, the princes assumed an exorbitant power, and had almost annihilated the constitution under the weight of their prerogative; as soon as the commons recovered from their lethargy, they seem to have been astonished at the danger, and were resolved to secure liberty by firmer barriers, than their ancestors had hitherto provided for it. (H 5.40)

Perhaps as a result, parliament in most of its early actions against James and Charles acted for practical purposes as one body (H 5.158).[58]

The parliamentarians, unlike their monarchs, knew that the English constitution was not clear but rather ambiguous; while the Stuarts studied theology and philosophy, parliament's leaders studied history. Those leaders also knew that the constitution's ambiguity made it necessary to change it so that it explicitly spelled out individual rights and parliamentary privileges. The status quo was not neutral but rather (through its tendency to produce recurrent emergencies, and government by prerogative in response to them) favored monarchical power (H 5.207). Finally, parliament's leaders knew that their excellent bargaining position made such a change possible. Their political alertness let them harness the new opportunities provided by urban politics, printing, mass petitions, and enthusiastic religion. And they had the qualities of mind and character necessary to pursue these hazardous and far-sighted political enterprises to a conclusion. All they lacked—and the lack was momentous—was the sense of legitimate constitutional authority, of the rightful limits of their own enthusiasm for liberty, that would have told them when to stop.

Though Hume's treatment of these subjects takes hundreds of pages, brief lessons on political ethics and strategy, illuminating for current purposes, can be listed in the schematic form of a prince's handbook.

PERCEIVING INCONSISTENCY

By Hume's time, it was common to describe the English constitution as a "fabric" (i.e., structure of a building): solid, built over generations, and worthy of English subjects' respect.[59] A generation after Hume's *History*, Burke would employ this metaphor to more or less conservative effect: he compared good citizens or subjects to tenants who should preserve a property for later generations rather than damaging it, and good constitutional reformers to good builders, who should never level an existing structure without cause when it is sound enough to be the basis for renovations.[60] Hume, in the course of his thesis that the myth of the ancient constitution was ridiculous, deployed it in a different way: "the constitution of England was, at that time [the early 1600s], an *inconsistent* fabric, whose jarring and discordant parts must soon destroy each other, and from the dissolution of the old, beget some new form of civil government, more uniform and consistent" (H 5.59; emphasis added).[61] The problem was not that there were no structures but that there was one ugly structure based on two impressive but mutually inconsistent architectures. The two conventions of monarchy and Magna Charta-based liberty were badly joined; given cultural and economic progress, "the several constitutent parts of the gothic governments, which seem to have lain long unactive, began, every where, to operate and encroach on each other" (H 5.18). To erect a proper building required one of two things. One could demolish one of the structure's two branches—James II's plan, and Cromwell's from the other side. Alternatively, and as eventually happened, one could engage in some very clever architecture-cum-masonry that would erect a new building ("new form of civil government") that looked enough like the old, unintentionally deconstructivist one to please architectural critics of both persuasions and make everyone comfortable.[62]

One difference between the parliamentarians and the early Stuart kings was one of political perception. Parliament's leaders knew that the fabric was inconsistent. (Hume notes that "men of the world" had come to rule the Commons [H 5.18]. Perhaps they, unlike monarchs trained in theology and philosophy, were suited by experience of market fluctuations to note and adjust to shifts in power, the "continual fluctuation" described below.) The Stuarts denied any inconsistency, thinking that there was only one structure: monarchical.[63] Even had the Stuart kings had the vigor for political action, they would have pursued an impossible end because they mistook their situation.

HARD BARGAINING

Hume notes that if James I's absolutism was more speculative than practical, parliament's assertion of its power was the reverse. It was, "though strongly supported by their present situation as well as disposition, . . . too new and recent to be as yet founded on systematical principles and opinions" (H 5.45). The members of Parliament, though many lacked skill at Greek and Latin, knew that a diamond flush could beat a pair of kings.

> The end, they esteemed beneficent and noble: The means, regular and constitutional. To grant or refuse supplies was the undoubted privilege of the commons. And as all human governments, particularly those of a mixed frame, are in continual fluctuation; it was as natural, in their opinion, and allowable, for popular assemblies to take advantage of favourable incidents, in order to secure the subject; as for monarchs, in order to extend their own authority. (H 5.160)[64]

Parliament also saw that the Tudor's previous absolutism had been based on economic accidents that now favored their own side. They had a sense of the secular "situation" (here meaning something more long-term and significant than mere "circumstance") that resulted from their own economic power and Elizabeth's previous sale of crown lands:

> The same advantage, we may remark, over the people, which the crown formerly reaped from that interval between the fall of the peers and rise of the commons, was now possessed by the people against the crown, during the continuance of a like interval. The sovereign had already lost that independant revenue, by which he could subsist without regular supplies from parliament; and he had not yet acquired the means of influencing those assemblies. (H 5.137)[65]

MASS POLITICS

When it comes to politics, Hume (unlike Machiavelli) was in a position to note the force of technological change. Printing in particular had a crucial adverbial role; while it did not itself cause any particular change in politics, religion or society, it "extremely facilitated" all of them (H 3.81). As in other areas, parliament was alert to change while the Stuart monarchs were not. The former, unlike the latter, made use not only of the local politics of "tumult" and "spectacle" with which Machiavelli was so familiar (though London's vast size allowed for urban politics on a scale not often seen in Europe since ancient Rome),[66] but of the modern political techniques that were starting to extend politics to a mass, national scale: religious ideologies and parties; public petitions that gave the parliamentarians' demands force while making the signers aware of collective power; the creation and propagation of popular martyrs and heroes through pamphlets and parliamentary speeches (made public for the first time).[67] In all this, parliament ran rings around the monarchy. With respect to Puritan and parliamentary agitation and mob action against an Anglican Convocation called by Charles, Hume notes that "[a]ll these instances of discontent were presages of some great revolution; had the court possessed sufficient skill to discern the danger, or sufficient power to provide against it" (H 5.278).

FORCE AND GUILE

I have noted that the parliamentarians wielded the supply power with new force. That said, they wielded it within old forms, "regular and constitutional," since "[t]o grant or refuse supplies was the undoubted privilege of the commons" (though one fallen into disuse). In general, parliament initially observed the formal rules of constitutional politics, even as it radically changed how the game was played. Hume expresses great praise for this formal restraint and the self-discipline that let members of parliament stick to it:

> To correct the late disorders in the administration required some new laws, which would, no doubt, appear harsh to a prince, so enamoured of his prerogative; and it was requisite to temper, by the decency and

> moderation of their debates, the rigour, which must necessarily attend their determinations. Nothing can give us a higher idea of the capacity of those men, who now guided the commons, and of the great authority, which they had acquired, than the forming and executing of so judicious and so difficult a plan of operations. (H 5.188)

This does not mean that parliament actually *felt* sentiments of "decency and moderation" toward the king: they feigned such until the king had bargained away many of his powers (without gaining popularity).

> And the torrent of general inclination and opinion ran so strongly against the court, that the king was in no situation to refuse any reasonable demands of the popular leaders, either for defining or limiting the powers of his prerogative. Even many exorbitant claims, in his present situation, would probably be made, and must necessarily be complied with. (H 5.284)

Parliament's addresses toward the king, initially courteous, turned insolent once its leaders judged that aggression would serve their cause better than politeness.[68]

That Hume's political figures are so often monarchs (one of his points being that monarchs and barons were the only actors who counted until the Stuart age) should not blind us to Hume's portrayal of parliament's leaders as natural politicians, possessing vast resources of skill and discipline unleashed by a new, commons-based freedom:

> This was the time, when genius and capacity of all kinds, freed from the restraint of authority, and nourished by unbounded hopes and projects, began to exert themselves, and be distinguished by the public. Then was celebrated the sagacity of Pym, more fitted for use than ornament; matured, not chilled, by his advanced age and long experience: Then was displayed the mighty ambition of Hambden, taught disguise, not moderation, from former constraint; supported by courage, conducted by prudence, embellished by modesty; but whether founded in a love of power or zeal for liberty, is still, from his untimely end, left doubtful and uncertain: Then too were known the dark, ardent, and dangerous character of St. John; the impetuous spirit of Hollis, violent and sincere, open and entire in his enmities and in his friendships; the enthusiastic genius of young Vane, extravagant in the ends which he pursued, sagacious and profound in the means which he employed; incited by the appearances of religion, negligent of the duties of morality. (H 5.293–4)[69]

As late as 1641, Hume proclaims parliament's actions more or less exemplary, worthy of "praise from all lovers of liberty." Parliament had not only remedied current grievances but forced through constitutional barriers to future ones: the Petition of Right, the Triennial Act, the abolition of arbitrary courts.

Under the circumstances Hume regards even a description of the parliamentarians' forceful methods as a proper occasion to praise their wisdom and excuse their excesses as unavoidable:

> [I]f the means, by which they obtained such advantages, savour often of artifice, sometimes of violence; it is to be considered, that revolutions of government cannot be effected by the mere force of argument and reasoning: And that factions being once excited, men can neither so firmly regulate the tempers of others, nor their own, as to ensure themselves against all exorbitancies. (H 5.330)[70]

Realism cuts both ways, and Hume's version was a mix of the "black" monarchical kind and the "red" variety that studied power in order to subvert it.[71] Given that kings naturally hate calling parliaments—and certainly Hume's story, which includes Charles I's eleven years of "personal rule," demonstrates that—Hume says of the Triennial Act, that it "was not entirely voluntary: It was of a nature too important to be voluntary" (H 5.308). After all, the solid establishment of Magna Charta had been "extorted" from King Edward I by similar means, and the extortion did the English "honour" (H 2.122, and see chapter 6).

The parliamentarians' understanding of power was not just static but dynamic. They understood momentum and initiative, and when they had a clear advantage, pressed it ever further. They kept some of their threats to withhold taxation as surprises to be sprung late in parliamentary sessions, when Charles lacked the resources to withstand them (H 5.202).[72] When met with royal claims of national necessity, the "sagacious and penetrating" parliamentarians, rather than acceding to them, took them as signs that the King feared he was losing—and in any case regarded the king's threats as non-credible; the parliamentary leaders were willing to risk a royal resort to emergency powers, since every instance of such only made the King less popular (H 5.271).[73] "And [the Parliamentary leaders] regarded the least moment of relaxation, in their invasion of royal authority, as highly impolitic, during the uninterrupted torrent of their successes" (H 5.374). That said, all of the parliamentarians' methods remained, in theory, peaceful. Parliament was merely asserting, and attaching ever more severe conditions to, its traditional power of supply. Nor is "extortion," strictly speaking, the right word (though Hume, as noted in the next chapter, is fond of it). If that means a demand for money upon the threat of force, it was Charles I, in his period of personal rule, who did more of that—as did Cromwell later. Parliament did the opposite: it demanded limits on, and ultimately control over, the executive power, on the threat of withholding money.

"SECRET REVOLUTION"

The outcome of these maneuvers, Machiavellian without being (very) physically violent, was what Hume calls a "secret revolution" (H 5.222). Old forms remained, but their mode of operation revealed a decisive shift in power. The clearest sign of this—still the hallmark of parliamentary government—was that Charles was forced, for the first time, to choose ministers on account of their "parliamentary interest or talents" rather than their loyal service to the throne (ibid.). The Petition of Right, which greatly circumscribed royal prerogative and safeguarded subjects' liberties through written laws, "produced such a change in the government, as was almost equivalent to a revolution"(H 5.200); what followed went even further. After the impeachment of Laud and Strafford, the parliament took a short rest since its conquest of power was all but complete, again without formal revolution. The commons had wrested away "[t]he whole sovereign power," and "the government, *without any seeming violence or disorder*, [had been] changed, in a moment, from a monarchy almost absolute, to a pure democracy" (H 5.293; emphasis added).[74] In general "the commons, though themselves the greatest innovators, employed the usual artifice of complaining against innovations, and pretending to recover the ancient and established government" (H 5.297). Hume means this as a compliment (as well as a dig at Whigs in his time who were credulous enough to take this innovating parliament at its mock-conservative word). This "artifice" allowed for huge and necessary shifts in governing structures without ruptures in governmental authority.

AN ENGINE TOO FAR

After Laud and Strafford's impeachment, Charles likened the parliament's activities to taking apart the workings of a clock:

> "You have taken the whole machinery of government in pieces," said Charles in a discourse to the parliament; "a practice frequent with skilful artists, when they desire to clear the wheels from any rust, which may have grown upon them. The engine," continued he, "may again be restored to its former use and motions, provided it be put up entire; so as not a pin of it be wanting." But this was far from the intention of the commons. The machine they thought, with some reason, was incumbered with many wheels and springs, which retarded and crossed its operations, and destroyed its utility. Happy! had they proceeded with moderation, and been contented, in their present plenitude of power, to remove such parts only as might justly be deemed superfluous and incongruous. (H 5.297–8)

The metaphor should be taken seriously. The Commons, in Hume's view, was not asserting any new constitutional principles. (That would in any case be a null set. What is new will lack the authority to be constitutional; it will be the creature of present power rather than being able, if necessary, to stand against it.) Many different programs were consistent with repairing the operations of the old one, whose parts clashed rather than cohering; compare the metaphor of the "jarring" fabric.

But the Commons eventually chose not to refashion the old conventions of Crown and Charter but to eradicate the former. From the perspective of Hume's political and constitutional morality, this was both strategically disastrous and, because it predictably undermined conventions of authority, morally culpable. Hereditary monarchy, which prevented the triumph of present social power over justice, was as much a part of subjects' constitutional rights as Magna Charta was:

> [T]he commons, not content with correcting the abuses of government, were carried, by the natural current of power and popularity, into the opposite extreme, and were committing violations, no less dangerous than the former, upon the English constitution. (H 5.392)[75]

The "prospect of sovereign power"—which Hume elsewhere (regarding Cromwell) says is "in general, irresistible to human nature" (H 5.450)—carried the parliament, which had been so zealous in pursuit of constitutional equilibrium, beyond that equilibrium and into an attempt to render the king at most a figurehead. Conscious that the people were still strongly attached to monarchy, the parliament soon became fearful of the same popular power it had so eagerly courted, and began to wield against the people the techniques it had practiced against the king. It saw that "invasion of the ancient constitution" would be possible only if it moved so quickly and at such short intervals as to allow the people no time for reflection (H 5.364; compare H 5.374 with respect to the king).

Upon the outbreak of Civil War, the silent revolution had rendered parliament secure and arbitrary monarchical government impossible. The main outstanding issue was whether parliament would wrest control of the army. At that point Hume judges the Commons' cause to be far less constitutionally tenable than the King's: the latter was "supporting the ancient government in church and state against the most illegal pretensions" (H 5.380–81).[76] Hume portrays parliament's actions as in accord with this judgment. Conscious that it would never command peaceful authority, parliament responded to Charles with an argument *ad baculum*:

> The commons were sensible, that monarchical government, which, during so many ages, had been established in England, would soon regain some degree of its former dignity, after the present tempest was overblown; nor would all their new-invented limitations be able totally to suppress an authority, to which the nation had ever been accustomed. The sword alone, to which all human ordinances must submit, could guard their acquired power, and fully ensure to them personal safety against the rising indignation of their sovereign. This point, therefore, became the chief object of their aims. (H 5.374)

From then on, the parliament "prudently avoided, as much as possible, all advances towards negotiation," since it could not win the public debate that would follow:

In opposition to the sacred authority of the laws, to the venerable precedents of many ages, the popular leaders were ashamed to plead nothing but fears and jealousies, which were not avowed by the constitution, and for which, neither the personal character of Charles, so full of virtue, nor his situation, so deprived of all independent authority, seemed to afford any reasonable foundation. Grievances which had been fully redressed; powers, either legal or illegal, which had been entirely renounced; it seemed unpopular, and invidious, and ungrateful, any farther to insist on. (H 5.431)[77]

From then on the Commons pursued a policy of violence and bombast for its own sake. The more reasonable the King's position, the more danger it posed to the Commons' authority.[78]

At issue was more than just an abstract political morality; the parliament was acting contrary to a higher prudence. Given that the monarchy commanded authority, according to public opinion, the parliament was courting an endless civil war with no plan for ending it. More than this, it was undercutting its own claims to legitimate authority. Hume argues that the Stuarts were intent upon asserting their prerogative out of lack of good alternatives. Since their authority rested on "the opinion of the people, influenced by ancient precedent and example," they could only hope to preserve that opinion by continually reasserting their authority (H 5.128–9). Parliament failed to learn the same lesson. When it made its ultimate appeal not to constitutional authority—and authority over taxation in particular—but to force, it should have known that it could not win. Parliament's relatively moderate, Presbyterian leaders were bound to be helpless against the greater fanaticism of the parliamentary and popular Independents, and they in turn helpless against Cromwell's coup. "[I]llegal violence, with whatever pretences it may be covered, and whatever object it may pursue, must inevitably end at last in the arbitrary and despotic government of a single person." Here "illegal," since it cannot mean "contrary to parliament's will," must mean contrary to *fundamental* law: a synonym for the non-Humean word "unconstitutional" (H 6.54).

Constitutions evolved as an alternative to primitive focal points: force, religious symbolism, present wealth, common knowledge through physical presence. Those who cast the fundamentals of the constitution in contempt will soon find themselves thrown back upon those primitive alternatives.

The dominion of the parliament was of short duration. No sooner had they subdued their sovereign, than their own servants rose against them, and tumbled them from their slippery throne. The sacred boundaries of the laws being once violated, nothing remained to confine the wild projects of zeal and ambition. And every successive revolution became a precedent for that which followed it. (H 5.492)

Conclusions

I have said that Humean constitutionalism represents a neglected liberal and democratic framework: one that works with the grain of prevailing passions, and that regards public opinion pertaining to political authority as normative rather than an obstruction to be circumvented. Hume's examples suggest several lessons that operate under such a framework. In Humean style, they will be both "positive" and "normative," as they give instrumental advice for furthering peace, prosperity, and liberty and refuse to distinguish moral from nonmoral virtues.

First, even among arms, certain laws are *not* silent. Fundamental conventions, once they exist, structure political actors' expectations of authority in relatively stable and predictable ways that suggest a limited number of possible roads to a durable, consensual settlement of disputes. Leaders alert to the requirements of constitutional peace—and disposed for whatever reason to prefer such peace to the advantage of profiting from continued war or military tyranny—will spend the time of relative chaos studying the fundamental conventions and thinking about how a future settlement might observe them.[79] Henry VII and General Monk did that. The Long Parliament—which eventually placed its own power over the realm's constitutional authority—did not, to its own costs and the country's.

Second, power can reshape authority but cannot create it. The pre-civil war parliaments commanded money; Monk commanded arms. Both used their advantages to bring about constitutional resolutions that were more to their taste than were certain alternatives. But there were severe limits to what their power could effect—especially since the prerequisites of power, whether military or monetary, are themselves grounded in conventions that a policy of extreme violence can destroy or render irrelevant. The members of the Commons were not walking granaries. Their power over their nation's wealth stemmed from their legitimate and representative *authority* to tax that wealth. They found out the hard way that this authority was contingent, when they forfeited it through anti-constitutional violence.

Third, even though the content of conventions varies hugely across time and place, durable lessons may be drawn from history regarding the *forms* of how conventions may be wielded and welded. Hume portrays the same forms being tried across very different realms. As noted, Hume regards the deliberate silence of the "naked bandwagon" strategy as a wise strategy for various politicians in different times and places. He portrays Henry II's confrontation with the Catholic Church under Thomas à Beckett in terms that precisely mirror those of parliament's confrontation with James I (and that way around: the King in 1163 occupied the pro-law, anti-arbitrary power position that parliament played in the early 1600s). When it came to Church authority over the civil magistrate, extreme doctrines in which the Church had always believed were suddenly made "open and visible": "the mask had at last been taken off." Under the circumstances, Henry "deemed it necessary to define with the same precision the limits of the civil power; to oppose his legal customs to their divine ordinances; to determine the exact boundaries of the rival jurisdictions" before Church claims "were fully consolidated, and could plead antiquity, as they already did a sacred authority, in their favour." (Unfortunately, the defenders of arbitrary power, the Church, won in this instance [H 1.314].)[80] The Cambridge School doctrine that all political concepts change over time may be true, as far as it goes, without being fully relevant to questions of leadership. Just as the rhetorical imperative to start with the assumptions held by the audience holds even though who the audience is and what it assumes will vary across historical cases, the forms of constitutional leadership may persist despite variation in their content, that is, in what the conventions are and what they govern.

Fourth, both leaders and theorists, prone to regard constitutional norms or fundamental conventions as constraints on the exciting possibilities of *virtù*, would do well to realize that norms and conventions are also the only levers that allow modern princes to move large objects. They define the parameters of winning mass support in ages less "disorderly" than Machiavelli's Florence (E: CL, 88), ages in which people surge most readily, not toward direct expressions of strength, nor away from acts of ferocity, but in accord with their accustomed opinions of who or what rightly commands authority. In the absence of such conventions, factional or religious loyalties—or else "ideology," their later, bastard offspring—can certainly rally subjects. But in addition to noting Hume's persistent normative critique of such solutions, one should point out that they provide no escape from mass politics. The Long Parliament, after attempting to wield faction and religion, was undone by them. Indeed, the forces of religion and faction constrained even Cromwell's options. Having risen to power through doctrines of saintly republicanism, he became unable to settle the regime along other lines (e.g., by founding a royal line of his own).[81]

Finally, there is a principled, non-accidental relationship between constitutionalism and pluralism. Factional or religious appeals are matters of substance—of what one dogmatically demands, or whom one considers religious friends. Constitutions are matters of form, allowing for the exercise of authority along lines at least partly independent of one's program or one's deepest moral commitments. Respect for constitutional fundamentals is not the only solution to political conflict. But it is the only *tolerant* solution, the only one that might command the unforced allegiance of multiple parties, religions, or ideologies rather than choosing one and suppressing the others.

This is perhaps Hume's most general lesson. The only pluralistic outcome to a civil war is a real or perceived restoration—and if perceived, it may as well be real—of ancient conventions of authority. Put differently, constitutional leadership is *the only* systematic alternative to a decisionist ethics by which the hallmark of authority is the ability to distinguish civil friends from public enemies. We face a choice: Hume *or* Carl Schmitt.

What I am calling the liberalism of enlargement has this as its deeper purpose: to erode, as much as possible, the difference between friends and enemies and the alleged necessity that there be a permanent difference. Constitutional leadership aims to preserve and perfect a state in which each of many factions has a place at a very long political table and a reason not to spoil the occasion.

Chapter 6

Vertical Inequality and the Extortion of Liberty

Had not his ambitious and active temper raised him [Edward I
"Longshanks"] so many foreign enemies, and obliged him to have
recourse so often to the assistance of his subjects, it is not likely
that those concessions [on reaffirming Magna Charta and a charter
limiting royal forestry rights] could ever have been extorted from
him. . . . Thus, after the contests of near a whole century, and
these ever accompanied with violent jealousies, often with public
convulsions, the Great Charter was finally established; and the
English nation have the honour of extorting, by their perseverance,
this concession from the ablest, the most warlike, and the most
ambitious of all their princes.

—H 2.121–2

To complain of the parliament's employing the power of taxation,
as the means of extorting concessions from their sovereign, were to
expect, that they would entirely disarm themselves, and renounce
the sole expedient, provided by the constitution, for enduring [*sic*]
to the kingdom a just and legal administration.

—H 5.568 (note [W])

The work so far has explored how Hume's theory of political convention and
change fits together: how structures of effective (though limited) authority
can arise in a world where cosmic or divine order can no longer be counted
on. Hume's theory is obviously attractive to those who live under conditions
of brutal civil war or anarchy, or who fear such. Not yet explained is why
it should appeal to everyone else. Contemporary citizens demand not just
order but other things: at the least, liberty, equality, and democracy. With
respect to the first two of these, at any rate, *Hume agreed* and rejected the
Hobbesian doctrine that order trumps all other goods. Englanders, in his
view, had reason to prize their modern institutions as providing "that noble
liberty, that sweet equality, and that happy security, by which they [were] at
present distinguished above all nations in the universe" (H 4.370).[1] But given

that Hume, in accord with his time and place,[2] had little use for natural rights language—or indeed the language of rights more generally—we are entitled to ask what this liberty and equality are supposed to rest on.

For those who prefer that problems take analytic form, we can regard the kind of political authority that arises as a solution to coordination problems as threatening to bring about two kinds of inequality (primarily with respect to power, but through the exercise of power, affecting wealth and other goods). These might be called *vertical* and *horizontal*.[3]

On the vertical level, leaders who solve coordination games can often demand a rent for doing so: they can arrogate some of the proceeds of peace and prosperity to themselves and their personal supporters.[4] On this point, Hume's *Treatise*, which talks about the magistrates' interest in administering justice (T 3.2.8.6–8, SBN 544–6), is both accurate as far as it goes and radically incomplete. Without further explanation of governmental structure, Hume's theory sets up magistrates with an interest in administering laws (by which they greatly increase their own power compared to a state of complete or partial lawlessness) *and* in using their authority over the laws to grab benefits for themselves, including the benefit of immunity from punishment if they do (departing from their supposed impartiality) violate others' conventional rights or harm their interests. Hume's "egregious tyranny" exception probably rules out the extreme case in which members of one group receive no benefits at all, are "subject to a leader's actions" but not "the followers of a leader."[5] Such governments, as noted in chapter 3, are for Hume the proper objects of violent rebellion or guiltless desertion. But it does not rule out the milder case in which the producers of "order and good government"[6] expropriate many but not all of the proceeds thereof.

Horizontal inequality involves not the diverging interests (and unequal power) of leaders and followers but those of different followers. In most coordination games, all parties benefit from reaching some solution, but benefit to a greater or lesser degree depending on which solution it is. Such games are called "impure" by game theorists and "biased," "unequal," or "discriminatory" by those attempting to describe the real-world consequences.[7]

Horizontal inequality will be the subject of the next chapter. This one will argue that Hume attacked vertical inequality, which goes by the classic names of monopoly, tyranny, and corruption, by disaggregating "government" very thoroughly—much more radically than many modern-day pluralists would be willing to countenance. Vertical inequality is to be fought through the power of the purse, which Hume called "the sole expedient, provided by the constitution, for [ensuring] to the kingdom a just and legal administration" (H 5.568, substituting "ensuring" for the text's "enduring," which seems a clear error). The power of the purse, sometimes called the supply power, was in England initially as blunt and borderline-criminal as it needed to be in order to check would-be absolute monarchs. Later, and to Britons' (and eventually Americans') benefit, it was quasi-institutionalized through a political body that masks its fiscal threats with speech: parliament (from *parler*: the body that talks). Nobles, later commoners as well, and eventually an ordered parliament that incorporated both but with the latter dominant, "extorted" concessions in favor of liberty, and extorted institutional guarantees for those concessions—Magna Charta, the Petition of Right, and for a time the Triennial Act.[8] Their weapon was the power of supply, exerted via threats to withhold the funds that the monarch needed to pay his or her armies. This tended to work most effectively when the monarch faced acute needs to fight domestic and foreign enemies. Though the previous chapter has noted its technical inaccuracy, Hume's blunt word "extortion" nicely describes a strategy in which parliaments and proto-parliaments essentially say "nice Crown you've got there." Liberty had its origins in barely sublimated violence: not always from the extorters, to be sure, but from those whose threats to the crown the extorters deliberately counted on and used.

The link of liberty to brinksmanship is not accidental. When conventions of authority predate those of liberty, those in charge of authority will have great power because they are indispensible. The citizens of a regime that, though absolute, ensures law and order and gives some protection against what would otherwise be near-omnipotent private warlords, would rather acquiesce to decisions that often disadvantage them than challenge that regime at the cost of civil strife. The advantage this gives to those at the top is profound. The possible methods of containing that power seem limited: (1) hoping that allegedly natural or supernatural sources of agreement ("right reason," "the voice of God within," "natural law," the "ideal speech situation") will render coordination problems moot; (2) increasing people's taste for civil war and bloody religious and ideological conflicts relative to their taste for peace and prosperity; (3) brinksmanship and statesmanship, a practice of threatening with disaster the government that coordinates authority, and hoping that prudent leaders and their liberty-loving challengers will cut a deal before anarchy or foreign conquest results; (4) institutionalizing liberty, through orders of governance and accountability that reliably produce authoritative decision makers while also reliably limiting the scope of their rule and allowing tyrannical or corrupt rulers to be both discovered and removed.

Defenders of the first method are swimming against centuries of modern skepticism that it is viable. The second method was once very much in play—it is, arguably, Locke's—but no longer attractive. Radical political theorists who think they support it would not want to live five minutes with the consequences (and probably wouldn't). Hume's story concerns the third and fourth methods. The third method was regularly tried in England, occasionally succeeding beyond all expectations and occasionally failing spectacularly. By trial and bloody error, England eventually groped its way to the fourth, constitutional method, and should keep it. So, as the Hume-influenced architects of the United States' institutions thought, should Americans.

Bargaining with the Prince: The Power
of Supply as the Basis of Liberty

As noted, Hume portrays English government in the Middle Ages as a barely tamed baronial anarchy. Powerful lords fought one another to the last commoner while coming together in mutual support of the idea that kings should be weak, laws silent, and most Englanders slaves. Royal power provided the first, blunt remedy for baronial violence, at the cost of arbitrariness. Tyrannical royal power—not even "absolutist" in any strict sense, because established theories of government never quite tracked practice—was both a necessary step in suppressing baronial domination and one with obvious disadvantages that Hume readily notes. While Tudor rule was better than the War of the Roses, Henry VII wins Hume's praise not for refraining from oppression but for making himself the "sole oppressor in his kingdom" (as opposed to the barons). And as already noted, Henry VIII's government was an out-and-out tyranny, justified only by the arguable alternative of religious war; and Elizabeth's rule differed from an "despotic and eastern monarchy" only because the people were armed and this particular despot was, by temperament, relatively benevolent.[9] In general, the constitution of England through the Tudor reign mixed not

> authority and liberty, which we have since enjoyed in this island, and which now subsist uniformly together; but . . . authority and anarchy, which perpetually shocked with each other, and which took place alternately, according as circumstances were more or less favourable to either of them. (H 5.556, note J; compare 5.550, note A)

The basic problem was that there was, until the seventeenth century, no fully *institutionalized* method of checking power—either baronial or royal—only force:

> The power of the Norman kings was also much supported by a great revenue; and by a revenue, that was fixed, perpetual, and independant [*sic*] of the subject. The people, without betaking themselves to arms, had no check upon the king, and no regular security for the due administration of justice. In those days of violence, many instances of oppression passed unheeded; and soon after were openly pleaded as precedents, which it was unlawful to dispute or controul. Princes and ministers were too ignorant to be themselves sensible of the advantages attending an equitable administration; and there *was no established council or assembly which could protect the people, and, by withdrawing supplies, regularly and peaceably admonish the king of his duty*, and ensure the execution of the laws. (H. 1.474–5 [Appendix II]; emphasis added)

"Withdrawing supplies"—refusing to approve the Crown's request for funds—would eventually become the chief safeguard of liberty, the basic check against oppressive royal authority.

Supply was not the tactic that originally secured Magna Charta. That would be, predictably, baronial force. A confederation of barons forced the king to surrender at discretion (and wrote terms that on Hume's account mostly though not exclusively benefited their own order [H 1.438–42]). But the later confirmations of Magna Charta, whose repetition (I have argued in chapter 4) made the Charter a fundamental convention that could not be eroded by disuse, were "extorted" from the "most warlike" Edward I through the withdrawal of moneys, not the force of arms. Hume considers this result superficially ironic, yet covered by clear and simple causal explanations: "necessities," not "chance" (H 2.109). On the one hand, Edward's military prowess was founded on the gradual growth of royal armies who served for wages. These replaced the "cumbersome and dangerous" feudal obligations that bound barons to furnish their own disorderly and personal armies, "often more formidable to their own prince than to foreign powers, against whom they were assembled" (H 2.99). The disuse of feudal obligation relieved the barons of a burden but also of a source of power: by the late thirteenth century, they no longer commanded ready-made armies that could challenge the king's. On the other hand, all these wars cost far more money than most English kings—blessed, in international comparison, by very large royal demesnes (H 1.475)—had ever needed. In this "distressful situation," the kings from the thirteenth century onward needed more money than they had. Being good politicians, they sought it from subjects who had money but no power (were in fact grateful to the king for such little security against the barons that they had): the lesser barons, the gentry, and the inhabitants of cities, which kings had enthusiastically chartered as counterweights against the barons (H 2.101–6).

Crucial to Hume's story, but often neglected, is the fact that the Commons' fiscal *powers* preceded its *authority*. The original negotiations between king and Commons were truly quasi-commercial bargains between a monarch who needed funds and those subjects who happened to be a position to supply them. They resembled current bond market auctions more than constitutional disputes. When Edward I in 1295 summoned the first Commons by formal and general writ, with the *quod omnes tangit* motto discussed in the next chapter, he in fact had the *formal* authority to levy taxes (in the form of "taillages") at pleasure (an authority, to Hume's mind, "utterly incompatible with all the principles of a free government," but fortunately impossible to exert in practice [H 2.106]). The king's inability to raise money was practical, not legal. The first parliament was likewise an *ad hoc* response to necessity, not a recognition of new legal authorities. Essentially, gathering the representatives of the moneyed together in one place was easier than requesting gifts from each separately.

But when the multiplied necessities of the crown produced a greater avidity for supply, the king, whose prerogative entitled him to exact it, found that he had not power sufficient to enforce his edicts, and that it was necessary, before he imposed taxes, to smooth the way for his demand, and to obtain the previous consent of the boroughs, by solicitations, remonstrances, and authority. The *inconvenience of transacting this business with every particular borough was soon felt*; and Edward became sensible, that the most *expeditious* way of obtaining supply, was to assemble the deputies of all the boroughs, to lay before them the necessities of the state, to discuss the matter in their presence, and to require their consent to the demands of their sovereign. (H 2.106; emphases added)

A lot, by the way, is packed into "expeditious." The monarchs needed not just a quick and easy way of levying funds, but one that would solve a public goods contributions game. Considered separately, each wealthy subject, even if willing to grant funds if others did, had individual incentives to withhold them if others would, or even might.[10] (Hume was an early student of such games, of course not calling them that.[11]) By assembling parliament in one place, Edward allowed for contract by convention and mutual surveillance. A common decision that bound all could be reached because each was present to say "aye" while watching others do the same, and knew in turn that he was being watched. No one could free ride, no one feared that others would free ride, and everyone knew that everyone knew all of this: the result was trust.[12] Ironically, by solving his own problems of speed and/or cooperation, Edward gave the representatives of the kingdom's wealth the future ability to solve what would otherwise be a radical problem of coordination. Burgesses and knights from various parts of the country would never have been able to mount successful resistance to ship money; "The House of Commons" easily could. "The *union* . . . of the representatives from the boroughs gave gradually more weight to the whole order . . ." (H 2.107, emphasis added),[13] and the collective actor that Edward I created, Charles I could not destroy.[14]

The ability to force very powerful and warlike monarchs to acknowledge checks on their power became strong and durable before it became institutional. Commoners wielded the power of the purse before the Commons did. The story is one of social and economic changes but also of the frictions and conflicts that occur when such changes outpace the political theory that would eventually accommodate them. (Hume in general has his own empirical version of Hegel's owl-of-Minerva theory. Theories of political authority, based on long trains of empirical evidence regarding what produces public benefits without endangering peace, *always* lag the changing balances of social forces; political progress is very often what we would now call "illegitimate."[15]) At the beginning, the Commons were grateful for the king's support and sanction. Legal protection from nobles, for instance through city charters, was sufficient recompense for large sums of money. We might call this a kind of inverted feudalism, and as such implicitly but not yet explicitly subversive. Grants, by grace, went upward to the king, in return for military protection offered downward. (Hume in one essay implies this parallel.[16])

Even the petitions of grievances, on the redress of which supply was soon made conditional, did not for a long time rise to the dignity of a share in formal legislation, which remained a matter of royal rather than parliamentary authority:

> [I]t became customary for them [the representatives of the boroughs], in return for the supplies which they granted, to prefer petitions to the crown for the redress of any particular grievance, of which they found reason to complain. The more the king's demands multiplied, the faster these petitions encreased both in number and authority; and the prince found it difficult to refuse men, whose grants had supported his throne, and to whose assistance he might so soon be again obliged to have recourse. The commons however were still much below the rank of legislators. Their petitions, though they received a verbal assent from the throne, were only the rudiments of laws: The judges were afterwards entrusted with the power of putting them into form: And the king, by adding to them the sanction of his authority, and that sometimes without the assent of the nobles, bestowed validity upon them. The age did not refine so much as to perceive the danger of these irregularities. (H 2.107–8)

The Commons' growing role in government was founded less on a theory of representation than on the Commons' increasing awareness of its bargaining power. Instances of particular royal need or vulnerability provided the opportunity. Only Edward I's need for money to fight foreign wars left him so in need of money that acknowledgment of the Great and Forestry charters could be "extorted" from him. Edward III, who was pursuing a claim to the French crown with more support in arms than in feudal law, was forced more than once to confirm the Charter under similar need (H 2.121, 206, 215). And of course the assertiveness of parliament against Charles I was made possible by the king's need of supply to pursue a foreign war (yet, crucially, not one in which parliament thought England itself threatened, given its island situation). Hume suggests that "the popular leaders" had welcomed war with this in view (H 5.160–1).[17] Hume endorses a paradoxical insight of Robertson's that in the age before regular parliaments, conquerors were the least tyrannical rulers, because they needed more money than those who stayed home (H 2.273, citing Book I of Robertson's *History of Scotland*). Religious rebellion was likewise favorable to the parliament's being able to assert itself through brinksmanship. The clergy wielded great power, from their command over legitimacy, administrative capacity, and land (in that order, as Hume normally portrays it). King John had famously been weakened by excommunication when he granted Magna Charta; Edward III faced an implicit threat of excommunication when in 1341 he was forced by parliament to confirm the Charter.[18]

Monarchs whose legitimacy rested most directly on public opinion were of course most dependent on it, and therefore on parliament. Henry IV (Lancaster), the parliament-created monarch who succeeded the hapless Richard II, was "obliged to court popularity" and parliamentary support. His usurpation, though bad for monarchy and the eventual cause of the Wars of the Roses, was good for parliamentary power. Under this monarch, parliament asserted the great powers and procedures that were later the core of its power: as conditions for granting supply it demanded the resignation of ministers, appointed auditors of royal expenses, and required that royal officers swear to articles of good administration that the parliament had drafted. Crucially, and early in Henry IV's reign, when his rule was most precarious, the house of commons—not merely the nobles—"insisted on maintaining the practice of not granting any supply before they received an answer to their petitions; which was a tacit manner of bargaining with the prince" (H 2.346). Whether petitions should precede supply or vice versa had previously been somewhat unsettled. If the parliament's authority had been legal and regular, the sequence would have made little difference. Because it rested on bargaining power, it made a huge difference.[19] Later, under Charles I, the Commons made

> [a] condition . . . in a very undisguised manner, with their sovereign. Under colour of redressing grievances, which, during this short reign, could not be very numerous; they were to proceed in regulating and controuling every part of government, which displeased them. And if the king either cut them short in this undertaking, or refused compliance with their demands, he must not expect any supply from the commons. (H 5.167)

Double-edged Purses

Hume certainly regards the threat to withdraw supply as a crucial source of English liberty. Without it, kings would have no reason to care who sat in the parliament, and until James I's reign they mostly didn't (H 5.58). With it, the Commons eventually "rescued the kingdom from aristocratical as well as from regal tyranny" and "afforded protection to the inferior orders of the state" (H 2.57). (The supply power is still the formal, constitutional basis for much of what the Commons does, from legislative debate to calling Ministers to account, though nobody much in Britain seems to think of things that way.[20]) Yet the supply power is a very blunt instrument that risks three basic dangers—dangers that are still relevant wherever executives, by whatever name, face parliaments, however styled.

First, the fact that the supply power is the remedy for all possible abuses under circumstances that cannot be known in advance requires that "it must be left unbounded by law: For who can foretell, how frequently grievances may occur, or what part of administration may be affected by them?" (H 5.568–9). For this reason, the check on arbitrary power will itself be a little bit arbitrary: it constitutes

> that circumstance in the English constitution, which it is most difficult, or rather altogether impossible, to regulate by laws, and which must be governed by certain delicate ideas of propriety and decency, rather than by any exact rule or prescription. (H 5.568)[21]

The proper use of the supply power does not, however, depend only on the executive abuse in question, but also, and embarrassingly for the kind of political science that seeks general rules, on the personal qualities of the executive. The same level of parliamentary self-assertion that created laudable and durable checks on Edward III's authority was sufficient to overthrow Richard II altogether—in favor of a baronial commission, and later a baron-created king (Henry IV), both of whose rules were steps backward in the progress of settled governmental authority and equal justice. That the terms of the bargain depended on the personal capacity of the monarch (Edward III bargained well, Richard badly) makes for gripping stories but not good government. "It were happy for society, did this contrast always depend on the justice or injustice of the measures which men embrace, and not rather on the different degrees of prudence and vigour, with which those measures are supported" (H 2.325). Hume thought the problem inherent in any mixed monarchy, but his reasoning applies to any government with a single executive facing a jealous legislature:

> as this person may have either a greater or less degree of ambition, capacity, courage, popularity, or fortune, the power, which is too great in one hand, may become too little in another . . . nor is it possible to assign to the crown such a determinate degree of power, as will, in every hand, form a proper counterbalance to the other parts of the constitution. (E: IP, 46)

The only remedy would be for legislatures to exert greater or lesser jealousy depending on their sober and accurate judgment of the executive's abilities and intentions. This call for perfect prudence is as useful as such counsels normally are. In practice, given how ambition operates, Hume predicted that the Commons would press its power maximally against all monarchs, reducing the monarchy's independent administrative authority to near nothing (H 5.569). So it has.[22]

Second, besides the power of the purse's being potentially too great when opposed to some executives but too feeble when opposed to others, it can also have dangerous or arbitrary objects. Parliaments can use their power for the general good, but there is no guarantee that they will: they may simply lunge for power. Hume dissented from the party-line Whig position that personal liberty and parliamentary liberty (or privileges, or powers) were conceptually equivalent. For Hume, the relationship was often close but causally contingent: the parliament's power might operate to safeguard private liberty, but one did not constitute the other.[23] Very often, the link broke down, and parliament endangered liberty in pursuit of popular causes or simply to further its collective ambition. From the late fifteenth century to the late sixteenth, on Hume's view, parliaments operated by "maxims" at once "ungenerous," "opposite to all principles of good government" and "contrary to the practice of present parliaments." They begrudged supply for necessary expenses, even wars favored by the parliament itself, but "they never scruple[d] to concur in the most flagrant act of injustice or tyranny, which [fell] on any individual, however distinguished by birth or merit" (H 2. 492). Until the reign of James I, parliaments gave no help to the victims of tyranny. They occasionally defied monarchs in defense of their own privileges, never in defense of ordinary subjects' liberty. Parliment was less often an opponent of the monarchical program of becoming "absolute master of the person and property of every individual" than an "instrument" through which monarchs pursued this program; parliament produced "tyranny converted into law" (H 3.68, 149, 244, 266, 299–300, 303, 310, 319–20, 323, 325, 363; quotations at 3.319–20, 305, 264).[24]

But it was not only during this early period that parliaments posed a threat to individual liberty. Even after the awakening of "civil liberty" that culminated in England's two revolutions, it was not the case that parliament opposed kings and protected subjects: it flexed its new-found strength against both. In the early years of King James, parliament threatened to imprison a bishop for writing in favor of union with Scotland (H 5.34. note "l"). Arbitrary "commitments" (what Americans would call criminal contempt of Congress) were, on Hume's view, *both* parliaments' only means of protecting their privileges against royal authority *and* a fine method for arresting parliament's enemies for factional rather than constitutional purposes and against the letter and spirit of Magna Charta (H 6.384–6). Persistently, in Hume's story, Parliaments under Charles I and Charles II used their powers to persecute Catholics, a tiny and more or less powerless minority, even as they talked fine words about civil liberty. In fact, persecuting and killing Catholics was considered a constitutive part of such liberty (among many other instances, see H 5.328). The relative friend of despised religious minorities was—equally under the Protestant James I and Charles I as under the more flexible and secretly pro-Catholic Charles II—the monarchy, the branch of government that did not face re-election. While Hume's particular historical conclusions—he regards Charles I's offenses against personal liberty as relatively trivial, and the Long Parliament's abuses as absolutely tyrannical (H 5.259, 411, 502; 6.13, 58, 117)—were controversial, then as now, it must be the case that a power strong enough to challenge the holder of military force is also strong enough to quash individual liberties. The power of both Britain's parliament and the U.S. congress to hold ministers to account is based on the implicit threat to withdraw supply. The sign that "liberty was thoroughly established" has always been that "popular assemblies entered into every branch of public business"—for better or worse (H 5.58). (One well-known head of the U.S. Senate's Committee on Government Operations was Joseph McCarthy.)

Hume is not clear on what "present parliaments" do better or which instances of investigating the executive, backed by the threat of withdrawing supply, he approves of. But his suggestion in various passages is that parliament in his day strikes a reasonable balance between zeal and self-aggrandizement. On the one hand, English liberty is by no means automatic and requires continued "jealousy" by the republican part of the constitution against the royal:

> [A]rbitrary power would steal in upon us, were we not careful to prevent its progress, and were there not an easy method of conveying the alarm from one end of the kingdom to the other. *The spirit of the people must frequently be rouzed, in order to curb the ambition of the court; and the dread of rouzing this spirit must be employed to prevent that ambition.* Nothing so effectual to this purpose as the liberty of the press, by which all the learning, wit, and genius of the nation may be employed on the side of freedom, and every one be animated to its defence. (E: LP, 12–13; emphasis added)

(Hume's point, again, involves coordination. The crown has the advantage of being a single actor; proper balance requires methods by which the public can be "animated" to act as if it were one, though it isn't.) At the same time, it seems, the kind of brinksmanship in the face of foreign threats that was required to vindicate public rights when the monarch's executive power was arbitrary and potentially unconstrained, is dangerous to the public in a time of relatively settled rights and real foreign dangers. If parliament wanted to destroy the crown's power—a very irresponsible thing, according to Hume—the peaceful way for it to do so would be "by making every grant conditional, and choosing their time so well, that their refusal of supply should only distress the government, *without* giving foreign powers any advantage over us" (E: IP, 44; emphasis added). Public opinion seems to make the difference: Hume notes that the public does not always rally to parliament. He alludes to the incident at the turn of the eighteenth century in which a Tory parliament that delayed in voting supplies for William III's war against France was met by angry petitions, not support (E: FPG, 35).[25]

A third problem, which can be woven together from Hume's first two concerns but was apparently opaque to Hume himself, arises when the first two are combined. A particularly arrogant and ambitious executive may overwhelm existing norms regarding the proper conduct of legislative opposition so that only a dangerous and unjust popular movement can, with great danger, restore balance. In effect, the contest between prerogative and rebellion, thought to have been relatively settled by constitutional norms, might break out again. Consider Hume's treatment of the "Wilkes and Liberty" movement.

Partisans of John Wilkes regarded his cause as a continuation of the Civil War (he was compared to Pym and Hambden, and sometimes Cromwell). Wilkes' offending writings protested above all against George III's atavistic royalism: his naming of a cabinet founded on his personal favor (with Lord Bute, not a member of the commons, at its head) rather than parliamentary support. The suppression of those writings and repeated bans against Wilkes' taking his elected seat in parliament raised issues of personal and parliamentary liberty as well as anti-royalism. Hume, on the other hand, opposed the Wilkesites as demagogic, thought their popularity presaged a new barbarism, and welcomed the rise of a pro-order, monarchist government opposed to Wilkes' claims. Hume blamed the Wilkesites for having no particular grievance and no pressing need to resort to extra-parliamentary protest; Hume's defenders (even more than Hume himself did) stress the virulence and real danger of Wilkes' anti-Scottish chauvinism in particular.[26]

The hard questions arise if both sides were right. Perhaps George III's policy did amount to a dangerous royalism that was no longer supported by prevailing opinion (a danger missed by Hume, who was blind to how much the strong-monarchy and weak-parliament norms of the early eighteenth century had changed) *and* Wilkes was an unprincipled ochlocrat and (proto-) racist, whose coordination of the English was bought at the price of stirring up hate against outsiders, i.e., the Scots, whose fate bothered him little.[27] If, as in Hume's theory, liberty, equality, and republican spirit have a contingent rather than a necessary connection, Hume's portrayal of the last as a crucial *but dangerous* weapon in support of the first two may retain more sense than first appears.

For all these reasons, Hume thinks it a very good thing that the disputes between parliament and crown be *settled*, the biggest questions no longer disputed. Mixed, constitutional government remained, on Hume's view, unstable. Either Commons or Crown would likely destroy the other's power in time, and meanwhile the jealousy between the two preserved liberty at the cost of factional and constitutional strife.[28] Still, England (later Britain) after the Glorious Revolution enjoyed a happy medium between uncontested authority and unconstrained contestation: "if not the best system of government, at least the most entire system of liberty" ever known (H 6.531).

From Status to Bargain: The Commercialization of Politics (and Vice Versa)

When he used the phrase "bargaining with the prince" to describe parliament's strategy of not granting supply until the monarch granted its petitions, Hume was pointing out something more radical than today's readers might realize. The embodiment of political authority (not that the convention ended with his or her body) was henceforth to be considered one political actor among many, who would pursue his or her interests in the full expectation that some of them would be frustrated. And the act of frustrating them—of turning down the king's requests as a matter not of natural law or divine right but of worldly power—was henceforth to be the proud badge of parliamentary ascendancy. It was not a matter of withdrawing consent to government. Government was necessary on all but a fantasy version of how societies could be ordered; and consent, the language of feudalism and baronial honor, was no challenge to medieval mythology. The language of interest and bargaining—and, more to the point, the practice it described—was something much more radical.

In chapter 3 I argued that the only government by consent that Hume regards as politically and historically significant is feudalism. Political allegiance based on personal fidelity to promises can exist only where political power is exercised by a few and those few recognize, or claim to recognize, the claims of personal honor rather than those of impartial justice. Strong, hereditary monarchy is for Hume a distinctive improvement over feudal order or its breakdown (baron-driven anarchy) because it embodies an impartial "principle of authority" independent of force and personal charisma and allows, though it does not guarantee, the equal application of law and civil rights.

The eclipse of feudal politics, the simultaneous decline of baronial and Church power, left a vacuum of authority. Government by opinion requires mechanisms of stability to prevent self-fulfilling doubts as to its basis. The constitutive conventions of monarchy and Magna Charta previously discussed can provide some such stability. But as static principles, they cannot accommodate change and disagreement. Crisis situations, the stuff of civil wars and succession crises, may be solved by artful reconstitution of one or both of these conventions (or to whichever conventions play the role in a given society that those play in England): unstable politics motivates a flight to quality in the market for legitimate authority. But the everyday politics of supply, as Hume noted, will not be fixed by general and constitutional rules. In the U.S. context the resulting crises are visible: given a written constitution, executive and legislative powers will clash, and everyone will assert constitutional positions when they do. In England, where the constitution is unwritten and even talk of constitutional law is a specialized rather than a mass taste, matters are different. Arguably, Britons like their constitution a bit arbitrary because they were convinced by philosophic radicals that fundamental conventions only serve vested interests and that the people are best served by keeping such interests in terror. (That a government, backed by parliament, strong enough to hold the powerful in fear can do the same toward the powerless seems of less concern.) But beyond that, the inchoate character of English constitutional checks may reflect their origins: not in legal status claims but in a blunt bargain—money for power—that eventually became governed by expectations but no explicitly constitutional laws.

The balance of power was a term from foreign policy whose domestic analogues (Hume mentions Athenian ostracism) Hume may have been among the first to note (E: BP, 332–41). It was, and remains, inherently subversive of older international-law theories that tried to reduce justice to right. Balance is a stronger metaphor than we think and compromise a stranger ideal than we realize. Regarding the force of one's claim as inherently relative, capable of outweighing or being outweighed by a counterclaim, entails rejecting the quest for explicit and permanent constitutional principles independent of circumstance. Bargaining need not reduce power to money. But it does reduce it to deal-making, in some literal or figurative currency.

Hume writes of a bill in parliament being "brought to maturity, all its conveniencies and inconveniences, weighed and balanced"; the result of this deliberation is "the unanimous desire of the people" (which kings won't dare to veto [E: IPC, 515]). This is the language of the bargaining table, not the law court. Each proposal involves conveniences and inconveniences (advantages and disadvantages) that can be balanced, not claims or counterclaims subject to confirmation or refutation. Parliamentary deliberations yield not a fictive agreement on a principle but a fictively unanimous desire. When Hamilton describes the House of Representatives as embodying "the purse" and therefore "WILL" (as the executive commands "the sword" and therefore "FORCE"), he voices the customary English way of regarding constitutional politics and political balance: it is money that talks, and the form of an effective political demand by a legislature is to put its money where its mouth is.[29]

The fictive idea that most principles can be reduced to interests has been called the basis of the politics of compromise (and of a "commitment to union" that strives for a basis of social coordination that transcends disagreements over principle).[30] One might call this the political counterpart of the Enlightenment quest to replace strife among sects and nations with peaceful commercial rivalry, passion with interest. Certainly the representatives of the old order did not regard this shift as a minor one in economics. The same was true when it came to the new politics. On Hume's account, one reason that Charles I could not reach a settlement with his parliamentary enemies is that he regarded parliamentary extortion, the limitation of his prerogative as the price demanded for supply, as "highly criminal and traitorous." Subjects, Charles haughtily thought, do not hold kings to ransom, and kings do not give up their prerogatives and principles for "pecuniary considerations" (H 5.161, 173–4, 210–11). The "express bargain" by which even a strong monarch like Edward III was forced to "sell some of his prerogatives for present supply" had always in royal eyes been a matter of necessity, not legality, and beneath royal dignity; even Edward equivocated and reneged as much and as soon he could (H 2.109, 325).

As Albert Hirschman has pointed out, the Enlightenment thinkers who thought that the politics of economic interest would leave no room for social strife and party struggle were not exactly vindicated.[31] One could extend this analogy to politics. The fact that we mostly argue over more or less spending for this or that rather than over prerogative and privilege, over the extent of government accountability and popular audit power rather than its basic legitimacy, does not render those arguments consensual or free of anger.

One objection to this would contest the conclusion. In international and historical comparison, our politics are both very peaceful and very consensual. A different and deeper objection, however, would take the opposite tack. Mixed government continues, as Hume feared and hoped it would, to combine jealous checks on government misconduct with the constant potential for brinksmanship in politics and a shutdown in government operations.[32] The language of compromise may be accurate but partly misleading. To stress extortion instead of bargaining—the implicit threat instead of the process through which one hopes to avoid its execution—is to show the extent to which constitutional politics can embody duress. Even peaceful bargains may be struck on very hard terms. Similarly, a view to the prehistory of checks and balances may reveal what is at stake in calls to lower the temperature. Otto Kirchheimer's class compromises, whose parties were whole social groups, were only technically peaceful: they embodied mutual retreats from the abyss, the penalty for failure being revolution or fascism.[33] What scholars call "comity" or "legal and political norms"[34] may play a similar role, diplomatic words masking deadly important things. Either the executive, who can assert the claims of military and economic security, or the legislature, who controls all of governments' resources, could potentially hold the other branch hostage. Those seeking excitement and radical possibilities can push this fact as far as they wish. Those preferring prosperity and government accountability must hope for a "power compromise" that preserves the fragile balance—while disagreeing over where the balance should rest.

Implications and Conclusions

The framework of this chapter helps illuminate a neglected political tradition that might be called populist constitutionalism. The tradition departs from traditionalistic conservatism, small-government libertarianism, and communitarian or radical nostalgism in stressing that centralized government power is (1) new, the product of historical changes rather than original design and no worse for that; (2) on balance good, necessary to vindicate personal liberty and security against threats from private interests and local religious (or in the United States, racial and ethnic) factions; and (3) dangerous: in need of effective, pervasive, and continual checks that a stylized Westminster majoritarianism alone cannot provide and neo-Hobbist partisans of absolute sovereignty cannot recognize. The idea that our economic welfare and peace depend on historically created but durable conventions of political authority yields the first two planks. Fear of the power that such conventions give the holders of government power, or the social groups they favor, yields the third.[35] Chapter 1 stressed how the circumstances of collective action bind the powerful for the same reason that they frustrate the aspiration to civic agency: that which I am not free to choose, would-be kingmakers also are not free to avoid. Here another logic points toward the same anti-Athenian end: those who oppose constitutional or representative forms of democracy would be hard-pressed to give a reason, once the respect for constitutional forms (and the tangible, universal interests they promote) has been demolished, why the powerful should address equality claims that they would much prefer to ignore.

Hume, in a late essay that sums up much of his *History* as well as his normative political philosophy, writes of this in terms of authority and liberty. The two struggle in every government. While all government means a "great sacrifice of liberty,"

> The government, which, in common appellation, receives the appellation of free, is that which admits of a partition of power among several members, whose united authority is no less, or is commonly greater than that of any monarch; but who, in the usual course of administration, must act by general and equal laws, that are previously known to all the members and to all their subjects. In this sense, it must be owned, that liberty is the perfection of civil society; but still authority must be acknowledged essential to its very existence: and in those contests, which so often take place between the one and the other, the latter may, on that account, challenge the preference. Unless perhaps one may say (and it may be said with some reason) that a circumstance, which is essential to the existence of civil society, must always support itself, and needs be guarded with less jealousy, than one that contributes only to its perfection, which the indolence of men is so apt to neglect, or their ignorance to overlook. (E: OG, 40–41)

We may explicate this in terms of coordination and vertical inequality. The struggle between authority and liberty is a struggle between the desire to coordinate at the cost of giving leaders power, and the desire to limit the power that comes from coordination authority at the cost of making coordination harder. The above passage is ambiguous as to whether the "partition of power" means that the monarch must govern by laws, or whether it involves a republic whose powers, combined, are greater than any monarch's would be. (The ambiguity accords with Hume's consistent position that law-based or "civilized" monarchies and well-designed republics are both fully legitimate or "legal" and fully modern.[36]) But Hume's key point is at the end. All governments need authority. But for that very reason we should stress liberty, which takes more energy to vindicate—coordination problems again?—and more thought to understand. Hume is well aware that the heirs of Hobbist theories possess a simplicity and surface realism that a complex theory of constitutional government lacks. Defenders of the latter must continually rebut both a false conceptual simplicity that places deductive analysis over observable experience and a facile realism that understands everything about power except its abuse.

Here, as in many areas, Hume's greatest influence was in English philosophy and American politics (whereas American philosophy and English politics have neglected him). Though Hume's anti-contractual theory of government was, and is, appreciated in Britain but mostly rejected in revolutionary America, his plan for government, though it would be rejected by Britain in pursuit of centralized and uncontested power, became entrenched in America, which placed force and administrative authority in an independently elected executive but the supply power in a separate legislature to prevent abuse of that authority.[37] *The Federalist*'s apparently baroque formulations (Louis Hartz called the American theory of sovereignty a "chaotic series of forays and retreats" in which both the national and state governments were called, incoherently, both sovereign and limited[38]) can likewise be seen as attempts to solve coordination games while limiting the solutions' abuses and inequalities.

The Tocquevillean thesis that America did not need a strong central government because it had no feudal institutions to overcome cannot explain the fact that the elite constitutional theory of the *Federalist* extolled checks and balances within a national government that its authors were desperately trying to *strengthen*.[39] The explanation, again, is that individual liberty and security require *both* established authority and checks against that authority, both coordination and established mechanisms for limiting the rents of coordinators. This was at the heart of John Adams' criticism of Turgot, who called for a strong central assembly to vindicate the people's will against particular interests but then neglected to prevent ambitious leaders or interests from controlling that assembly and wielding it against most citizens' interests.[40] More famously, Madison argued that men not being angels,

> In framing a government which is to be administered by men over men, the great difficulty lies in this: you must first enable the government to control the governed; and in the next place oblige it to control itself. A dependence on the people is, no doubt, the primary control on the government; but experience has taught mankind the necessity of auxiliary precautions. This policy of supplying, by opposite and rival interests, the defect of better motives, might be traced through the whole system of human affairs, private as well as public.[41]

"Opposite and rival interests" solve a complex problem. That problem is not merely the abuse of power, but the need to simultaneously establish and strengthen the national government's power *and* check its abuses.

In spite of Madison's ingenuity and erudition, there remains a clear note of pessimism: there is no perfect solution. Still, the American solution (as corrected by a Bill of Rights that the centralizers at first resisted) is true both to theory and to one, idealized version of English practice. A double convention that defines both constitutional authority and a separate charter of liberties allows citizens to place more trust in the government than would be rational if the government faced no limits, and allows government to exert less violence than if such trust were lacking.

A vigorous executive governs through the leadership power that comes from coordination. Its defenders stress the need for good government to ensure order and protect the weak against attacks by the strong, and praise the virtues of coordination: "[d]ecision, activity, secrecy, and dispatch."[42] The legislature's job, on the other hand, is not to coordinate policy but to bargain over the terms of coordination. Armed with a purse, expert in compromise, and dedicated to the proposition that everything in government should happen slowly, a legislature is completely unable to speak with one voice. (As Jeremy Waldron has argued, it can accommodate diverse interests and adjudicate conceptions of justice precisely because it speaks with many.[43]) Its function from the perspective of constitutional liberty is to extort the terms on which the executive can speak. It forces the executive branch to acknowledge grievances and reveal corruption, and serves as an agent that transforms public grievances into tense but authoritative bargains between the outraged and the objects of outrage. Where executive power and popular representation remain separate, each with partisans or quasi-partisans who wish to stress and expand their champion's claims, the result can embody the same sort of combination of efficiency and deference to public rights that Hume saw (or took one party to see) in the Glorious Revolution. "The people cherish monarchy [or executive power], because protected by it: The monarch favours liberty, because created by it [i.e., in the American context, though not what Hume intended, the executive derives legitimacy from election]. And thus every advantage is obtained by the new establishment, as far as human skill and wisdom can extend itself" (E: PS, 506).[44]

Finally, Hume's treatment shows that his rejection of social contract theory and natural rights need not involve a rejection of either liberty or equality in politics. Social contract theory, in its real or hypothetical forms, begins with an imagined original liberty and equality and treats legitimate government as a set of enumerated exceptions to natural anarchy, justified by consent (or in some versions, justified by what the political theorist putting forth the theory takes to be good reasons). Another approach to liberal equality starts with the imperative of strong and ordered government, in whose absence or weakness powerful private actors, from barons to corporations, rule unchecked at the expense of the weak. It then asks, as older, conservative defenders of authority did not, how such government can over time be made consistent with a liberty and equality that should be all the more prized because they are not natural. Our safety, a product of government, should be prized because the alternative is arbitrary domination. Our liberty and equality—a product of threats to hold government hostage, at calculated risk to our safety—have been hard won through canny politics. We respect and keep them best, not by

crediting the illusion that there is anything natural about them, but by studying the strategies by which liberty and equality were wrested. The point is not
to venerate the past but to notice the logic that motivated past solutions that
retain present relevance. That logic motivates the search for an effective and
authoritative executive authority combined with "watchful *jealousy* over the
magistrates, to remove all discretionary power, and to secure every one's life
and fortune by general and inflexible laws" (E: LP, 12, emphasis in original).

Neither God nor Reason being reliable checks on executive violence, the
guarantor of liberty is politics. The best way to remind ourselves of that is by
studying the ways in which it used to be something even cruder than politics.
To appreciate constitutions, we must stop seeing them as climb-downs from
reason and principle. They are, instead, steps up from violence and extortion.

Chapter 7

What Touches All

Equality, Parliamentarism, and Contested Authority

The last chapter suggested how the separation of monetary from executive power may maximize the compatibility of authority with liberty. Such separation helps correct for the vertical biases built into crude solutions to coordination games. The power that administers government has every reason to grab power (and rents); the power that funds it has every incentive to prevent it from doing so. This chapter addresses the horizontal biases of coordination: the ability of those holding government office to systematically favor some over others in the distribution of public goods or even of legal protection (though unless *some* protection is offered, subjects or citizens have no relationship to the government deeper than the relationship of kidnapper to captor; they are not party to a convention of authority and allegiance).

My thesis is unoriginal, though a bit unpopular among many U.S. political theorists: the main guarantor of equality, in the face of the inequality that governing elites would otherwise prefer, is—and historically was—*parliaments*: legislative assemblies, grounded on a franchise that became more equal over time. And it continues to be such assemblies, which simultaneously participate in government, assume the legitimacy of governance, and insist on a fair canvassing of claims and opinions as to the justice of government's operations. Hume, who lived in an unequal society with a restricted franchise and a political class restricted to a small elite, told only the beginning of this story. But his theory, I will argue, contains the resources for explaining its underlying logic and making sense of its future progress.

A Humean approach to horizontal bias most productively starts by modernizing the medieval roots of parliamentary theory. Church conciliarists and their public-law disciples developed a theory of parliamentary representation and consent in which the consent of all members of society was required for the legality of any decision that affected them all. What this theory did not do was question the need for such decisions or assert the option of citizens' withdrawing consent from government itself. Government was, on this view, a natural part of the human and cosmic order; consent concerned its specific operations, not its existence.[1] The Humean redefinition of "laws of nature" as what everywhere and always serves mutual advantage, given observed regularities in human psychology, allows a Humean to keep the structure of parliamentary consent theory while changing its ultimate justification.[2] Authority may not be cosmically ordained, but no one who prizes large, diverse, and wealthy societies can consistently oppose it. Legislative assemblies exist to demand that state officials ask the people's representatives what shall be done before doing it. These assemblies do not, and should not, contest the need for them to do anything at all. All citizens, all the time, benefit from there being an authority. Legislatures exist to discuss not whether the benefits of authority are greater than zero but how they are, and ought to be, distributed.

I have argued that government for Hume is not really a "parliamentary" matter. The executive governs; the parliament serves as a corrective to how it governs. Parliament operates more through its economic-political power than through explicit authority, and its role in Hume's scheme, while crucial, is not fully constitutional. In the two and a half centuries since Hume wrote, however, we can safely say that things have changed—certainly (and not surprisingly) in England, but generally in legitimate modern governments. Most modern constitutional governments are representative democracies, and none can easily sustain authority without granting a specified and central role to representative and, crucially, *plural* assemblies where disagreements over the justice of state action can be debated and provisionally resolved.[3] As modern societies have developed and their citizens have gained in both wealth and cultural breadth, citizens nowhere are prone to acquiesce to a government that makes decisions without consulting a representative body. Perhaps not just the usefulness of authority conventions but their long-term dependence on discussion by parliamentary assemblies are things we now know, even if Hume did not, to be political laws of nature.

It is widely denied that there is much room for equality or social justice in Hume's scheme. In fact, Hume's theory of property is often seen as endorsing a very biased game. As many commentators have argued, while Hume may be right that each agent is better off with some rules of property than none, Hume implicitly (and wrongly) assumes that all viable rules of property are equal in point of justice. At the very least he exaggerates the costs, and slights the possible benefits, of moving from one convention of property to another or at least of debating adjustments to property schemes at the margin.[4] Perhaps Hume might accept, say, a redistributive welfare state once it was established and widely accepted. (As Neil McArthur has noted, Hume's "what is established?" standard may be conservative but is in principle never reactionary: once a new scheme has gained the solidity of a convention through custom and prescriptive acceptance, it should be kept.[5]) But Hume is wisely thought to lack a principled reason for advocating this (or any other reform) ex ante, since he clearly believes that having some rule of property is so much more important than what it is that to risk one rule to aim at an allegedly better one is almost never worth it. To the extent that "judgments about the justice of laws . . . have to do not with their over-all advantageousness but with the distribution of the costs and benefits of compliance among those subject to the law," Hume's theory, says one critic, culpably denies that we ought to aim at such judgments—or, on some readings, that the enterprise of doing so is even coherent.[6]

Again, though, the *Treatise* story of conjectural origins may deeply mislead us. Justice in the loose, non-Humean sense that the critics intend concerns not where social conventions come from or what makes their existence worthwhile, but the distribution of advantages from those conventions: the standards and processes needed to correct or perfect property and other conventions *after* they arise. Hume's philosophical works treat the foundations of conventions rather than their perfection. The *History* is the other way around, and is therefore where we must turn if we are looking for justice (or at least a possible and potential model for justice). Parliaments, on Hume's account, possess an inherent capacity to accommodate new economic and social grievances after these grievances gather strength outside of parliament, though for the most part no sooner. Even crude schemes of representation embody a "pretence" (or focal point) of non-hereditary authority, which allows for such accommodation when a regime without representation could keep power and property out of sync for generations. Better schemes do this better.

Those who say that Hume lacks a normative "theory" of justice must be right.[7] But given our failure to arrive at versions of those theories that convince all philosophers, let alone ten thousand or so ordinary citizens per country, this is not necessarily a flaw. If Hume had had such a theory, it would probably have involved an elaborate justification of his own social prejudices, including his own relative indifference toward any kind of equality except equal security under law. (Liberty is a constant and explicit theme in Hume's work and a central reason for his joy at parliament's progress. Equality, except the kind that means freedom from feudal and ascriptive legal domination, is not.) As it is, Hume's account of how parliaments accommodate grievances of all kinds—including every manner of accusation that the gains of social conventions are being arrogated by a select group rather than shared equitably— allows Hume's scheme to be more open to equality than he was. If he lacks the kind of justice "theory" that normative scholars often demand, Hume displays an openness to the mechanisms for resolving disagreement about such theories that such scholars sometimes lack.

A parliamentary solution to the problem of equality is therefore Humean but not Hume's. It requires inventive construction from Humean materials, with the goal of continuity with his overall scheme, rather than interpretation of what Hume himself intended or wanted. Those readers who care about the substance of a theory and do not care who said it may now skip ahead to the next section. Those concerned with violence to Hume's intentions, perhaps out of fear that his system might not hold together if too many parts are discarded or enlarged, should note that flexibility in the pursuit of grievances is fully in accord with Hume's constitutional theory, including its institutional "conservatism." Hume's theory of fundamental conventions—monarchy and Magna Charta—is, except in crisis cases, fairly static on a human scale. Such conventions evolve over hundreds of years, and we should not expect to see new ones in the space of a generation or two. But Hume's account of parliament's effective role, which I have argued takes place outside those fundamental conventions, is dynamic and evolutionary: as society changes and new grievances and actors feel their power, the political role of parliament will change to follow. While Hume often wrote as if the English constitution of his time was the best achievable, at least with respect to its promotion of liberty, he did so in a pessimistic voice: he expected it to end, to yield to something else.[8] Given this, we would betray the general message of Hume's political analysis—though not, perhaps, Hume's personal politics or prejudices—by assuming that the role of parliaments, those powerful, protean actors on Hume's stage, can or should remain unchanged. We carry that analysis forward, developing the political science to which Hume saw himself as an early rather than a final contributor, by assuming that legislative assemblies will change their role, as they always have, when formerly powerless groups find their voice and assert their importance. Structures of representation and consent are, according to Hume, bound to follow changes in property—or, as we may generalize, in whatever forms of social power whose allegiance government cannot do without. Growing social equality will eventually be reflected in growing political equality. Groups previously disadvantaged by the policies sustained by state power will over time be able to press their demands for adjustment in those policies.

Quod omnes tangit: Politics as Powers of Attorney

As discussed in the last chapter, parliament solved two coordination problems: one on purpose, one by accident but with very good effects. An expedient that kings originally dreamt up in order to render more efficient their requests for financial contributions eventually ended up solving not only their own but the people's coordination problems. The representatives of those petitioning for liberty were gathered in one place and could bargain collectively, money for rights. Hume was a mostly self-made man alert to money, and I have noted the element of the counting house in his account. But he was also a former student of the law who knew how intimately legal forms governed

English political theory. And it turns out that those forms matter more for the progress of political equality than for that of liberty. Here is how Hume puts it:

> Edward [I] became sensible, that the most expeditious way of obtaining supply, was to assemble the deputies of all the boroughs, to lay before them the necessities of the state, to discuss the matter in their presence, and to require their consent to the demands of their sovereign. For this reason, he issued writs to the sheriffs, enjoining them to send to parliament, along with two knights of the shire, two deputies from each borough within their county, and these provided with sufficient powers from their community, to consent, in their name, to what he and his council should require of them. *As it is a most equitable rule,* says he, in his preamble to this writ, *that what concerns all should be approved of by all; and common dangers be repelled by united efforts;* a noble principle, which may seem to indicate a liberal mind in the king, and which laid the foundation of a free and an equitable government. (H 2.106)

Many terms in that passage ("required," "united efforts," "common dangers," "necessities") will be discussed later. For now we may focus on the "noble principle." "What concerns all should be approved of by all" is an English rendering of *Quod omnes tangit ab omnibus approbetur*—a famous formula in European law and medieval political theory, which scholars often abbreviate as *quod omnes tangit* or *q.o.t.*[9] Its use in 1295 is regarded by Hume—and many modern scholars agree—as a turning point. It was a sign that monarchs could no longer define the realm's "common profit" unilaterally. Henceforth their full authority would always require the concurrence not only of the magnates or peers but of those summoned by writs to localities demanding representatives—eventually a full-blown "House of Commons."[10]

"What touches all should be approved of by all" seems from the perspective of a methodological individualist to involve two fictions: few things affect everyone, and no scheme of any size or scope can function through a unanimity rule. The first fiction is only a slight modification of reality. Parliaments arose as a response to universal concerns, that is, warfare and consent to public subsidies in support of warfare (a.k.a. death and taxes). While people disagree about what government should do, the idea of *some kind* of a common good and a body that must settle it seems relatively unproblematic as long as security and scarcity continue to be problems; we may call this the "circumstances of parliaments." The second fiction is harder, but we do not need to solve it anew. What might seem abstract and arcane parliamentary theories can in fact be seen as the result of past attempts to solve a giant collective action problem in *private* law.

In Roman law, the *quod omnes tangit* motto originally arose from the private law of trusts: when a ward had more than one trustee, matters touching all the trustees could not be decided by one alone. The compilers of the ancient

Roman code wrenched it out of this context and listed it as a free-standing maxim. After the rediscovery of that code in 1130, q.o.t.'s meaning was gradually extended by canon lawyers to the public representation of church bodies; eventually it was extended by English civil lawyers, influenced by church law, to the representative bodies now called parliaments.[11] The generalizations and rationalizations through which *quod omnes tangit* and related concepts expanded outward from probate law to parliaments can be seen as responses to the continuing problem of forging one common policy out of thousands of private grievances—a problem of coordination.

While the details of medieval law and parliamentary custom are intricate and beyond this book's scope, a few key themes seem uncontroversial and particularly instructive.

First, public business arose out of private rights (legal rights, not natural). Q.o.t. was essentially a due process notion: if the accustomed distribution of rights was challenged by an authority, those who previously had possession of rights were entitled to defend the previous arrangement and to demand that the public power give an account of why change was being required. The medieval way of conceptualizing these matters was in this way initially conservative and legalistic. But one can easily see how an updated version could readily translate matters from property rights to economic and social interests in ways that would allow for compromise and bargaining, and might also discard the backward-looking bias that tilts the scale in favor of status-quo interests.[12] Arguably, modern representative government became possible through this translation: an individual entitlement to defend one's legal rights expanded into an entitlement to participate in negotiating both minor adjustments in the adjudication of interests and, occasionally, major changes in the definition of which interests would be publicly recognized and promoted.[13]

Second, for political purposes it became clear—that is, public lawyers insistent that public business be done made it their business to render it clear—that the "all" that were affected were not individuals but corporate groups or communities. That is what made it possible for a majority to bind the rest rather than a rule of unanimity frustrating all change. Initially, the communities represented in proto-parliamentary processes included what would now seem economic or ethnic communities—the King treated with representatives of the Jews, and with the merchants of certain towns, for special taxes. But eventually, these special communities dropped away (in the case of the Jews literally; they were expelled *en masse* in 1290, five years before Edward's famous writ), and the only communities represented in the civil parliament were geographic ones.[14]

Crucially, the shires—geographic units roughly equivalent to the United States' counties—had long been recognized as being the right kind of communal and corporate unit, the kind capable of being represented, as a whole, with one voice. (So were the boroughs, which were later called towns, though as compact and self-consciously vulnerable urban centers these present in some sense an easier case.) Since time immemorial, meaning no later than 1166, shires had been regarded as the kind of bodies that could authorize representatives.[15] Scholars seem to take one of two positions on why this was. One portrays shires as quasi-natural. A shire was regarded as a true *communitas*, "an organic body with common knowledge."[16] The shires were considered as unified bodies by canon law, which may or may not have been widely recognized. More to the point, they were perceived as units in the sentimental and subjective life of residents, forged by common experiences and senses of place and boundary:

> Both shires and towns were, in fact, real communities in the sense that they had self-consciousness, self-government, and self-purpose; and the composition of the House of Commons in the later middle ages quite exceptionally reflected the reality. The knights and burgesses could speak for the realm because the areas which they represented covered both territory and opinion to a remarkable degree.[17]

On another account, local communities were more pragmatic or fictive in origin. It behooved a borough or locality to take on a corporate identity to facilitate the granting of legal privileges and the ability to defend local interests with one voice. Representation on the basis of community was a "convenient fiction" that worked because those communities tracked familiar legal jurisdictions that long preceded political representation.[18] Helen Maud Cam argues that the natural logic of representation—a group that has reached "an agreement on action" will choose one to act for the whole—suggests that corporate representation of all kinds could have had common-law or traditional roots, and might not have required a canon-law justification that probably came later. Representation will be invented whenever there "is an active community upon which some external demand is made."[19]

Both historical interpretations could be given congenial Humean readings. The first would correspond to Hume's view that conventions are generally found, not made; the second, to his emphasis that conventions are artificial rather than organic or cosmic in origin: their goodness tracks their advantages. The fictive reading of shire identity in no way discredits the reading that stresses communities of local feeling, though it may breed a sense of irony toward those communities' origins and justification. As with the artificial virtues, artificial communities can come to *seem* natural, and there is nothing wrong with this: the stability of convention is greatly enhanced by practices of mutually teaching and internalizing conventions rather than always calculating them. We now recognize that even business corporations, which everyone knows to be useful fictions, not organic essences, can solve coordination problems through fostering a corporate culture in which employees sincerely believe.[20]

Shire and borough representation had certain conceptual advantages in finessing the transition away from feudal theories of governance.[21] Of more contemporary interest, however, the concept of local unity solved collective action problems by allowing representatives to speak, deliberate, and bargain for their shires and boroughs as a whole, not just in their own name or even just the name of those in the community who had supported their election. When a parliament met, the representatives were not seen as speaking for certain individuals in their communities rather than others; rather, "the communities *were there, by proxy.*"[22] And just as a corporate attorney can influence momentous decisions by virtue of speaking on behalf of a great body rather than for himself, the commons asserted its supremacy over the peers by claiming that the magnates spoke only for themselves, while the knights spoke "for their shire."[23] It is not clear that modern theories of district-based representation—whether philosophical or folk—have a coherent theory that does better than this one at explaining why those who voted against their current representative (or did not vote) should regard laws passed by the assembly of representatives as authoritative or binding on them.[24]

This brings up a third aspect of medieval theory. The powers held by members of parliament—that is, the common members, though the commons were not yet deemed a formal "House"—were what we would call powers of attorney: a full power within the sphere of representation, but for limited purposes.[25] (The medieval phrase was *plena potestas*: the representative— originally called a *procurator*, whence our "proxy," had "full power" to decide on the principal's behalf.[26]) The community could not disown the attorney's act. The Member of Parliament, as he was later called, was authorized not merely to negotiate and bring the terms of a deal back to his community, but to *settle* business on authority already granted.

The logic here is clear and unusually powerful. The monarch needed a parliament that was empowered to act on authority of the communities it represented, lest calling it not be worth the effort. But because parliament both consented to crucial public goods and potentially allocated those goods in asymmetric ways, each community also had an interest in giving its representative full power, lest its own interests and grievances be neglected by a body impatient to consult only those who had authority to decide. The interests of monarchs and communities coincided, and soon found a legal justification. This explanation also makes sense of the fact that MPs' power of attorney was for limited purposes (in Clarke's words, "both temporary and general"[27]). The knights and burgesses who eventually were styled members of parliament had full power "to do what shall be ordained by the common counsel" *and nothing else*: not, for instance, to accede to the arbitrary command of a king or baron, nor to engage in legal or financial business that would have bound their communities under private law.[28] Where the communities' interest in *plena potestas* ended—that is, where there was no permanent advantage to be gained by empowering a proxy—so did the power of attorney and the theory of public law that justified it.

Thus, parliaments involved an unusually effective feedback loop between necessity and distributional interests. Public business needed to be done.

Monarchs needed widespread agreement to taxation in order to do it, and cared more that it be done than about the details of distributing or implementing public goods decisions. On the other hand each community had, in accord with collective action theory but without needing such a theory, only a small interest in contributing to the public good. But it had an intense interest, for distributional reasons (given competition with other communities), in electing one or more representatives and giving them full backing once they were elected, giving them free rein to negotiate and decide. Once the communities did that, however, mutual surveillance in parliament guaranteed that no representative could avoid responsibility for the public good. None could claim a particular right to exempt his own community because all knew that all had been present and had had an equal chance to debate and dissent before deciding. The system united with remarkable efficiency the executive's interest in power and national security, the communities' interest in a fair distribution of burdens and benefits, and the public interest in avoiding free riders.

Parliamentary Equality: Mutual Advantage and Consent as Political Practice

Hume's Third Theory of Justice

Brian Barry, arguing (as most social and political philosophers who read Hume do) exclusively from Hume's *Treatise* and second *Enquiry*, has argued that Hume has two theories of justice. One appeals to mutual advantage; the other, to impartiality. The mutual advantage theory, which limits the scope of justice to those who can affect our interests, is, on Barry's view, not about justice at all. "Justice is normally thought of not as ceasing to be relevant in conditions of extreme inequality in power but, rather, as being especially relevant to such conditions." A theory of justice worth the name is only to be found in what Barry calls Hume's second theory of justice: when we seek to arrive at moral judgments in common with others, our private opinions, which characteristically give great weight to our "particular interest," must alter and adapt so that they can be justified in terms of "general interests."[29] But by leaving out Hume's *History*, his only book about politics, Barry neglects a third alternative. What might be called "parliamentary equality"—or parliamentary justice, if one wants to apply the term where Hume would not—occupies a principled middle ground between "mutual advantage" and rational "justification."

Parliamentary justice is a kind of mutual advantage theory; "common profit" was the formula, starting in the medieval era, for that about which parliament deliberated.[30] But it is not the kind of mutual advantage theory whose vulnerability to asymmetries of power prompts despair that the result will track "justice" as we normally use the word. Notoriously, advantage in private deals respects equality in only the narrowest formal sense. The parties equally have the right to make a deal or to walk away, but since the stronger party has more resources to contribute to any common effort and can weather the costs of non-agreement much more easily, it can leverage its power to force the weaker into desperate bargains. The resulting relationship neither embodies equal status nor is likely to result in fair outcomes. But the workings of a representative assembly, while still based on power, work very differently in two respects.

First, representative assemblies typically assume, and require for their functioning, a permanent political equality among all representatives.[31] (That is: each representative in congress or parliament gets one vote, none more than one.) In chapter 4, I noted how the royal "principle of authority" allowed for a legal and constitutional order independent of personal strength and aggressiveness. Over time the principle came to allow subjects to enjoy the blessings of legal order without having to defer to accidents of baronial blood. Through parliamentary representation, something similar could occur in legislation. *Quod omnes*, when worked out by canon lawyers, meant that in a decision involving a religious corporation, an attorney or other agent must be appointed either by the whole corporation or at least with its consent (depending on whether the interests of the whole or primarily those of the prelate were at issue), not by the head of the order or chapter.[32] Since the clerical officer—an abbot, Dean, or the like—remained higher in ecclesiastical rank, *quod omnes* was a serious though indirect attack on the privileges of that rank when it came to dealings with outsiders. The parallel triumph of the doctrine *maior pars* ("greater part"), which defined a corporate body's will as the vote of a majority of its members rather than as the decision of its head, was similarly epochal. *Maior pars* embodied a slow revolution, first in canon law as applied to religious chapters and then with respect to civil representation (both in the selection of knights and burgesses by electors and with respect to these representatives' voting rule in parliament). Without the canonists, we would lack "majority" rule as a normative concept. Here again, majority rule originally applied only to corporate bodies. Individuals could not be deprived of a right (in person or property) or a privilege unless they personally consented, but a right attaching to a corporation of any kind could be ceded or traded with the consent of a majority.[33]

Second, parliaments are committed to *agreement*, at least on budgets and expenditures. The parties to a private bargain may threaten to walk away. The legislative assembly member who does the same typically just loses the chance to affect the outcome. This structural and conceptual difference between public and private bargains is related to the previous one. Without a majority decision rule, public business involves an imperative to agree. But that imperative then works against political equality rather than for it, giving imperious minorities the means to insist on horizontal inequalities as the price of their consent to public business. To cite one prominent formal theorist,

In all cases where justice or the general good might require new laws to be passed, or active measures to be pursued, the fundamental principle of free government would be reversed. It would be no longer the majority that would rule: the power would be transferred to the minority. Were the defensive privilege limited to particular cases, an interested minority might take advantage of it to screen themselves from equitable sacrifices to the general weal, or, in particular emergencies, to extort unreasonable indulgences.[34]

The two-thirds rule favored by those who want politics to resemble private, Pareto-optimal transactions[35] can be criticized (as Barry criticized it) precisely for mirroring their flaws.

Another Individualism: Making Consent Work

Jeremy Waldron once defined liberalism as the idea that "all aspects of the social order should either be made acceptable or be capable of being made acceptable to every last individual." The determination to ground legitimate government on such acceptability, or loosely "consent," reflects the need to address two concerns at once: the "individual need for control" and the "desirability of our interaction with others." (In politics, these are articulated as "liberty and autonomy" on the one hand and the "potential gains from social cooperation" on the other.) The goal is "a basis on which these gains can be realized without any serious threat to freedom."[36]

Unfortunately, universal consent is not to be had. Requiring that legitimate government gain the consent of literally all would prevent there being any government. Hypothetical or rational consent—the "capable of being made acceptable" above—prevents this problem but creates another: It threatens to render government completely illegitimate in the eyes of those whose goals or self-conceptions do not mirror the ones that the theorist attributes to all rational beings (for instance the formal goal of being able to pursue a conception of the good on an individual basis without prejudice to others' doing the same).[37] Rationalist liberals are typically troubled by this problem but determined to forge on. One method is to define as "unreasonable" those whose goals differ too much from those they find appropriate. (In its more honest versions this solution abandons the aspiration to neutrality.) Another, characteristic of multicultural liberals, is to carve out special exemptions, where possible, for those whose plans of life are not liberal. Both these solutions, however, obscure the fact that the original goal was not neutrality but *legitimacy* or general acceptability. To the extent that a self-styled liberal government explicitly either failed to represent the wills of some citizens or failed to give some citizens reasons they could acknowledge as valid, it would lack legitimate authority over those left out, whether its defenders responded to this lack by bullying the dissenters or by flattering them. For it would have professed a universal consent standard for legitimacy while professedly falling well short of that standard.

Niklas Luhmann, in response to Jürgen Habermas' problems along similar lines, cites *quod omnes tangit* in an ironic mode. Since what touches all will never really be approved by all, we should give up on Kantian or ideal forms of liberalism and focus on studying the kinds of reasons that people really use and the empirical ways in which actual social structures gain legitimacy.[38] Jan-Werner Müller, noting a similar impasse in the debate between John Rawls' "neutrality" and Ronald Dworkin's "autonomy," proposes that liberalism re-examine its relationship to the Kantian aspiration that all government measures be justifiable to each citizen: "internal critics of liberalism might have explored other liberal traditions."[39] Humean parliamentarism is one such tradition. It grounds a mitigated and benignly fictive form of universal consent in mutual advantage—subject to institutionalized challenges, on the basis of political equality, to how the State proposes to cash out that concept—rather than in autonomy.[40]

Again one might start with Hume's master formula regarding good government: "limited . . . authority and conditional allegiance."[41] In the case of parliamentary elections, this formula was not the product of Humean theory but closely tracked political reality. A version of the formula was explicitly agreed to: it was in the writs that monarchs issued to call parliaments. The liberal (but not only liberal) justificationists' idea that one subject should not be bound by the decision of another was recognized, but in a mode defined by both form and custom so that it constrained both authority and choice, avoiding the extremes of raw coercion and philosophical anarchy. The king issued writs for calling a parliament under a claim of necessity (*necessitas*, a technical Roman/canon-law term) "by which all subjects were obliged to contribute when the welfare or existence of the realm was endangered." (*Quod omnes* had a flip side: what touched all *should be approved* by all, though the details and direction of the approval could be negotiated.)[42] Those officials were bound to call an election but not required to bring electors to the polls, nor to support the King's program. The electors were free not to attend—at the pain of having no influence on the outcome. If the electors did show up, they could elect whom they chose on the condition of agreeing to be bound by any decisions their representatives might arrive at in concert with their fellow MPs. The members of parliament could approve the king's requests (usually for money but sometimes for other legislation), disapprove them, or vote for some outcome in between, on the condition that they agreed that a non-unanimous vote, soon resolved into a majority vote, would be binding, given the claims of urgency. Over time, such grants were of course made conditional on all sorts of petitions regarding rights and property; this was not only the origin of civil rights but a substantial check against monarchs who would call parliaments, and claim urgency, without cause. The only choice that was never available was to ignore the king's assertion of urgency, neither approving nor disapproving it, while neither voting for a representative in parliament nor (if elected as such a representative) attending parliament. But one might reasonably ask whether the freedom to do *that* was ever morally praiseworthy. The system was imperfect and built in many assumptions. But as a way of combining universal consent with necessary authority, it embodied an evolved, institutional brilliance.

The previous statement perhaps overstresses the claim of necessity at the expense of the substance of parliamentary conditions; it takes up what I have described as the monarch's standpoint.[43] But one can tell the same story in terms of subjects' interests, from the bottom up. Here I follow, or attempt to follow, Clarke: "The theory of consent was generally admitted, but, on the one hand, it was impossible to secure unanimity and, on the other, it was impossible to consult all persons whose interests were involved."[44] The story is complicated, but seems to be this: customary taxes started to seem illegitimate given that the individuals' consent had not been given. It was actually advantageous for boroughs (Clarke here neglects shires) to be able to consent to taxation. For they could get something from the king, namely liberties, in return for consent—but could get nothing from obstinate refusal. Therefore it was the *local bodies* that were eager to say that the consent of representatives sent to Westminster bound the whole. We may, though Clarke of course does not, compare this to the modern economic doctrine that the ability to be bound by a contract is a great economic advantage, allowing one to strike deals that would never be reached if everyone knew they could be easily backed out of.

On this story, we are attributing something to citizens in common. We have a universal interest not in autonomy or the pursuit of the good but in liberty (with respect to the king but also private actors, as Hume stressed though Clarke doesn't) and in national defense. As the theory, and more important the practice, developed, it became natural to recognize a common interest in being able to obtain what we take to be our rightful share of goods that are public but can be unequally distributed: schools, roads, and so on, and on the negative side, taxes. The picture just painted—government tries to exercise sovereignty and asks for resources to do that, and we are able to have our say on its plans and its taxes to the extent that we vote and demonstrate our good faith in abiding by the results of votes—seems close to ordinary citizens' view of what government does and how citizens can influence it.[45] The high-liberal or neo-Kantian view that society is a scheme of mutual cooperation directed toward giving everyone an equal ability to pursue his or her conception of the good seems somewhat further from that.

Shaping Coordination: "Participation at Sovereign Command"

John Roskell defined the role and purpose of early parliamentarism as "participation in government at the sovereign's command."[46] If this is an excellent summary of parliaments, it is also an excellent summary of both coordination solutions—the command—and the role of parliamentary equality or justice in addressing the horizontal inequality to which those solutions give rise. To a striking extent, the ways in which Roskell and his colleagues and students have been able to make sense of parliamentary theory can be rephrased in the language of coordination problems.

Royal government through the course of the thirteenth century saw, says one of these scholars,

> a dramatic increase in the scope of government which impinged on the interests of a substantially wider sector of the community but at the same time provided facilities for subjects to assert and defend their rights. This is the context in which parliament came to fulfill its unique function as both an instrument of royal government and the voice of the community.[47]

The development of parliamentary practices from 1295 onward increased the power of, but one could argue did not revolutionize in theory, a body that characteristically "reviewed, co-ordinated and decided matters which had often originated elsewhere."[48] Even in the fourteenth century, parliament could not generally oppose taxation demanded for a war, nor even attach strong political demands to the grant, but could "safeguard their rights and limit their commitments" on the occasion of being called to register their approval. Parliament, even when it was an assembly of nobles rather than common representatives, had always had the "dual character of an organ of royal government and the instrument through which the magnates might place constraints upon the king. These apparently conflicting roles were in fact complementary aspects of its essential purpose, to further the business and common good of the realm."[49] Even the formula that currently represents British sovereign authority, "the Queen (or King) in Parliament," represents what we might call mitigated coordination: a "single (mixed) sovereign body."[50]

The kind of equality that results from such a theory is, as stated, a limited-purpose equality. All politically relevant members of the polity (on which more below) are equally able to shape the government's course of action. But they cannot change the form of government, the agents of government, or even the agenda of government—except by placing conditions on an agenda already set. This is equality expressed in a power to deliberate and correct, not directly to act. But as G. R. Elton points out, the "whiggish blinkers" that lead some to value parliament's historical role only to the extent that it confronted monarchs, pitting the people's liberties against royal prerogatives, can blind us to parliament's value in another role: as a participant in, and shaper of, public business. Elton persuasively argues that the English parliament survived and became a body that monarchs could not do without precisely because it generally said *yes* to royal demands. Continental parliaments ended up resembling their name—bodies that *parlent* (speak)—quite literally. They *only* talked, predictably and constantly asserted that ancient rights had been violated, and never gave consent to government action. They therefore came to be safely and wisely ignored by monarchs who found, out of necessity, other ways of enlisting money and popular support behind their measures.[51] Parliamentary equality succeeds by stealth, and builds up more and more power, because it never threatens the existence of authority or its ultimate exercise while always, and more thoroughly over time, constraining how it operates and whom it favors.

The Progress of Peerage: The Expansion of Political Classes

The principle that what touches all should be treated by all may seem obvious once promulgated. But the question remains of who counts as being "touched" by a decision. This question is neither empirical nor logical but a matter of political controversy. To answer it is to define the political class, the set of people who are seen to make up the politically relevant population rather than being rightly subordinated to it. Elton, like Hume, is deeply impressed by the way economic and social forces gradually transformed the concept of a feudal kingdom based on ties between monarch and barons (the body politic being the head and the noble peers the members[52]) into that of a *communitas Anglie* set up on a more inclusive and increasingly Commons-led basis. He stresses clearly that the political nation reflected in parliamentary practice meant "all political interests": "those interests powerful and concerned enough to engage in the activities which constituted the politics of the day," whoever they were and came to be.[53] When the theory of *quod omnes* was first being used to argue that the representatives of a chapter were to be chosen by all the clergy who made it up, the laity over whom the clergy claimed spiritual authority (and often economic authority: the clergy ran the poorhouses) were never consulted. What a chapter "was," conceptually, was what we might call the upper religious "class," not the lower; proto-democratic ideas applied only *within* the former.[54] "The feudal doctrine of consent was drawn out of the contracts of individuals; the ecclesiastical doctrine arose out of the professional privilege of an international body, claiming superiority over the whole of secular society."[55]

But Hume's most central thesis about parliamentarism is that it is hard for a political class to keep out new members. Political power will eventually track social power, and the forms and practices of parliamentary representation smooth the way. Public opinion came to be of account (a threat even to kings), and laws something of more than paper value, as a result of "the gradual progress of arts in England, as well as in other parts of Europe" (H 2.439). To recap Hume's story: what we would now call technological change in the late middle ages led to new occupations that challenged the pre-eminence of military men (nearly always men); the progress of the market led barons to prefer consumer goods to "rustic hospitality" and command of personal armies; this both undermined nobles' ability to challenge general laws and rendered money rents more popular than villainage because they were more profitable (H 2.522–4, on "rustic hospitality" see H 1.463–8, 2.428). "Thus *personal* freedom became almost general in Europe; an advantage which paved the way for the encrease of *political* or *civil* liberty" (H 2.524, emphasis in original).

Parliamentarism, along with the *quod omnes* idea that it represents, are such powerful instruments of equality not because they exclude no one in principle—their principles are fully compatible with exclusion—but because they provide an obvious and peaceful mechanism for accommodating new groups in practice: the method is literally to *enfranchise* them.[56] (That is a radical, though gradual, activity. In its earliest meanings it meant either to grant someone the privileges of a city or to manumit a slave.[57]) It has often been noted that *quod omnes* blurs, or better, has little place for, the modern distinction between public and private concerns. Medieval political thought lacked a theory of "politics" or "the state" but addressed crucial matters of authority in the course of inquiries "seemingly *prima facie* 'social,' 'economic,' 'ecclesiastical' or even 'spiritual.'"[58] Clarke even argued that parliamentary lawmaking in its origins was justified as "necessary to provide a remedy for the failure of the courts to do right to all men."[59] In this instance the ambiguity is a great benefit. If political right is separated from private interests, perhaps being considered a matter of blood or else divine grace, no change in real or perceived interests can easily be translated into legitimate political power: political progress will be revolutionary, not peaceful. But if representation is seen as the rightful solution to the problem of protecting *private* interests against unjust or unequal government policy, it is hard to grant legal rights (or social rights, which will look like much the same thing) without eventual political legitimacy. And legal rights—in particular, effective access to, and protection by, the property convention—are the kind of things that elites will find it difficult, over time, not grant. For they are very, very good for business.

While Hume never explicitly puts forth the above line of thinking, he repeatedly practices it. The reason that Magna Charta "without seeming anywise to innovate in the distribution of political power, became a kind of epoch in the constitution" and brought the government "a little nearer to that end, for which it was originally instituted, the distribution of justice, and the equal protection of the citizens" was partly a matter of personal security but more specifically a matter of declaring that everyone's injuries mattered as a matter of public concern:

> Acts of violence and iniquity in the crown, which before were only deemed injurious to individuals, and were hazardous chiefly in propor-
> tion to the number, power, and dignity of the persons affected by them, were now regarded, in some degree, as public injuries, and as infringe-
> ments of a charter, calculated for general security. (H 1.488)

This was as yet tentative and theoretical, but later developments were more concrete. The "new plan of liberty" that culminated in 1689, founded on "the privileges of the commons," had its roots in economic causes. The barons' desire for luxury led them to prefer paying tenants to armed retainers; cities swelled their population with the hands thereby made redundant, and via the protection of Kings; "the middle rank of men began to be rich and powerful" (H 4.384–5). Again, subtle and apparently private causes, not alterations in formal institutions, had profound political effects. "[T]he change of manners" (social causes, as we would now say)

> was the chief cause of the secret revolution of government, and subverted the power of the barons. There appears in this reign [Elizabeth I's] some remains of the ancient slavery of boors and peasants, but none afterwards. (H 4.385)[60]

This is true in particular of the House of Commons, whose preponderant power in the English government stems from the wealth it came to represent due to economic growth:

> The lower house is the support of our popular government; and all the world acknowledges, that it owed its chief influence and consideration to the encrease of commerce, which threw such a balance of property into the hands of the commons.[61]

As noted earlier, social and economic causes (as we would now call them) are not in themselves enough to ensure peaceful change and political progress. The public will regard assertions to power by new social groups to be "usurpations" unless the constitution gives a "share of power, though small," to those who have come to have that power. If that small share exists, "it is easy for them gradually to stretch their authority, and bring the balance of power to coincide with that of property. This has been the case with the house of commons [sic] in ENGLAND."[62] Though Hume did not live to see it, he would not have been at all surprised to learn that the Third Estate in France found peaceful change a far more difficult proposition than it was for non-nobles in England, given that that Estate's constitutional status in France was novel in the eyes of everyone living, and had been effaced by centuries of absolutist prescription. (Similarly, though not using the same language, John Danford sees Hume's stress on the rediscovery of Justinian's *Pandects* in the twelfth century as involving a "trigger" theory. Those who preferred civil to military occupations needed a non-feudal source of legitimacy to grant them license to hold property on non-feudal grounds. In Roman Law, they got it.[63])

As noted, Hume did not continue the story, but we can. In the case of class, Harvey Chisick has shown that Hume's contempt for the poor was founded partly on the same Greek and Latin classics that brought so many of his educated contemporaries to despise "the rabble," but partly on hard sociological realism: the poor were ignorant and unreflective because they needed all waking hours to pursue subsistence.[64] Chisick notes that Hume's "Perfect Commonwealth" essay, by envisioning a franchise based exclusively on wealth, "was, in the context of the time, progressive" in being based purely on a kind of ability. For in Hume's time the privilege of birth still played a major role in determining political rights.[65] One might add that it was progressive in a temporal as well as an evaluative sense. The fact that Hume's dismissal of the common people as political agents was based on their situation rather than their birth suggests that as their economic condition improved and their education and leisure increased, their political status would legitimately increase as well.

In the case of women, Annette Baier has suggested that Hume was saved from casting women outside the circle of justice only by his recognition of men's self-interest in procreation; she implies that Hume was counseling women to adopt a *Lysistrata* solution to their social and political weakness.[66] Whether or not she is right about that—I would claim that Hume is talking about men's interest not just in sex but in society and companionship with women[67]—this all presupposes, as Baier notes, that women are both tied down by childrearing and cut off from paid work (so that they are dependent on men for their own subsistence and their children's). Given that Hume's theory is, regarding sex as well as class, one based on "station" or "situation" rather than inborn inequality of talent, it is not hard to construct a theory for how typewriters and reliable contraception would change the bargaining situation.[68]

In none of these cases is economics short-term destiny. Under a "pretence" theory of constitutional change, a widely held ascriptive prejudice of why a certain group cannot in principle participate in government can delay that group's progress a very long time. (Compare the relative length of time it took to obtain voting rights for many working-class white men on the one hand and for African Americans in the U.S. South on the other.) Still, on these matters the fluid and geographical theory of government represented by parliamentarism seems at least no less likely than other theories to allow for entry into the electoral class. Kant thought that political rights should be based on reason; Bentham, on the capacity to have interests and feel happiness or unhappiness. But Kant solved the problem of women and the poor by saying that the former were mentally different from men and the latter necessarily dependent on employers. Bentham was more consistent, but many seemed able to follow Bentham while blithely rejecting his support for democracy and (quietly) for women's suffrage. There is one way of describing the politically disenfranchised that is inherently hard to rationalize away: the class of people who can strike bargains with the state, by contributing to the workforce and the support of public goods if the state gives them a say in its decisions, and staying home (or sitting in, or breaking windows) if not.[69]

Conclusion: Humean Equality, Convention, and Autonomy

When it comes to political equality, Hume's scheme provides, once again, an alternative to Kantian liberalism. It shares some of liberalism's greatest goals but denies the grounds on which those goals are often said to rest. Humean theory is liberal in the contemporary sense (the political meaning of liberal was not current in Hume's time) in a great many meanings of that word. It denies natural hierarchy. It does not believe in religion, tradition, or non-instrumental authority, and it praises reform and progress in the realm of policy and society.[70] But it denies the existence of natural rights, autonomy, the social contract, the right of revolution (except in truly extraordinary cases), popular sovereignty, and Reason as any but an instrumental faculty. In politics, at any rate, Hume's proto-liberalism starts from the advantages to be gained from a common government carrying out a common program (meaning no more or less than one approved by the accepted authority). It becomes more proto-liberal, if that means favorable to liberty and equality, in welcoming the development of institutions that consult every member of society on the content and direction of that program—as well as on its extent, given that common projects compete with private ones. To the extent that Hume favors liberty and can be stretched to favor equality, he does so by calling on excluded or neglected interests to have their grievances heard and accommodated in parliamentary debate, rather than pretending that we can aim at a rational order in which no grievances worth the name will exist. There will always be grievances as long as people disagree on how much government will do and on what basis it will be paid for.

There is no space here to argue that the things that Hume failed to believe in merited his disbelief (though in the Conclusion I will suggest reasons to believe that *political* theory and practice can dispense with them). On the current point we might argue from experience rather than a priori and note that Humean political theory assumes a different paradigm or model of political life than Kantian theory. The former takes as a model a large, diverse society in which individuals and communities that differ in their opinions, interests, or sentiments must reach agreement, or at least acquiescence, in a common assembly in order to produce public goods and give all an equal and palpable stake in the process that produces them. A deliberative or autonomy-based view takes as the paradigm of political right primitive city-states, or sometimes the "civic" republics that expanded on that form, or as a final possibility the Stoic "cosmopolis" that sought to extend the political and intellectual unity and equality of the *polis* to accommodate all humankind. Under any of these models, the political realm as a whole is required to have a single will grounded in reason, or at the very least in agreement on the proper modes of non-negotiable action that are supposed to sustain citizens in their common life.

I submit that diverse modern societies are more hospitable to the former idea than the latter. Our aspirations and self-definitions diverge much more than rationalists or critical theorists posit that they should. And the resulting gains in economic and cultural dynamism, not to mention individual choice and the chance to fulfill diverse, particular projects, are too precious to be worth risking for the sake of a rational legitimacy or civic unity to which few actual citizens feel any calling to aspire.

Glossing the admittedly unorthodox William of Ockham, Antonio Marongiu has portrayed *quod omnes tangit* as a formula for reconciling public business with private interests:

> Q.o.t. is therefore the foundation of the best organized collectivity, in which the sovereign, or indeed the public power in general, can demand of citizens what is strictly necessary for accomplishing its institutional purposes without depriving them of their liberty, their goods, their rights.[71]

Of Ockham's direct application of the q.o.t. formula to politics, he asks simply: "could one have a clearer expression of democracy?"[72]

Conclusion

On the account given so far, Hume's account of authority, and the politics of authority, is at root quite simple. Governmental authority is the product of conventions. It persists because of our universal interest in observing those conventions. It faces a crisis when governing conventions are not yet stable or when transitions between one convention and another are taking place (due to social, economic, or cultural changes that have unsettled the old ones or made new ones seem imaginable for the first time). Government is universally necessary in the first instance as the only actor that can settle disputes about property (and by implication other disputed conventions); once in place, it also furthers public goods of all kinds and is perceived to be ever more necessary the more it does that. All these things being obvious, either prospectively or retro-spectively, the main problem individual actors face is not whether to support government at all, but which among more than one plausible government to support: they face a coordination problem (chapter 1). The pre-history of stable government (conceptually, not quite chronologically; it occurs in spurts and stages during the long period in which proto-modern governments are finding their footing) involves the acknowledgment by key actors and social groups that they can achieve more of what they value through large-scale conventions of peace and prosperity than through enjoying domination and glory on a smaller scale. Once modern governments have been in place for many genera-tions, most relevant citizens and political groupings recognize this. Those who don't still end up better off, though ungratefully so, than they would be under medieval poverty and near-anarchy (chapter 2). That done, coordination prob-lems can be, and in lucky countries are, solved by conventions that establish "authority" if looking at a whole system or from the top down, or "allegiance" if one is considering individual virtues from the bottom up. Keeping the conventional status of authority and allegiance in mind reveals that "government" and "people" are not two separate things but two different ways of looking at the same thing, namely the tendency of a group of people to follow the directives of magistrates or political officers who gain and hold power according to express or tacit rules that are commonly accepted (chapter 3). Because ways of solving coordination problems by what I have called "primitive" methods—focal points or local common knowledge—are limited with respect to space and unstable with respect to time, successful politics must develop what I have called "fundamental conventions" that define the rules for choosing government officials and limiting governmental authority; in England those fundamental conventions are hereditary monarchy and Magna Charta (chapter 4). Questions of crisis leadership are best understood as attempts to address contradictions both within and between these conventions (chapter 5). As coordination problems involve the potential for both what I have called "vertical" inequality (tyranny by the governors) and "horizontal inequality" (solutions that differentially benefit different social groups), it is extraordinarily desirable, though not strictly necessary for governmental authority, that some sort of legislature develop to check the power of the magistrates and reflect the demands of emerging social groups. Liberty and equality are therefore late-emerging though very welcome refinements of governmental conventions rather than natural or pre-political attributes of isolated individuals (chapters 6–7).

This story—the one suggested both by Hume's theory and by his philosophical *History*, which if both theory and history are based on evidence should come to the same thing—is both coherent and comprehensive. Properly developed, it would answer many big questions about politics, both causal and normative: the nature of authority and leadership, the basis for and justification of formal and informal constitutional norms, the difference between modern and ancient government, the proper standards for political ethics, the status of liberty and equality and their relationship to government and order. It would also have a great deal to say about questions of "origin" or "foundation" that can confusingly seem to be both causal and normative—though Hume, once he comes to consider the question thoroughly in his later work, suggests that origins and foundations are two radically different things. The reasons for government and the ways in which it promotes our purposes are best seen not at government's birth but in its maturity.

The account, admittedly, leaves out many things, in fact most things, that appear in Hume's *History* on the one hand and the world of politics on the other. It follows one simple explanation of an endlessly complex political and historical world (though with the excuse that government itself is a universally useful mechanism for keeping this complexity from defeating all of our long-term and sophisticated projects). What the account leaves out on the empirical side is obvious: the whole study of social forces and large-scale causes that I have called science (1) and that modern social science and history have carried far beyond anything Hume could have achieved. As said, Hume's formal or strategic political science, which I have called science (2), is the only part of his science that we should expect to have lasting relevance.

As a political theorist (in the traditional sense, not the one that means a producer and consumer of formal models), my main concern is with questions of political value: the standards for political judgment and action. The question then is whether the story presented here culpably fails to address crucial problems of value. I submit that it does not. One reason Hume's political theory is so important is that it shows how we can put forth and justify a set of evaluative standards for political life without making any reference to the concepts normally regarded as necessary for doing so: autonomy, justifications that no one could reasonably reject, dignity, hypothetical consent, social and distributive justice. In this conclusion I shall briefly suggest why Hume's striking theory is both viable and good, and his rejection of these concepts, for political purposes, not inappropriate.

In effect, I shall be explaining some continuing implications of a very old debate. Hume's attack on an older, Lockean form of social contract theory—an account that portrayed actual consent as unlikely, tacit consent as incoherent, and neither one as necessary, since governments are supported by opinion and are justified by their furtherance of common advantage—is famous. After reading it in Hume's *Treatise* Bentham "felt as if scales had fallen from [his] eyes" and judged that the "chimera" of the original contract had been "effectually demolished" (metaphor was not Bentham's forte).[1] Christopher Berry has argued that this forced later social contract theory to take its current form: hypothetical, based on exploring what rational citizens *would* agree to, and not particularly interested in actual consent.[2]

But Hume's account of politics poses a different type of threat to modern, mutated contract theory as well. Unlike Lockean or Whig accounts of contract, hypothetical contract theory cannot be refuted empirically. (Such is its genius: it's a closed system.) But it can be, in a rough sense, superseded or outcompeted if an alternative account of political value and judgment is shown to do all that it can and more, while avoiding some difficulties that it faces. Humean political theory provides such an alternative.[3] Though the following can only outline its implications, Hume's treatment of most questions of political value is, given its coherence and comprehensiveness, potentially, and to a great extent actually, a systematic alternative to hypothetical consent and its brethren. Vindicating its relevance and validity as an alternative, however, requires going beyond what Hume said and defending his theory against allegedly superior alternatives (some, but not all, Kantian or neo-Kantian) that came after him.

The Liberalism of Enlargement versus the Liberalism of Dignity

Hume famously denied the distinction between moral and nonmoral virtues, in other words, between moral qualities and talents: "[w]ho did ever say, except by way of irony, that such a one was a man of great virtue, but an egregious blockhead?" (EPM App. 4.2.23–5, SBN 314). This stance entails more than is commonly understood. Once we refuse to give one human virtue pride of place over all others, we lose the rationale for privileging one human *capacity* over another, or for judging the moral and political world exclusively by how it accommodates one human demand or aspiration, given that there are others. More concretely, a Humean polity cannot be one in which we judge citizens exclusively by their tendency to show one another respect, or in which we judge a political order by its tendency to grant recognition.

It is a striking fact about those who assume that politics must be about autonomy or respect that they rarely defend the Kantian metaphysics that would render that assumption plausible. (If they do defend it, they have to admit that the basis for their political demands is opaque to many, some would say most, fellow citizens.)[4] Similarly, the "politics of recognition" has Hegelian origins but hardly posits rigorous Hegelian arguments. It has rightly been seen as growing out of both the transition from ancient honor to modern dignity (positing, a bit too quickly it might seem, that the former no longer speaks to us) and a contemporary cult of authenticity[5]—in other words, from an eclectic mixture of components that seem scarcely compatible if we were to take the foundational arguments seriously.

Since the politics of dignity or recognition—the liberal and communitarian positions that at least until recently have divided up the terrain of normative political theory—cannot reliably rest on rationalist grounds, many have sought to support them by adducing alternative, sentimentalist arguments for them. Something like the politics of recognition could be—and on one account, actually was by Adam Smith—arrived at by combining the universal passion of vanity with Smithian sympathy (whereby I imagine your hurt at being insulted by me or others). And something akin to neo-Kantian impartiality, though in a form that more fully engages our passions, can be arrived at by combining Hume's somewhat different theory of sympathy with his account of how our moral and esthetic judgments can and should be improved.[6]

But such projects, however ingenious, beg the question of why it makes sense to give dignity, impartiality, and recognition such a disproportionate role in our politics once we doubt that "reason" places them above other values. From a Humean perspective, to be sure, vanity (the raw material, on the sentimentalist view, of dignity and recognition) is "a social passion, and a bond of union among men" (T 3.2.2.12, SBN 491). It is a passion that almost all people attempt to satisfy, and their attempts to satisfy it are likely to benefit others by motivating attempts on their part to become more useful or agreeable to others. But it is only *one* such passion among many others. Along with vanity as the common springs of human actions, Hume lists "[a]mbition, avarice, self-love, friendship, generosity, public spirit" (EHU 8.7.14, SBN 83). Commercial society provides plenty of opportunities for the complex, corrected (or channeled) satisfaction of vanity, and for actions that satisfy others' vanity,[7] but also for complex, corrected, or channeled satisfactions of ambition, friendship, generosity, and of course (but not uniquely) avarice. To place dignity or recognition above all other social goals would be to bias the society in favor of people whose ruling passion is vanity or esteem—or who are particularly gifted at engaging our sympathies toward that passion, or at making vivid the obstacles toward its satisfaction—at the expense of those whose ruling passions run elsewhere.[8]

Most of us being vain, or stated more positively, desirous of esteem, we want to achieve a certain dignity in the face of our fellows and win a certain recognition from them. But most or all of us (it does not much matter) also want wealth, peaceful forms of social power and influence, friends, family ties, a sense of contribution to larger wholes, and a sense of civic purpose. Many also yearn for the fulfillment of particular projects that are not universal and lack a place in catalogues of typical human passions but for that reason set each person proudly apart from others; such projects appeal not to all but to each. Surely the most "liberal" position is not to say, with Kant, that these other things lack all value when they conflict to any degree with dignity (i.e., socialized vanity), but to seek out a society in which peace, prosperity, and the advantages of scale render less and less frequent the necessity to choose among them. Within such a society, we may duly respect those who are greatly sensitive to the demand for recognition in themselves or others as having a perfectly legitimate but minority taste, and a specialized job waiting for them as advocates for very important civil rights.

The same goes for the deliberative democrat's sense of reciprocity, said to be founded on "the capacity to seek fair terms of social cooperation for their own sake."[9] That all of us have this capacity to some degree, and some to a very great degree, seems correct (though some economists would deny it). But there seems no reason, absent a Kantian metaphysics that most deliberative democrats seek to avoid, to demand that this capacity deserves *above all others* to be the basis for politics and social morality. The capacity to make and appreciate art, to selflessly love family members who may need special care, or to better one's economic condition also reflect capacities that are present in almost everyone, though differentially prominent in some as compared to others. All these capacities give rise to a certain weak claim, grounded on sympathy, that we welcome occasions for the capacity's fulfillment when that fulfillment does not harm others and may benefit them. And all these capacities ground not so much of universal duties or demands as particular job descriptions. Someone who possesses to an unusual degree the capacity and propensity to seek fair terms of social cooperation might do very well as a mediator, a marriage counselor, or a particularly nice kind of legislator, but there is no reason to suppose that he or she exceeds others in the ability to serve as a generic citizen. And a spectator who values that capacity to an unusual degree is engaged not in a generic and universal practice of mutual respect but in an admiration for that kind of work—an admiration which may or may not be either universal or mutual among all citizens, and does not need to be.

While the liberalism of dignity and recognition is often contrasted to utilitarianism, that of enlargement is best contrasted to communitarianism. The project of enlargement, of seeking conventions that extend ever further beyond the narrow bounds of religion, ethnicity, or culture—is directly opposed to a conservative, communitarian politics that not only glories in the narrowness of our cooperative and conversational circles but claims that intellectual and political praise for such narrowness is the basis for our humanity.[10] Hume's program is rightly seen as part of a larger Scottish effort to say that human capacities were best fulfilled not by a one-dimensional assertion of civic virtue or dignity but by commercial and cultural progress, which would allow the fuller flowering and employment of all human capacities—what Pocock has called the politics of "manners" (as opposed to virtue) and I have called a politics of enlargement. Modern republicans often accuse liberals of valuing only negative liberty, freedom from restraint. While that may be true for some, it is not true for the liberal who prizes commerce, manners, and the enlargement of human interests and projects. Such a liberal prizes societies in which "relationships and interactions with other social beings, and with their products, bec[o]me increasingly complex and various, modifying and developing more and more aspects of [one's] personality."[11]

One advantage of the manners view is that it does not require an obsession with the state.[12] On the enlargement view, our actual opportunities and the extent of our protection against arbitrary state power matter greatly, but the precise formulas that lawyers and bureaucrats choose to apply to things matter hardly at all as long as their mouthings sustain a decent set of rules (whereas for dignity theorists such formulas often matter hugely, since whether the state insults me is, by stipulation, central to my self-worth). The liberalism of manners or enlargement also allows for a relative lack of obsession with language and ideology generally. Whatever conventions work to bring more people together for their mutual benefit should be embraced, regardless of whether they express "respect" for our favored symbols. To the extent that this kind of liberalism worries about new, trans-ethnic or transnational conventions, it will be only for instrumental reasons, if it seems that new conventions might undermine the operation of more durable ones that enable a commonly acknowledged authority and that limit authority's reach, without doing the same jobs well themselves. Hume's tendency to analyze philosophical disputes as "merely verbal" and of no tangible consequence may, once again, be generalized.

The difference can be seen through the question of whether a dignified and respect-driven poverty trumps a culturally messy opportunity. One would think that no one would say, except by way of irony, that a polity does all it should to protect and promote the aspirations of its citizens if it maintains them all in equal poverty through deliberate policy, when huge gains in prosperity and choice for all—at the cost of slightly less equality in social and political status—are on offer. In fact, the former alternative persistently finds fervent defenders. In Hume's time it was necessary to attack the self-styled republican thesis that a policy of poverty would maximize Spartan civic virtue. As we have seen, Hume regarded the virtue argument as so popular that he phrased his argument that we should "comply with the common bent of mankind, and give it all the improvements of which it is susceptible" in the only terms the neo-Spartans would understand: he claimed that commerce could outdo virtuous poverty when it came to military readiness (E: C, 260).[13] In our time it has been cogently argued that Kantian considerations require maximizing fair and equal opportunity even if this means having to accept a higher incidence of poverty, since discrimination undermines "self-respect" and prevents us from being "full and equal participants in the basic structure of a well-ordered society," whereas lacking the minimum resources needed to live decently and pursue my projects does not.[14] From a Humean perspective, neither discrimination nor universal poverty may be desirable but the latter is much worse. To the extent that I am able to flourish and pursue my own projects, I can literally afford to laugh off insults. (And, as in the story of parliament's development in the last two chapters, I can over time demand, from a position of social power, that the magistrates stop pursuing policies that favor the desires that those insults reflect.)

Hume greatly prized "true liberty of thought, which engaged men of letters, however different in their abstract opinions, to maintain a mutual friendship and regard; and never to quarrel about principles, while they agreed in inclinations and manners."[15] Hume thought that only "ancient times" allowed for such liberty—faction having spoiled it for modern times—but as usual he undersold the potential of liberal democracy. The beauty of a society in which people need not affirm a particular theory of government, society, or culture provided that they observe the same conventions others do, and resist departures from them, may have great mass appeal to the culturally marginal or political inept. More generally it may appeal to those who have a greater taste for mutual exchange, the division of labor, and personal choice than for disputation in a political sphere ruled by complex cultural constraints, in which those best socialized in a specialized, sophisticated elite discourse are likely to prevail. At the risk of patriotic digression: It has been said that Hume's political theory is inconsistent with American democracy, in particular with the United States' folk doctrines of popular sovereignty.[16] Perhaps so (though whether most ordinary citizens are intellectually attached to *any* foundational theory of politics may be doubted). But the politics of dignity and recognition, in which the right kind of citizenship is said to depend not on hard work, toleration, and getting along with others—minimal requirements, easily mastered by newcomers—but on mastering complex codes that define culturally appropriate individual or group self-assertion as well as the parameters of mutual deference, is equally at odds with the American Dream.

Conventional Virtue and the Ethics of Change

The difference between Humean and Kantian approaches may be clearest in the realm of political ethics. It will be no surprise that all Humean imperatives are "hypothetical," making reference to our desires or goals, rather than "categorical," deriving ought statements from pure practical reason. Even those who know little of Hume have generally heard his claim that "[r]eason is, and ought only to be the slave of the passions, and can never pretend to any other office than to serve and obey them" (T 2.3.3.4, SBN 415). But there is a deeper reason why praiseworthy political choices, for Hume, will always be what Kantians call "heteronomous," not determined solely by reason. That is: in politics, the content of what we ought to do depends, not incidentally but fundamentally and always, on what others are doing.

All collective action, in private as well as in public, relies for its success on others' choices: individual agents choose strategies, not outcomes. When it comes to private endeavors, this often does not much matter, since we are not necessarily judging actions by their actual outcomes. If I display public gratitude toward a benefactor who turns out not to want his generosity to be acknowledged, and who angrily withdraws his gift when it is acknowledged, I have caused harm but no one will blame me (unless I violated a promise). We praise qualities of character that are *typically* useful and agreeable to oneself or others, even if circumstances prevent the success of particular actions expressing those virtues: "Virtue in rags is still virtue" (T 3.3.1.19, SBN 584). But gratitude, for Hume, is a *natural* virtue, not an artificial one; its praiseworthiness, though not its specific expression, is independent of convention.[17] The artificial virtues are a different matter. Conventions create them and create them *for a particular reason*: because they produce mutual advantages. The virtue itself would make no sense—would not be a virtue—apart from those advantages. It is certainly possible, for Hume, for a particular act to be a requirement of justice, allegiance, or fidelity (i.e., promise-keeping) though it causes harm in a particular case.[18] But in situations where a convention has lost its overall utility, has come to harm a whole society or a huge chunk of it, we should abandon it for the duration of such situations—as constitutional rules yield, in Hume's view, in cases of necessity (see chapter 3), and property rights in times of famine (EPM 3.1.8, 186–7). By implication, and extending Hume's argument beyond the emergency case: if a convention as a whole *consistently* causes more harm or less good than an actually available alternative convention, abiding by it is no virtue. Crucially, however, the alternative convention must be a *convention*: something that we can anticipate everyone will observe. For a society in which different conceptions of property or authority compete for our observance is no better than one in which no such rules exist at all (and may be worse: in the anarchic case we may flock to any reasonable solution; in the partisan case we may stubbornly stick to multiple and incompatible solutions at great cost to us all).

This may appear to have conservative results—we should stick to the conventions we have—though of course not reactionary ones, since once new conventions have been established we should observe those too.[19] But the logic of the argument is more complicated than that and suggests a more interesting set of conclusions.

(1) Given authority, one may modify property. Hume is well aware that there can be disputes over conventions. Even when (like property) a convention is defined by formal legal rules, hard or ambiguous cases will produce disagreement. In such circumstances the solution is to appeal to an agreed authority for settling disputes: that is one reason for government's existence and its continuing roles (T 3.2.7, SBN 534–8, and most explicitly EPM 3.2.34–5, SBN 197–8).[20] Though Hume never says so directly, the argument suggests government can also be a force for changing conventions *as a whole* with some expectation that new conventions will stick. Disembodied reform proposals are vain or mischievous since a reformed convention will only be beneficial if everyone simultaneously comes to believe it beneficial.[21] But a reform backed by governmental authority, if unambiguous, *names* the new convention, and anyone in doubt as to whether to observe it will consult authority and answer yes. In cases of existential threat—the rough cultural equivalent of Hume's "egregious tyranny" in politics (or else of foreign conquest), whole peoples may adopt new languages, or *linguae francae*, that become de facto national languages.[22]

Hume clearly judges that reason of state rightly trumped property rights in at least two cases. One is Henry VII's breaking of noble entails (discussed above), a break whose radical character can be difficult for members of modern non-aristocratic countries to appreciate.[23] Another occurred during Britain's Civil War era: the parliamentary side seized royalist land, sometimes directly through attainder but more commonly indirectly, through huge forced loans conditioned on the victims' suspected politics. Hume considers these acts more "severe and arbitrary" than any previously seen in England and says that the royalists were "plundered." But when discussing the Restoration he is notably silent about the fact that the royalists during the Restoration got very little of that land back: Hume praises the lenience of the new regime's policy toward its old enemies, and letting Roundheads keep the land was presumably part of that (H 5.528, 6.4, 158–9).[24]

That reasons of state would have justified a twentieth-century Humean in enacting progressive taxation and labor regulation—in other words, changes in old property conventions—in response to real threats of civil war and revolution, is in no way fanciful. (In the real world, as opposed to conjectural intellectual history, large changes in property arrangements are typically the product of political, economic, or social crises that make the old arrangements unsustainable, not philosophical arguments that in a vacuum prove them unphilosophical.) The ends that property serves and the natural grooves of our mental habits set limits on how much of this is possible. Though Hume thinks that in departing from an equal property distribution we "rob the poor of more satisfaction than we add to the rich" (Hume is clearly no skeptic regarding interpersonal utility comparisons), he thinks that equal distribution is *not* a viable property convention, as any inequality of "art, care, and industry" would immediately disturb it and only "tyranny" and a "rigorous inquisition" could enforce it (EPM 3.25–6, SBN 194). But we should not over-emphasize that extreme example. Not only might a Humean, as noted, wel-come some sort of welfare state after the fact. He or she might even consis-tently move to *enact* it given evidence that a contemporary state that wishes to maintain its citizens' allegiance can no longer limit itself to a nightwatch-man role. Property is alterable precisely because allegiance is fixed. In fact, its being alterable might be the precondition for allegiance's remaining fixed.[25]

What goes for property goes equally for other things commonly called conventions. Some of them serve no purpose at all, may persist in spite of nearly universal irritation with them. They may be quickly and rightly scrapped once a social movement (or even a random event) has disrupted an equilibrium that binds all but serves few or none.[26] A great many social prac-tices asserted by conservatives to be traditional and therefore good may be in this category. There is no reason to think that abandoning them will cause anarchy, or (put differently) that anarchy in certain areas of personal choice is necessarily a bad thing. Other conventions, to be sure, may involve real tradeoffs—such as norms of politeness, in which the real goods of facilitating conversation and fellowship among strangers compete with the real costs of learning complex social codes as well as with the likelihood that facility with those codes will be made an occasion for snobbery and class distinctions.

But in any case, conventions of authority are the *only* ones with respect to which the "conservative" argument for sticking with whatever we have has great force—and even then, as noted, modifications of the effective exercise of authority may be compatible with retaining the forms of authority that allow for peaceful transition. The same conservative logic simply does not apply to conventions other than authority. The belief that constitutional and social change must move together probably rests on the assumption that governing institutions reflect and ought to reflect our fundamental values—so that hav-ing the same institutions as our grandparents is a sign (comforting to con-servatives, offensive to progressives) that we must think as they did on social and cultural questions too.[27] But on a Humean perspective this is false. Any given convention of authority represents only one accidental and customary method, among many possible others, whereby the universal need for au-thority has come to be structured in a particular time and place.[28] An author-ity convention will be most durable to the extent that it is compatible with *any number* of private and social moralities, and many authority conventions will do this adequately well. So understood, constitutional conservatism is fully consistent with social liberalism or radicalism—and may even facilitate it by making it safer. (Openness to liberalism when it comes to alleged conventions that may be pseudo-conventions also makes radicalism safer. If one wants to switch from a state in which one practice is normative and an alternative one widely despised to a state in which the opposite is true, it helps if one finds tolerable the state in which this attempt fails, leaving the practice up to individuals. Arguably, this has happened in many modern societies with respect to prior norms regarding religion, sexuality, gender roles, and various in-group loyalties to one's ethnic group, class, and so on. Attempts at radical change have succeeded partially, and more in some parts of society than others, leaving the operative rules both largely up to individuals and a common occasion for confusion and misunderstanding.) As long as something prevents us from killing one another, there are many ways of arranging our conventions of talking to, living beside, doing business with, or marrying one another. Sweden is still a kingdom.

(2) *Conventions may be criticized for any reason except violation of the virtues they establish.* Alistair Macleod has noted that a Humean cannot consistently attack property arrangements on the grounds of justice—only those of utility.[29] This is true but less significant than it seems. Property arrangements cannot be called unjust because Hume *defined* justice as observance of existing property arrangements. (A precise synonym for justice as Hume defines it would be "non-theft," if that were a word; since it is not, he uses "justice.") That property arrangements cannot be unjust is true by definition—just as triangles cannot have four sides—but not interesting. It merely means that criticism of property relations must use some language other than justice, and it can be very strong language. Exercising their parliamentary role, politicians can attack property arrangements and refuse to address the government's program of administration and taxation until their constituents' demands for relief and opportunity are met. Either politicians or philosophers may say—in the course of parliamentary debates, or outside them—that existing property relations are inhumane, incredibly foolish, or subversive of public welfare; that they cause needless suffering on a massive scale; that they are narrow-minded and bigoted in denying to a great many people the benefits of property, industry, and trade; that they callously ruin people's lives; that they reduce to criminality or beggary people who have the desire and ability to be productive and peaceful; even that they result in people being killed or brutally harmed (disapproval of murder and assault being a matter of natural virtue for Hume, not convention).[30] As noted, Hume himself thought that a more equal distribution of property tended to produce the most "satisfaction." And of course we can argue that without a certain standard of subsistence, the personal security that forms the justification for authority has little meaning.[31]

Of course any of these claims might also fail—but not because the language needed to express them is lacking. Perhaps we want to be able to call property rules *unjust* as well—and force the Humean to use a different word for the narrow convention of non-theft. But on the level of specialized political theory, as opposed to everyday political rhetoric, it does not much matter. It is again a verbal dispute. One is fighting, after all, over the equivalent of the right to call the sexual double-standard "unchaste"—instead of just (say) out of step with contraceptive technology, silly, unequal, or wrong—or to say that a debased currency "isn't really money" as opposed to merely noting that it has caused hyperinflation.

(3) *The sanctity of allegiance is contingent* and grounded in experience and utility; new political discoveries may erode it. Authority for Hume is qualitatively different from other conventions in that there is no appeal from it. Disagreements about property are settled by authority; disagreements about authority are settled by guns. To actively act against conventions of authority therefore seems the height of irresponsibility—the word *evil* might often be apt, since the chance of actual harm is so high—since that rejection will commonly bring about not a new convention of authority but strife over clashing proposals for different ones. Rejecting *fundamental* conventions is even more irresponsible. The pretender who seizes a throne might at least hope that his or her own claim will eventually and retrospectively become solid; the revolutionary who topples an entire monarchy will have to rely on the so-called people's army alone (at some risk to actual people on the other side).

But these are contingent matters. Hume's conviction that new conventions of authority will always be radically disputed and fragile compared to old ones was a counsel of history and experience that later experience might be said to have challenged. It has been noted that as more countries have become democratic and human rights norms have been enshrined in treaties, those who sought to overthrow non-democracies have had not just courage on their side but normative examples.[32] In Humean terms, one could say not only that older regimes' doctrines of authority became suspect (though Hume might have disagreed, since his standards for tyranny were so strict) but that the likely result of overthrowing existing constitutions was no longer anarchy, nor civil war. As a result of comparative experience and global norms, an electoral democracy that acknowledges human rights constraints is the assumed default when dictatorships fall, and this lowers to some degree the likely costs of felling them. Similarly, Hume's assumption that citizens facing authority have limited options—essentially, obedience or rebellion—may have reflected both the political experience of his time and the position of the major parties (Tory and Whig). But it has since been rendered doubtful by the invention of civil disobedience—a political technology that uniquely combines limited diallegiance to current regimes with a demonstrated willingness to cooperate with fellow citizens under new arrangements.[33] Civil disobedience is in this way the opposite of regicide, which Hume hated so much because it signaled the opposite intention. (Cromwell, in effect, was saying "most English subjects think constitutional monarchy is the sole legitimate form of government; we intend to slay the monarch and abolish monarchy; therefore you can trust that we plan to subdue our enemies by naked force.")

Matters of democratic transition and consolidation, and the role of protest within them, are the subject of intense empirical debate. The intent here
is not to summarize that debate but to point out why, on Humean terms, it
matters for ethics. Our political actions should take account of what others
might do, and the best guide to what they might do is what they demonstrably have been known to do. Experience with an immeasurably greater
variety of regimes—and of decent regimes—than Hume knew of makes a
huge difference for how we do politics. One of the many weaknesses of ideal
or Kantian theory is that it takes pride in willful ignorance of that experience
(willful because one deliberately abstracts from most of what one knows).
Against this, the politics of convention is a politics of invention. If a regime is
an arrangement for the common advantage, new discoveries in the political
realm imply an ethical requirement to consider new conventions—and new
possibilities for dynamic transition from one to another.

This empirical, historical view of things helps judge revolution in terms
more helpful than those of "the right to rebel" or "political obligation." The
right of things depends on the likely outcome of one's actions, and that in
turn depends on whether destruction of an existing convention of authority
is likely to result in a quick and consensual attachment to a new one. Locke's
stance on what came to be called the Glorious Revolution was correct not
because a return to a primeval, constitutive state of "society" or "community," and the erection of a new government, would have been anything but
a disaster, but because nothing of the kind was going to happen and Locke
knew it. He assumed that powerful political actors would only unite against
James II in the name of a return to traditional conventions of limited monarchy, parliament, and legal due process. These were both an obvious rallying
point and a popular one, and everyone knew them to be both. The matter has
nothing to do with whether one "trusts the will of the people."[34] The question is whether one thinks that the will of the people actually exists—as opposed to reflecting a fallacy of composition—or whether convention must
take its place. Similarly, the (fair) assumption that Hume would have hated
the French Revolution, while he demonstrably acquiesced in the American,
is neither inconsistent nor a matter of ideological "moderation." It expresses
a coherent view that revolutions can produce a new order, one not based on
terror, only when obvious post-revolutionary conventions exist. They did
in America (whose self-governing structures were solid and customary, as
Hume understood).[35] They did not in France.

Richard Dees is right that the Eastern European revolutions of 1989 present a similar case to "orderly violent revolutions, like the American," but his
preferred framework of "normative" consent theory does not allow him to see
why.[36] An Eastern European citizen in 1989, with at least intermittent access to
Western mass media, knew at least vaguely what a "typical" European regime,
that is, a parliamentary democracy that observed human rights, looked like;
knew that he or she wanted it, and knew that others knew. The EU provided

a vague but serviceable set of conventions that served as a standing and obvious rallying point for any Eastern European revolution that found its own regime tyrannical. Whether such rallying points are available throughout the world, or whether on the contrary they are limited to particular regions or require certain cultural preconditions, is a matter of *empirical* dispute. Our attitude toward revolutions in any but the most egregious tyrannies (where even a protracted civil war or brutal authoritarian rule may improve on the status quo) ought to track our position on that dispute. It does not make moral sense to back revolution for its own sake when the alternative to a bad or brutal regime is what Hume would have predicted: a mix of unstable government, nostalgia for the old order, and a turn to strongmen whose rule is often more tyrannical than that of the regime they replace.

In the course of rightly rejecting a disembodied "critical" perspective that attempts to lay down normative rules independent of social experience,[37] Humeans need not reject the possibility of serious reform or even, when actually superior alternatives are common knowledge, useful revolutions. Whether such reforms will have good or bad results, whether they will move in a "progressive" or "conservative" direction, and whether they will be recognized as legitimate (what Hume would call "lawful") are, as they should be, *empirical* questions. It all depends on which conventions are likely to stick at which times and places. Hume's reticence on matters of revolution may reflect not coyness on the a priori question but his stated belief that political science in his time was primitive.[38]

All of this sounds very exciting and laudably flexible, but there remain limits—limits different from those a more Kantian perspective would suggest. Hume's opposition to utopians and "projectors" is not, like Burke's, an attack on hubris and a lament that revolutions displace a sense of sublime mystical awe from our governors (where in Burke's view it belonged) to a revolutionary process.[39] It is almost the opposite: a prohibition on magical thinking. Hume attacks projectors in the context of noting how constitutions are not like machines. "Supposed argument and philosophy" should not be appealed to in making supposed improvements to a constitution at a great and predictable cost to its custom-based authority.[40] In our day, pacifists who destroy military hardware or ascetic anarchists who blow up government buildings, not in reasonable expectation of a new arrangement but in the hope that everyone else will be inspired by their selfless example to end war or acquisitiveness, culpably flout their responsibility to act on the best available evidence regarding how large groups of people choose to arrange their affairs, and how societies usually respond to destructive protests in the name of utopian goals (i.e., by punishing the protestors and dismissing the goals). Similarly, those who hope that "deliberation" can substitute for institutional forms (as opposed to being a proper mode of discussion within those forms, which is very different) should be asked what deliberative reason—by stipulation independent of convention—would point to concerning the appropriate term of legislators, the number of justices on the Supreme Court, or the proper term of patent protection. If reason cannot settle these things, something else must. If that thing is not to be force, it must be convention.

Conventional Idealism

England's conventions are famously unwritten, historical, and gradualist (and its constitutional conventions can remain so even when governments style themselves as radical: no change in local government or education funding approaches an open disavowal of monarchy, parliamentarism, or *habeas corpus*). That is not so everywhere. Countries that were founded in the name of ideals often mix conventions of authority—constitutions, typically written ones—with conventional adherence to ideals that transcend all authorities: for example, liberty, equality, fraternity, the pursuit of happiness. Samuel Huntington thought this gave rise to an "Ideas vs. Institutions gap," which he saw to be a perennial and permanent source of disaffection in countries founded on ideals (like the United States). The problem is that no set of governing institutions—which by definition embody some constraint, and inequality between government and governed—can ever fully respect the ideals in whose name those institutions govern.[41] In the Humean context, Donald Livingston has portrayed Thomas Jefferson's hatred of Hume's *History* as reflecting a "mythical" and permanent battle between the radical and "rationalistic Declaration with its doctrine of natural rights and its claim to moral authority" and "the more sceptical Constitution with its historically grounded system of checks and balances." A good Humean, on his view, should choose the latter, rejecting the former.[42]

Those more attuned than these conservative thinkers tend to be to the dangers of horizontal and vertical inequality might see things another way. References to founding ideals may have the effect of undermining governing conventions—or they may simply serve as the pretext for rallying around political reform within those conventions. It is, again, an *empirical* question. Appeals to liberty and equality led the American constitution to lose authority (deservedly) during the crisis leading up to the Civil War. But in retrospect, it is clear that they did no such thing in the United States in the 1960s. In that period, they served to motivate far-reaching reforms, bordering on social revolutions. The absence of those reforms would have presented a much greater danger to government authority, in the form of creeping disallegiance, than change did. In the course of this, the basic outlines of constitutional authority were *not* challenged, except to the extent that enfranchisement itself is, as usual, radical.

It may be dangerously antinomian to demand (as students and academics do far more often than political actors of any stripe) that only social ideals, and not government itself, be treated as legitimate. But the contrary demand, that government be allowed to function without reference to any such ideals, can be dangerously oblivious to governments' tendencies to tyranny and self-dealing when unchecked. A set of conventions that simultaneously endorses governing institutions *and* principles that no institution could possibly observe is incoherent when presented as an account of what single individuals should believe. But it may be both viable and valuable as an account of how groups of individuals might achieve both the advantages of coordination solutions and the ability to contest these solutions' biases.

It is still the case that if governmental authority were to be ripped up at the roots, the Declaration of Independence or the Rights of Man would produce indeterminate and anarchic solutions, culminating ultimately in the rule of force (and, perhaps later, in a restoration). But there is no reason to expect this vertiginous outcome to be likely. For the most part, fears that it is likely can be attributed to the same false "necessity" that led Charles I to think he "had to" govern without parliament—when what was truly necessary was listening to its grievances and acting to address most of them.

Three Faces of Realism

Hume's politics exemplifies the ways in which political theory, rather than philosophy on the one hand or modes of political inquiry modeled on economics on the other, has a distinctive set of concerns and can make a distinctive contribution. Philosophers are prone to study the conditions for rational consensus, and economists the conditions for mutual gains through market exchange. But politics is above all the study of conflict: what happens when reason gives no determinate answer and when market exchange is either not relevant or itself the source of conflict. And the evaluation of political institutions is the study of entities that enable binding, authoritative decisions in the face of deep social disagreement—something that neither seminar rooms nor commodity exchanges typically do.

But it is a particular kind of political theory that has affinities with Hume, and Hume's *History*. This is not the so-called ideal theory that judges all existing institutions as wanting compared against a constructed standard, but a realist theory that explores how institutions and frameworks for decisions that are mutually acceptable (or not) can arise, and how those institutions and decision frameworks can be challenged through political interactions and under the operation of strategic or prudential decisions. Self-styled realism takes many forms, and many diverse implications can be drawn from it.[43] Here I would stress three.

The first thing realism does is challenge a magical or mythical history in which one's favored institutions or principles are described as having an essential nature that persists unchanged throughout time and explains a variety of events non-causally, since the principle was "meant" to be vindicated.

The most revolutionary lesson of Hume's *History* is that why something arose has almost nothing to do with why it is (or is not) now valuable or worth preserving. As a corollary, the fact that something would be good does not constitute evidence that it is likely to arise or is worth thinking about on the basis that it somehow might arise. Hume's position frustrates all ideological or partisan doctrines that, in Hume's time as ours, write philosophy in the style of politics, as if a sense of common endeavor, founded if necessary on common myths, were more important than pursuing the best possible judgments about how things stand in the world.[44] The *History*, in attempting to teach "the great mixture of accident, which commonly concurs with a small ingredient of wisdom and foresight, in erecting the complicated fabric of the most perfect government"(H 2.525) attempted, however quixotically, to universalize a distaste for historical myth.

In the face of myth-based accounts of our past and present, Hume teaches a few things that are no less counterintuitive for being near tautologies once one points them out: that not every cause tracks a coherent moral or intellectual reason; and that history being complex, any version of the past that is simple enough for a party pamphlet, a school text, or the conjectural-history section of a philosophical treatise will necessarily lie about almost everything. It also teaches some things that frustrate grand narratives in fascinating and non-obvious ways: Though actors in the past did not act to serve our purposes, they may by accident have served them very well. The most successful long-term political strategies succeed not by determining future situations but through systematically favoring the kind of pursuits whose devotees will not want the same things their ancestors did. Modern societies, compared to premodern ones, provide greater opportunities for those who profess ancient values as well as modern ones, and promise greater fame for reactionaries as well as modernizers. Conventions can persist even when people's understanding of them changes radically, provided that their understanding changes in rough concert. In any case conventions need not be consciously understood and actively endorsed, but do most of their work through being habitually followed as if they were natural (though they aren't).

All this suggests that political concepts, as opposed to the actions they describe or recommend, are of critical importance largely in crisis situations in which the prevailing convention is unclear. They are otherwise less crucial than students of them imagine, and play far less of a role than custom and habit do in determining the terms of human interactions. This is the second face of realism: a modest attitude toward what political theory can accomplish and toward the status it can rightly claim. There are three reasons for adopting such modesty. The first is negative: custom can be an annoying constraint on the reasonable expectation that principles should be consistent. Regarding Henry's marriage to Catherine of Aragon, Hume writes that "principles of sound philosophy" definitively prove that the laws and conventions against incest should not have been applied in such a case, but "Henry had custom and precedent on his side, the principle by which men are almost wholly governed in their actions and opinions."[45] The second, related reason to adopt a chastened attitude toward political theory is that it is only likely to gain political importance through an alliance with either superstition or force. (In the contemporary age one might add democratic numbers, though philosophy can only muster those by transforming itself into ideology.) During the delicious French factional wars between the Burgundy and Armagnac factions, Hume notes that the dons in Paris came to have some influence due to the credence paid to religious interpretation: "this connection between literature and superstition had bestowed on the former a weight, to which reason and knowledge are not, of themselves, any wise entitled among men." That said, Hume judges the academics' influence minor compared to that of Paris's butchers and carpenters, whose arguments had more of an edge to them (H 2.360). The final reason why theory should not vaunt itself too greatly involves the need to cash political concepts out into the operations of political institutions. Realist theory need not neglect questions of justice, liberty, and equality, but it will tend to treat them in a particular way. Justice is what results when relatively weak actors manage to pool their political resources so as to prevent the powerful from taking their own will as the only measure of right and wrong. Liberty, politically speaking, is what we call the agreed limits on the use of such resources; otherwise stated, the condition in which those who command the power of government can be reliably prevented from using it in certain ways. Equality, politically speaking, is primarily the condition in which those in charge of government are constrained from using it to systematically favor some groups or individuals over others. In practice, this requires an institution through which all members of society come to have an equal right to control the mechanisms that hold state actors to account. The development of liberty—always mediated by, or as a corrective to, authority—is widely taken to be a central story of Hume's *History*. The development of equality can be our own contribution to a political theory based on the *History*'s account. In all cases, it is a mistake to study an idealized condition in which nobody would have a desire to disturb our desired equilibrium. Societies and economies evolve; preferences and power constellations shift; relatively durable political institutions will be those that can accommodate such changes rather than denying them.

The third face of Humean realism is a refusal to pretend that political problems are more tractable than they are. The problems of authority, order, and change, of human interaction in an indifferent cosmos, seem mild in the kind of societies most of us live in only because we are so compliant in accepting the hard-won solutions to them: conventions of authority, and in particular of fundamental authority. Our freedom to talk about popular sovereignty—and to disagree in fundamental and theoretically dangerous ways over what we would do with it—is safe only because we have no intention of pursuing such sovereignty. In practice, almost all of us will stick with decent and unchosen constitutions where we find them. And when we change such constitutions we will do so very much in accordance with—equally unchosen—rules for doing so. Like it or not, even a parliament that in theory (often its own theory) can change constitutional rules at will is never able to make such power stick in practice. As Hume pointed out, positive law itself is authorized by constitutional authority, and it is not clear than an attempt of the former to utterly change the forms of the latter would succeed.[46] To make matters concrete: if (say) a New Zealand parliament passed a law suspending all future elections and making its current members MPs for life, the law would violate no written constitution—but would still have zero probability of being obeyed.

Raymond Geuss has noted the disjuncture between the topics of idealist theory and the experiences of the past century (or any other for that matter):

> Are reflections about the correct distribution of goods and service [sic] in a "well-ordered society" the right *kind* of intellectual response to slavery, torture, and mass murder? Was the problem in the Third Reich that people in extermination camps didn't get the slice of the economic pie that they ought to have had, if everyone had discussed the matter freely and under the right conditions? Should political philosophy really be essentially about questions of fairness of distribution of resources? Aren't security and the control of violence far more important? How about the coordination of action, the sharing of information, the cultivation of trust, the development and deployment of human individual and social capacities, the management of relations of power and authority, the balancing of the demands of stability and reform, the provision for a viable social future?[47]

If Geuss' list of topics seems uncannily to mirror Hume's own agenda, this is in one sense accidental but in another inevitable. While there is no particular reason to believe that Geuss has either read Hume closely or would endorse his political theory if he did, Geuss and Hume have something in common because they derive their agenda from something that they share and that all of us are free to observe: the real world of politics.

The Politics of Faith and the Politics of Charm

One reason the realist can do with fewer illusions than the idealist—though never none—is that she need not fill a yawning gap between duty and happiness. Kant judged human actions according to their ability to follow duty strictly, independent of inclination; Rousseau defined the general will as that which triumphed in opposition to each individual's particular will. The great "metanarratives" that took as their subject the progress of *Geist* on the one hand or political freedom on the other can be seen as responses to the fact that these ideals were deliberately unpleasant—hence Kant's lament that humanity's timber, not his theory, was crooked—with the result that Reason and Freedom's progress in the face of recalcitrant human passions was necessarily slow (or, in the view of later skeptics, nonexistent).[48]

There are many potential problems with Hume's theory, but not this one. For him, a human virtue, or its impersonal counterpart, a "convention," was to be judged by whether it was useful or agreeable to oneself or others. Upbraided by Hutcheson for "lacking warmth in the cause of virtue," Hume responded not by making himself warmer but by portraying virtue as hotter. The "philosophical truths" of his theory are also advantageous to society because they "represent virtue in all her genuine and most engaging charms, and make us approach her with ease, familiarity and affection":

> The dismal dress falls off, with which many divines, and some philosophers have covered her; and nothing appears but gentleness, humanity, beneficence, affability; nay even, at proper intervals, play, frolic, and gaiety. She talks not of useless austerities and rigours, suffering and self-denial. She declares, that her sole purpose is, to make her votaries and all mankind, during every instant of their existence, if possible, cheerful and happy; nor does she ever willingly part with any pleasure but in hopes of ample compensation in some other period of their lives. . . . And if any austere pretenders approach her, enemies to joy and pleasure, she either rejects them as hypocrites and deceivers; or if she admit them in her train, they are ranked however, among the least favoured of her votaries. (EPM 9.2.15, SBN 279)

In Hume's view an austere moral theory is not only wrong but hopeless. "[E]ngaging mankind" to a morality of "austerity and rigor" is impossible; a moral theory that does not speak of universal advantage cannot serve "any useful purpose" (ibid.).

That Hume's appeal to "moral charm, and other sexy virtues" is shocking in its non-Christianity has been noted by Annette Baier.[49] We might further note that it more or less dissolves the problem of hope. Humean hope, if such it be, is based on the likelihood that a system of virtue will *actually attract support*, through engaging our passions.[50] It does not require the kind of faith, proudly independent of evidence, that imagines that a theory of providence or history guarantees the success of some artificial system that we choose to call rational in spite of its having won no support in the past. If Hume's revised motto of Enlightenment is "dare to be enlarged—think of innovative ways of expanding the scope of mutually beneficial cooperation," hope is both more contingent than if we are seeking the kingdom of ends and more achievable. Opportunities for such cooperation may or may not exist in a given situation, but there is no cause for despair if they don't: situations change, and if we cannot draw more people into a convention now, we may be able to later. Here, as often, Hume provides a bridge between a non-rationalist strand of

"Enlightenment" (to use a term not current in his time) and postmodernism. He also bridges postmodernism and so-called rational choice, which have in common the determination to work with rather than against human passions, and to build ethical theories on the likely results of that rather than imagining we can rise above those passions.

It is common for both the friends of the Scottish Enlightenment and its enemies to see it as optimistic: everyone's interests will automatically harmonize if we only leave them alone. Istvan Hont has stressed how misleading this is. The Scottish Enlightenment studied the equilibria that *might* arise out of human interactions—there was no guarantee—because they thought no other source of order was credible. It was attempting to build a new order, as best one could, from the ruins of the belief that a providential God would take care of things for us. The social ideals of the Scottish Enlightenment arose out of pessimism with respect to that earlier belief system, and out of a realistic attitude toward the problems and possibilities of human cooperation, not out of optimism. Authority was a crucial topic of study because nothing beyond human interactions guaranteed its success.[51] Hont rightly argues that Hume's theory was rooted in anguish and anxiety. We might add that the reason it does not seem that way is that Hume did not think *solving* the problem of authority required obsessively *naming* it. The politics of opinion was to draw its stability not from the anticipated future results of endless appeals to reason but from the existing and predictable fact that human mental habits followed custom, and the predictable human desire for stable mutual expectations.

Hume's political theory, even more than Smith's economics, attempted to build an indefinitely long bridge, broad and solid enough to carry both those who felt like looking down and the majority who would rather look at one another (or else ahead), over what he fully knew to be an abyss. Politics rested either on convention or on nothing—fortunately, most of the time, the former.

Hume himself did not just look ahead and to the side. He was not just a historian and political theorist but a philosopher. His small but steady smiles in all the known portraits reflected not self-delusion but self-command. He did look into the abyss; it looked back. One of them blinked and it wasn't Hume.

Notes

Introduction

1. David Hume, *The History of England* (1983): 4: 354–5 (henceforth H: followed by volume and page number; see references for abbreviations).

2. Ordinal game theory, the kind preferred by Hardin (1999, 2007), posits agents who know how they and others rank the available outcomes but rules out as incoherent the question of how strong those preferences are. That is, it ranks preferences but does not quantify payoffs. Ordinal game theory in one sense captures constitutional politics' pervasive uncertainty—at the cost of effacing one of politics' central questions: who stands to gain *more than others* from any proposed outcome or change in outcomes. I thank Gerry Mackie for discussion on this.

3. Clarendon had been England's Thucydides: the careful chronicler of a key event (Britain's civil war) in which he himself had participated. Eighteenth-century Britain took the Tacitus and Thucydides models very seriously: see Hicks (1996).

4. "Most political theorists agree that modern political thought began with Machiavelli and that David Hume was a modern philosopher who made a notable contribution to political theory. Most philosophers do not spend great amounts of time either with Machiavelli or with Hume's political philosophy, and political theorists (with some Rawlsian exceptions) largely ignore Hume's ethics, epistemology, or histories"—Hiskes (2005: 181). Honorable recent exceptions include Krause (2008), Frazer (2010), Whelan (2004), and Hanvelt (2012)—and, in philosophy, Baier (2008, 2010). But the first two of these works primarily treat Hume as a moral psychologist who might provide an alternative, non-rationalist foundation for positions normally regarded as resting on neo-Kantian practical reason, and the last three use Hume's *History* as occasions for adding nuance to interpretations on Hume based overwhelmingly on the *Treatise* and *Essays*. Only Whelan (2004: esp. 127–8) gives a central and independent role both to *politics* as the central topic of discussion and to the *History* as the most helpful text for exploring Hume's contributions to it. As a one-word summary of Hume's politics, Whelan's "realist" is certainly far better than "skeptical" or "conservative."

5. The absence of a political treatise is noted by Stewart (1963: v). Forbes (1975: 84) notes that Hume's "political philosophy, as we have it in the *Treatise* and the [second] *Enquiry*, is a section of an argument about the nature of moral judgements" and is therefore shorter than a traditional treatise that aims to cover the fundamentals of politics as a whole.

6. Almost all recent Hume scholars believe that he endorsed both skepticism toward rationalist epistemology and a trust in empirical evidence in all practical moral, political, and social contexts. (Ridge [2003] carefully traces prevalent accounts of how this is possible and defends a nuanced position.) No reader of Hume's *History*, whose attention to evidence is minute, can doubt this (see, e.g., H 6.295 and H 6.412). For a letter that seals the point, establishing Hume's acute concern with empirical accuracy, see L 1.354–6.

7. Political theorists seeking quick knowledge of Hume often turn to Wolin (1954). His portrait of Hume as an odd sort of conservative—out of skepticism rather than a belief in religion or tradition—has been hugely influential. It combines all too easily with a belief that Hume was too indolent and complacent to hold any strong beliefs at all.

8. Russell (1945: 673).

9. Hume wrote that the system of human conventions was "advantageous to the public; tho' it be not intended for that purpose by the inventors" (T 3.2.6.6, SBN 529). He readily acknowledged, though some readers miss it, that the account in the *Treatise* telescoped and simplified a historical process in order to highlight a theory of origin: it supposed conventions "to be form'd at once, which in fact arise insensibly and by degrees" (T 3.2.3.3, SBN 503).

10. Haakonssen (1981). Haakonssen (1993: 213), an attempt to treat Hume's political theory generally, contains a similar emphasis, treating Adam Smith's jurisprudence as "the sharpest reading Hume's *politics* has received" (emphasis added). Christopher Berry, while treating Hume's thought more fully, like Haakonssen sees reliance on rules as the link between Hume's epistemology and psychology and his politics: general rules grounded in repeated experience allow for the predictability and reliability needed for economic and social progress, just as they provide the "cement of the universe" in the face of what would otherwise be epistemological chaos (2009: 43). Even Neil McArthur's lively defense of Hume as a reformer and scholar of social change largely mirrors this approach. While it portrays Hume as describing and welcoming change in the social, economic, and religious spheres, its description of civilized government focuses on the existence of "general laws" and their impartial administration (2007: 10 and passim).

11. Hume's conventionalism was, however, radical in his own time, in which human conventions were regarded as morally inferior to ties that bound human beings to God (e.g., through oaths). See Forbes (1975: 66–8).

12. As McArthur (2007: 14) points out, doing so requires that we not restrict our studies to work that looks like "philosophy" as that subject is now conceived. Most of Hume's political reflections in the *Essays* and *History*, unlike those in the *Treatise* and second *Enquiry*, look more like "political science."

13. Forbes (1975).

14. Kramnick (1968: 123–4, 127, 152, 181); Pocock (1975: chapters 13 and 14); Forbes (1975: chapter 6). The last source is (rightly) more prone than the first two to stress Hume's sympathy toward Country positions on some points. Phillipson (1989:

chapter 2) alertly notes that while Hume largely adopted the Court defense of modern manners and interests and the commerce that produced them, he improved on writers like Defoe in systematically exploring what these new views of virtue and human nature entailed regarding political and constitutional questions.

15. Miller (1981).

16. Stuart Hampshire (1989: 81, 103) refers to Hume as "ample and amiable . . . sceptically smiling"—an uncanny description of his appearance in the Ramsay portrait—and repeats the view, still common among non-specialists, that because of Hume's skeptical stance, "his moral philosophy has a profoundly conservative tendency; it is as if his Toryism was built into his epistemology."

17. Phillipson (1989: 139).

18. Stewart (1963: 298); the same sentiment is endorsed in broad terms by Forbes (1975: 264) and implied, though not in so many words, by Phillipson.

19. See Stewart (1963: chapter 12); Stewart (1992); McArthur (2007); and to some degree Skinner (1993). A somewhat different version of this tradition, present in Annette Baier's unclassifiable work (1991: chapter 12; compare 2010: 51) as well as Krause (2008), lauds Hume as the prophet of a different kind of modern reason that consists in practices of open, mutual, and continual justification—"deliberative" reason, as it is sometimes called, though without the Kantian grounding that self-styled deliberative democrats often assume. Our sense of Hume's contribution will then depend on the degree to which we think such practices of justification are, as sometimes claimed, the fundamental basis of modern government and society.

20. Lewis (1969: 3–4 and passim; Gauthier (1979); Baier (1991: esp. chapter 10); Miller (1981: 68, without using the word coordination but employing "unforced agreement" and "natural point of convergence" to the same effect; compare 75); Hardin (2007). I do not mean to deny huge theoretical and normative differences, sometimes explicit and on occasion testy, among these authors. Donald Livingston's reading of Humean convention (1984: especially 66ff.) is importantly different and rooted in historicist and hermeneutic philosophic assumptions that I shall not pursue in detail here.

21. Danford (1990: 160).

22. Schelling (2006a: 26).

23. Even Baier, who notes how central questions of transition must be in Hume's account of authority, quickly turns away from these questions in favor of noting Hume's departure from more familiar theories of contract and legitimacy (1991: 264ff.).

24. Compare Geisel (1969).

25. McArthur (2007: 125 and chapter 6 passim).

26. H 4.355, Appendix III, cited by McArthur (2007: 127) as a concession to politics that does not fundamentally alter Hume's radical and reformist approach to policy.

27. See H 4.341 on the "specious arguments" that induced Queen Elizabeth to debase the currency. This passage and H 2.484–5 (in which conquerors' "sanguine" hopes are dashed) contain two of the only instances in Hume of truly awful puns.

28. See Schelling (1980 [1960]: Appendices A–C; esp. 302, where Schelling calls the questions involved "a fruitful meeting ground for game theory and sociology").

29. I prefer "partial" to "self-interested" given Hume's repeated and highly detailed attacks on the self-love hypothesis favored by Mandeville. See especially T 3.2.2.5, SBN 486–7; E: DMHN, 84–6, and EPM App. 2, SBN 247–54. But the text argument works even assuming, for argument, self-interested motives.

30. To oversimplify greatly, one strand of the school regards political language as a series of illocutionary utterances (also called speech-acts), while another focuses on language systems as instances of highly complex and differentiated Kuhnian paradigms, and the history of thought as "a history of change in the employment of paradigms" as well as in second- and third-order reflections on paradigms. See, respectively, Skinner (2002: chapter 6 and passim) and Pocock (1971: 23).

31. Lewis (1969).

32. On the last see Hanvelt (2012).

33. Skinner (1969: 52) seems to admit this possibility ("there may be apparently perennial questions, if these are sufficiently abstractly framed"). The much-revised version of this essay in Skinner (2002) omits this passage.

34. Forbes (1975: 121, 222) and elsewhere notes how Hume believed science appropriate to the politics of regular institutions in which individual idiosyncrasies mattered comparatively little, and on page 227 stresses that Hume's alternative to party views of political change was to view politics in terms of self-interest. Phillipson (1989: 140–41) concludes similarly. Pocock (1975: chapters 14 and 15) develops similar themes at length. See especially page 497: Hume was "a great historian in the eighteenth century" largely because he "saw commerce and passion as dynamic forces contributing both to the construction of political society and to an active and kinetic history, and . . . was by no means incapable of taking a sanguine view of the present and future, in which ultimate corruption might be averted for a very long time." His successors, one might add to Pocock's account, would improve on this theory by changing "a very long time" to "forever."

35. Skinner (2002: 77–8).

36. This answer follows, roughly, Hardin (2007).

37. Hume scholars who agree on little concur that the ancient and medieval volumes are less interesting or significant than the later ones. (See, e.g., Stewart 1963: 261; Forbes 1975: 324. This focus on the Stuart volumes is not new: see Potkay 2001: 33, with citations). Braudy (2003 [1970]: 95 and chapter 3 passim) is the only source I know of who contests this judgment. The first two volumes of Hume's *History* are in many ways the most theoretically instructive since Hume's sources are, by his own admission, suspect—and he freely rewrites what accounts he does have. Since factual details, beyond bare outlines, are not in question, Hume freely uses his ancient and medieval history to make points in political theory.

38. E: MOL, xxxviii.

39. Quotation on EHU 12.3.31, SBN 165; comparison of historical to physical experiments on EHU 8.1.7, SBN 83–4. Moore (1977: 810–13) is an excellent short treatment of this kind of science in Hume.

40. See Pocock (1999: 1–25, 199–221). As Forbes (1975: 121) notes, someone who knew of Hume only from his philosophical works might have expected him to write a more thoroughly "social" history than the one he actually wrote—which has been faulted (including by Forbes) for being "too narrowly political." Phillipson (1989: 140) and McArthur (2007) agree that Hume took a certain kind of legal government, rather than pre-political social and economic forces, to be the primary driver of civilization, but unlike Forbes, approve of this view. Stewart (1963: 299) goes so far as to say that "The *History* is a political history, *not* a history of civilization in England" (emphasis added).

41. Eric Schliesser has stressed the instances in which Hume said certain moral (we would say social-scientific) predictions were just as precise as those in natural philosophy or science, including Newton's (Schliesser 2009, citing *inter alia*, DP 6.19; T 1.3.14.33; EHU 8.1.19, 8.1.16; T 1.3.2.16, 1.3.12.16, 1.3.14.33; as well as E: BT, 313 and EHU 8.1.16ff., where the examples are particularly vivid). In E: RPAS, 112–13, domestic constitutional theory and economic policy are claimed to be the most susceptible of the moral sciences to the identification of "determinate and known causes"; compare E: C, 253–5; M, 289–90; I, 304). On the other hand, Hume repeatedly warned against expecting too much precision from his own generalizations, especially in politics (see, e.g., T 1.3.15.11, SBN 175, and E: PRS, 16; BG, 47–8; CL, 87–8; NC, 203; C, 255–6; PC, 357; SRC, 366). The two conclusions are not hard to reconcile. Human actions can be subject to deterministic causal laws in principle while the content of those laws remains, necessarily, partly inaccessible to human beings. For one thing, and contingently, Hume's infallible social laws are based on palpable and repeated experience (money flows toward economic activity unless forcibly prevented; jailers don't let prisoners go for no reason; a full purse left at Charing Cross won't be there in an hour). But if the question is which constitutional forms have which results, Hume thinks we have too little experience—too few cases, in today's terminology—to judge. (We might note that in Hume's time there was only one known mixed parliamentary monarchy on Britain's model, only a few republics, and *no* representative democracies, with equal adult suffrage, of the contemporary type.) Further experience since Hume's time leaves us in relative ignorance given that new institutional forms keep being invented and proposed. Hume's own historical argument regarding reforms like toleration and freedom of the press can be glossed as lamenting that historical actors had to judge those reforms without having the proper basis for judging them, namely experience (see Sabl 2002). Forbes (1975: chapters 4 and 9) is excellent on Hume's proto-social science as a whole; see also Frazer (1970) on the special role played by historical uncertainty.

42. One result of this is to blame past figures less than partisan or ideological histories would. For what they had reason to expect others to do, because it was normative at the time, shaped their actions more than we would realize before reconstructing their situation. See Forbes (1975: chapter 8, esp. 284–5) and Wertz (1996: 350ff.).

43. Hume's virtuosity in doing this greatly impressed his contemporaries. See the review in the *Critical Review* reprinted in Fieser (2002: 289–97, esp. 292).

44. Livingston (1984: 191); Capaldi (1978: 121) and passim; Wertz (1975, 1996).

45. See the discussion of this and similar passages in Jones (1990: 3–5).

46. Capaldi (1978); Jones (1990). Herdt (1997: 120) notes a similar link. She not unreasonably regards Hume as jumping too quickly to explanations involving irrationality when religion is remotely concerned.

47. See Oren (2009: 290–91), who cites Weber (2004: 314): "This construct of rigorous, instrumentally rational action therefore furthers the evident clarity and understandability of a sociology whose lucidity is founded upon rationality. In this way a *type* is presented ("ideal type") from which real action, influenced by all manner of irrationalities (emotions, errors), can be presented as a 'deviation' from processes directed by purely rational conduct" (emphasis in original). For a more thorough treatment see Ringer (2004: 89–104, 176ff.). A key illustration of this method in the *History* occurs at 1.331: Thomas à Becket's "violent" measures should not be as-

sumed the result of "passions alone" but were rather a desperate attempt to forestall royal actions that he rightly foresaw.

48. Other brief attempts to revive the Weberian use of rational choice assumptions for *Verstehen* purposes include Friedmann (1996:15) and Tsebelis (1990: 44–5). The latter, asserting that rational choice explanation is superior to interpretive history because it does not rely on empathy and attributes the same law of action (rational choice) to all actors in all cases, misses Weber's point: the simple and universal hypothesis has the flaw of being false.

49. Hampsher-Monk and Hindmoor (2010: 57–60). The law of anticipated reactions was formulated by Friedrich (1968); I thank Gerry Mackie for pointing out its relevance here.

50. The third point is not controversial. For the first two, see respectively Whelan (2004: 145–51, and the citations of Hume therein) and Whelan (2001), citing forty-one instances of "perverse effects" or unintended consequences in Hume's *History* (sometimes supplemented by examples from Adam Smith).

51. Compare Hardin (2003).

52. See Tucker (1970); for more on this kind of charisma, see chapter 1.

53. A distinction made by Elton (1973: 208).

54. I would therefore disagree with Whelan's claim (2004: 57) that the survival of something like Machiavelli's *virtù* in Hume's *History* frustrates scientific explanation. As suggested previously, Hume does not think he has access to deterministic laws of politics—or, perhaps, that we can ever know such. But, unlike Machiavelli, he systematically accounts for, rather than attributing to *fortuna*, the circumstances that *determine the range of choices* available to actors. These circumstances themselves derive from others' choices both in those actors' own time and in their past. To use Whelan's example: Henry VII chose at "the crisis of his fortune" to seize the throne after the Battle of Bosworth Field (H 3.4). But Hume adds that Henry was "obliged suddenly to determine himself": there was a brief opportunity to seize the throne but it would soon pass. And one might add that *only* Henry—the heir of the house of Lancaster—and a few other actors were in a position to seize the throne, due to conventions of hereditary succession that were not up to him. (For more on this see chapter 5 in this book.)

55. Braudy (2003 [1970]: 95); Capaldi (1978: 113).

56. Pocock (1999: 207–8).

57. Ibid., 208. Braudy (2003 [1970]: chapter 3) portrays in roughly similar terms the tension between "character" and "cause" in Hume's *History*, though dissenting from Pocock's judgment that Hume resolved it masterfully throughout the work.

58. Hume himself drew attention to this problem (E: CL, 87–8). We might add that when he was talking about political regimes involving representation, Hume was drawing on a handful of cases; when it came to representative democracies, zero. See note 41 above.

59. As noted by Stockton (1976: 315–16).

60. Hardin (2007: 25; compare vii).

61. A great many evaluative words in politics conceal empirical claims or rest on empirical premises: constitutional, peaceful, "in accord with prevailing *mores*," authority, democratic. On such "crossover" words in morality, see MacIntyre (1978), which convincingly argues that while Hume famously denied that ought could be "deduced" from is, logically speaking, all his work assumes that the two can be

related non-deductively. As MacIntyre argues, one of the key moral categories in Hume is that of "common interests" as the source of moral rules; if Marxists are right that there are no common interests, those rules cease to be moral. Sabl (2011) attempts to identify similar crossover categories in political, as opposed to moral, theory.

62. Throughout I shall use the spelling "Charta" instead of "Carta" since Hume does. Both spellings are still in use. Hume usually uses the English "Great Charter" (often in all capital letters) in any case.

63. Hume typically leaves "Parliament" in lower-case letters, as part of his general program of demystification. (He commonly does the same with other words often capitalized as honorifics: commons, lords, king, queen, bishop, pope, god.) I shall mainly do so as well, for ease and consistency.

Chapter 1. Coordination and Convention

1. Hardin (2007: vii).
2. Schelling (1980 [1960]: 58).
3. These are all taken from Schelling (1980 [1960]: 54–6).
4. Schelling (1980 [1960]: 56).
5. Ibid., 58). The implicit and explicit fans of coordination games are truly ecumenical and not limited to those who prize formal theory. The explicit camp includes MacIntyre (1984: 102), who sees the meeting-in-New-York game as a perfect example of his anti-rational and tradition-based approach to moral questions.
6. Schelling (1980 [1960]: 58–77).
7. Ibid., 298).
8. Moshe et al. (1611: 1 Samuel 8–9).
9. See Goodin (1976: 27).
10. Here Lagerspetz (1995: 200) is particularly clear.
11. "[T]he bigger a coordination coalition the better it is" Goodin (1976: 41).
12. Cardinal utility assumes that it makes sense to quantify the value of outcomes. Agents know precisely how much happier one outcome would make them as compared to another, as in "getting this job would make me eight times as happy as getting that one" (intrapersonal cardinality). And this comparison makes sense across agents as well, as in "if he gets that job and I get this one, he'll have gotten three times as much happiness as I have" (interpersonal cardinality). Both kinds of cardinality are fiercely controversial. Ever since Pareto, many economists have been skeptical of interpersonal comparisons of utility and have argued that one state of affairs can only be called unambiguously better than another if all parties affected would prefer it (voluntary market exchange being the paradigm). Such skepticism has obvious political implications (explicit in, and intended by, Pareto himself and many of his followers). That is, it undercuts one of the classic utilitarian arguments for redistributing income, namely that the rich gain less happiness from each extra dollar than the poor. Less obviously political, and to my mind possibly a little stronger in some cases, is the argument against intrapersonal utility. Many of us know that we would strongly prefer one outcome to another while having no idea how to quantify by how much. A common way of "solving" this problem, by asking how much we would pay to get one outcome versus another (or a given chance of one outcome versus the same chance of another) merely distorts things further,

given human beings' psychologically complex, nonlinear attitude toward risk and the fact that I may care ever less about an extra dollar as the imagined absolute amounts grow higher. In other words, the plausible assumption that increases in income produce decreasing marginal utility may be an argument *for* interpersonal comparisons of utility, roughly speaking, but *against* intrapersonal ones!

13. As argued in Hardin (2007).

14. However, Russell Hardin's arguments (1999: 132 and chapter 5) suggest that a certain absence of obvious cardinal imbalances—this is not his language—might be necessary. If a constitution permanently and explicitly locks in certain relative gains and losses, it will be unsustainable. A constitution will be the object of a rough consensus only if nobody can predict the relative winners and losers it will produce in the future. Moreover, if a constitution entrenches a theory of economics or other policy positions at time T that is supposed to bind actors at time T + n, it will probably be a bad theory since policy knowledge is progressive.

15. Here Hume means interested in the sense of instrumental rationality, not narrow self-interest. In 1477, both Charles VII of France and Edward IV of England are led by irrational passions—"animosity and revenge" for Charles, "indolence and pleasure" for Edward—to perform actions that frustrate the geopolitical ends they intend to pursue.

16. Lagerspetz (1995: 32–3).

17. See Hume, E: PAN.

18. Lagerspetz (1995: 38) notes this possibility but does not stress it.

19. Compare Albert Hirshmann (1977: 4–5) on the development of commerce and interest theories in opposition to earlier values of glory and religious virtue: his story entails "the identification of a sequence of concatenated ideas and propositions whose final outcome is necessarily hidden from the proponents of the individual links, at least in the early stages of the process; for they would have shuddered—and revised their thinking—had they realized where their ideas would ultimately lead." On the ubiquity of unintended consequences in Hume's thought, especially his *History*, see Whelan (2001); on the impossibility in principle of predicting the social consequences of technological change, Popper (1988 [1982]).

20. Lagerspetz (1995: 33ff., 43–50; quotation at 50).

21. Whelan's (1985: chapter 5) careful reading of Hume's "skepticism" is similar, though it does not use rational choice language.

22. Schelling (1980 [1960]: 77).

23. Ibid., Appendix C, 294–6).

24. See Luce and Raiffa (1957: 5.3, 90–94). Luce and Raiffa are, however, wiser than many of their followers in stressing that without clues or communication this game is potentially "wilder" than many others and immune to easy equilibrium solutions.

25. Chwe (2001: 97–9).

26. Calvert (1992); Dickson (forthcoming); and more briefly Hardin (1982: 209).

27. Hardin (1999).

28. Hardin (2007).

29. Goodin (1980: 211ff.). That said, taking the point further suggests that one remedy against such manipulation is to pick a very old map over a "new and improved" one on the grounds that the former could not possibly have been manipulated to serve present cartographers' purposes.

30. Chwe (2001).

31. "But where no force interposes, and election takes place; what is this election so highly vaunted? It is either the combination of a few great men, who decide for the whole, and will allow of no opposition: Or it is the fury of a multitude, that follow a seditious ringleader, who is not known, perhaps, to a dozen among them, and who owes his advancement merely to his own impudence, or to the momentary caprice of his fellows" (E: OC, 472). For more on this passage see chapter 3, under "General Consent."

32. The first use of "communicative" in the sense "Of, relating to, or characterized by the communication of information" occurs only in the seventeenth century (OED, meaning 7). It was recently made famous as a political concept by Habermas (1987).

33. I use the non Humean term "ordinary" partly to avoid having to choose between the adjectives "artificial" and "natural," which would both be accurate in Hume's terminology: the conventions in question are artificial because they correspond to what Hume in individualist mode calls artificial virtues, and natural because they correct flaws of human nature that always and everywhere need correction. Conventions arise by "laws of nature" in that sense (T 3.2.1.19, SBN 484).

34. All but the last three are discussed in the *Treatise*. Hume in EPM.Dial.19, 32, SBN 331, 335, strongly suggests that French gallantry, which licensed adultery but not fornication, is a viable alternative to English chastity and the double standard. One might speculate that the necessary good to be furthered in each case, in an age of traditional economic roles and before artificial contraception, is avoiding babies' being born with no means of support. Good manners (taking turns in conversation, feigned modesty to cover natural self-regard, etc.) appears briefly, and seems to have all the characteristics of an ordinary convention (E: RPAS, 132). On toleration, see Sabl (2009a); on money, Wennerlind (2008). For a slightly different list see Hardin (2007: 85).

35. On simple societies see T 3.2.8.1–3, SBN 539–41. The details of how these sorts of conventions get started, either historically or conceptually, are the subject of intense debate among Hume scholars. To my mind the most adequate treatment is Garrett (2007).

36. See Hardin (2007), citing repeated instances in Hume (see esp. E: OC, 473).

37. Indeterminacy is Russell Hardin's (2003) term. Schelling (1980 [1960]: 65) uses "arbitrary" in a similar sense, but "indeterminate" is better in our context since Hume uses "arbitrary" to describe a convention that could just as well not exist, rather than one that must exist but can take many forms.

38. See Stewart (1992) and McArthur (2007); the "precautionary" label is used by the latter.

39. On these exceptional cases see E: IPC, 513, and chapter 5 of this text. Dees (1992: 241), citing Hume's treatment of feudal property in H 1.456–61, notes that different property conventions might be suited to different political structures. He draws from this a relativist conclusion, but one might equally draw a progress-oriented one if desired and if one believes, as Hume does, that political structures themselves can be ranked.

40. Or else, in more skeptical mode, they will stress the ways in which Humean outcomes frustrate individual intentions, using either the language of collective action problems (in which individuals choose strategies rather than outcomes) or that of skeptical social and political philosophers who doubt that planned orders can improve on evolved or spontaneous ones. See respectively Hardin (2007: 171) and

Berry (2009: chapter 4). Berry claims affinities between Hume and both Oake-shott and Hayek on this score. At least with respect to politics, the former analogy is more persuasive. But I am not sure that any of these skeptical readings counts as "conservative" in any usual sense or necessarily entails politically conservative conclusions.

41. See Sabl (2002).

42. H 4.354, Appendix III.

43. As claimed by Dees (1992: 241).

44. Or else linguistic, as in the classic treatment by Lewis (1969). The parallels between linguistic and constitutional conventions—and between changes in each—deserve separate treatment. For some quick reflections, see the Conclusion, note 22.

45. This is why Hume praises the effects of religion in the Middle Ages: the content of religion was absurd, but the presence of a formal authority independent of baronial dominaton was a good in itself (H 2.14).

46. In the first edition of his *History*, in a passage which the attacks of MacQueen (1990 [1756]) forced him to withdraw, Hume described the "local and temporary" religious opinions known as Catholicism and Protestantism, implying that future ages would not know what either sect was. See Todd (1982: xiv–xviii). "Prevailing" is Hume's persistently skeptical word for customs that must be pragmatically respected but are fundamentally wrongheaded, not to be missed when they disappear. Hume uses it in the *Essays* to describe past fashions that we are well rid of or popular opinions that he is about to refute (E: ST, 246; M, 342), and in the *History* to describe the irresistible force of religion (H 1.235, 242, 324; 2.402; 5.304; 6.347, 380) or faction (6.523) or in general practices or opinions that are popular, therefore perhaps warranting pragmatic accommodation, but silly or destructive (H 2.83, 170; 287; 3.169). According to Adam Smith's famous account of Hume's death, Hume imagined himself begging Charon for more time in this world so as to "'have the satisfaction of seeing the downfal [*sic*] of some of the prevailing systems of superstition,'" only to be upbraided for seeking a stay of "'many hundred years'" (Smith to William Strahan, November 9, 1776; reprinted in E: xlvi).

47. On religion see E: PG, 60–61, and Korsgaard (1999); on faction, E: IP 43 and Sabl (2006a). Herdt's (1997) treatment of both subjects is subtle and searching at the cost of great complexity.

48. Mackie (1996).

49. See Sabl (2009a).

50. "Even the clergy, as their duty leads them to inculcate morality, may justly be thought, so far as regards this world, to have no other useful object of their institution [than 'the support of the twelve judges']" (E: OG, 37–8). For Hume's view that all existing religions tend to have a "bad influence . . . on morality" rather than a good one, see NHR 14.70–73.

51. See Baier (2008: 81–99), with excellent citations to the scholarship (especially Siebert [1990: chapter 1] and Herdt [1990: 196ff.]) on religion's portrayal in the *History*. Baier notes (90, 82) that "[t]here is not the same sort of obvious case for uniformity of religious worship in a community that there is for, say, uniform acceptance of the same conventions concerning property, or rules of the road," and that while one of Hume's characters says "true" religion ought to "regulate the heart of men, humanize their conduct, and infuse the spirit of temperance, order, and obedience," actual religion in the *History* generally perverts human virtues, drowns

out salutary human feelings, and inspires political violence. Chapter 2 will cite evidence on this point.

52. Hume suggests that an unwillingness to change religion for pragmatic reasons is a Protestant vice that must be acknowledged as universal but should still be lamented (H 3.431–41; 4.18–19, 395–6 [note "Q"]; and especially H 4.322). Compare Hume's apparent approval of ordinary people's policy, during the English Civil War, "always to adhere to any power, which was uppermost, and to support the established government" (H 6.60). As Hume would have had closely in mind, such political flexibility would also have required religious flexibility, switching back and forth between Anglicanism on the one hand and Puritan or Independent forms of Protestantism on the other, since royalists prohibited the latter and Commonwealthmen the former.

53. Smith to Alexander Wedderburn, August 14, 1776, cited in Baier (2008: 99).

54. McArthur (2007: 129); compare Berry (2009: 70ff.).

55. Calvert (1992: 19).

56. Ibid., 15–16. Compare 17: "Close control of the leader is possible in principle, but may be undesirable in practice because the cost of coordination failure is too great."

57. Calvert's treatment of "authority" as a convention that evolves over the fairly short term and is fragile in the face of self-fulfilling doubts in the leader's authority (1992: 15) is strangely anarchic, better suited to the study of factions within legislatures than the study of why legislatures have authority in the first place. Those who do hold elected office are immune, to a first approximation, from immediately losing office when they lose face. Chapter 4 has more on this.

58. Przeworski (1986: 52–5; quotations on 55 and 52, respectively). Compare Przeworski (1998) claiming that when a corporation buys advertising in its own name, it seeks not to persuade on the substance of the ad but to signal the fact that it and other corporations have the capacity to control common media knowledge.

59. E: BG, 52.

60. In a special case: if the people rebel against conventions of authority but not those of property, a rebellion led by elites may lead to a "new order" resembling the old one except with regard to formal political forms—the case of the Scottish rebellion against Charles I, which established an effective "republic" while retaining the (absent) king as a mere figurehead (H 5.257; compare H 5.262, 263, 266, 347, 421, and 6.7).

61. Tucker (1970: 81–2).

62. See Sabl (2009b).

63. Shulman (1998).

64. Hardin (2003: 2); compare Hardin (2007: 171).

65. This is to dispute the arguments of Baier (1993)—who at the point of writing that work had studied carefully mostly Hume's *Treatise*, not (as later) the *History* as well.

66. Waldron (1999: 117).

67. Lasswell (1936).

Chapter 2. Coordinating Interests: The Liberalism of Enlargement

1. See Hardin (1999: 99ff.) on the anti-Federalists.

2. Under some circumstances, tribalism may be more rational for individuals than impartial conventions of property and government (Hardin 1995). The case envi-

sioned here is different: impartial conventions that would work and would further each individual's interest are available, but something psychologically prevents people from adopting them.

3. See chapter 1, "Circumstances of Authority and Qualitative Coordination."

4. The clearest statement of this is in H 5.67; instances in which Hume adduces this phenomenon include (among many others), H 2.401; H 4.18; H 5. 80, 112, 146, 214, 221, 223, 243, 252, 258, 260, 262, 323, 441–2, 513, 527, 538–9; H 6.8–9, 61, 80, 106, 143–4. Particularly vivid examples and statements include H 1.250; H 4.221; H 5.342–5, 380, 493–4, 514; H 6.3–4, 113, 128–9.

5. Among a great many other examples, see H 1.85, 104, 152, 215, 217, 286, 309–10. But Hume, with his usual mild anti-anti-Catholicism, takes "protestant writers [*sic*: lower case]" to task for over-stressing this point (2.3–5), gives credit to the Church for its real contributions in preserving learning and checking (however occasionally and imperfectly) what would otherwise have been near-absolute power of those who commanded armed force (H 2.14, 258, 518, 520, 537 [note T]), and concedes that many who pursued Church power in medieval times were subjectively sincere in their piety (H 1.333).

6. See NHR 14.71–2 (unmotivated "austerities" are "distinguished marks of devotion"); compare H 1.139 and NHR 14.73 on how priests promote "unaccountable" duties to cement their own power.

7. Thus "[c]elibacy, fasting, penance, mortification, self-denial, humility, silence, solitude, and the whole train of monkish virtues" are "rejected by men of sense" (or, better in Hume's view, counted as vices) because they "serve to no manner of purpose" with respect to either interest or entertainment (EPM 9.1.3, SBN 270). Here Hume seems to blame superstition for providing the theoretical basis for praising these vices as virtues, and "gloomy, hair-brained" enthusiasm for being more likely to make people actually practice such vices.

8. In DNR 12.221–2, Philo, the skeptical character whose views are often assumed to be largely (if not totally) Hume's, claims that "superstition and enthusiasm" have little durably good effect on conduct but rather by "the raising up a new and frivolous species of merit" weaken our mundane moral motives and weaken our benevolence in favor of a self-seeking desire for salvation. Illustrations of this theme are a very common motif in the *History's* early volumes: see, e.g., H 1.30, 41, 49, 61, 51, 90–91 (on which see Siebert 1990: 74); 92, 93, 99, 124–5, 133, 282. Herdt (1997: 168–88) contains a much fuller discussion.

9. Compare H 6.4 in which radical Protestants after Charles I's murder adopt extreme, anarchical positions but even "those among the republicans, who adopted not such extravagancies, were so intoxicated with their saintly character, that they supposed themselves possessed of peculiar privileges; and all professions, oaths, laws, and engagements had, in a great measure, lost their influence over them. The bands of society were every where loosened; and the irregular passions of men were encouraged by speculative principles, still more unsocial and irregular." Individual, antinomian fanaticism is in one sense the best case. When a whole party is suffused with religious fanaticism, the result is not to undermine attachment to conventions but to turn those conventions' ability to coordinate and to be self-enforcing to partisan purposes: the social virtues, enlisted in the service of party, become a "virulent poison" (H 5.380). The only other time Hume refers to a "virulent . . . poison" is in E: S, 578—in discussing superstition.

10. This is a deliberate reference to Hobbes' assertion (1991: 226, chapter 29) that fear of sovereign authority, which he calls tyrannophobia, is like rabies, sometimes called "hydrophobia," because it leads its victims to shun the very thing (water, or authority) that would save them. Since Hume's theory of authority is not dictatorial, the Humean counterpart to Hume's fear of tyranny is a fear of convention.

11. See the discussion of this passage in Siebert (1990: 19–20) and Sabl (2006b 555–6).

12. See Sabl (2006a) for further explication.

13. Among many other examples, see H 6.519, 533.

14. This is true of factions of "interest" and "affection" as well as those of principle. "Interest" means not economic welfare but political office, and competition over place is both zero-sum and fierce. And parties of affection, for Hume, are above all those that want one royal family or another to be in power—the potential source of civil war (see E: PG, 59, 63; OC, PO, PS CP, passim). The "Coalition of Parties" and "Protestant Succession" essays argue in effect that issues of affection—in particular the Tory attachment to the Stuart succession—are getting in the way of recognizing that the status quo constitution embodies a reasonable accommodation of both parties' principles (on this see in particular E: PGB, 71). Hume's proposed "coalition of parties" is in fact an example of conflicts over principle being *more* tractable than conflicts over place. The existing English constitution should please both partisans of authority and those of liberty—but those who seek *office* under the Whig or Tory banners can only succeed by displacing the other team.

15. Hume notes that the escalating effect of party strife, whereby "imitating" the outrages of the opposite party serves by a contrary logic to "justify" further retaliations, is obvious to outside observers but not to partisans (H 2.310). The partisan desire to take revenge—the "usual violence of party" is opposed to both the "common sense of mankind, in more peaceable times," and to the "maxims of equity and justice" (if there's a difference) (H 2.459–60).

16. Compare Hardin's (1995) account of dueling as a class marker for the eighteenth- and nineteenth-century European aristocracy.

17. Herdt (1997: 15). One might add that the remedy works specifically against *superstition*, which involves fear of unknown causes. Enthusiasm, which seems to be a theological reflection of a stubborn hyper-individualism and of discontent with the compromises required for modern conventions to succeed (koinophobia), may be less easily cured.

18. On extensive sympathy see Herdt (1997: xii, 47–9, 100–101 and passim). Herdt in different places suggests at least five main mechanisms through which she sees Hume as trying to extend or correct our sympathies: irony; sentimentalism in the purpose of making vivid others' suffering or the consequences of factional strife; the historical form itself (which renders us interested in characters but not attached to their [past] partisan allegiances); the moderation and liberalization of religion; the correction of moral taste through the deliberate taking on of multiple points of view; and dramatic or theatrical presentations that unexpectedly interest us in the troubles of fictional protagonists. She also suggests, not unreasonably, that Hume's immoderate disdain for religion limited his own sympathies and led him to tar all religious aspirations as absurd. Krause (2008: chapter 5) calls for both appreciating and expanding on the ways in which political deliberation and argument, as well as civic education, can be employed to similar ends. Compare Michael Frazer's argument (2010: 46–64) that only "corrected" sentiments that take on a "general"

point of view have normative worth. He too (at 178–82) takes deliberation and civic education to be the methods or mechanisms by which sentiments are corrected. This whole literature builds, of course, on work explicating Hume's story of how we correct our *moral* sentiments so as to move from a partial to a general point of view (see, e.g., Baier 1991; Korsgaard 1999). It tends to take for granted that a common moral language is desirable and necessary for politics.

19. Hume's central treatments of extensive sympathy occur at T 2.2.9.15–17, 3.3.1.11, and 3.3.6.3, SBN 387–8, 578–9, 619. Hume's well-known claim that "extensive sympathy" is consistent with "limited generosity" (my sympathy with another gives me pain when presented with something that gives another "uneasiness," "tho' I may not be willing to sacrifice any thing of my own interest, or cross any of my passions, for his satisfaction") is at T 3.3.1.23, SBN 586.

20. Unlike economists, concerned with momentary market demand, and political scientists concerned with the short-term translation of preferences into votes and other political actions, the political theorist on a historical scale simply has no reason to deny that preferences change over time or to regard political strategy as having no effect on that change. Hume makes this explicit. The assumption that "[s]overeigns must take mankind as they find them, and cannot pretend to introduce any violent change in their principles and ways of thinking," is true only in the short term: "A long course of time, with a variety of accidents and circumstances, are requisite to produce those great revolutions, which so much diversify the face of human affairs" (E: OC, 260). Hume says the "most important law in its consequences" of Henry VII's reign was "that by which the nobility and gentry acquired a power of breaking the ancient entails, and of alienating their estates" (H 3.77). This hastened the transition from birth to wealth as the basis of status and political power (i.e., the Commons rose). Granted, the relationship between structure and agency in Hume's account is complicated: for further discussion see Danford (1990: 177); Forbes (1975: 313–14). I would suggest that what public-policy scholars now call "policy learning"—the most effective and political agency often consists in learning what has happened by accident elsewhere and adopting it purposely in another—both reconciles the two views and is very true to Hume's position (e.g., in E: PRS, 24 and E: RPAS, 125).

21. See Clark (2000: 143–9).

22. See *Le Gout Des Autres* (2000).

23. "[W]here the ideas of morality and decency alter from one age to another, and where vicious manners are described, without being marked with the proper characters of blame and disapprobation . . . I cannot, nor is it proper I should, enter into such sentiments. . . . The want of humanity and of decency, so conspicuous in the characters drawn by several of the ancient poets, even sometimes by HOMER and the GREEK tragedians, diminishes considerably the merit of their noble performances. . . . We are not interested in the fortunes and sentiments of such rough heroes: We are displeased to find the limits of vice and virtue so much confounded: And whatever indulgence we may give to the writer on account of his prejudices, we cannot prevail on ourselves to enter into his sentiments, or bear an affection to characters, which we plainly discover to be blameable" (E: ST, 246).

24. See Hardin (2007: chapter 4).

25. See, e.g., Raphael (2001: chapter 9); Hume writes that "love of gain" or "avidity . . . of acquiring goods and possessions for ourselves and our nearest friends" is the

only passion "insatiable, perpetual, universal, and directly destructive of society" (T 3.2.2.12–13, SBN 491–2). Albert Hirschman, a historical sociologist keen to explain the link between the goals of Enlightenment thought and the blind spots of capitalist society, focuses on Hume's economic essays in portraying him as the quintessential exponent of the view that pre-modern destructive passions must be channeled toward the single goal of peacefully pursuing wealth: Hirschman (1977: esp. 26, 37 [on "love of gain" as synonym for "passion or interest"], 66). Hume, however, is more like Hirschman than the latter realizes in stressing how commerce is not simply peaceful but gives rise to new social divisions and conflicts. For a more extended defense of the primacy of economics thesis regarding Hume, see Stewart (1963: 305–6).

26. The quotation is from Pocock (1983: 252). Livingston (1990: 115) briefly suggests a similar reading of Hume in particular. For fuller treatments see Pocock (1975: chapters 13–15; 1985: 37–50), as well as Finlay (2004), Phillipson (1981), and Robertson (1983: 157–69). As O'Neill (2010: 566) has pointed out, Kalyvas and Katznelson (2008) have largely rediscovered this theme. He might have added that what Pocock described but valued skeptically at best, the latter writers mostly favor. On the civil/civic distinction more generally, see Berger (2011: 47–9).

27. Hume does not expect too much from this thought process. Rather cynically, he describes the hallmark of an "enlarged" mind as the need to come up with complicated *reasons* for hating the enemy general (as most inevitably will) beyond the fact of his being the enemy. Though Hume suggests that forgetting personal enmity may be possible in esthetic matters (see E: ST, 239–40), he does not portray politics the same way.

28. See also E: I, 299–300, one of the epigraphs of this chapter.

29. See also E: JT, 331; H 5.246; L 1.272, and again EPM 3.1.21, SBN 192, where the same logic that suggests that family or clan units should extend rules of justice across a whole society also suggests that "several distinct societies" might benefit from a similar process. Hume praises elites for transcending the "vulgar motive of national antipathy" (H 5.34). For an attack on Hume that effusively praises vulgar motives, see MacIntyre (1988: chapters 15 and 16).

30. This essay, though one of four in which Hume tries on various positions on human existence, is widely thought to be not too far from Hume's own view. A more moderate version of the same sentiment, noting that enlarged views take note of the great variety of tastes around the world but not despairing of a standard that would pronounce some inferior to others, appears at E: ST, 227.

31. A third kind, the geographic "enlargement" made famous by *Federalist* No. 10, works well but contingently. Because Madison assumes a large and heterogeneous country where no faction will have more than local influence, a politics covering the whole country will necessarily fail to track faction (Hamilton et al. 2001 [1788]: No. 10, 47–48). (The only great, national factions that in the event endangered social stability were those centered around slavery, which was not a domestic political cause in Great Britain.) Because Hume (implicitly) assumes the opposite premise, a fairly small and homogeneous country in which factions, unchecked, will be national in scope (Hume's Great Britain was one-eighth the size of the American colonies), Hume proposes essentially the *opposite* strategy—breaking Britain up into a federal republic of ten thousand parishes, so that the political passions of one will not, by "influence and example," cause another to be "infected" (or, in another

metaphor, so that "the force of popular currents and tides" will be "broken") See E: IPC, 523 and 512–29 passim; E: FPG, 36).

32. See Immerwahr (1992: 305ff.). For treatments of the *History* as a project aimed at undermining partisan passions (both in the particular case and more generally by encouraging good mental habits), see Forbes (1975) and Jones (1990: 20 and passim).

33. See note 14 earlier in this chapter.

34. Immerwahr (1992: 299) portrays this as a violent passion being overcome by a calm one. The text does not seem to warrant this reading. The benevolent concern for others triumphs only when it itself becomes fairly violent.

35. Hume attributes disinterested zeal to *both* parties at the outset of the English civil war. The problem, given that conventions of authority were in dispute, was that each party in principle preferred consensus and peace to partisan strife but had no idea how best to achieve it. But this is a very different situation than one in which the parties actually desired each other's extermination, and explains why a bloodless restoration (on the basis, more or less, of a return to the constitution that existed before the war) was later possible.

36. Hardin (2007: 23) claims that Hume's naturalism, which he glosses as value-free social science (a bit anachronistically in my view), ought to prevent him from recommending as good particular virtues or actions—Hume's regrettable "panegyric moments" notwithstanding.

37. On justice as founded on self-interest but reinforced by "*education, and the artifices of politicians*" (emphases in original), see T 3.2.5.12, SBN 523.

38. Forbes (1975: 136 and ff.).

39. On the Glorious Revolution coalition—Hume's own marginal note is "Coalition of Parties," just as in his Essay by that name—see H 6.502ff. In the end "every one from principle, interest, or animosity" united against James II (6.518). (The 99 percent figure is on 6.290.) On the unity of Scotland against Wilkes and the "mad and wicked Rage against the Scots" that he promoted, see L 1.492; 2.224. Forbes points out that Hume saw the stakes as "constitution" vs. "mob" (Forbes 1975: 191, citing L 2.218). For the influence of Wilkes' hate speech on Hume, see Pocock (1985: chapter 7) and Stewart (1992: 303–7; the anti-Semitism comparison is on 303, citing and endorsing Lewis Namier and John Brooke, *The History of Parliament. The House of Commons, 1754–1790* [3 vols., London: Her Majesty's Stationery Office, 1964]: 1:168). See also chapter 6 in this book.

40. "Let us therefore try, if it be possible, from the foregoing doctrine, to draw a lesson of moderation with regard to the parties, into which our country is at present divided; at the same time, that we allow not this moderation to abate the industry and passion, with which every individual is bound to pursue the good of his country" (E: PRS, 27; internal citation omitted).

41. Baier, noting that for Hume "we naturally desire what is forbid" (T 2.3.4.5, SBN 421), makes the fascinating point that Hume's morality aims to "minimize flat prohibitions" because such prohibitions are not just vain but counterproductive (1991: 169). But Hume's political theory does not rest strongly on this maxim of moral psychology.

42. Immerwahr (1992: 306).

43. Sabl (2009a).

44. "[N]othing opens the eyes of men so readily as their interest" (H 1.306). The metaphor is also used in the same sense, to indicate dissent against a corrupt Church,

on H 1.441; 2.171; see similarly H 2.9, 70, 71, 278–9, 325, 348–9, 356–7, 374. Perhaps parliamentarism can be seen as magnifying this effect: particular individuals might place a taste for religious authority over economic interest, even for a lifetime, but the assembled representatives of the nation's wealth are less likely to do so.

45. Forbes (1975); Miller (1981: 192–205).

46. Compare Krause (2004: 634ff.).

47. See Sabl (2006b: 551–4), with extensive citations to the *History*. "[D]emolition of the hero" is from Hirshman 1977: 11, citing Paul Bénichou, *Morales du grand siècle* (Paris: Gallimard, Collection Idées, 1948: 155–80).

48. T 3.3.2.12–15, SBN 559–601.

49. Hume's military heroes who display some or all of these qualities include, besides Monk (see chapter 5), Lucius Carey, viscount Falkland, a constitutional moderate and reluctant (though brave) participant in the Civil War (5.416–17); several admirals including Blake ("one of the most perfect characters of the age" [6.84]), Sprague, de Ruyter, and Tromp the Elder (6.41, 47–50, 66, 77, 83–4, 202–4, 260–62, 279–80); and the Duke of Bedford (who inherited a project of conquest but wins Hume's praise as a "great man" through his conduct in retreating from it [2.405]). For de Ruyter's decision to withdraw from a naval battle in order "as long as possible, to render service to his country" in spite of others' urging him "to turn upon the English, and render his life a dear purchase to the victors," see 6.204; on how modern battles may be preferred to ancient because they allow for orderly retreats, see E: PAN, 405. For Hume's derogation of conquests that serve "glory" rather than "interest," see H 2.423. Hume's praise in volume 2 of the *History* of Bertrand du Guesclin, constable of France during the Hundred Years' War, is particularly worth studying. Hume praises Guesclin's strategic and logistical judgment over his valor, admires Guesclin for his skeptical attitude toward the Pope (whose ability to grant absolution Gueslin regards as less important than his ability to grant money [2.264]), and avoids mentioning Guesclin's flamboyant nickname, "Eagle of Brittany." See H 2.264ff. on the "character" (i.e., reputation) of Guesclin. Hume calls him "one of the most accomplished characters of the age" at 2.262 and "the first consummate general that had yet appeared in Europe" (as of about 1370) at 2.270. In general, and not surprisingly, Hume favors the Fabian style of warfare, which puts a premium on discipline and resources—and almost by definition is a style that favors defenders over conquerors; the army with the longest supply lines loses. Examples of Hume's palpable appreciation for good military plans, whether strategic or logistical, include (inter alia) H 2.229, 248–9, 256–7, 258, 262, 266, 270; H 5.220.

50. The domestic convention of toleration, though very rough at the time, also played a key role: many English Catholics, far from supporting Spain, enlisted in the English navy, subscribed English ships, or mustered troops for home defense (H 4.265–6 and see Sabl 2009a: 531–2).

51. Compare 2.135, where an inferior army gives its commander no chance of "signalizing that valour, which had formerly made him so terrible to his enemies." Dees (1992: 236n47) notes that the first observation is among the *History*'s "wonderful ironies": the ship-money whose levying caused Charles I's downfall was responsible for Cromwell's later glory. See too H 6.262: a "sense of honour" is indeed useful in desperate circumstances when an army is clearly overmatched—but this only allows an army to keep the field, not to win. Hume in general refuses to describe

the "[n]umberless feats of valour" that are the only things that occupy medieval chroniclers (H 2.395; compare the irony of H 2.266: "Historians of that age are commonly very copious in describing the shock of armies in battle, the valour of the combatants, the slaughter and various successes of the day").

52. When Rollo the Dane around the turn of the ninth century "united all the valour of his countrymen with the policy of more civilized nations," England, with its "most excellent military as well as civil institutions" established by Alfred the Great, was impervious to his invasions. But France had "no means of defence" and had to let Rollo settle in some of the provinces he had conquered—what became "Normandy," named after the norsemen (H 1.112–13). Compare Cromwell's ability to combine "prudence" with "valour" (H 5.473). Valour alone is not one of the passions that Hume describes as "calm" or "settled" but is rather flighty: "precarious in most men," as in Prince Rupert who fought with bravery on the field but then surrendered a fortified town for no good reason (H 5.475).

53. On the sea, the contrary thesis that reckless courage is a virtue only seems true but isn't (H 3.101, note "p").

54. See especially Robertson (1983).

55. Regarding liberty see, e.g., H 6.187–8 and 2.456; "regular militia" at H 1.70.

56. On Henry II's proto-regular armies, made possible by replacing some feudal dues with scutage (so-called shield-money) see H 1.304, 350, 374.

57. H 1.249; H 2.195, 233–4, 266; "miserable state" at 2.193; no "order in great armies" at 2.266 (and contrast 2.388, where "discipline, however imperfect," allows for "some appearance of order"); long quotation at 2.230. Compare the similar point at E: PAN, 405: "The long thin lines, required by fire-arms, and the quick decision of the fray, render our modern engagements but partial reencounters, and enable the general, who is foiled in the beginning of the day, to draw off the greater part of his army, sound and entire." At H 2.340 Hume suggests that around 1400 the maximum manageable size of an army was about 12,000.

58. See H 2.449: Richard Duke of York lost his life because "he thought, that he should be for ever disgraced, if, by taking shelter behind walls, he should for a moment resign the victory to a woman" (the woman being Margaret of Anjou, Henry VI's queen, whom Shakespeare's characters call "she-wolf" and "tigress"; Hume's assessment of her "ferocity" is on H 2.488).

59. Buchan (2006: 176) argues, with good evidence, that in Hume and other Scottish Enlightenment thinkers, "'civilization' was used to explain how domestic processes of pacification created civil societies connected to powerful sovereign states with enhanced capacities for the successful waging of war." His evidence that Hume actually wanted civilized states to spend resources on subjugating "barbarous" peoples is thin. But Buchan's broader thesis could be amply demonstrated by focusing on what Hume says not about the New World but about Ireland: e.g., H 5.47, 313, 336, 338. Even when Hume blames English colonists (as of 1599) for refusing the Irish the protection of the laws and for treating the Irish as "inhuman masters" treat "wild beasts" (H 4.311), his complaint is not that the English conquered the Irish but that they failed to use force for civilizing ends: failed to impose on the Irish the "civility and slavery" that the Romans had imposed on the Britons (H 4.312; similarly H 1.345).

60. For Hume's determination to be fairer to France than "vulgar Whig" sentiment allowed, see Forbes (1975), chapter 5.

61. Goodin (1976: 27). Compare Hardin's (1999: 295) observation that the United States' Anti-Federalists "wanted to be oligarchs in their small worlds rather than more nearly equal citizens in a larger world"—and not unreasonably, given this, sought to ground government in the shared values that applied only to the former.

62. Stewart 1963: 224ff. is particularly good on this.

63. Here I dissent from Danford's view (1990: 169–70, 182) that Hume portrays the barons' life as contrary to the usual tendencies of human nature, requiring only a "trigger" to reset things to a more natural equilibrium (in analogy to the Spartan regime that Hume calls "a prodigy," founded on a "violent" policy "contrary to the more natural and usual course of things" [E: OC, 259–60]). While the fact that a whole society only honored "the military profession" (H 2.522), may, as Danford says, imply a sort of perversity, for the *barons specifically* to favor feudalism and military values was, or at least seemed, perfectly in accord with their own interests. Though it made everyone else miserable, it gave their own order power.

64. H 2.179. Compare 2.428 on Warwic (dubbed "the Kingmaker" during the War of the Roses), the last of these politically dangerous barons.

65. Hume does not give details, but he may mean the progress of enclosures for sheep and the wool trade, through which estates (to extrapolate beyond Hume's explicit argument) came to produce a surplus in money rather than food. The progress of enclosures, which progressed under the Tudors, is a subject Hume pays much attention to elsewhere, e.g., 5.36–7, 138, 236. Hume, while sympathetic to rebellions by yeomen and peasants forced off the land by enclosures, calls "the converting of arable land into pasture" "the general turn of that age, which no laws could prevent" (including the Star Chamber [5.236]) because meat was clearly more profitable than grain. But with regard to an earlier period Hume clearly thinks the main driving force of enclosures was the sale of wool, whose manufacture outcompeted agriculture because it was easier to make new discoveries in the former than in the latter (3.369).

66. On learning and consumption see 2.174–5: The Knights Templar, having taken their Crusade booty back to Europe, were, "being all men of birth, educated, according to the custom of that age, without any tincture of letters." They therefore had to choose between a monastic life and the "fashionable amusements of hunting, gallantry, and the pleasures of the table" and had the good sense to prefer the latter. The nobility in general before the Tudor era "valued themselves on ignorance as their privilege, and left learning to monks and schoolmasters" (H 2.477).

67. Danford (1990: 172, 183ff.) stresses this passage, and notes its resemblance to the passages in (E: PAN, 383–4) that make a similar point with respect to ancient masters and slaves as Hume makes in the *History* with respect to barons and villains. Smith (1981 [1776]: 3.4.10–15) makes a similar argument, citing Hume.

68. Danford (1990: 177).

69. "Robbers" appears on H 2.189, 279, and esp. 1.288; "gangs" on 2.190.

70. "[A]ll the considerable traders will be tempted to throw up their commerce, in order to purchase some of those employments, to which privileges and honours are annexed"; thus "[c]ommerce . . . is apt to decay in absolute governments, not because it is there less *secure*, but because it is less *honourable*" (E: CL, 93 [emphasis in original]).

71. "Riches are valuable at all times, and to all men; because they always purchase pleasures, such as men are accustomed to, and desire: Nor can any thing restrain

or regulate the love of money, but a sense of honour and virtue; which, if it be not nearly equal at all times, will naturally abound most in ages of knowledge and refinement" (E: RA, 276).

72. See H 1.16; the Saxons were so bent on war that they tried to undermine the alternative occupations that would have competed with it: "anxious to prevent any improvements of that nature . . . the leaders, by annually distributing anew all the land among the inhabitants of each village, kept them from attaching themselves to particular possessions, or making such progress in agriculture as might divert their attention from military expeditions, the chief occupation of the community" (H 1.16). Compare H 1.5, 81–2; 2.54.

73. Compare H 1.164. That security of property is the basic prerequisite for further progress has been named as one of Hume's central claims, and not wrongly (see McArthur 2007: 46ff., who stresses the central importance of "general laws"). But as Danford (1990: 163–4, 162) has pointed out, the causation goes both ways: "The insecurity of property and want of liberty (really two sides of the same coin) precluded the development of trade and commerce, and the lack of economic progress in turn contributed to insecurity"—by allowing barons to deliberately sabotage alternatives For further evidence see 1.166.

74. Hume begins a new chapter with this passage, which merits its own marginal gloss "Institution of the Garter." It is rare for Hume to spend two chapters on one monarch, and it seems significant that this event was the occasion for a break. In mocking the manners of James I's realm, Hume writes that "[c]ivil honours, which now hold the first place, were, at that time, subordinate to the military. The fury of duels too prevailed more than at any time before or since. This was the turn, that the romantic chivalry, for which the nation was formerly so renowned, had lately taken" (H 5.133, Appendix 4).

75. Berger (1970).

76. "Though the persons, of whom [the Parliament] was chiefly composed, seemed to enjoy great independance, they really possessed no true liberty; and the security of each individual among them, was not so much derived from the general protection of law, as from his own private power and that of his confederates. *The authority of the monarch, though far from absolute, was irregular, and might often reach him: The current of a faction might overwhelm him: A hundred considerations, of benefits and injuries, friendships and animosities, hopes and fears, were able to influence his conduct*; and amidst these motives a regard to equity and law and justice was commonly, in those rude ages, of little moment. Nor did any man entertain thoughts of opposing present power, who did not deem himself strong enough to dispute the field with it by force, and was not prepared to give battle to the sovereign or the ruling party" (H 2.179–80 [emphasis added]).

77. Compare Hume's comment on H 2.530 Note "E": while different sectors of nonnobles used the Commons ever-more systematically over time to vindicate their common interest in redressing grievances, "[t]he barons had few petitions. Their privileges were of more ancient date: Grievances seldom affected them: They were themselves the chief oppressors."

78. Hume is placing sentiments in the mouth of the Bishop of Carlisle (at the deposition of Richard II in 1399) that are really his own. The original source (Hayward 1610: 101–110, whom Hume calls "Heywarde") contains almost none of the ideas that Hume is allegedly summarizing and on the contrary stresses biblical arguments.

79. Whelan (2004: 6–8, 127–31, 130, 293).

80. Whelan (2004: chapter 3). This is not the place for a detailed assessment of Whelan's reading. I would stress more than he does the possibility that when Hume describes rulers acting with expedience he is often engaging in satire rather than praise.

81. This section draws on Sabl (2006b: 551–4), which contains a slightly different treatment.

82. Compare 263, where Spartan principles are called "too disinterested and too difficult to support." On this point Manzer (1996: 492–3) is excellent.

83. Though Hume knew this only from study, not from personal experience. In letters to Gilbert Elliot (L 2.161) and Turgot (L 2.181) he seems not even to consider the possibility that a government minister could find power and the execution of policy desirable for its own sake. He told Montesquieu he had consecrated his life to the "peaceful ambition" of philosophy and belles-lettres (L 1.138).

84. Compare 2.451: even at his accession, Edward displayed "every popular quality" and thereby won great "public favour."

85. Braudy (2003 [1970]: 70) notes that Hume's historical heroes are "men of moderation . . . who possessed 'disinterested zeal' and contributed to the smooth running of a state too often disrupted by a profusion of drama, gestures, and striking personalities."

86. In addition to passages otherwise cited here, uses of these adjectives in more or less this sense include: "magnificent" (H 1.129, 239, 386; 2.419; 3.40; 4.268; 5.494, 552–3, 6.302; and esp. 2.26); "splendid" (H 1.217, 387; 2.29, 30–31, 270, 276–7, 380; 5.265; and esp. 2.244, 255, 267); "noisy" (H 2.270, 6.115, 128); "spectacle"(H 1.129, 4.268). When Hume does contrast showy behavior to Christian humility, he does so in the course of praising the former as fun and the latter as ridiculous in its opposition to pleasure: H 3.355; 4.198. To be sure, Hume realizes that showy gestures can be instrumentally useful, as a device for gaining popularity, the source of a salutary ceremony, or a commitment device. For the popularity function see H 1.192; 3.8; 4.216; for ceremony H 6.43 (the Commonwealth's "magnificent funeral" for Ireton was appropriate, and the kind of thing on which the public spirit of a republic is founded); for commitment H 3.4 (Henry VII's acceptance of a "magnificent present"—an ornamental crown—declares his decisive intention to claim the crown; compare the "splendor" and "spectacle" of his formal coronation on H 3.9).

87. See Hanvelt (2012).

88. The last phrase Hume credits to the Tudor historian Polydore Vergil. Henry VIII's house historian is widely seen as biased against Henry VII; but what Polydore may have considered satire, Hume takes as praise.

89. Compare 1.392, and on the Crusades generally 1.234ff. Hume doubts that the Crusades were primarily a matter of religious devotion: "the passion for Crusades was really in that age the passion for glory" (2.144). Certainly England's most notorious crusader, Richard Lionheart, was in Hume's view "impelled more by the love of military glory than by superstition" (1.378).

90. Hume waxes both melancholy and bitter on the fact that Henry VIII, a violent tyrant, has a better reputation in the eighteenth century than Charles I, who made comparatively mild and honest constitutional mistakes (History 5.583, note KK). See similarly 2.271: "The English are apt to consider with peculiar fondness" Edward III on account of his "glorious" victories, ignoring his domestic good government.

91. A point made, with good citations, by Whelan (2004: 16).
92. This is partly a point about military discipline: only a professional army, funded through the taxes that a surplus makes possible, can be properly trained.
93. Hardin (1999: 17 and passim).
94. Price (1965: 102).
95. Hume here calls Edward's policy "generous." He cannot mean loose with money, of which there is little evidence here. Earlier senses connoting nobility and/or valour (OED 2, 3) seem apt.
96. "In restoring a loan, or paying a debt, his divinity is nowise beholden to him; because these acts of justice are what he was bound to perform, and what many would have performed, were there no god in the universe. But if he fast a day, or give himself a sound whipping; this has a direct reference, in his opinion, to the service of God. No other motive could engage him to such austerities" (NHR 14.72).
97. Baier (1991: 212) writes of Hume that "[c]ourage has to be transferred from the battlefield to more peaceful fields (or to merely domestic battlefields), before it gets approved as a virtue. Once there, it becomes scarcely distinguishable from patience, serenity and the virtues that Hume usually puts under the heading of the 'amiable' rather then [sic] the 'awful,' the good rather than the great." To the extent that that is true, courage will cease to be immediately agreeable; what is merely good is not sublime or noble.
98. Siebert (1990: 168). Siebert mentions Bacon as an example, but Hume considers him inferior to Galileo and Kepler (H 5.153). Better examples, besides Galileo, would be Newton, "the greatest and rarest genius that ever arose for the ornament and instruction of the species" (H 6.542), and in particular John Napier, the inventor of logarithms, whom Hume calls "the person to whom the title of a GREAT MAN is more justly due, than to any other, whom his country [Scotland] ever produced"—as a conspicuous digression in the middle of a passage describing the military adventures of Montrose (H 5.462).
99. Here I gently dissent from Krause (2004: 636) and the sources she cites; she claims that Hume opposed "heroic virtue" altogether as a standard or ideal for modern life.
100. Hume clearly intends a theoretical point, since he tells the story in spite of believing, as he admits in a footnote, that it was all made up (H 2.531note "G").
101. H 2.238 (internal citation, admitting the unlikelihood of the story, omitted). The six burghers of Calais, and Eustace de St. Pierre in particular, have in fact been remembered: in innumerable tellings and many works of art, including a Rodin statue.
102. I cannot help suspecting that Mark Twain, a great admirer and reader of Hume's *History*, had this passage in mind when he wrote the smallpox-hut chapter of *A Connecticut Yankee in King Arthur's Court*. When the King carries a child with smallpox to his dying mother, at great risk of infecting himself, the narrator, deeply touched, writes, "He was great now; sublimely great. The rude statues of his ancestors in his palace should have an addition—I would see to that; and it would not be a mailed king killing a giant or a dragon, like the rest, it would be a king in commoner's garb bearing death in his arms that a peasant mother might look her last upon her child and be comforted" (Twain, 1917: 282, 284).
103. Compare 2.246; the Black Prince, praised for his humanity toward the captured King of France, had previously reduced several conquered towns to ashes: "ravages and devastations" were "the mode of war in that age."

104. Indeed, the Black Prince's example, which soon became general English and allied practice, was not only humane but lucrative: the English side made a tidy profit from ransoming its noble prisoners rather than killing them (2.252).

105. "There seldom has been a treaty of so great importance so faithfully executed by both parties" (H 2.260).

106. Forbes (1975: 296–323) notes that Hume treated barbarism and civilization as legal and political categories, departing from the Scottish Enlightenment practice of treating them as socioeconomic ones (barbarism being pastoral and civilization agricultural). Actually things are more complex. The stages-of-society meaning of barbarism vs. civilization appears at H 1.27, 31–2, 112–13, 160–61, 179–80, 249 (the Christians in the era of the Crusades are the superstitious barbarians), 272, 339, 345; H 4.312; arguably H 1.246–7, and especially 2.518, 528–9. But the moralized meaning is also very common and very consistently, regardless of the age described, means mistreatment of prisoners or unnecessary cruelty in war; see, e.g., H 1.116, 250, 393; 2.376, 407–10, 413, 429, 449–50, 508; 5.345; 6.462–3. H 2.82 is particularly striking: the agricultural English, upon subduing the pastoralist Welsh, adopt a "barbarous, though not absurd policy" of exterminating all the bards to prevent future culturally based resistance.

107. Waldron (1999: 102).

108. Forbes (1975: 87–8).

109. E: RA, 270 (emphasis added). Similarly, "[o]f all EUROPEAN kingdoms, POLAND seems the most defective in the arts of war as well as peace, mechanical as well as liberal"—ibid., 276.

110. Compare the third epigraph to this chapter.

111. Compare Whelan (1985: 166ff., and esp. 167) stressing that Hume's account of motivation is "not monistic."

112. Hume calls Machiavelli a "great genius" on that page, and says that the *Discourses* displayed "great judgment and genius" in an early variant of E: BP, 634.

113. The Advocates' Library had by Hume's estimate 30,000 volumes; being appointed as its librarian enabled Hume to write the *History*. The Detroit Public Library holds nearly 8 million. (*American Library Directory*, www.americanlibrarydirectory.com, search for "Detroit Public Library," accessed 26 December 2011.)

114. Compare the ironic, narrative demonstration of this point at 2.313.

115. See, e.g., Taylor (1989).

116. OED "enlarged" 1 (from mid-eighteenth century); compare "liberal" 4 (first example from 1772). The antonym "illiberal," however, was used in the sense of narrow-minded somewhat earlier (OED 2). Hume makes this meaning of enlarged explicit on occasion: one who is enlarged is unusually open to the "principles of liberty" and lacks the "illiberal prejudices" that come from lack of acquaintance with foreign cultures (H 5.550, 1.103)

117. On legislators see H 5.483; on philosophers EPM App. 4.11, SBN 318 (and E: OC, 469, where Hume suggests that "philosophers, who have embraced a party" is a "contradiction in terms"); on the affinities between the two with respect to general rules, see E: OC, 254–5. In a democracy, unlike in Hume's mixed government with franchise restrictions, Hume's fairly strict division of labor does not seem viable. A critical mass of citizens must at least appreciate salutary conventions strongly enough not to punish politicians who promote them and who impose sanctions against departures from them.

118. In Hardin's formulation, Humean order is "grounded in individual values, whatever those may be. Political philosophy need have no value theory at base. It can merely posit the structure of institutions that enable people to seek their own individual values" (2007: 196). In this respect the closest parallel between Hume and Oakeshott lies in the latter's *On Human Conduct* (1975), which denies that a modern state has ends of its own, rather than in Oakeshott's not particularly Humean and somewhat overheated attacks on rationalism and reform. The purpose of reform may be to enable as many divergent and possibly contradictory ends as possible to be pursued at once.

119. Smith (1981 [1776]: 1.1.9).

120. "In times when industry and the arts flourish, men are kept in perpetual occupation, and enjoy, as their reward, the occupation itself, as well as those pleasures which are the fruit of their labour" (E: RA, 270).

121. Goodin (1976: 41). Goodin notes the contrast between this and situations, e.g., the forming of parliamentary majorities, in which "members divide a relatively fixed total amount of goods" and have an interest in the "minimum winning coalition" that enables each member to be on the winning side while sharing the spoils with as few others as possible.

122. On this see Hardin (1995, though he would not use this language; also 1999: 295).

123. Hardin (2007: 150).

124. Hobbes (1991 [1651]: chapters 15, 26).

Chapter 3. Convention and Allegiance

1. See, e.g., E. Miller (1990); Wexler (1979: 19); and more equivocally Forbes (1975: 298–9).

2. I leave aside chastity, clearly one of Hume's artificial conventions, as of limited relevance to the topics of this book. Other lists include (on the strength of EPM 8.1-2, SBN 261-2, and EPM 5.2.44, SBN 231) good manners, and honor. Much depends on how one classifies Hume's three different ways of describing conventions: from the perspective of social conventions (property, justice, civil government), laws of nature (stability of possession, transference by consent, performance of promises [T 3.2.6.1, SBN 526]), or artificial "virtues" that individuals can possess or display (fidelity, justice, allegiance). In theory, the three formulations should be equivalent; whether Hume's theory is in fact consistent across these formulations is controversial.

3. We should note that *all* apparent history appealed to in the *Treatise* is likely to be conjectural. Hume is discussing the forces that could motivate compliance with the conventions we observe, and in particular denying their divine provenance, rather than tracing the causal mechanisms that produced them, which would require evidence that he never adduces. In the passage cited in the text, Hume presents his speculations on societies without government to distinguish himself from "some philosophers" who think "that men are utterly incapable of society without government" (T 3.2.8.1, SBN 539).

4. Compare T 3.2.8.7, SBN 546: "Tho' there was no such thing as a promise in the world, government wou'd still be necessary in all large and civiliz'd societies."

5. Hayek (1966). In accord with his jurisprudential and evolutionary focus, Hayek ignores Hume's doctrine that in wealthy societies, government is an absolute ne-

cessity, and writes (p. 338) that the *History of England* contains "improved formulations" and popularizations as compared to the *Treatise*, but "little that is new." Baier (2010: 18) stresses how Hume's *History* adds to the *Treatise's* conjectures, but her insights have mostly to do with ethics rather than politics.

6. Hume in the *History* uses "citizen" in its historical sense: to mean an inhabitant of a city or partaker in its corporate privileges. But in his political essays (and at least once in the *History*, when making a general and theoretical point) he uses it with its modern meaning, an ordinary member of a state—often, though not always, a republic; often, though not always, with the meaning of a "civilized person" as opposed to a barbarian; sometimes interchangeably with a term like "person." Excluding references to the "citizens" of ancient republics, who called themselves such, see E: LP, OG, PG, STO, NC, C, RA, Int., JT, PC, PAN; 10, 38, 39, 60, 148, 212, 265, 271, 301, 329, 354, 361, 398—and crucially, H 6.528. Hume's more typical terms for the parties to a convention are less convenient: "men," or even more typically, "we."

7. Compare Locke (1960: §19; and similarly §§168, 186, 232).

8. Baier (1991: 256).

9. Stewart (1963: 191, and esp. 123) links the lack of mystery to the state's status as a "play" or invented artifice, which lacks independent status as an object apart from its constituents.

10. The connection between authority and allegiance is ubiquitous in Hume, particularly in the *History*, but looser than that between justice and property in the *Treatise*, which systematically portrays that virtue and convention as a matched pair. A full treatment of how the connection plays out, and changes, throughout Hume's work is beyond the scope of this book. Key citations include T 3.2.8.2, SBN 540, and 3.2.10.2 SBN 554; E: OC, 470, 471, 478–9, 80; H 1.50, 215, 284, 299, 315; 2.6–7, 13, 161–2, 301, 307, 337, 436; 3.205, 445–6; 4.137, 188–9; 5.462–3, 544–5; 6.7–8, 111–12. Stewart's (1963: 123ff.) treatment of authority and allegiance in Hume comes closer than any other I have seen to capturing the spirit of the connection—but with insufficient textual evidence given Stewart's focus on the *Treatise* in those passages. True, Hume in certain passages refers to a kind of authority that comes from force and fear (more usually, "awe") alone. In such cases, there is "acquiescence" but no allegiance (see, e.g., E: OC, 477–8; H 1.285, 314 (ambiguously), 388–9; 2.350; 3.296, 397–8, 5.291, 372–3). Such instances render understandable Livingston's assertion (1990: 119) that authority in Hume refers to "commands of the sovereign independent of the rule of law," though that claim is not valid more generally. But the link between allegiance and lawful or legitimate authority is otherwise strong.

11. "A small degree of experience and observation suffices to teach us that society cannot possibly be maintained without the authority of magistrates, and that this authority must soon fall into contempt, where exact obedience is not payed to it. The observation of these general and obvious interests is the source of all allegiance, and of that moral obligation, which we attribute to it" (E: OC, 480).

12. More precisely, and tracking approximately the language of Raz (1979), authority is a convention that designates certain identifiable people whose ordering X gives us reason to do X whether or not we independently and antecedently have reasons to do X (in fact, for Raz as for Hume, coordination problems are often an essential second-order reason for establishing authorities that pre-empt first-order reflection on what to do in some area). And allegiance means exactly the same thing from a different perspective: recognition of a good reason to do as magistrates say,

whether or not it is what one individually would have chosen to do absent the knowledge that one has the same understanding of allegiance as others.

13. On such education and correction see chapter 2.

14. Hume, describing the "solid arguments" that the leaders of the House of Commons "might" have used but didn't (6.527), may be regarded as speaking in his own voice, though he concedes that his theoretical arguments would have been impolitic in this situation (in hammering out the settlement of the Glorious Revolution).

15. Besides the citations that follow, see Stewart (1963: 305–13); Macleod (1981); Waldron (1994: 102ff.).

16. Thus Baier (1991: 234–5) writes that "for this first convention to be taken as the solution to a coordination problem, we must be able to see it as really in everyone's best interest to go along with the cooperative scheme that institutes property rights. . . . Only if the state of nature were much more Hobbesian than Hume seriously wants to portray it would it be sensible to risk beggary, let alone risk slavery, for the sake of stability. *To have the stable possession of almost no property would be no improvement over unstable possession of ever varying amounts of goods*, which is what one could expect when cooperation was restricted to families and friends" (emphasis added). (Waldron [1994: 102–7] argues very similarly.) Actually, it would be a substantial improvement if one adds considerations of ability and force and thinks in dynamic, historical terms: Under conditions of justice and property there is some chance that the poor will build up property over time (and Hume gives the greatest cynic a concrete account of how they did so: their masters perceive that they will work harder, and produce more for their overlords, if given secure title in some of their work's products [H 2.523 and see the discussion in the previous chapter]). Without a property convention, the poor have no hope at all: whatever they can steal will be minimal and easily stolen back by someone better off (armor and swords being costly).

17. See Lecaldano (2008: 270). On his account benevolence, however limited in Hume, will sufficiently motivate people to refrain from gratuitous bodily injury. This requires that our sentiments on matters like others' bodily harm be generalized or socialized in the way that Hume thinks our reflections on virtues ought to be and often are, especially when personal enmity is not at issue. (One passage supporting this claim would be T 3.1.1.26, SBN 468; see also the discussion of similar points in Korsgaard [1999: 4–5].)

18. Here I respectfully differ with Baier's argument (2010: chapter 4) that the *History* contains an "enlargement" of the concept of justice itself, so as to cover personal safety, due process, and other goods besides property. I would argue that her reading fails to fully acknowledge the role of authority conventions in Hume's account. The examples she adduces of a wider sense of "injustice" in the *History* almost all involve the non- or mal-*administration* of justice, i.e., the abuse of authority or a willful refusal to extend its protection equally to all. The miscarriages of justice that she discusses at greatest length include Parliament's impeachments of Strafford and Laud and its trial of Charles, which Hume considered the result of misplaced authority. (On 5.457, in a passage Baier cites, Hume writes that "popular assemblies," due to the faction-inspired shamelessness noted in chapter 2, are prone to "acts of the greatest tyranny and injustice" when they "exceed the bounds of law" as they did in these cases—and the Commons did so in pursuit of radical, anti-monarchical designs.) The U.S. Constitution, which explicitly stipulates that

impeachment can bring about only removal from office, not criminal punishment, may be said to reflect Hume's concerns.

19. While human beings wherever they are found will be social, the state of nature is a "philosophical fiction" or thought-experiment representing what would happen if we acted on the "blind motions" of our affections or passions without the "direction" of understanding (T 3.2.2.14–15, SBN 492–3). Hume brings up the state of nature in the middle of a passage on justice, and right before he discusses the scarcity and limited generosity that Rawls would later call the "circumstances of justice."

20. To be sure, this is a section on the origin of government, not on property, but Hume in these passages is arguing that the purpose of government is mostly to correct for imperfect observation of the justice convention.

21. Baier (2010: 84) makes a similar point regarding this section of the *History*, that is, Appendix 1: leaders preceded property.

22. The corsnet, usually spelled "corsned," was a version of trial by ordeal. The accused was fed a consecrated barley cake that the guilty supposedly could not chew and swallow.

23. Hume relentlessly documented pre-Tudor slavery in England, stressed that other countries made progress against slavery before England did, and rejected euphemisms for the word slave—as part of his program of mocking those who appealed to allegedly ancient English liberties (H 1.171–2, 1.437, 463, 1.469; 2.99, 105–6, 522). In the late fourteenth century, Hume stresses, slavery was the "universal" state of the common people, and England had a higher proportion of slaves than any other country in Europe (H 2.201, 289).

24. Hume's use of "generous" seems to reflect OED meaning 2a: "noble of spirit, honourable, principled," or in modern, weaker usage "unselfish, magnanimous, kind." In this sense, "generous" and "enlarged" are near-synonyms.

25. As commonly noted: see, e.g., Manzer (1996: 492–4); Capaldi and Livingston (1990); and, most carefully, Whelan (1985: 356–63).

26. On the lesser gentry, the vassals of the great barons, see 1.462: the vassals were utterly dependent on the greater lord for military training, room and board, amusement, gratification of ambition or the desire for honor, and protection from one another and (more important) from other barons. It was of course "natural for the king to court the friendship of the lesser barons and knights, whose influence was no ways dangerous to him, and who, being exposed to oppression from their powerful neighbours, sought a legal protection under the shadow of the throne." This is part of Hume's story of the development of the Commons (2.103–4).

27. "The execution of justice" and the "suppression of robbery or violence" are, Hume takes for granted, synonymous with demolishing nobles' castles. H 1.301. Compare 1.284, 2.524–5.

28. H 3.267 defines prerogative as "a power, which was exercised on a particular emergence, and which must be justified by the present expedience or necessity."

29. H 5.127, mocking political theories during the realm of James I that saw prerogative as eternal in this way. In exactly the same vein, Hume also mocked ideological defenders of thinkers like Locke and Sidney for extolling the partisans of liberty in a one-sided manner over the defenders of authority. The "moderation" and distaste for "extremes of all kinds" expressed in the latter passage (6.533–4) is not so much a temperamental moderation as an active defense of durable constitutional safeguards, where they exist, against both rebellion and prerogative.

30. Here, as in H 5.128, the telltale sign of an immature or imperfect constitution is that royal prerogative is asserted to exist not just in cases of "necessity" but for the sake of mere "convenience." There is no stable and clear convention defining authority and its use. Here as often in Hume, political theory provides a formal criterion, but one that does not reduce merely to context or prevailing opinions. Any mature constitution will define authority and its limits clearly, and certain political goods will follow from its doing so. But the content of that definition will depend on particular historical paths.

31. Walzer (1973: 178–9).

32. Compare E; PO, 489: Hume writes of the "virtue" of "the execution of justice" [i.e., authority] having to "give place to public utility, in such extraordinary and such pressing emergencies." In T 3.2.10.18, SBN 565, Hume (true to form) makes much the same point in the language of moral psychology as the text quotation and this one make in more institutional terms.

33. This is the argument of the court party in H 5.380. Hume puts it in the mouth of the king's party, but the fact that he does not provide the opposing argument makes it reasonable to gloss it as Hume's own view. The partisans of Hampden (who was on the opposite side of the party dispute, and whose arguments are likewise presented by Hume as unrebutted) make a similar claim about necessity at 5.247. (H 5.376 is along the same lines: parliament and king are arguing about whether, as parliament says, a certain measure is "necessary for public safety" due to "urgent dangers," or whether existing institutions were, as Hume thinks, capable of addressing the emergency. But they do not argue about the criterion.) It is fair to say that on Hume's view, reasonable partisans would be arguing over whether a given plea of necessity was strong enough to excuse departure from constitutional rules, not whether this is the right standard.

34. "I seek, therefore, some such interest more immediately connected with government, and which may be at once the original motive to its institution, and the source of our obedience to it. This interest I find to consist in the security and protection which we enjoy in political society, and which we can never attain, when perfectly free and independent. As interest, therefore, is the immediate sanction of government, the one can have no longer being than the other; and whenever the civil magistrate carries his oppression so far as to render his authority perfectly intolerable, we are no longer bound to submit to it. The cause ceases; the effect must cease also" (T 3.2.9.2, SBN 551). Compare E: PO, 492: "a right without a remedy would be an absurdity; the remedy in this case, is the extraordinary one of resistance, when affairs come to that extremity, that the constitution can be defended by it alone."

35. Hume does not think Charles himself put these arguments well or drew the right conclusions. He took prerogative too far, though his doing so was excusable given the constitutional theory of the time (see chapter 5). The House of Lords adopted de facto the policy Hume thought the constitution sadly lacked: they endorsed a temporary suspension with the king having a responsibility to declare the cause of imprisonment "within a *convenient* time" (H 6.196 [emphasis in original]).

36. "Not only the prince, in cases of extreme distress, is exempted from the ordinary rules of administration: All orders of men are then levelled; and any individual may consult the public safety by any expedient, which his situation enables him to employ. But to produce so violent an effect, and so hazardous to every community,

an ordinary danger or difficulty is not sufficient; much less, a necessity, which is merely factitious and pretended. Where the peril is urgent and extreme, it will be palpable to every member of the society; and though all ancient rules of government are in that case abrogated, men will readily, of themselves, submit to that irregular authority, which is exerted for their preservation" (H 5.246).

37. Forbes (1975: 277).

38. See, respectively, E: PO, 492; ibid., 490; and H 5.502 (where Hume, writing of England's Commonwealth era, refers to "that slavery, into which the nation, from the too eager pursuit of liberty, had fallen"). Charles I in 1642 is reduced to making a personal appeal to parliament not to imitate the false claims of necessity that he himself had employed. In Hume's opinion, settled institutional safeguards against Charles' future power were, tragically, available but not widely recognized and therefore moot (H 5.380).

39. For more on this see Sabl (2002).

40. Compare H 6.293–4 (Hume's own view put in the mouth of "such as could maintain a calm indifference").

41. The full story is very complicated, and Whig arguments from consent often sat uneasily with their love for a constitution allegedly ancient and immemorial. See Kramnick (1968); Pocock (1975); Forbes (1975).

42. This is to oversimplify hugely E: OC, 465–87. Incidentally, though it is a complicated question involving much scholarly debate, I regard the general opinion argument (which at first sounds silly, since Hume rejects popular moral standards all the time) as being essentially privative and as making perfect sense in the particular context of opposition to contract theory. It is perfectly reasonable to say that nobody can be bound *by a contract* that he or she has no awareness of having signed. Ignorance of the contract would then be evidence of either forgery, fraud, or diminished capacity. Contract arguments for authority, and they alone, rest on the parties' conscious will. This also keeps the argument from working the other way, that is, that if people believe consent to be the true basis of obligation it for that reason becomes so [Dees 2008: 395]. A contract may be void if I have no knowledge of having signed it and never had any; but it is not valid merely by virtue of my thinking that I have signed it when I haven't. If, say, Americans were demonstrably prone to *enforce* the terms of Lockean consent theory against one another, and against government, that might establish the constitutional validity of that theory on a convention-based view. But we are not.

43. Hume takes seriously the possibility that actual governments arose by consent in only one place: in the *Treatise*, where he imagines (without evidence) that government at its first and primitive founding could have been based on a promise. "When men have once perceiv'd the necessity of government to maintain peace, and execute justice, they wou'd naturally assemble together, wou'd choose magistrates, determine their power, and *promise* them obedience" (T 3.2.8.3, SBN 541). In later writings, Hume was more likely to portray the origin of government as force and accident. See E: OG39ff., and the discussion in Stewart (1963: 158ff.) and, most definitively, Haakonssen (1993). But even in the *Treatise*, Hume doubts that consent is relevant to *current* political obligation, which is founded on the utility of government (and our sympathy with all those who would suffer from its absence, not just us), as well as social and political education in "loyalty" (T 3.2.8.7, SBN 545). E: IPC, 513, concedes a hypothetical possibility that "a dissolution of some old government,

or ... the combination of men to form a new one, in some distant part of the world" would allow for a constitution to be formed from scratch on ideal lines—but Hume explicitly denies that any practical conclusions for existing governments follow.

44. On a small scale, it might be a different matter: see H 1.167–8 on the Anglo-Saxon mutual defense pacts called *sodalitia*.

45. Of Hume's claim that the people are "unfit to choose for themselves" their leaders, Chisick (1989: 15) writes, "It is hard to think of a more forceful assertion of the political nullity of the people." But Hume's point seems to concern the unfavorable *circumstances* of choice, not any intellectual or moral failing of ordinary subjects as individuals. I accept Chisick's broader point that Hume, in common with most Enlightenment thinkers and indeed most elites of his time, granted the poor some sympathy but little regard and almost no respect.

46. Hume actually thinks that Cromwell *had* a plausible title to rule by acquiescence: "Though Cromwel's administration was less odious to every party than that of any other party, yet was it entirely acceptable to none (6.69). It is the sham of consent to which he objects. Compare 6.98, and 1.146–7 on the accession of King Harold, in which silence under fear of arms was taken for consent and the "suffrages of the people."

47. The Restoration, similarly, was relatively peaceful and consensual because the parties were exhausted and had a natural alternative leader (the Stuart King, Charles). Even then, General Monk could probably have seized power had he chosen to. See chapter 5.

48. Allegiance is in origin a feudal word. As Baier notes (1991: 271), it comes from *liege*, which may have once meant a person unbound by political commitments. "Liege" is of doubtful etymology, but one school traces it to a Middle German form of modern German *ledig*—free, without obligations (or "unmarried"!). See OED "allegiance," "liege."

49. Similarly, the existence of the convention of promising did not entail enforcement; barons could go back on a promise if they could plead an obscure rule of honor against it, as they generally could. Glocester's pledge of course followed on his prior violation of his fealty oath; also at the end of Edward III's reign, barons promised in parliament not to harbor lawbreakers but repeatedly broke those promises (H 2.279).

50. As Hume's narrative suggests, these terms hardly *guaranteed* baronial obedience. In fact (as later with Hobbes) they licensed a cascade of disallegiance once the original liege seemed to be losing to another (H 1.283).

51. Hume calls him "Sixtus Quintus," perhaps to imply that his purposes were imperial as well as spiritual.

52. Compare 4.176–7 regarding the pope's initial bull, in response to which Elizabeth "established no inquisition into men's bosoms."

53. During Elizabeth's reign and after, the people could be trusted to render an impersonal allegiance without needing to take oaths endorsing the monarch's Supremacy. Such oaths were required only of office holders, since they were still seen as the necessary religious cement for promises of active service (H 4.176–7, 6.276) (seen, that is, by the people, not necessarily by Hume, who thinks James I's avoidance of such oaths sound policy though bad politics [H 5.32]). There were certainly instances after that in which ordinary subjects were asked to swear oaths of allegiance and supremacy, but Hume portrays these demands as oppressive and fanatical, the result of religious

faction rather than the policy of statesmen in established governments. Except in Scotland, where Charles II (reacting to his own ill treatment by Scottish covenanters as a youth) countenanced extreme religious and political oppression, it was kings who resisted such oaths and parliamentary entrepreneurs who demanded them. Scottish covenanters who excommunicated King Charles and renounced their allegiance on religious grounds are likewise portrayed by Hume as throwbacks, though their extreme response to oppression was understandable (H 6.395, 418, 415–16).

54. Compare Baier (1991: 273): "We invest liberty, in the hopes of a return in more secure rights and liberties."

55. I owe this formulation to discussion with Mark A. R. Kleiman.

56. Hume in fact describes the English government under Henry VIII and Elizabeth I as in form more despotic than any in the East, though less so in practice due to these monarchs' relative restraint and a lack of state capacity (H 3.244, 4.360, 370).

57. On this point see Dees (1992): 231n35.

58. Among numerous other instances, see H 3.244, 279, 285, 287–8. On 3.321–2 Hume says that Henry deserves to be called "great" but not "good" (due to his "tyranny and barbarity"), and concedes that "the danger of a revolt from his superstitious subjects, seemed to require the most extreme severity." On this point see E. Miller (1990: 76f).

59. For the phrase "egregious tyranny" see T 3.2.9.1, SBN 549; "flagrant instances of tyranny and oppression": T 3.2.9.4, SBN 552; "grievous tyranny and oppression": T 3.2.10.1, SBN 554; "tyranny, and violence, and oppression": E: CP, 501.

60. True to form, Hume also adduces many instances of alleged tyranny and oppression while expressing skepticism that they in fact met that standard. See H 2.322, 3.55, 5.193 (a close case), 6.53.

61. Hume in general is prone to call the Irish barbarians, and sometimes to insult their mores and religion, but ultimately blames the English for not providing them the laws and institutions that would have helped them advance from that state. See *History* 5.47, 313, 336, 338, 425.

62. The Norman barons, feeling that their incompetent and superstitious duke provided no "regular government" and had let Normandy become "a scene of violence and depredation"—mostly at the hands of other barons—were "more disposed to pay submission to [England's Henry I] than to their legal sovereign," and readily let themselves be conquered by that foreign prince (H 1.258–9).

63. See, among others, H 5.503 (the army hoped "by terror alone, to effect all their purposes"), 5.513–14, and esp. 5.522 ("The terror of the army kept the citizens in subjection. The parliament was . . . over-awed" and many members had "withdrawn, from terror of the army") and 509: the independents in the commons "expected, by the terror of the sword, to impose a more perfect system of liberty on the reluctant nation." (They failed.)

64. Hardin (2007: 212–24).

65. Vieira and Runciman (2008).

66. L 2.210, 213, and see Livingston (1990: 145). The text reading (and Livingston's) is admittedly a bit speculative.

67. For precommitment see Elster (1984), Holmes (1988); on coordination, Hardin (1999).

68. The Marxist doctrine that working people have no country and should feel instead an intense loyalty to their class stands and falls with the doctrine that bourgeoisie

and proletariat are the primary *political* designations within both an individual workplace and in the larger society.

69. On this point I am told that Converse (1964) has never been refuted, nor his findings falsified by later data.

70. Przeworski and Teune (1970, chapter 1).

Chapter 4. Crown and Charter: Fundamental Conventions as Principles of Authority

1. Schelling (2006a: 250).

2. Hume in the *Treatise* seems to doubt (ambiguously) whether a positive law can overturn a constitutional fundamental, given that legislative authority is drawn from those fundamentals except in cases of an "evident tendency to the public good," which in context seems to involve a very high standard (T 3.2.10.14, SBN 561; for more see the text below). In the *History*, Hume puts a more uncompromising form of this thesis in the mouths of various parties but never, it seems, in his own voice. In his own voice he mocks the idea "that a free legislative body could do anything illegal" (H 2.215); though perhaps the monarch who called the act illegal made a mistake, in Hume's view, in not calling it *irregular* or contrary to the constitution's foundations.

3. "Rule" and "regular" (or "irregular"): H 1. 48, 161, 324, 407, 410–11 (ambiguously), 485; 2.179, 319, 381, 436, 437, 525, 536 (ambiguously); 4.355; 5.50, 551; and in E: MOL xxxviii; IP, 43 and 46n2; BG, 50; TA, 348, RC, 368–9, 371, 374, 375; OC, 468, 478. (This excludes the many cases in which Hume uses "regular" to mean stable or predictable—i.e., in accord with scientific rather than human-made laws.) "Foundation" and "fundamental" appear rarely in the constitutional sense: aside from the *Treatise* passage discussed below, and usually in the phrase "ancient foundations": see 2.333, 2.346, 2.436 (where "ancient and natural basis" is used as a synonym) 2.438; 6.181; "Maxim": H 1.372, 2.320, 2.437, 492, 525; 5.193, 240; 6.74 (a maxim can also be merely a prudential or political counsel of wise conduct, and some of these instances shade into that usage); "principle" 1.161, 407–8, 464; 2.320, 347–8, 430; 4.194; 5.583, 6.38, and OG 40–41.

4. Livingston (1991: 162) claims that all conventions and customs are constitutive to varying degrees. Depending on how one pursues the argument, this may be right; the kind of events that make us change our language or our ideas of justice challenge our sense of self, just as those that make us change our fundamental political institutions do. But in the case of a polity, which may contain a variety of customs and traditions, political conventions seem most relevant.

5. Hamilton et al. (2001: No. 1, p. 1). Whelan (2004: 328n115) cites scholarship suggesting that Hamilton in posing this alternative was acknowledging Hume, the theorist of accident and force, as a worthy opponent. For a subtle discussion of the differences and similarities between the authors of the *Federalist* and Hume on this matter, see Manzer (2001). Essentially, the *Federalist* in his view embodies a fairly Humean theory with mostly verbal concessions to the widespread American myth of popular sovereignty.

6. Hobbes (1971: 140).

7. Hobbes (1991 [1651]: chapter 14).

8. Hardin (1999).

9. Moshe et al. (1611: Ecclesiastes 9:11).

10. The question is complex and in need of separate treatment. The analyses of Day (1965) and Miller (1981: 85–92) provide excellent starting points.

11. See similarly H 1.162: "The idea of an hereditary succession in authority is . . . natural to men, and is . . . fortified by the usual rule in transmitting private possessions."

12. Hume calls the English gentry's "loyalty to their sovereign" during the Commonwealth era a "noble and generous principle, inferior only in excellence to the more enlarged and more enlightened affection towards a legal constitution"—though in the Commonwealth context, which Hume calls "military usurpation," the two coincided (H 6.38).

13. Hume's essay "Of the Origin of Government" contains an early exploration, but one that lacks both detail and causal explanation. "It is probable, that the first ascendant of one man over multitudes begun during a state of war; where the superiority of courage and of genius discovers itself most visibly, where unanimity and concert are most requisite, and where the pernicious effects of disorder are most sensibly felt. The long continuance of that state, an incident common among savage tribes, enured the people to submission; and if the chieftain possessed as much equity as prudence and valour, he became, even during peace, the arbiter of all differences, and could gradually, by a mixture of force and consent, establish his authority. The benefit sensibly felt from his influence, made it be cherished by the people, at least by the peaceable and well disposed among them; and if his son enjoyed the same good qualities, *government advanced the sooner to maturity and perfection*; but was still in a feeble state, till the farther progress of improvement procured the magistrate a revenue, and enabled him to bestow rewards on the several instruments of his administration, and to inflict punishments on the refractory and disobedient." (E: OG, 39–40, emphasis added). The preconditions of "maturity and perfection" and the political decisions that secure them are the subject of this chapter. The "progress of improvement" that allows modern taxation and other instruments of state are the subject of what I have called science (1), the causal story of political development, and will not be discussed here.

14. Forbes (1975: 301).

15. Hume's "Of the Original Contract" (E: OC, 478) contains a very similar, though much briefer, account of the Roman Empire: "The condition of the people, in that mighty monarchy, was to be lamented, not because the choice of the emperor was never left to them; for that was impracticable: But because they never fell under any succession of masters, who might regularly follow each other. As to the violence and wars and bloodshed, occasioned by every new settlement; these were not blameable, because they were inevitable."

16. Jean Hampton's Hobbesian solution to the problem of choosing leaders (Hampton 1986: chapter 6, esp. 161–73)—all agree on the need for a ruler, and then the ruler's identity is settled through a process of repeated votes, or else repeated violence, and bandwagoning around the early winner either way—neglects the time dimension and the importance of focal points. When a state of non-rule can be anticipated, e.g., when the current monarch is ill, each prospective (or for that matter current) ruler, anticipating a state of non-rule, has an interest in eliminating other plausible candidates. As long as there are any primitive focal points, i.e., anything that would make one future ruler more salient than another (wealth, force, birth, height, religious authority), command over those focal points is a very useful thing to have

when a new monarch is being chosen and a very dangerous thing to have when it is generally anticipated that a new monarch may soon be chosen (or the existing monarch fears a challenge). At that point salience means a target on one's back. Reasoning backwards, since the monarch could die at any time, salience will always provide such a target; it will motivate, rather than preventing, civil war. This is not a criticism of Hampton, who puts forth this solution as Hobbes', not hers, and goes on to criticize it. She is quite persuasive that Hobbes proposed something like this. If so, Hobbes' proposal reveals the limits of the kind of deductive and analytic method that fails to do justice to the complications of history.

17. Thus Hume considers the "Salic law" in France, excluding female heirs, as founded on a precedent that no longer has reason behind it—though still legitimate due to long precedent and positive law.

18. The British idea of a constitution as a combination of laws, customary practices, and norms of political morality no doubt makes it easier to grasp the universal truth that all government—including government under a written constitution—rests on conventions and opinions.

19. Hume's citation is to Aeschines, *Against Ctesiphon*, §§5–8. He notes that the Thirty Tyrants, as their first action upon dissolving the democratic regime, abolished the indictment for illegality.

20. Representation is the principle that when a king dies, with his eldest son having died before him, the king's eldest son's sons, not the king's younger sons, become king. If that rule is confusing, it proves the point. The principle is non-obvious and far from natural: a convention of authority.

21. Primogeniture, writes Hume, is bad for private society "by producing and maintaining an unequal division of private property"—but "advantageous, in another respect," because it means that succession rules will, by analogy to the private rule, clearly favor the eldest, preventing succession struggles (1.486).

22. Hume knew a great deal about English queens, was born during the reign of one (Anne), thought the English rule permitting their succession was in modern circumstances superior to the French one forbidding it, and wrote a whole book about one of their reigns (H 4 on Elizabeth). Yet he still habitually referred to holders of the throne as "men" (which could barely be considered gender-neutral) and of monarchs as "kings" (which cannot).

23. Similarly, Hume writes that the Glorious Revolution established not a "new king" but a "new *family*" (H 6.531, emphasis added).

24. Here I disagree with Manzer (2001), who thinks that Hume wants constitutional allegiance to depend on the substantive, scientific goodness of particular constitutional arrangements. The passage just quoted suggests the opposite: there *was* a constitutional content to the mere rule of allegiance to the rightful monarch. I would also challenge Manzer's claim that Hume wanted an Enlightened public mind to accept "the authority of 'a science of politics' " (ibid., 511). Hume's scientific aim was real enough and he drew on it to suggest reforms, but *authority* as opposed to utility or the quality of governmental institutions lay in long experience with the constitution, not in the science that studied that authority.

25. Stewart (1963: 132).

26. Henry IV's "present possession" was such a "precarious foundation" for rule that it was, "by its very nature, . . . liable to be overthrown by every faction of the great, or prejudice of the people" (2.334). The fact that Henry's "authority could with dif-

ficulty be brought to equal that of his predecessors," along with several other crude focal points on his side, favored the claim of Richard II's young heir (Roger Mortimer, fourth Earl of March) so thoroughly that Henry would have been in great danger from that pretender had Roger lived longer (2.334). Northumberland, who had helped make Henry king, also tried to overthrow him in short order, "tempted" by "the precarious title" (2.339).

27. David Miller's claim (1981: 87) that Hume conflates "the authority which is attributed to a whole complex of institutions, and thus derivatively to those persons who hold institutional positions" with "the authority which is accorded to a person on the basis of some characteristic he is thought to possess" results from his failing to distinguish between crude or barbaric monarchy and the constitutional kind that results from subjects' acknowledging allegiance to rules of succession regardless of monarchs' personal qualities.

28. To be sure, Mathilda's claims against Stephen could not be vindicated by claims of legitimate succession alone, which were not yet a "fixed" convention. Nor in retaking the crown did she seek authority from "the states of the kingdom, the measure which the constitution, had it been either fixed or regarded, seemed necessarily to require," but only from an ecclesiastical synod (H 1.289). Hume's uncharacteristic emphasis on Mathilda may have had a party-political subtext. A claim of descent from Mathilda was one rather lame way in which partisans of the House of Hanover claimed that that line's title was not merely parliamentary (Clark [2000: 95, 287]); Hume in stressing this ancient civil war may be reinforcing his common doctrine that unearthing ancient titles only undermines all stable authority.

29. Incidentally, talk of "fluctuation" in Hume is often, though not always, an indication of an occasion where convention would be useful: everyone would like a common standard for action but there is no agreement on what it should be.

30. Arthur had support in France, where representation was more secure.

31. Hume is putting his own sentiments in Carlisle's mouth: see chapter 2, note 78.

32. The Glorious Revolution occurred in 1688 according to the Old Style English calendar (a Julian calendar, as England did not recognize Pope Gregory, and with a year that started for some reason in March) but 1689 by current calendar dating, which is used in the United States. I will use 1688 in the context of Hume's narrative, 1689 when speaking in my own voice.

33. Hume likewise says that when Lancaster had Richard II "solemnly deposed in parliament for his pretended tyranny and misconduct," he acted "notwithstanding the danger of the precedent to himself and his posterity" (2.317). The danger to himself is clear enough—Lancaster was fully aware throughout his entire reign as Henry IV that his kingship, founded on a poor title, was far from secure. "Uneasy lies the head that wears a crown" (*Henry IV, Part II*, Act III, scene 1) was a statement about monarchs in his circumstances, not monarchy generally. In terms of our analysis, posterity is more important. The meta-principle that departures from the royal line constitute no precedent was not yet solid enough to stand on its own: in the event, Richard II's deposition constituted only a momentary precedent that later would be referred to only in extreme circumstances.

34. Hume partly excuses Lancaster's own actions because of extenuating circumstances and security dilemmas surrounding his accession—but the larger constitutional point remains. Compare H 2.340, 344.

35. Note the singular verb: "the establishment of political society, and of an order in succession" are to Hume's mind not two things but one. Dees (1992: 239n54) is very good on the implications of Bolingbroke's usurpation, but does not link them to the existence of a fundamental convention.

36. With particularly heavy irony, Hume places *legitimist* arguments, and an opposition to crude focal points based on royal talent, in the mouths of Henry VI's Lancastrian partisans: "though the present king enjoyed not the shining talents, which had appeared in his father and grandfather, he might still have a son, who should be endowed with them; he is himself eminent for the most harmless and inoffensive manners; and if active princes were dethroned on pretence of tyranny, and indolent ones on the plea of incapacity, there would thence forth remain in the constitution no established rule of obedience to any sovereign" (2.437).

37. This occurred in France under Charles V as well as in England, much of the time, under Henry VI (who in addition had a weak title): H 2.369, 384–5, 426.

38. In this context, "evident" unmistakably means something very close to "self-evident, incapable of being disputed" rather than merely "clear" or "supported by evidence." If it were the latter, the fundamental law could hardly limit the sovereign—and could hardly, as the Salic law did for centuries of French history, have prevented any queens from ruling on their own behalf. The "evident tendency to the public good" standard is analogous to the "egregious tyranny" standard for resisting existing governments: it names the conditions for very rare exceptions to fundamental conventions when the existing convention is truly intolerable and a better alternative seems plausibly available.

39. For Hobbes (1991: chapter 19, 135–8), limits on a sovereign's right to choose his/her/ its successor are void as limitations on sovereignty; rules of succession operate only in default of an express will and testament; and a monarch may name any domestic or foreign person as his or her successor.

40. The foreign imports were, most famously, Justinian's code, but even William the Conqueror's feudal law had good points in comparison to Anglo-Saxon law at the time. On ancient constitutionalism see Pocock (1987). For Hume's contrasts with this tradition, see in general Forbes (1975: 267ff.) and specific to Magna Charta, McArthur (2007: 105–7), E. Miller (1990: 71ff.), Phillipson (1989: 129), and in the primary text, especially H 1.444ff., 487–8, 2.283–4.

41. Hume, it is true, does use Magna Charta to "conjecture" about the laws of Edward the Confessor. Since the barons claimed to be vindicating ancient laws that have since been lost, the legal rights of Magna Charta might well, he supposes, resemble those of Edward (H 1.446). Yet this conjectured antiquity did not, in Hume's view, add to the Charter's legitimacy. On the same page, Hume approves of the barons for putting the king's pragmatic need for funds ahead of ancient prohibitions on the king's preferred means of raising them (wardships, i.e., impounding the income of a deceased noble's estate during the period in which the heir was a minor).

42. Here I think the OED's second definition, "easy to remember, able to be remembered; memorizable" is more relevant than the more familiar first one, "worthy of remembrance or note; worth remembering; not to be forgotten." Of course Hume thinks it was both.

43. The other medieval institution that possessed authority independent of present force, and therefore could check such force, was the Church (H 2.14, 212–13). It is no accident that those who distrust constitutional conventions as the sources of

political allegiance are forced to assert that moral principles can replace church authority as the judge of allegiance and the source of limits on power—and forced to ignore the disagreements about morality that prevent moral systems, as they came to prevent Churches, from serving as uncontroversial sources of such allegiance and such limits.

44. This is what Hume thinks Henry should have done, not what he did do: "Instead of reducing the dangerous power of his nobles, by obliging them to observe the laws towards their inferiors, and setting them the salutary example in his own government; he was seduced to imitate their conduct, and to make his arbitrary will, or rather that of his ministers, the rule of his actions" (2.64-5). Hume thinks that Henry III's reinforcement of the Magna Charta convention *would* have reduced baronial power had he practiced such, would have lent authority to Henry's more direct application of royal force.

45. Of an earlier confirmation in 1222, Hume writes that "a law in those times seemed to lose its validity, if not frequently renewed" (H 2.12–13). The people of England were fortunate to have bad theories of law. The repetition that reflected bad law was, by accident, extremely good politics and essential for solidifying the new convention.

46. See Braudy (2003 [1970] 78ff.).

47. In this Essay, Hume mentions Hampden's "heroism" in opposing ship-money. Hume's mature opinion in the *History* is considerably less favorable to Hampden personally, though it does not question the need to quickly oppose government encroachments.

48. Forbes (1975: 245) notes that the idea that English rights gained rather than lost authority through repeated reassertions of them in the face of violations, and through formal parliamentary denials that violations constituted precedents, was a doctrine of Country party ideologist Henry St. John, Viscount Bolingbroke. Perhaps because he assumes the ancient and medieval volumes of the *History* to be relatively unimportant, he fails to note that Hume takes the same position and in fact asserts it at greater length. Hume adapted the arguments of ancient constitutionalists to justify his own, modern version of constitutionalism.

49. For the Court arguments see H 5.173-4.

50. Here Hume is summarizing the best arguments that Parliamentarians could have made against Charles I. Hume unequivocally calls these arguments "better founded" than the royalists', even though the royalists' arguments were "perhaps . . . more solid, more safe, and more legal" according to the "established maxims of lawyers and politicians" at the time (ibid., 500).

51. Article XI petitions (in modernized spelling) "that Your Majesty would also vouchsafe to declare, that the Awards, Doings and Proceedings, to the Prejudice of Your People in any of the Premises shall not be drawn hereafter into Consequence or Example" "The Petition of Right, 1628," at http://www.nationalarchives.gov.uk/pathways/citizenship/rise_parliament/transcripts/petition_right.htm, accessed 29 July 2009.

52. This must be, at least partly, a joke at the expense of defenders of the ancient constitution. The substance of the political science "rul[e]" that Hume is vindicating is that "violent innovations"—especially by legislatures—do more harm than good. Old Whig ideology held that English liberties were fundamental, and that violations were not to be drawn into precedent, but that the right to revolution was sac-

rosanct and that the form of government could rightly be changed through revolution. Hume is essentially saying that if the old Whigs claim that we should draw no lessons from repeated violations of English liberties, political scientists are entitled to draw no lessons from (much rarer) instances of revolutions that happen to do more good than harm.

53. The "false and dangerous precedent," referring to Edward II's deposition by "successful violence," was decried by the bishop of Carlisle in his speech in defense of Richard II against Lancaster's charges—a speech that clearly has Hume's sympathies since he makes it up with disregard for the original source (see chapter 2, note 78). As Hume imagines Carlisle to argue, "it was sufficiently to be lamented, that crimes were so often committed in the world, without establishing principles which might justify and authorize them" (H 2.320).

54. While one should hesitate to use irony as the explanation of difficult passages (a shame, since Hume's irony is so delicious: see Price 1965); this one is avowedly in the mouth of one party; uses language ("sacred") that Hume never employs in his own voice, and describes the Charter as "never-failing" in ways that Hume's own account refutes overwhelmingly and at great length.

55. Examples of the restrictive use from adjacent pages in the same text: "as they lived at a distance, they would be little awed by shame or remorse, in employing every lucrative expedient, which was suggested to them" (H 2.4); "All the forests, which had been enclosed since the reign of Henry 2, were desaforested" (H 2.6). Hume uses "which" like this very frequently. Talk of "the which that's really a that" is common among those who study his work.

56. McArthur (2007: 134).

57. Livingston (1995: 163–4n14, citing as well EPM, SBN 190). Livingston claims that this is the only place "where Hume, speaking in his own voice, affirms what appears to be a doctrine of natural rights" (163). McArthur disagrees, citing H 1.450 and 2:319, and the Essays "Of Public Credit" and a variant reading of "Of the Liberty of the Press" (E: PC, 362; LP, 604). Livingston's case seems better. The other passages are either sketchy and vague (discussing "self-preservation" but no other rights), arguably not in Hume's own voice, or omitted from late editions in which Hume thought better of them (regarding press liberty).

58. OED, definition 1b.

59. See Stewart (1963: 127); cf. McArthur (2005: 72–3). The congruence between Magna Charta rights and laws of nature raises extremely complex questions. Perhaps Hume really means it when he calls England's government "singular and happy," because of what we would now call Millian freedom, to be restrained by no prerogative or power but only the authority of laws (H 5.114, though "happy" was added only in late editions). Through accident and history, England has enacted some universally useful legal rights. Or perhaps the point is that although philosophers can understand a utilitarian basis for rights, this understanding does not matter in describing politics, since philosophical conclusions on their own cannot affect political action generally and the actions of crowds in particular. We might add that philosophical truth is perhaps the least likely candidate for a standard that could serve as a coordinating convention that will rally ordinary members of a polity. By definition, even philosophers radically disagree about it (since nothing philosophically interesting is noncontroversial), and most ordinary people have never thought about it.

60. Livingston (1995: 164n14).
61. Whelan 1995; Capaldi 1990: 198–9.
62. Here I differ with Capaldi, who asks the question "when do unconstitutional practices become hallowed by custom?" and eventually answers that "the appeal to the unwritten British Constitution" can be seen in retrospect as doing so (1990: 201–2). His answer, to my mind, begs the question: there could be no unwritten constitution if there were not some convention that no custom can erode. Only fundamental conventions provide a non-question-begging answer to Capaldi's question.
63. On the distinction between absolute and arbitrary governments in Hume, D. Miller (1981: 145–7) is excellent.
64. See the careful treatment by E. Miller (1990: 56–7).
65. Wentworth's remarks are at H 5.191. Hume argues in T 3.2.10.5, SBN 556–7, that since what counts as "long" is relative to context, hereditary succession is harder to change than civil rights. For a usurper will always have held office for a short time compared to the life of a kingdom, while rights are judged on a more human scale. Hence "a shorter period of time will suffice to give a prince a title to any additional power he may usurp, than will serve to fix his right, where the whole is an usurpation. The kings of *France* have not been possess'd of absolute power for above two reigns; and yet nothing will appear more extravagant to *Frenchmen* than to talk of their liberties." But Hume's example here refers to France, *which had no fundamental convention regarding rights*. In England, attempts to abrogate Magna Charta are likewise judged as of short duration *compared to the duration of Magna Charta*, which approaches that of the kingdom. The same might be said about the relative authority of the United States' Constitution and the Declaration of Independence: accidentally, their age and authority are roughly the same.
66. Apologies are due to Huntington (1968: 1).
67. D. Miller (1981: 154, 168).
68. This is a rough gloss of T 3.2.2.22, SBN 497.
69. Barry (1989): 148–52, 169–73.
70. Among many other citations, see H 2.147, 160, 173–4, 243–4, 283–4, 323–4, 344–5, 426, and especially 3.24, 6.448. Whelan (2004: 21) notes that while Hume's ethical theory seems to have much more in common (as he avowed) with Cicero than with Machiavelli's aggressively anti-Ciceronian *virtù*, his "descriptions and assessments of the qualities of political figures, especially in his *History*" possess many more affinities to Machiavelli, though without ever adopting radical anti-moralism. In particular, Hume's insistence that political ability and non-moral virtues generally be counted as a kind of virtue has affinities to the realist or reason-of-state tradition generally. Compare 30n21, 85, 129–31, 208 (on James I's lack of *virtù*), 265, 276, as well as Sabl (2009b).
71. Machiavelli (1996 [1531]: 3.9.1–3, pp. 239–40).
72. To be sure, this became more true several decades after Hume's death, when monarchs became mere figureheads, than in his own time, when they retained substantial power. Hume saw the latter state as a problem inseparable from a mixed monarchy: because England gave substantial ruling powers to the monarch, whose personal qualities could vary widely, its constitution could never balance parliament's powers with the monarchy's perfectly and durably (E: IP, 46).
73. Manzer 2001: 508.

Chapter 5. Leadership and Constitutional Crises

1. Whelan (2004: 129–34), with specific cites to Humean passages that broadly resemble Machiavellian positions. Whelan's reading of Machiavelli is "Tacitist" or realist rather than humanist or republican (2004: 28n11). Asserting Hume's affinity with this strand of Machiavellianism is therefore consistent with interpretations of Hume that stress his opposition to the civic-republican tradition (Finlay 2004; Forbes 1979; Moore 1977) or his partial, equivocal relationship to it (Pocock 1985; Robertson 1983).

2. See Mayhew (2000: 192–3) on the tradition of political science and political theory that sees politics in terms of what he calls "steering": "the management of states or governments by leaders."

3. Montesquieu (2000 [1721]: Chapter 1, p. 90, alternate reading). My translation.

4. Whelan (1995) is a neglected classic on these matters. I shall draw on it heavily while contesting some of its conclusions.

5. Hobbes (1971 [1681]: 140).

6. As astutely noted by Baier (1991: 221 and passim).

7. Whelan 1995: 112ff., and see chapter 4.

8. Whelan (1995: 114–15), summarizing H 3.4–6. Henry VII's Lancastrian claim was ambiguous because his descent from John of Gaunt was illegitimate, the line having been legitimized only retroactively and under controversy.

9. H 3.5. The future Henry VIII owed his Latin skills (whence his skill in theology and writing, and the religious arrogance that went with it) to his father's acute knowledge that old dynasties might threaten new ones: "His father [Henry VII], in order to remove him [Henry VIII] from the knowledge of public business, had hitherto occupied him entirely in the pursuits of literature" (H 3.84). Conventional monarchy was planted on the grave of *virtù*. Henry VIII could live to be an undisputed, legitimate king only because his father deliberately kept from him the political nous he would have needed to pursue an independent, Yorkist claim by force.

10. H 3.3–12, 63–4.

11. As Henry VII and Elizabeth of York's great-great grandson through Henry VIII's sister, James I's title was unaffected by the latter's marital disputes as well as by dynastic struggle between Lancaster and York.

12. The parts of the *History* on Henry VII were in some editions part of the medieval volumes rather than the Tudor ones. There remain two different valedictories to the "barbarous" or medieval age in the *History*: one preceding Henry VII's reign, one following it. The idea that Henry VII's odd title and Machiavellian governing style rendered his reign an in-between stage between the War of the Roses and the beginning of a truly uncontested royal line with Henry VIII was also common among those monarchs' contemporaries. See Penn (2011: 385–6).

13. See Hume's account of the Catholic rising in the North of England (H 4.130), of the Duke of Norfolk's attempted conspiracy to free, and marry, Mary Queen of Scots (but allegedly and initially not to dethrone Queen Elizabeth; H 4.157), and of William of Orange's "total silence" with respect to English parties before the Glorious Revolution" (6.529). Henry Bolingbroke/Lancaster can be said to have installed himself as King Henry IV by a similar method, but it gets complicated. On Hume's account, his naked bandwagon seems to have fooled not only Richard II and his allies but even Lancaster himself.

14. "English" is correct: Scotland's distinctive institutions and strong attachment to Presbyterianism ensured that its interests would not track England's (though both recognized the same royal line).

15. E. Miller (1990: 97) notes that the party extremes' having fought each other to exhaustion was a necessary condition for the success of Monk's strategy and successful restoration.

16. The military regime had considerable support among rank-and-file soldiers: Even after a free parliament had been elected, a rally by General Lambert, an old Cromwellian, threatened to successfully disperse it and was only narrowly prevented—by undermining a strategy in fact quite similar to Monk's (H 6.137–8).

17. Hume presumably is referring to the ancient civil wars within Greek city-states, in which a victorious party habitually massacred or exiled the other party *en masse*—what we might now call "factional cleansing." See E: PAN, 406–7.

18. See chapter 4.

19. Schelling (1980 [1960]: 298).

20. Monk's brother had been sent as an agent by royalists (i.e., a group that should have been sympathetic to Monk's goals). Monk refused to talk to him once he found that his brother had betrayed his own mission to a man *whom Monk himself would have trusted*. The general took reticence to laudable extremes.

21. E. Miller (1990: 97).

22. At least, that is my understanding. Since Henry VIII had married his third wife, Jane Seymour, after Catherine of Aragon was dead, and they were married by someone who had been ordained as a Catholic priest, even Catholics must have conceded that Henry's marriage to Jane was legitimate, and Edward therefore a legitimate heir. Incidentally, the rule of succession had always been that younger male heirs succeeded to the throne ahead of older sisters.

23. The first known use of "Anglican" as a noun occurred in 1710; as an adjective, 1598 (OED).

24. On both accounts, if the Queen in question had no children, the Scottish line (which by the time we are discussing meant Mary Queen of Scots, followed by James VI of Scotland, both Henry VII's direct descendants through the female line) was to succeed next—as in fact eventually happened.

25. The first succession oath, declaring Henry's marriage to Catherine of Aragon void and requiring the recognition of Anne Boleyn's heirs, was imposed by parliament in 1534 (H 3.204). After Anne fell out of Henry's favor and into an elm-wood coffin, a parliament in 1536 declared her marriage to Henry VIII null and void as well, not only declaring both Mary and Elizabeth illegitimate but making it treason to assert the contrary (H 3.240). In 1544, an Act of parliament fixed the order of succession as Edward, Prince of Wales followed by *both* Mary and Elizabeth. Hume calls this Act "a reasonable piece of justice" that "corrected what the king's former violence had thrown into confusion"—but notes that it was rendered problematic by Henry's refusal to "allow the acts to be reversed, which had declared [Mary and Elizabeth] illegitimate." (This made their succession logically incoherent, since no constitutional theory held that illegitimate heirs should succeed in preference to legitimate ones [H 3.303]). In 1552 a Regency parliament imposed severe punishments on anyone who would call "the king or any of his heirs . . . heretic, schismatic, tyrant, infidel, or usurper of the crown." But since "the king and his next heir, the lady Mary, were professedly of different religions; and religions, which

threw on each other the imputation of heresy, schism, idolatry . . . [i]t was almost impossible . . . for the people, if they spoke at all on these subjects, not to fall into the crime, so severely punished by statute" (H 3.391). Hume calls the Commons on this point not "very active, vigilant, or clear-sighted."

26. Henry VIII's will passed over the Scottish line—since constant warfare against Scotland had left the king with an irrational animus toward Scots—but in terms that left ambiguous whether some of them might count as "lawful heirs" in default of children from Mary or Elizabeth. In any case, there seems no good theory whereby the King could by such an act of will countermand the rules of royal succession, which were by then constitutional and embedded deeply in tradition. Hume considers the will utterly capricious (H 3.321). Edward VI's will, passing over Mary and skipping over to Lady Jane Grey on no very coherent theory, is portrayed by Hume (as was common in his time, though now contested) as extorted by the Duke of Northumberland—and as in any case unlawful absent parliamentary approval (H 3.397–8). Neither will was respected by the people in the event. Hume has great fun with these statutes and the will; they display both Henry's caprice and the effectiveness of his tyranny, as against the Whig theory of a Tudor constitution under which the parliament was strong and assertive.

27. The fact that both Mary and Elizabeth were on paper attainted as illegitimate, and that the latter mounted no challenge to the former, must have helped. Lady Jane Grey, whose title was bad and whose supporters were widely hated as factional schemers, was no great threat to the legitimate line of succession on Hume's account.

28. Only the intercession of Philip, who preferred Elizabeth to the Scottish line for geopolitical reasons, prevented violence (H 3.428, 459). Philip protected Elizabeth not out of mercy but to forestall the accession of Mary Queen of Scots, whose French upbringing and connections made her a likely enemy to Spain.

29. Hume thinks it "probable" that the Queen of Scots herself had a hand in the bull (H 4.137, 177).

30. A book written by a learned Catholic—Hume, probably ironically, calls him "Dr. Allen"—"served farther to efface . . . scruples, with regard to the murder of an heretical prince"; such ideas became widely propagated among English Catholics (4.211). The bull was rendered all the more powerful by a later clarification that paid homage to collective action problems: those Catholics who would otherwise have rejected the bull as counseling hopeless rebellions were assured that they could "in conscience" bide their time until "the sovereign pontiff" signaled that circumstances were ripe (4.188). (This tacitly recognized one of Elizabeth's main advantages: as long as the Queen of Scots was imprisoned, the Catholics had "no head who could conduct their dangerous enterprizes," no leader around whom to rally [4.194].)

31. Mary's at least tacit claim to England: H 4.159. Conspiracies: H 4.128, 132, 174; Mary "willingly gave her concurrence" to conspiracy: 4.156; similarly 159, 185, 227, 243.

32. Elizabeth's successor on the theory of the will's validity would have been Catherine Grey, lady Jane's younger sister. (As far as I know, she would also be heir if one adhered to Edward VI's will, but nobody did.) Elizabeth's fear of Catherine Grey's potential heirs (H 4.49–50; more on this below) suggests that she felt at least some Protestant enemies might rally to the Greys.

33. Elizabeth went to great, often extreme, lengths to undermine potential successors by preventing them from marrying and reproducing, lest their having heirs make their lines seem more reliable than hers (H 4.49–50, 220).

34. Hume, to be sure, mentions this in the context of making an opposite argument, that the Queen of Scots was *not* dangerous because she would die soon. He puts this argument, however, in the mouths of a minority of Elizabeth's counselors. The argument from desperate courage seems to have prevailed.

35. One could read Elizabeth's strategy, though Hume does not clearly do so, as one involving credible commitment. By eliminating some future options (a natural heir, once Elizabeth was past a certain age, was impossible) and declining others for the moment (a designated successor, should Elizabeth die suddenly), Elizabeth guaranteed that her reign was something Protestants would fiercely defend, since the alternative was so uncertain. This happened: a league was subscribed in her defense, and became so popular that even the Queen of Scots tried to sign up as well in her own protection (H 4.204–5; for more on this see Collinson 1994: chapter 2). But commitment strategies, as Schelling points out, are double edged: they increase one's bargaining power at the cost of limiting one's own and one's allies' future options (Schelling 2006b). By the time the Queen of Scots' plots got truly dangerous, Elizabeth's counselors thought Mary's death the only way of safeguarding their own lives: "they personal safety, as well as the safety of the public, seemed to depend alone on the queen's life, who was now somewhat advanced in years," and they were "even more anxious than the queen herself, to prevent [the Queen of Scots] from ever mounting the throne of England" (4.229). This of course was incentive for them to kill the Queen of Scots whether or not the accusations of conspiracy and treason were accurate. Unlike Elizabeth, they had equal reason to fear Mary's succession to the throne whether it was violent or peaceful.

36. Hume always portrays two sides to a historical argument when he thinks there are two, but in this case the "Reasons for the executions of Mary" presented to Elizabeth by her advisers, from which this is taken, stands alone. I submit that Hume sees no sound rebuttal: the text represents his own view.

37. "[Mary] was at last engaged in designs, which afforded her enemies, who watched the opportunity, a *pretence or reason* for effecting her final ruin" (4.223, emphasis added); "The queen had now brought affairs with Mary to that *situation*, which she had long ardently desired; and had found a *plausible reason for executing vengeance on a competitor*, whom, from the beginning of her reign, she had ever equally dreaded and hated" (4.236, emphases added).

38. Hume also stresses that Henry VIII was so capricious that his will was not to be trusted; besides, Elizabeth in her dying breath had countermanded that will and endorsed James' title (H 5.4).

39. After the Queen of Scots' death, the pope desperately endorsed the last Catholic hope, that is, invasion by Philip's Armada and the complete uprooting of Elizabeth's line through right of conquest. In fact, he literally designated the Armada invasion a crusade (H 4.265). This had no effect in England, whose Catholic subjects felt relatively well-treated by Elizabeth and had no interest in becoming part of Spain. Even highly ranked gentlemen, barred from service as English officers, enlisted as private soldiers and sailors for England; Catholic noblemen sponsored English ships (under Protestant command) and encouraged their tenants to prepare for homeland defense (H 4.266).

40. On 5.551, Hume notes that the puritan party in parliament "did not think proper to dispute this great constitutional point": in other words, if they had any reservations about hereditary succession, or yearnings for a Howard succession, they kept them quiet.

41. For James' assumptions, see H 5.19. For the thesis that Henry VIII and Elizabeth had governed in a quasi-absolute manner, so that *recent* precedents were all on the monarchy's side and contrary to Parliament's claims, see all of H 4.Appendix III, 4.354–71, and much of H 5 but especially Appendix IV, 5.124–9.

42. To summarize a very complex argument, the commons had come, by the course of the sixteenth century, to own most of the land (while the Crown, by the end of Elizabeth's reign, had sold almost all its assets); it was starting to demand the rule of law, in line with general European progress in letters, manufactures, trade, and liberal arts; and the particular form its assertions tended to take were both individualistic and (irrationally) courageous because of religion: Puritanism, which makes every individual a spiritual authority, brought a zeal for civil liberty. For the economic bases of the changes in parliament, see H 4.384, 5.22, 38–40, 134–5, 187, 371, 558; also E. Miller (1990: 83–6). For the "general, but insensible revolution" spurred by arts, manufactures, and letters, see H 5.18–19. McArthur (2007), consistent with that and many other passages, takes Hume's doctrine to be that social and economic conditions demand a "civilized" government involving the rule of law but do not determine whether civilized government will take a monarchical or parliamentary form. For the Puritan basis of civil liberty, see especially 4.145–6, 5.177–8, and 5.559 note J as well as 5.35 and E: SE, 73–9.

43. James I assumed the title "King of Great Britain" and declared that anyone born in either England or Scotland was a natural citizen of both, without having passed a formal act of union through either country's parliament. Hume points out that the English and Scottish people could be the same, when they had the same king and different parliaments, only if we "suppose, that the sovereign authority resided chiefly in the prince, and that these popular assemblies were rather instituted to assist with money and advice, than endowed with any controuling or active powers in the government." Bacon, arguing James' case on the point, did assume something very like this. "It would seem from this reasoning, that the idea of a *hereditary, limited* monarchy, though implicitly supposed in many public transactions, had scarcely ever, as yet, been expressly formed by any English lawyer or politician" (H 5.35, emphasis in original). Compare 5.170: "No one was at that time [1626] sufficiently sensible of the great weight, which the commons bore in the balance of the constitution. The history of England had never hitherto afforded one instance, where any great movement or revolution had proceeded from the lower house." At 5.562, Hume claims that no sixteenth-century writer had described England as a "limited monarchy": they called it instead "an absolute one, where the people have many privileges."

44. Hume is deliberately coy. He writes "we, in this island, have ever since enjoyed, if not the best system of government, at least the most entire system of liberty." That "if not" was, in Hume's time as now, ambiguous between denial and tentative affirmation. Hume's view of England's form of government in his own time is complex. The safest summary might be that he thinks it good for liberty (perhaps too good; maintaining it requires a more unlimited freedom of the press than he thinks wise), potentially deficient in producing public order, and likely not to last very long. See E: LP, 9–13, and BG, 47–53.

45. There was also a security dilemma once war had begun: "power alone could ensure safety; and the power of one side was necessarily attended with danger to the other" (H 5.455).

46. Hume adds two caveats. First, there must be a "pretence," such as a parliament, whereby new social forces can smoothly and legitimately enter the seats of power. Second, a single holder of a large property can exert much more political influence than dispersed holders who in combination own more property—partly because of coordination considerations: "it is difficult to make many persons combine in the same views and measures" (see respectively E: FPG, 35; and E: BG, 48).

47. "Though justly sensible, that no part of civil administration required greater care or a nicer judgment than the conduct of religious parties; he [James I] had not perceived, that, in the same proportion as this practical knowledge of theology is requisite, the speculative refinements in it are mean, and even dangerous in a monarch. By entering zealously into frivolous disputes, James gave them an air of importance and dignity, which they could not otherwise have acquired; and being himself inlisted in the quarrel, he could no longer have recourse to contempt and ridicule, the only proper method of appeasing it" (H 5.11–12). James should have learned from experience: the Puritan clergy, though "of mean education," had showed no reluctance to contradict James' religious positions in public (H 5.10–11).

48. On 5.562, Hume suggests that the "king's love of general, speculative principles" was not the only cause of the veil's being removed; the "rising spirit of the parliament" was bound to lead to demands for further constitutional clarity. But we might say that James should have picked his time better—and should have framed his declarations according to his ability practically to vindicate them, not his conviction of their theoretical validity.

49. "Charles' capacity shone not equally in action as in reasoning" (H 5.524).

50. "There is nothing, which tends more to excuse, if not to justify, the extreme rigour of the commons towards Charles, than his open encouragement and avowal of such general principles, as were altogether incompatible with a limited government" (H 5.198). By ordering Anglican priests to put such sentiments in sermons, Charles discredited the Anglican church—and encouraged the opposing party to resort to Puritan counter-preaching—without helping himself (H 5.177–8).

51. Hume notes this belief repeatedly (e.g., on 5.140: "While James was vaunting his divine vicegerency, and boasting of his high prerogative, he possessed not so much as a single regiment of guards to maintain his extensive claims"). To be sure, Hume is sometimes so carried away by his outrage at Charles I's execution that he seems to forgive or even view favorably the divine-right claim—in complete opposition to his usual views (see 5.536).

52. Comparing excessive pliability to excessive assertions of prerogative, Hume says "that this new extreme into which the king, for want of proper counsel or support was fallen, became no less dangerous to the constitution, and pernicious to public peace, than the other, in which he had so long and so unfortunately persevered" (H 5.306). Hume suggests that while Charles was right to acquiesce in the Petition of Right, the Triennial Act, and other measures to safeguard personal liberty and parliamentary privileges, agreeing to let parliament control or choose the instruments of the law's execution, especially the army, was another matter (H 5.334, 384–5). By the time Charles came to realize that his concessions to Parliamentary power had gone too far, his prerogative was "defenceless" (5.328).

53. Rather than pursuing the initiative when his army was facing the Scots, Charles I agreed at the decisive moment to a cease-fire and to the disbanding of his army at great loss of time and money. Charles' actions here and the associated expense were

the precipitating cause of his having to call two parliaments, the second of which never disbanded and eventually killed him. Hume calls Charles' character "not sufficiently vigorous or decisive" on H 5.268 (cf. 276).

54. Of the start of the English Civil War, Hume writes that "From the mixed character, indeed, of Charles, arose in part the misfortunes, in which England was at this time involved. His political errors, or rather weaknesses, had raised him inveterate enemies: His eminent moral virtues had procured him zealous partizans. And between the hatred of the one, and the affections of the other, was the nation agitated with the most violent convulsions" (H 5.384).

55. On personal honor, H 5.330 and especially H 5.273–4, where Hume puts in the mouth of Court apologists the argument that Charles would keep his word because he had promised "not only on the word of a prince, but also on that of a gentleman (the expression which he had been pleased to use)." Hume proceeds, as usual, to list arguments at least equally compelling on the side of Parliament. On Hume's belief that Charles would have upheld his late, constitutional concessions even without fierce coercion, see H 5.394, 430–31. Hume is ambiguous, and in places suggests that Charles should have been trusted not because he was unwilling to challenge the new constitutional limits that parliament had forced on him, but because those limits had left him *unable* to do so. See below.

56. Dees (1992: 235). Contrast Hume's assessment of the Earl of Argyle: "A man equally supple and inflexible, cautious and determined, and entirely qualified to make a figure during a factious and turbulent period" (H 5.263).

57. Machiavelli (1996 [1531]: 1.9.2, p. 29).

58. Hume at one point notes that parliament was a false collective—its members had "various dispositions" and did not have "the same motives" (H 5.207). But not until after parliament has scored all its decisive constitutional victories over the monarchy does Hume have cause to draw any practical implications from this fact. To be clearer: every parliamentarian faced a prisoner's dilemma problem—they were safe collectively but their leaders highly vulnerable as individuals. (As previously noted [see chapter 2 on negative conventions], Hume believes that only irrational religious motives could and did overcome this problem.) But parliament did not face a *coordination* problem: those who wanted to act were agreed on what to aim at.

59. Most famously by Bolingbroke in his "Dissertation Upon Parties" (1997: 94).

60. E. Burke (1987 [1790]): tenants metaphor on 83; builders on 19, 115.

61. Elsewhere Hume calls the English constitution of the early Stuart reigns "turbulent" (5.96) and inaccurate (5.43, 207); he speaks of its "inaccurate genius" (5.207; here genius means "prevailing character or spirit, general drift, characteristic method or procedure" [OED 3c]).

62. One reason why Hume sounds much more "conservative" in his *Essays* than in his *History* is that by his own time he considers the fabric well-formed and consistent, though dangerous in its substance because its attachment to liberty is so strong. If Hume's treatment of the wise statesman who "will . . . adjust his innovations, as much as possible, to the ancient fabric, and preserve entire the chief pillars and supports of the constitution" sounds proto-Burkean, it is a Burkeanism relative to changed circumstances and a new constitution (E: IPC, 512–13).

63. Hume considers this a view held by "a great many," thus forgivable in the Stuarts, but wrong (H 5.127, Appendix IV). James lacked the "penetration" to see that "neither his circumstances nor his character" let him act as Elizabeth did, but the "en-

creasing knowledge" of his "people" (really the Parliament, the only popular actor in the early stages) "discovered [i.e. revealed] to them that advantage, which they had obtained, and made them sensible of the inestimable value of civil liberty" (H 5.558 note "J").

64. Forbes (1975: 310–11) notes that the story of English liberty, unlike so much in Hume, is in some sense *not* a matter of unintended consequences. Forbes' gloss of Hume is that the commons' leaders "knew what they wanted and adapted means (control of supplies) to this end."

65. For this meaning of situation see also H 5.159.

66. The Commons had the allegiance of the City of London—which as a "place of general rendezvous and society" faced far fewer common-knowledge problems than the countryside—and used the City ruthlessly by inciting mob violence against key royalist figures and measures. See H 5.367, 320–21, 323, 362–3, 367ff.; 372–3; quotation at 5.294. Bongie (2000) has noted that French conservatives and reactionaries referred constantly to the *History* in National Assembly debates. Whether the French Left may have studied Parliament's actions in the *History* as a kind of organizing manual is, to my knowledge, yet to be explored.

67. Parliamentary speeches were "first published and dispersed" at this time and used to rally public opinion. Political sermons by "puritanical preachers and lecturers . . . resounded with faction and fanaticism"; these sermons were often not only directed toward political topics but organized by political figures (H 5. 294–5). On sermons see also 299–300, 362, and esp. 445–7. The press "swarmed with productions" that Hume looks down on as lacking "art or eloquence": he means the political pamphlet, newly invented and of a potency Hume recognizes (H 5.295). On petitions see 5.296, 496; again Hume, always the elitist, is suspicious of many petitions, especially in later stages, given that many of their signers were poor or even female (5.371), and praises later restrictions placed on petitioning under Charles II (6.173). One should be careful not to go to the other extreme and romanticize petitions as faithful heralds of public opinion. Hume notes that parliament not only disregarded but *arrested* circulators of petitions in favor of monarchy or the Anglican hierarchy, explicitly stating that those who supported the status quo had no need of petitions (5.372).

68. "The policy pursued by the commons, and which had hitherto succeeded to admiration, was, to astonish the king by the boldness of their enterprizes, to intermingle no sweetness with their severity, to employ expressions no less violent than their pretensions, and to make him sensible in what little estimation they held both his person and his dignity. To a bill so destructive of royal authority, they prefixed, with an insolence seemingly wanton, a preamble equally dishonourable to the personal character of the king" (H 5.375). Charles actually refused this particular demand— that the King appoint as army officers a set of persons named by parliament and responsive to their wishes—but by then his bargaining position was so weak that parliament stood to gain from the resulting civil war.

69. The criticisms that Hume makes of Hambden (his spelling of Hampden) and Pym in particular have to do more with the populist and religious form of their rhetoric—not that this is trivial for Hume—than with the effectual truth of their policy: "Profound capacity, indeed, undaunted courage, extensive enterprise" were "polluted with mysterious jargon, and full of the lowest and most vulgar hypocrisy" (i.e., enthusiastic religion: 5.304).

70. Hume dissents only from Strafford's attainder, which he calls a "complication of cruel iniquity."

71. The distinction between red (republican) and black (royalist or imperial) theory, from scholarship on different schools of neo-Tacitist political thought, stems from Giuseppe Toffanin in 1921. For modern treatments see P. Burke (1969) and, with specific reference to eighteenth-century Britain, Weinbrot (1993).

72. When Charles asked the parliamentary leaders at one point to name "all the concessions, which they deemed requisite for the settlement of the nation," they refused; it is not good negotiation strategy to name one's reservation price (H 5.376).

73. Hume also suggests that Charles' claims of necessity had a boy-who-cried-wolf quality: "the employing, so long, [of] the plea of a necessity, which appeared distant and doubtful, rendered it impossible for him to avail himself of a necessity, which was now at least become real, urgent, and inevitable" (5.281; compare 5.545). The parliamentarians were not only "sagacious and penetrating" but "implacable and artful"; Hume is here multiplying synonyms for "lion and fox" (5.200).

74. Compare H 5.308, where the Triennial Act is called "so great an innovation in the constitution" that the whole nation rejoiced (and promised to grant the king supply, for a while).

75. On this point I take Hume to be more than usually in accord with Burke, who would later write that "The people of England . . . look upon the legal hereditary succession of their crown as among their rights, not as among their wrongs; . . . as a security for their liberty, not as a badge of servitude" (1987: 23).

76. The King's arguments on this point displayed, in Hume's opinion, "justness of reasoning and propriety of expression" (H 5.381).

77. "Sacred," by the way, has a strange meaning for Hume: it certainly has nothing to do with divinity, but rather has to do with fundamental *conventions* that are inviolable sources of authority. This general, not distinctly religious meaning "secured by religious sentiment, reverence, sense of justice, or the like, against violation, infringement, or encroachment" was not always uncommon: see OED 5a.

78. "While he [Charles I] offered a toleration and indulgence to tender consciences; they threatened the utter extirpation of prelacy. To his professions of lenity, they opposed declarations of rigour: And the more the ancient tenor of the laws inculcated a respectful subordination to the crown, the more careful were they, by their lofty pretensions, to cover that defect, under which they laboured" (H 5.435).

79. The dispositions may not have purely moral origins. Hume suggests that Monk brought about the restoration of Charles II and a free parliament, rather than pursuing "the same grandeur and authority, which had been assumed by Cromwel" (an "exhorbitant, if not impossible" project—again the ambiguous "if not" does and does not rule it out), due to "the natural tranquillity and moderation of his temper, [and] the calmness and solidity of his genius, *not to mention his age, now upon the decline*" (H 6.125, emphasis added; compare 6.247, where Monk, by then the Duke of Albemarle, is also said to lack greed). His circumstances mattered as well as his character.

80. As in the English Civil War, opportunities for compromise were wasted because imperfect constitutional theory obscured their likely shape (2.324). The parallels deserve further study.

81. For further discussion of these issues see Sabl (2009b).

Chapter 6. Vertical Inequality and the Extortion of Liberty

1. Whelan (1985: 358) claims that "Liberty is not an especially prominent theme in Hume's writings"—and then proceeds to give a very fine account of the prominent role it plays. Whelan clearly means, in context, that Hume had little use for a *natural* or pre-political account of liberty; liberty for Hume was something "defined and maintained as an aspect of government, in the general context of allegiance" (ibid.). Compare Capaldi and Livingston (1990).

2. Hunt (2007: 122 and chapter 3 passim), by counting book titles, reckons the 1750s the decade among all others, before or since, in which talk of rights was least common in the United Kingdom. This was the decade in which Hume wrote his *History* and in which most of the volumes were published.

3. Given that inequality in power is what is primarily at issue, words like "exploitation," "domination," or even "oppression" (which Hume freely uses in this context, H 1.475) might capture the intended meaning somewhat better than "inequality." But inequality captures the overall similarity between the vertical and horizontal cases.

4. This is a common theme of many rational choice accounts of coordination. See, e.g., Calvert (1992); Fiorina and Shepsle (1989: 32–5).

5. For the distinction between "followers of a leader" and "those who are merely subject to a leader's action" see Calvert (1992: 20). Calvert treats a stylized case in which there are no institutions. The legal-constitutional version of this extreme case would be a government by a ruling group that coordinates among itself but rules another group through mere terror. This has been analyzed under the headings of a "dual" regime (Dahl 1971: 93–4), a "*Herrenvolk* democracy" (R. Smith 1997), or a "piecewise just society" (Sabl 2001).

6. The phrase "order and good government" occurs not just famously in Canada's national charter (less famously in New Zealand's as well, and perhaps others) but twice in Hume: H 4.97; NHR, 30.

7. Compare Luce and Raiffa (1957: 5.3, 90–94), Hardin (1999: 305–9), and Schelling (1980 [1960]: 64, 87, 300). As mentioned earlier, Hume's general attitude that constitutional settlements are fragile could be made compatible with the view (though it seems not to be Hume's own view) that the advantages of constitutional authority are so great as to overwhelm any inequality in how they are distributed. Those receiving a permanently inferior share of power will accordingly—especially if inferior in numbers, wealth, or other politically relevant resources—be urged to accept a counsel of acquiescence. They are unlikely, by risking civil war, to win more than what they receive under an unfair peace. This sort of inequality often shades in practice into vertical inequality, since the ruling coalition may well consist of members of the socially superior group. Analytically, however, the two are distinct. To illustrate the distinction: when horizontal inequality is deeply implicated in an existing order, even a leader who is a member of the disfavored group may be easily able to grab spoils for close associates but unable substantially to challenge the larger inequalities of power in the polity or society. To do so would require risking disorder on a broader scale than either she or her fellow members of the disfavored group would find acceptable.

8. Hume endorsed this part of the so-called Country program. Of the triennial act he writes that "nothing could be more necessary than such a statute, for complet-

ing a regular plan of law and liberty" given monarchs' natural reluctance to assemble parliaments and the constant temptation they faced to settle public business through extra-legislative "acts of state" (5.307–8). The Act was never enforced and had been repealed by Hume's time (as of 1716). Some of the Commonwealth's more populist outposts (Australia, New Zealand) continue to have a three-year term for parliaments. In the United States, the House of Representatives' term is two years, largely due to the same kind of Country reasoning.

9. "Sole oppressor" is at H 3.49; "despotic and eastern monarchy" is at H 4.370.

10. Clarke (1936: 256–7) notes the historical, not just theoretical problem of taxing people without a proper practice of representation: in the early thirteenth century there were magnates who refused to pay taxes voted by the peers on the grounds that they had not been personally present in parliament and therefore had no obligation to observe its decisions.

11. Hume was certainly aware of public goods contribution games before they were called that; see T 3.2.7.8, SBN 538–9.

12. On contract by convention, see Hardin (1982); on mutual surveillance, Chwe (2001).

13. For the collective action problems faced by representatives before the body was fully institutionalized, see 5.557, note J. Conversely, "the first symptom of a regular association and plan of liberty" among the English barons was the result of a botched royal attempt at expedition: King John in 1201 "summoned together" the barons to demand military service; they "unanimously" refused to do so until he restored their privileges. John on that occasion was able through threats to panic the barons and break their "association." The barons not being used to collective action, "affairs were not yet fully ripe for the revolution projected" (H 1.410–11).

14. Hardin (1995: 28ff.; 2007: 89, 96–7) stresses this "dual coordination" origin of governmental power: the central authority has a unique ability to set the agenda and declare a default set of norms or behaviors, and gains power from people's recognition that such common understandings tend to produce peace and economic gains; the opposition is inherently scattered, unable to coordinate on a unique alternative to governmental claims—and a central government has, among other things, the power to scatter it further and disrupt its communications. Less formally and more historically, Post (1964: 204n150) notes that "the king's business of administration and taxation was equally important, and perhaps prior to justice, in that the summoning of representatives of the communities for taxes and the like, or for bearing the record, gave the communities the opportunity, or rather acquainted them with the means, to pursue their own interests in Parliament." Hume at 5.134 notes, however, that the alternative to gathering nobles (and later gentry) together did not work. When James banished members of parliament to the countryside because he reasoned "that, by their living together, they became more sensible of their own strength, and were apt to indulge too curious researches into matters of government," the MPs and Lords merely became richer and more obstreperous by cultivating wealth and power in the country. Parliament had to be summoned if national resources were to be drawn on.

15. See Sabl (2002).

16. Discussing the Commons' supply power in his own time, Hume stresses how easy it would be to reduce the monarch to total dependence (which, as we now know, happened within a few decades). "Did the house of commons [*sic* for lower case] depend in the same manner on the king, and had none of the members any prop-

erty but from his gift, would not he command all their resolutions, and be from that moment absolute?" (E: IP, 44).

17. H 5.272 is even clearer: parliament took aim at royal prerogative by driving hard bargains in return for supply when England faced an invasion from Scotland. Here Parliament's bargaining power was extreme because pseudo-conventions were felt unequally by the parties. Parliament, which shared the Scots' (Puritan or Calvinist) religion, did not regard a possible Scottish invasion as really a foreign conquest, whereas Charles feared it intensely. Thus, Parliament's threats were extremely credible and extremely forceful.

18. On King John, see chapter 3 above; on Edward III, see H 2.213.

19. Hume stressed the same point in his criticism of Harrington's *Oceana*, in arguing that a royal veto would squelch liberty if allowed at the beginning of the legislative process instead of at the end, when public opinion would render its use very rare (in fact, we might note, never used in England since Queen Anne's reign). "[C]ould the King crush a disagreeable bill in embryo (as was the case, for some time, in the SCOTTISH parliament, by means of the lords of the articles), the BRITISH government would have no balance, nor would grievances ever be redressed." (E: IPC, 515; internal citation omitted).

20. Griffith and Ryle 1989: 7–8.

21. On these passages see Forbes (1975: 170–71).

22. Hume thought in this passage and elsewhere, including E: IP, that what the Country party called "corruption" or the offering of government office to ensure pliant parliaments, would keep the executive-legislative balance in check. Something like this in fact occurred in England during and after Hume's time. The U.S. Constitution purposely bans it.

23. Forbes (1975): 304–5; Livingston (1990: 117); E. Miller (1990: 92–4).

24. At H 5.58, Hume notes that, as of 1614, parliament had refused supply only "thrice in six hundred years."

25. Madison, in the course of a very Humean account of the development of the House of Commons from "an infant and humble and representation of the people, gradually enlarging the sphere of its activity and importance," grants similar importance to how representatives will view "the dignity of their country in the eyes of other nations": the House of Commons has sustained its power over money bills by *not* displaying "absolute inflexibility" to the point of bringing about "general confusion." Hamilton, Madison, and Jay (2001 [1788]: No. 58 [Madison]).

26. See Hume, L 2.178, 210, 221, 235; Livingston (1990: 145); Mossner (1980: 421, 469, 552–3); Pocock (1985: 137–41); Stewart (1992: 302–7); for a pro-Wilkes view (which does not to my mind answer the charge of ethnic bigotry) Thomas (1996).

27. See Hardin (1995: chapter 4) on the us-versus-them method of overcoming collective action problems. Essentially, a communal or ethnic norm can function as what I have called a negative convention, one which is stable and self-enforcing in pursuit of a smaller gain than would be possible if those excluded were let in.

28. See E: BG, passim.

29. Hamilton, Madison, and Jay (2001 [1788]: No. 78 [Hamilton]).

30. Carens (1979: 136).

31. Hirschman (1977).

32. This potential becomes actual in mixed governments when all or part of the body that controls supply fails to provide it on terms the administration will accept—as

in the U.S. budget shutdown of 1995/6, the "Dismissal" crisis in Australia in 1975, or any year in California.

33. Kirchheimer (1969). The particular phrase "class compromise" appears to have come from a later summary of Kirchheimer's views.

34. Schlesinger (1973); Krishnakumar (1998: 591).

35. This combination, which (now) has a New Deal flavor, has escaped analysis by a political theory discipline whose tendencies are New Left. The most complete modern treatments mix empirical, policy-oriented, and normative analysis and as such lie to some degree outside the subfield of "political theory" narrowly understood: Beer (1993); Holmes and Sunstein (1999); Schlesinger (1998 [1949]); and perhaps most seriously, Huntington (1968)—whose focus on the need for developing polities to centralize power has obscured his concession that in mature polities this should be followed by dispersing it. The last book (which lacks the negative references to immigration that discredited Huntington's later work) perhaps best echoes Hume's historical theory; the first three better mirror Hume's simultaneous attachment to centralized authority and personal liberty. On a more popular level see Lind (1995) and Starr (2007), both of which have more or less fallen dead-born from the press.

36. Hume wrote to Catherine Macaulay in 1764 that he regarded "all kinds of subdivision of power, from the monarchy of France to the freest democracy of some Swiss Cantons, to be equally legal, if established by custom and authority" (NL, 81).

37. Van Holthoon (2008: 2) notes that "Hume had a view of the separation of powers not unlike that of the Founding Fathers. Their [America's] president as elective king should take care of daily business and an intricate system of controls to be handled by Congress was designed to keep him out of mischief."

38. Hartz (1955: 44–5).

39. On both the coherence of this pro-government program and its limits and discontents, persisting to the present day (in particular the characteristic U.S. fear of taxation by the federal government), see Edling (2003).

40. Adams (1794: e.g., 1.128).

41. Hamilton, Madison, and Jay (2001 [1788]: No. 51 [Madison]).

42. Hamilton, Madison, and Jay (2001 [1788]: No. 70 [Hamilton]). The same paper declares in favor of a "numerous legislature."

43. Waldron (1999: chapters 2–4).

44. One should note that Hume writes these words not in his own voice but to characterize the position of Whig optimists. His own position is neither Whig nor Tory but ambiguous—and, of course, necessarily contingent on which conventions have come to be customarily recognized.

Chapter 7. What Touches All: Equality, Parliamentarism, and Contested Authority

1. "[F]or even the most philosophically-minded among the representatives of this latter tradition [starting with the conciliar movement and extending through the "constitutionalists and resistance theorists of the sixteenth and early seventeenth centuries"] . . . consent appears finally to have remained what it had been even for the most advanced' of medieval consent theorists: not, that is, the assent of a concatenation of free and equal individuals imposing on themselves an obligation which of their ulti-

mate autonomy they could well avoid, but the consent instead of free communities, possessed at a minimum of the original right to choose their rulers, perhaps also to choose the form of government under which they were to live, maybe even to participate on some sort of continuing basis in the governmental process—those choices, however, 'conditioned by the principle that authority must exist,' that it was 'necessary and in some sense natural to man'" (Oakley 1983: 324; final quotation is from Ewart Lewis, *Medieval Political Ideas*, 2 vols. [London: Routledge & Paul, 1954]: 1.160).

2. "Mankind is an inventive species; and where an invention is obvious and absolutely necessary, it may as properly be said to be natural as any thing that proceeds immediately from original principles, without the intervention of thought or reflexion" T 3.2.1.19, SBN 484.

3. For the crucial role of a numerous assembly, as opposed to a single ruler or small group claiming a representative role, see Waldron (1999: chapters 2–4).

4. For the latter point see Waldron (1994: 121).

5. McArthur (2007: 123). The argument that the welfare state (as well as "the liberation of women") might on Humean grounds legitimately arise as a modification to prior property conventions, and might on Humean grounds deserve retrospective praise (without being available as a critical standard or normative requirement ahead of time), appears in Nagel (1995: 208).

6. Macleod (1981: 76). Compare Barry (1989: 168–75); Miller (1981: 74–5). Hume's distinction in the second *Enquiry* between "the necessity of a separation and constancy in men's possession" that is "obvious, strong, and invincible" and "the rules, which assign particular objects to particular persons," which "depend on a public utility more light and frivolous, on the sentiment of private humanity and aversion to private hardship, on positive laws, on precedents, analogies, and very fine connexions and turns of the imagination" (EPM [EPM App. 3.11n65], SBN 310) certainly invites this reading: see the treatment in Hiskes (1977). The current chapter pursues the possibility that Hume's quasi-theory of justice is what Hiskes calls "formal." That is: many different arrangements could be equally acceptable; which one counts as just is settled by law and the authority convention.

7. Livingston (1990) argues that Hume's historical method rules out the possibility of a theory of this kind and demonstrates the vanity of seeking one. He may overstate his case, but only slightly.

8. This is a strong theme of the *Essays*. See especially E: BG, 47–53.

9. Clarke (1936: 248–9) calls this formula and *quod principi placuit* ("what has pleased the prince has the full force of law" on account of the people's grant of *imperium* to him) "the main political contribution of Rome to Western Europe." The short version of *quod omnes tangit* actually obscures some important questions arising from different variants of what follows those three words. In various versions of the principle, "what touches all" should be either "treated by" (*tractari*) "approved/ confirmed by" (*comprobetur, approbari*), or "heard by" (*vocandi*) all, or should be subject to the will (*voluntas*) or agreement (*consensus*) of those affected (Post 1964: 173ff.; Luhmann 1998; grammatical inconsistency in the original phrases, which vary in how the formula is put together). "Treated by" (*tractari*) is most common, but may overstate the extent to which the parties were able to negotiate from strength or universally recognized power: the word was used in the period before regular parliaments to mean little beyond discussion and the exchange of information (Holt 1981: 21; Post 1964: 180).

10. Harriss (1981: 30).
11. Stein (1988: 47); Post (1964).
12. Or one could retain that bias on (libertarian) purpose. Watner (2005) is a plausible attempt in this vein.
13. See Harriss (1981). Compare Clarke's assertion that the idea of consent was, as it would be in current matters of private law, originally "archaic and obstructive": any change in a customary legal arrangement would violate rights unless consent was given (1936: 247).
14. See Holt (1981: 2, 21–2); Elton (1974: 23). Hume (H 2.529–30, note (E)), noting the case of the merchants, blames the incongruity, in the eyes of his own time, on "the maxims of all the feudal governments, that every order of the state should give their consent to the acts which more immediately concerned them," the other orders' consent not being necessary, since their interests were not at issue. The eventual abandonment of occupationally based, non-geographic taxation showed that "the notion of a political system" had become "well understood"—though even then Hume adduces economic rather than distinctly political reasoning: "the commons [by the reign of Edward III] had then observed that the people paid these duties, though the merchants advanced them; and they therefore remonstrated against this practice." Harriss (1981: 43) gives a more "political" explanation: briefly, the commons distrusted the existence of an independent body of tax grantors not subject to its own jurisdiction, and asserted the right to judge the "common profit," as opposed to the "singular profit" of the merchant companies.
15. Cam (1970: 270).
16. Edwards (1970: 144). Elton notes that before the sixteenth century the modern British practice of MPs not being residents of their districts was uncommon (1974: 43–4). It is still prohibited by law or convention in some countries and by a strong political norm in the United States—though not by the federal Constitution, which requires only that representatives reside in the state that sends them, not the community or district.
17. Elton (1974: 41). M.V. Clarke waxes poetic on the theme:
    > This steady application of the representative principle through the jury would have been impossible without that framework of local boundaries and institutions which was the richest part of the Anglo-Saxon inheritance. The whole of England was honeycombed with small and seemingly insignificant districts to which tradition and geography had given a natural unity. By the thirteenth century even the youngest of the shires had been a centre of public life for three hundred years; the hundreds, whatever their origin, were also ancient, and in their courts quarrels and common business had been heard and examined by generations of neighbors. Though many boroughs were relatively upstart, the narrow circle of their walls had compressed their inhabitants into a unity more obvious, if no deeper, than the slowly growing cohesion of rural communities. . . . Either by the king at the centre or by the ordinary man in his village, political geography was deemed to determine something essential. John Green was not only a freeman of the parish and vill of Cow Honeybourne, he was also a member of the hundred of Kiftsgate, and, through that membership, had his part in the county of Gloucester. Each form of membership had its corresponding form of activity in the courts of the vill, the hundred and the shire. Clarke (1936: 285)

18. Clarke (1936: 286). Post (1964: 236–7) likewise notes that knights and burgesses may have learned to engage in public-law assertions of rights to be present, and to give consent when taxes were demanded, from their experience of similar rights in private lawsuits, as parties or jurors.

19. Cam (1970: 270). See similarly Holt (1981: 24); and Clarke (1936: 161, 246–7), who, taking a middle position, places great weight on the *quod omnes tangit* formula but stresses its lack of settled acceptance until 1311 or possibly later.

20. Kreps (1990).

21. Essentially, such representation made it possible for the old idea of the kingdom as the system of grants of land from king to magnates in fee to yield (for purposes of politics, though not law) to a more inclusive geographical notion: "if the king's business touched the kingdom, it touched all who represented the community and communities of the realm, and all these must be summoned" (Post 1964: 233).

22. Elton (1974: 43).

23. Clarke (1936: 13), citing a late fourteenth century document.

24. Matters are of course very complex. Senates in federal systems can easily adapt the medieval theory, as perhaps can political parties under a party-list system (since parties represent, to some extent, communities of interest and identification). Obviously the kind of "pluralist" theories that have sought to divide consent-based representation (or in radical versions, sovereignty) among parliaments, religious bodies, and groupings based on occupation, class, or union membership theoretically solve this problem as well (and have often appealed directly to medieval models). They do so, however, at the cost of creating the much bigger problem that the precise relationship among these different sources of authority is left in limbo. The pluralists have often forgotten that parliaments were developed because ad-hoc, pluralist representation of diverse bodies whose membership was defined heterogeneously *had not worked*. Public business could not be done when each group's support had to be canvassed separately and each could strike a separate bargain in return for its political and financial support.

25. Clarke (1936: 200, 180) notes how *attornati* was sometimes the word used to describe representatives sent from the shires, and argues that *quod omnes* was originally a formula to ensure that no body's rights could be taken away without proper notice to appear at trial, and proper opportunity to appear personally or through counsel. Post (1964: 164 and passim) gives a very similar account, culminating in the argument that q.o.t. was originally a sort of due process guarantee (p. 226).

26. Post (1964: chapter 3). Edwards (1970: 137); Elton (1974: 48).

27. Clarke (1936: 291).

28. Edwards (1970: 146). Edwards argues, without apparent evidence, that this solution implied a vision of England as "the community of the realm," possessing a common will of its own. (See similarly Clarke [1936: 13].) This seems unnecessary: parliament could in both legal theory and practice be a private association without corporate identity, so to speak an "executive committee for managing the common affairs of the shires." Cam (1970: 273) implies some such view. As in the case of local communities, fictive and organic views of national community are probably two ways of describing the same set of conventions, which existed because they were useful but were only useful if largely unquestioned.

29. Barry (1989: 163, 164–8).

30. Harriss (1981: 30, 32).

31. Again, this is consistent with voters having unequal weight in the decision, for instance in a federal system in which states send an equal number of representatives to the center, or an unequal number but one not proportional to population. The principle of one-person, one-vote, can only result from a separate, democratic principle that may be consistent with Humean ideas but is not contained or even "intimated" by them. But of course Barry's preferred method of impartial justification, with its implied requirement for universal though hypothetical agreement, also is notorious for having available no particularly persuasive arguments for one-person, one-vote—or for voting of any kind.

32. Berman (1983: 221).

33. Post (1964: 207, 211, 212n180).

34. Hamilton et al. 2001 (1788): No. 58 (Madison). Compare ibid.: No. 75 (Hamilton).

35. Buchanan and Tullock (1962).

36. Waldron (1987: 128, 137).

37. Ibid., 140–45.

38. Luhmann (1998).

39. Müller (2003: 236).

40. Clarke (1936: 267–77) reads consent through parliament as a direct response to the problem of securing unanimous consent. Waldron's (1999) endorsement of parliamentary solutions to problems of disagreement, especially regarding justice, represents a tacit acknowledgment that we best accommodate individual interests and the diversity of opinions in a large society by stressing the category of public business, and the need for fair discussion of the burdens of that business, rather than that of rational justification.

41. See chapters 3 and 4. "Good government" (even in the capacious sense this phrase takes on in the Commonwealth, as opposed to its U.S. connotation of a government that is merely honest and competent) may be too narrow to capture the concept intended: a government that is recognized as having authority because in general it effects the ends for which government exists, and in particular respects the fundamental conventions that, in a particular place and time, ground authority. Most of the adjectives that correspond roughly to this idea ("legitimate," "consensual") are biased toward non-Humean answers to the relevant questions. If there were an adjective form of the verb "acquiesce," as consensual derives from consent, attaching that adjective to government would serve. But there isn't. I thank Marc Hanvelt for discussion on this question.

42. Harriss (1981: 41). Harriss stresses that the claims of necessity were serious and "reflected in the procedures of parliament, where the chancellor's speech detailed, often graphically, the danger to the realm which the commons were then charged to consider and provide for" (ibid.). (Compare Oakley's [1983] argument cited above.) This was an explicit and vivid instance in formal speech of Jeremy Waldron's doctrine that legislative give-and-take is the product of "our sense of the moral urgency and importance of the problems that it is necessary for us to address—the things that (morally) *need* to be done and must be done by us, in our millions, together, if they are to be done at all" (1999: 117; emphasis in original).

43. Scholars differ on whether the king's assertion of "necessity" was of crucial importance in legally justifying the request for funds and placing the onus on parliament to approve them. See the contrasting arguments by Prestwich (1988: especially 423–4, 455) and Harriss (1975). The importance of something like necessity

or urgency to the general logic of authority need not turn on this historical/ legal point.

44. Clarke (1936: 267).

45. It is also close to Hume's view: "the people are apt to attach themselves more to the house of commons, than to any other member of the constitution; that house being chosen by them as their representatives, and as the public guardians of their liberty" (E: FPG, 35).

46. Roskell (1970: 322). In Davies and Denton's excellent book of edited essays (1981), every chapter expands on this theme. Roskell's view, incidentally, tends to confirm Hume's basic position that the full power of parliament was, contrary to Whig myths regarding the ancient constitution, intermittent and largely potential until the constitutional settlements of the seventeenth century.

47. Harriss (1981: 35).

48. Ibid.

49. Harriss (1981: 42, 53).

50. Elton (1974): 35.

51. Ibid., 32, 48, 59 and passim. Charles I in 1626 threatened, in Continental style, to dispense with parliament in favor of "new counsels" but lacked the standing army and tax-collection technologies requisite to vindicate the threat in the long term (H 5.171, 175ff., 188).

52. See Clarke (1936: 12). As late as the deposition of Edward II (1327), Clarke documents calls for all "estates" to renounce their "homage," in feudal style—but those estates now included "knights, justices, and others," not just nobles and clergy (1936: 183ff.).

53. Elton (1974): 50, 47; see also 58–9.

54. Berman (1983: 221).

55. Clarke (1936: 259).

56. This is not to say that enfranchisement in an existing parliament is the only way of accommodating an excluded social group. Sometimes recognition of local self-government, partial or complete, will serve the purpose better, and in a colonial context this alternative may be more apt (as Hume himself suspected with respect to the American colonies). Here a Humean perspective, which insists on their being some authority but does not demand that all authorities share a common standard of moral justification beyond some very basic constraints, may at least have no fewer resources than a rationalist perspective for recognizing the diverse ways in which good government may be achieved. Again I thank Marc Hanvelt for discussion on the point.

57. OED "enfranchise," I.1.(a), II.4. Parliamentary forms and the language of access to the mechanisms of defending one's interests are sometimes said to be ill-suited to the "politics of recognition" or the addressing of inequality based on caste and culture. If this were the case, participants in the women's suffrage and civil rights movements would seem to have massively misunderstood their own interests. I have received as a gift, and have hanging in my home, a photograph in which a voting rights worker in the Jim Crow South bears a hand-lettered sign: "Be a First-Class Citizen. Register. Vote."

58. Burns (1988b: 2–3); Pollock and Maitland (1968 [1898]: 1.230); quotation from Burns (2–3). Harriss (1981: 49–50) notes that most of what we now consider public business originated as early as the fourteenth century in petitions that were private

in form but rightly directed at parliament as matters of common interest. During that century, private petitions gradually declined in favor of "common" petitions, but the evolution was gradual and it does not seem that a sharp public-private distinction was ever drawn. Parliament, as the combined representative of the realm's communities, settled all private matters that clearly required a settlement involving more than private and particular interests. "Bill" originally meant "petition" (Madicott 1981: 62; Clarke 1936: 230ff.). The late fourteenth century model of the commons as vindicator of the "grievances of the kingdom" was formed "within an older structure" in which grievances had been glossed as private in origin—the main difference in theory, though again the shift was gradual, being that the commons, not the barons, now embodied the "community" of the realm (Brown 1981: first two quotations on 111, last on 131).

59. Clarke (1936: 244).

60. Adam Smith's account of the decline of the barons and the end of slavery (1981 [1776]: 3.2.8–15; 3.4.10–15) relies heavily on Hume's *History*, though Smith adds more detail and brings out the intermediate stages between slavery and full freedom.

61. E: RA, 278. Compare H 4.384, 5.40; Dees (1992: 235).

62. E: FPG, 35. In E: BG, 48, Hume mentions another caveat: a single holder of a large property can exert much more political influence than dispersed holders who combined own more property—partly because of coordination considerations: "it is difficult to make many persons combine in the same views and measures."

63. Danford (1990: 169–70).

64. Chisick (1989: 12–14). Chisick also richly documents Hume's fear and contempt for the vulgar in politics: (14ff.)—but again it's a matter of situational ignorance, not ascriptive incapacity.

65. Chisick (1989: 31–2n80).

66. Baier (1989: 43–5).

67. "Were the human species so framed by nature as that each individual possessed within himself every faculty, requisite both for his own preservation and for the propagation of his kind: Were all society and intercourse cut off between man and man, by the primary intention of the supreme Creator: It seems evident, that so solitary a being would be as much incapable of justice, as of social discourse and conversation" (Hume, EPM 3.1.20, SBN 191).

68. Baier (1989: 45; 2010: 69–71) suggests some arguments along these lines.

69. I would therefore differ with Sharon Krause's conclusion (2008: 14) that Hume's relative indifference to "the negative effects that the wrong social and political arrangements can have on the impartiality of judgment" entails an indifference to equality as such. The parliamentary model is one in which politics first accommodates an ever-growing variety of *partial* judgments, leading to changes in the allocation of social goods and bads. These changes come to be seen as the product of "impartiality" only later, if at all, as the victories gained by new social groups come to be taken for granted and internalized even by those outside those groups. On a Humean view, impartiality is more likely to be the result of political equality than its cause.

70. See Wolin (1954); Stewart (1992); McArthur (2007).

71. Marongiu (1961: 106). My translation from the French.

72. Ibid., 107.

Conclusion

1. Bentham 1988 (1776: 1.36 [text and notes 1–2]). (Bentham's editors rightly judge that he was referring to T 3.2.8, SBN 539–49. Bentham does not cite Hume's essay "Of the Original Contract," and may not have read it.) Hume's *History*, which Bentham also cites lavishly in the *Fragment*, was explicitly an attempt at portraying an alternative view in which some "wisdom and foresight" and a great deal of accident lead over time to a "most finished and most noble" government, a "complicated fabric" or constitution, that was stable, effective, and lawful or legitimate without at any time having required for its lawfulness the conscious and deliberate consent of the governed (2.525).

2. Berry (2009: 110–11).

3. Here I take a very different approach from that of Russell Hardin (2007), who portrays Hume as a purely empirical and formal theorist who has no "normative" standpoint or "moral theory" at all. Simpson (2008) points out that this claim in its strict form is implausible given Hume's explicit aim to further "practical morality," and that Hardin can sustain his claim only by defining moral or normative theory in extremely restrictive (essentially Kantian) terms. But this definition surely stipulates too much of the other party's case. While the claim that no theory counts as normative if not (in effect, though not always avowedly) Kantian is common, it is Kantians who should maintain it, not Humeans.

4. Or, if "political liberals," they may personally believe the Kantian metaphysics but concede that it will never be the basis of a polity-wide consensus; reasonable people will differ on such "comprehensive" philosophical matters (Rawls 1996).

5. Taylor (1994: 25–37).

6. On Smith, see Kalyvas and Katznelson (2008; chapter 2); on Hume, see Krause (2008: 108 and chapter 3 passim). Hanley (2009: 36–38 and chapter 4 passim) points out that Smith takes vanity, the desire for esteem or recognition, to be a universal but potentially destructive passion that must be civilized and moralized into love of praiseworthiness. The desire for recognition, one might say, is in its native form a social vice rather than a virtue.

7. Baier (2010: 52) fascinatingly suggests that Hume's conventions of good manners are needed to restrain our vanity given the scarcity of opportunities to satisfy human vanity in a crowded social world ("scarcity of room to preen and boast," as Baier puts it), just as property arises from the need to satisfy, through channeling, the desire for economic self-interest.

8. This is the political equivalent of the one-sidedness that Annette Baier (1991: 217) attributes to Kantian ethics, which requires "most of each person's passions to face the survey of one privileged one."

9. Gutmann and Thompson (1996: 52–3): compare 79 (mutual respect is an "excellence of character") and 92 (reciprocity is a "virtue").

10. For a polemical but not unfair discussion of the contrast, see Hardin (1995): chapters 7–8.

11. Pocock (1985: 49). For more on this see chapter 2, note 26 and accompanying text. Similarly, Livingston (1995: 158) compares Hume's "humanistic, historical, rhetorical, and virtue-centered liberalism" to that of Tocqueville, Constant, Berlin, and John Gray rather than that of Bentham (also a target of Pocock's humanism). I differ with Livingston's distinctly conservative reading of that pluralist pantheon.

12. Phillipson (1981) argues that avoiding the obsession with politics and civic liberty was a constant project of the Scottish Enlightenment—necessarily, since after Union with England, politics was run by a parliament in which the Scots had barely any representation.

13. Compare E: A, 571–2: since extreme avarice is incurable, the best response to it is satire—which does nothing to make the avaricious less so, but amuses everyone else.

14. Taylor (2004: quotation at 346).

15. Dedication to Hume, *Dissertations*: ii.

16. Manzer (1996, 2001). Dees (2008) contains a more involved claim to the effect that the ideological justification of modern democracy embodies the consent theory that Hume rejects. A Humean would reply that while radical consent *theory* may endanger convention, democratic authorization of officials might itself *be* a convention—something we recognize as a hard-won and collective civil right, not remotely pre-political or natural.

17. That the specific *expression* of a virtue is deeply dependent on convention is obvious: how one appropriately gives thanks depends not only on language but on subtler social conventions, and if I get either language or manners wrong I may not even be recognized as having given thanks. Hume puts no anthropologists out of business.

18. Here the parallel to "virtue in rags" is close but often missed. When I restore gold from a poor thief to a rich miser, my action is virtuous in its general tendency—and even the thief benefits from living in a society with secure property rules, which are responsible for the wealth he is trying to steal—even though an accident of distribution prevents it from doing good.

19. On this see McArthur (2007: 122–4). True reaction, a determination to return to an old order regardless of consequences, would seem most consistent with an anti-instrumentalist, romantic, honor-oriented ethos that deliberately refuses to think in terms of strategy and consequences—in other words, the cult of the Lost Cause. Nineteenth-century French monarchists upheld precisely such an ethos (Cubitt 1997). Hume contains nothing like it.

20. Not all conventions are formal and not all of them are subject to legal authority. In Edith Wharton's *Age of Innocence*, an ambiguous dispute over marital and sexual propriety—over "chastity," in Hume's language—is adjudicated by a couple whose judgment of propriety is acknowledged by everyone (they are the "arbiters of fashion," the "Court of Last Appeal," because "Everybody in New York knows what [they] represent" (2008 [1920]: 43)). The couple successfully ends the dispute by inviting the victim, whom they consider innocent, to a dinner party. The book does not leave the reader convinced that the convention thus upheld is worth upholding.

21. See the excellent discussion in D. Miller (1981: 75–7).

22. Here one may endorse Livingston's (1991) discussion of language as the paradigm for human conventions while dissenting from his view that change in conventions must reflect spontaneous evolution. Israel presents the case of a language convention constructed from scratch—not the Hebrew language but its conventional status, the practice of using it in everyday speech, was unprecedented—in response to existential threat. Indonesia represents the case of a lingua franca deliberately adopted by a new, postcolonial country in order to forestall civil war. Conquest may produce a similar effect and one Hume demonstrably welcomes, as in his claim that

the most elegant parts of English come from French (H 1.208–9). Whole countries may conduct official business in the written language of former colonial oppressors to avoid disputes over which local language or dialect to adopt (as in much of Africa but also Switzerland, whose leading written language is High German, not any of the different dialects of *Switzerdütsch*, none of which is closer to German than modern Dutch is). Finally, one can prefer formality to spontaneous evolution for the sake of greater precision in formal communication or even for esthetic reasons. The spontaneous evolution argument would suggest that Hume would welcome the absence in English of standard dictionaries or grammars. But he doesn't; he greatly laments it (E: CL 91).

23. I owe my own appreciation of it to Baier (2010: 92).

24. Compare H 6.376, where Hume suggests that Charles' apparent ingratitude toward the "cavalier party" was part of a laudable attempt to "abolish the distinction of parties."

25. Waldron (1994: 120–21) points out that James Buchanan, by acknowledging that the better off have an interest in accepting new property distributions when extremes of inequality make the old ones extremely vulnerable to violation (see Buchanan [1975: 79]), renders himself "no longer in a position to condemn unilateral or fractional or majoritarian attacks on the status quo in this situation, for it is precisely the recognition of the possibility and rationality of such attacks that is going to motivate the property-holder to acquiesce willingly in the renegotiation of his holding."

26. Here again see Mackie (1996).

27. That is the radical version of the worry. The conservative version would say that conventions arise from experience and reasons, and principles arise from abstractions from that experience—so that rational criticism of conventions is inapt, practically a contradiction in terms (Livingston 1991: 161ff.). This would seem an argument that applies only to *rationalist* reform proposals, not to the kind that would derive new rules from the experienced adequacy of new ways of life. Proposals to instantiate equality with respect to a formerly hierarchical social characteristic (race, sex, sexual orientation) are at least as commonly the latter as the former.

28. This is true as a first cut. Hume certainly feels that different modes of government are allied with social practices in some respects; for example, true politeness is difficult without a monarchy that concentrates subjects' attention upward (see E: CL and Tolonen [2010]). This work is concerned with the political goods of peace, prosperity, liberty, and equality, and frankly assumes that achievement in these areas outweighs any potential, and likely small, differences in how a given regime affects intellectual and artistic practices.

29. Macleod (1981: 74).

30. Lecaldano (2008: 270).

31. If it is a question of what might motivate agents to pursue reform in the property convention, again the artificial virtue of justice counsels acting in accord with existing conventions, but the natural virtue of "equity" might motivate reforming them, and is a common theme of Hume's earlier writings. Arguably, "humanity" plays a similar role in the later ones. On equity see Baier (2010: 78 and chapter 3 passim); on humanity, Hanley (2011).

32. Huntington (1991: chapter 2).

33. At least, I have argued (Sabl 2001) that civil disobedience is best understood in these, "forward-looking" terms.

34. As Dees (2008: 396) summarizes the difference between Locke and Hume.

35. Hume drew attention in a letter to the American colonies' existing governing institutions. He claimed that all such institutions would have to be overthrown if "Arbitrary Power" on the part of the English mother country were to attempt "Acts of destructive Violence" in the course of a "Scheme of *conquering* the Colonies" (emphasis added: in Hume's view they were already de facto self-governing). "We must [if we wanted to accomplish this conquest] annul all the Charters, abolish every democratical Power in every Colony; repeal the Habeas Corpus Act with regard to them; invest every Governor with full discretionary or arbitrary Powers; confiscate the Estates of all the chief Planters; and hang three fourths of their Clergy" (L 2.300–301).

36. Dees (2008: 396).

37. As with Livingston (1991: 164).

38. See Introduction, note 41.

39. Burke 1987 (1790: compare 76, 81, 84, 145 to 72).

40. "Of all mankind there are none so pernicious as political projectors, if they have power; nor so ridiculous, if they want it: As on the other hand, a wise politician is the most beneficial character in nature, if accompanied with authority; and the most innocent, and not altogether useless, even if deprived of it" (E: IPC, 647). On the machine-design argument that Hume adduces here, see chapter 3, "Authority and Allegiance."

41. Huntington (1981).

42. Livingston (1976: 17–18).

43. Realist political theory has recently burgeoned, especially in England. Seminal contributions include Farrelly (2007), Galston (2010), Geuss (2005, 2007), Philp (2007), Sabl (2011), Stears (2005, 2007), Williams (2005). The best treatment of Hume as a realist is of course Whelan (2004), who alertly notes (p. 324) that realist theory is centrally and characteristically concerned with the questions of transition that "ideal theory" slights or ignores.

44. Without attempting a study on the scale of Livingston's treatise on it (1998), one might summarize what Hume calls "false philosophy" as the attempt to address philosophical questions with moral tools while under the delusion that one is doing the opposite.

45. H 3.192. Hume's argument is that the need to prevent undue intimacy in the home was not at issue given the tradition of royal exogamy (observed in spades in this case; Henry and Catherine had not grown up in the same country). The desire to sustain a general rule against incest was inapt since a meta-convention (papal dispensation) was in place for ensuring that such marriages would be exceptional. One might add that the idea that marrying a brother's ex-wife was incestuous in the first place relied on a theological "one flesh" fiction rather than on any good secular reason for prohibiting true incest.

46. See chapter 4, note 2 and text section on "The First Constitutional Regime."

47. Geuss (2005: 31), emphasis in original.

48. On the two meta-narratives see Lyotard (1984). O'Neill (1996: 287ff.) discusses briefly how Kant's philosophy of history grew (like his argument for postulating the existence of God) from the need to grapple with the gap between duty and happiness and from the need to assert the presence of moral intention in a world otherwise ruled by mechanical causality. Bonnie Honig (1993: 51, 14) takes issue with

the crooked timber remark, saying that if humanity is made from crooked timber "this is a reason to give up on the ideal of straightness"; and in general support of her dissent cites, if not Hume, several admirers of Hume over the ages from Mill to Bernard Williams (1993: 51, 14).

49. Baier (1991: 203).

50. Here Krause (2008) is excellent.

51. Hont (1994). Compare Peter Gay (1966: 418–19):

> David Hume was both courageous and modern; he understood the implications of his philosophy and did not shrink from them. He was so courageous that he did not have to insist on his courage; he followed his thinking where it lead him, and he provided through his own life (and, Samuel Johnson to the contrary, in the face of death) a pagan ideal to which many aspired but which few realized. He was willing to live with uncertainty, with no supernatural justifications, no complete explanations, no promise of permanent stability, with guides of merely probable validity. . . . Hume, therefore, more decisively than many of his brethren in the Enlightenment, stands at the threshold of modernity and exhibits its risks and its possibilities. Without melodrama but with the sober eloquence one would expect from an accomplished classicist, Hume makes plain that since God is silent, man is his own master: he must live in a disenchanted world, submit everything to criticism, and make his own way.

References

Works by Hume

DNR: David Hume, *Dialogues Concerning Natural Religion*. Ed. Norman Kemp Smith. Indianapolis, IN, Bobbs-Merrill Educational Publishing (Library of Liberal Arts), 1947. Cited by section and page number.

DP: David Hume, *A Dissertation on the Passions*. In *A Dissertation on the Passions; The Natural History of Religion*. Ed. Tom Beauchamp. Oxford: Oxford University Press, 2008.

Dissertations: Four Dissertations. London: A. Millar, 1757. Accessed from Eighteenth Century Collections Online. Gale. University of California–Los Angeles, August 26, 2010. http://find.galegroup.com/ecco/infomark.do?&contentSet=ECCOArticles &type=multipage&tabID=T001&prodId=ECCO&docId=CW125288867& source=gale&userGroupName=uclosangeles&version=1.0&docLevel=FASCI MILE

EHU: David Hume, *An Enquiry Concerning Human Understanding*. Ed. Tom L. Beauchamp. Oxford: Oxford University Press (Clarendon Press), 2000. Cited by section and paragraph number, followed by the page number in the (previously standard) "SBN" edition: *Enquiries Concerning Human Understanding and Concerning the Principles of Morals*. Third edition. Ed. L. A. Selby-Bigge and P. H. Nidditch. Oxford: Clarendon Press, 1975.

EPM: David Hume, *An Enquiry concerning the Principles of Morals*. Ed. Tom L. Beauchamp. Oxford: Oxford University Press (Clarendon Press), 1998. Cited by section number, part, and paragraph number followed by the page number in the SBN edition: David Hume, *Enquiries Concerning Human Understanding and Concerning the Principles of Morals* (see entry under EHU).

Essays: Individual essays cited as "E" followed by the abbreviated title listed below, followed by the page number appearing in David Hume, *Essays Moral, Political, and Literary*. Revised edition. Ed. Eugene F. Miller. Indianapolis: Liberty Fund, 1987.

A: "Of Avarice"
BG: "Whether the British Government Inclines More to Absolute Monarchy, or to a Republic"
BP: "Of the Balance of Power"
BT: "Of the Balance of Trade"
C: "Of Commerce"
CL: "Of Civil Liberty"
CP: "Of the Coalition of Parties"
DMHN: "Of the Dignity or Meanness of Human Nature"
EL: "Of Eloquence"
FPG: "Of the First Principles of Government"
I: "Of Interest"
IP: "Of the Independency of Parliament"
IPC: "Idea of a Perfect Commonwealth"
JT: "Of the Jealousy of Trade"
LP: "Of the Liberty of the Press"
M: "Of Money"
MOL   (not technically an essay but cited from this edition): "My Own Life"
NC: "Of National Characters"
OC: "Of the Original Contract"
OG: "Of the Origin of Government"
PAN: "Of the Populousness of Ancient Nations"
PC: "Of Public Credit"
PG: "Of Parties in General"
PGB: "Of the Parties of Great Britain"
PO: "Of Passive Obedience"
PRS: "That Politics May Be Reduced to a Science"
PS: "Of the Protestant Succession"
RA: "Of Refinement in the Arts"
RPAS: "Of the Rise and Progress of the Arts and Sciences"
S: "Of Suicide"
SC: "The Sceptic"
SE: "Of Superstition and Enthusiasm"
SH: "Of the Study of History"
SRC: "Of Some Remarkable Customs"
ST: "Of the Standard of Taste"

H: David Hume, *The History of England from the Invasion of Julius Caesar to the Revolution in 1688*. 6 vols. Ed. William B. Todd. Indianapolis: Liberty Fund, 1983. Cited by volume and page number.

L: *The Letters of David Hume*. Ed. J.Y.T. Greig. 2 vols. Oxford: Clarendon Press, 1932.

NL: *New Letters of David Hume*. Ed. Raymond Kilbansky and Ernest C. Mossner. Oxford: Clarendon Press, 1954.

NHR: David Hume, *The Natural History of Religion*. Ed. H. E. Root. Stanford, CA: Stanford University Press, 1957. Cited by section number and page number.

T: David Hume. *A Treatise of Human Nature*. Ed. David Fate Norton and Mary J. Norton. Oxford: Oxford University Press, 2000. Cited by book, part, section, and paragraph number of the paragraph, followed by the page number in the (previously standard) "SBN" edition: *A Treatise of Human Nature*. Ed. L. A. Selby-Bigge. Revised by P. H. Nidditch. Oxford: Clarendon Press, 1978.

Secondary and Contemporary Works

Adams, John, 1794. *A Defence of the Constitutions of Government of the United States of America Against the Attack of M. Turgot in his Letter to Dr. Price*. 3 vols. London: John Stockdale.

Baier, Annette C., 1989. "Hume on Women's Complexion." In Jones 1989, 33–53.

———, 1991. *A Progress of Sentiments: Reflections on Hume's* Treatise. Cambridge, MA: Harvard University Press.

———, 1993. "How Can Individualists Share Responsibility?" *Political Theory* 21, no. 2 (May): 228–48.

———, 2008. *Death and Character: Further Reflections on Hume*. Cambridge, MA: Harvard University Press.

———, 2010. *The Cautious Jealous Virtue: Hume on Justice*. Cambridge, MA: Harvard University Press.

Barry, Brian, 1989. *Theories of Justice*. Berkeley: University of California Press.

Beer, Samuel H., 1993. *To Make a Nation: the Rediscovery of American Federalism*. Cambridge, MA: Harvard University Press.

Bentham, Jeremy, 1988 (1776). *A Fragment on Government*. Ed. J. H. Burns and H.L.A. Hart. Cambridge, UK: Cambridge University Press.

Berger, Ben, 2011. *Attention Deficit Democracy: The Paradox of Civic Engagement*. Princeton, NJ: Princeton University Press.

Berger, Peter, 1970. "On the Obsolescence of the Concept of Honor." *European Journal of Sociology* 11: 339–47.

Berman, Harold J., 1983. *Law and Revolution*. Cambridge, MA: Harvard University Press.

Berry, Christopher J., 2009. *David Hume*. (Major Conservative and Libertarian Thinkers, Vol. 3). New York and London: Continuum.

Bolingbroke (Henry St. John, Viscount), 1997. *Political Writings*. Ed. David Armitage. Cambridge, UK: Cambridge University Press.

Bongie, Lawrence, 2000. *David Hume: Prophet of the Counter-Revolution*. 2d ed. Indianapolis: Liberty Fund.

Braudy, Leo, 2003 (1970). *The Plot of Time: Narrative Form in Hume, Fielding, and Gibbon*. With a Preface by Hayden White. Los Angeles: Figueroa Press. (Originally published as *Narrative Form in History and Fiction: Hume, Fielding, and Gibbon* [Princeton, NJ: Princeton University Press, 1970].)

Brown, A. L., 1981. "Parliament, c. 1377–1422." In Davies and Denton 1981, 109–40.

Buchan, Bruce, 2006. "Civilisation, Sovereignty and War: The Scottish Enlightenment and International Relations." *International Relations* 20, no. 2 (2006): 175–92.

Buchanan, James M., 1975. *The Limits of Liberty: Between Anarchy and Leviathan*. Chicago: University of Chicago Press.

Buchanan, James M., and Gordon Tullock, 1962. *The Calculus of Consent: Logical Foundations of Constitutional Democracy*. Ann Arbor: University of Michigan Press.

Burke, Edmund, 1987 (1790). *Reflections on the Revolution in France*. Ed. J.G.A. Pocock. Indianapolis: Hackett Publishing.

Burke, P[eter], 1969. "Tacitism." In *Tacitus*, ed. T. A. Dorey, 149–71. London: Routledge and Kegan Paul.

Burns, J. H., ed., 1988a. *The Cambridge History of Medieval Political Thought c. 350–c. 1450.* Cambridge, UK: Cambridge University Press.

———, 1988b. "Introduction." In Burns 1988a: 1–8.

Calvert, Randall, 1992. "Leadership and Its Basis in Problems of Social Coordination." *International Political Science Review* 13, no. 1: 7–24.

Cam, H. M., 1970. "Representation in Medieval England." In Fryde and Miller 1970, 1.262–78.

Capaldi, Nicholas, 1978. "Hume as Social Scientist." *Review of Metaphysics* 32, no. 1 (September): 99–123.

———, 1990. "The Preservation of Liberty." In Capaldi and Livingston 1990, 195–224.

Capaldi, Nicholas, and Donald W. Livingston, eds., 1990. Liberty *in Hume's* History of England. Dordrecht, The Netherlands, and Norwell, MA: Kluwer Academic Publishers.

Carens, Joseph H., 1979. "Compromises in Politics." In *Compromise in Ethics, Law, and Politics (Nomos,* vol. 21), ed. J. Roland Pennock and John W. Chapman, 123–41. New York: New York University Press.

Chisick, Harvey, 1989. "David Hume and the Common People." In Jones 1989, 5–32.

Chwe, Michael Suk-Young, 2001. *Rational Ritual: Culture, Coordination, and Common Knowledge.* Princeton, NJ: Princeton University Press.

Clark, J.C.D., 2000. *English Society, 1660–1832: Religion, Ideology and Politics during the Ancien Regime.* 2d ed. Cambridge, UK: Cambridge University Press.

Clarke, M. V., 1936. *Medieval Representation and Consent.* London: Longmans, Green and Co. Ltd.

Collinson, Patrick, 1994. *Elizabethan Essays.* London and Rio Grande, OH: Hambledon Press.

Converse, Philip E., 1964. "The Nature of Belief Systems in Mass Publics." In *Ideology and Discontent,* ed. David Apter, 206–61. Glencoe, IL: Free Press.

Cubitt, Geoffrey, 1997. "Legitimism and the Cult of Bourbon Royalty." In *The Right in France, 1789–1997,* ed. Nicholas Atkin and Frank Tallett, 51–70. London and New York: I. B. Tauris.

Dahl, Robert A., 1971. *Polyarchy: Participation and Opposition.* New Haven and London: Yale University Press.

Danford, John W., 1990. "Hume's *History* and the Parameters of Economic Development." In Capaldi and Livingston 1990, 157–94.

Davies, R. G., and J. H. Denton, eds., 1981. *The English Parliament in the Middle Ages.* Manchester, UK: Manchester University Press.

Day, John, 1965. "Hume on Justice and Allegiance." *Philosophy* 40, no. 151 (January): 35–56.

Dees, Richard H., 1992. "Hume and the Contexts of Politics." *Journal of the History of Philosophy* 30, no. 2 (April): 219–42.

———, 2008. "'One of the Finest and Most Subtle Inventions': Hume on Government." In Radcliffe 2008, 388–405.

Dickson, Eric, forthcoming. "Leadership, Followership, and Beliefs About the World: An Experiment." *British Journal of Political Science.*

Edling, Max, 2003. *A Revolution in Favor of Government: Origins of the U.S. Constitution and the Making of the American State.* New York and Oxford: Oxford University Press.

Edwards, J. G., 1970. "The *Plena Potestas* of English Parliamentary Representatives." In Fryde and Miller 1970, 1.136–49.

Elster, Jon, 1984. *Ulysses and the Sirens*. Rev. ed. Cambridge, UK: Cambridge University Press.

Elton, G. R., 1973. Review of Lawrence Stone, *The Causes of the English Revolution* (London: Routledge and Kegan Paul, 1972), *Historical Journal* 16, no. 1 (March): 205–8.

———, 1974 (1969). "'The Body of the Whole Realm': Parliament and Representation in Medieval and Tudor England." In *Studies in Tudor and Stuart Politics and Government*. 2 vols. Cambridge, UK: Cambridge University Press, 1974. Volume 2:19–61.

Farrelly, Colin, 2007. "Justice in Ideal Theory: A Refutation." *Political Studies* 55, no. 4: 844–64.

Fieser, James, ed., 2002. *Early Responses to Hume's* History of England. 2 vols. Bristol, UK: Thoemmes Press.

Finlay, Christopher J., 2004. "Hume's Theory of Civil Society." *European Journal of Political Theory* 3, no. 4 (October): 369–71.

Fiorina, Morris P., and Kenneth A. Shepsle, 1989. "Formal Theories of Leadership: Agents, Agenda Setters, and Entrepreneurs." In *New Perspectives in Political Science*, ed. Bryan D. Jones: 17–40. Lawrence: University Press of Kansas.

Forbes, Duncan, 1975. *Hume's Philosophical Politics*. Cambridge, UK: Cambridge University Press.

———, 1979. "Hume and the Scottish Enlightenment." In *Philosophers of the Enlightenment*, ed. S. C Brown, 94–109. Brighton, UK: Harvester Press; Atlantic Highlands, NJ: Humanities Press.

Frazer, Catherine S., 1970. "Pattern and Predictability in Hume's *History*." *Enlightenment Essays* 1, no. 1 (Spring): 27–32.

Frazer, Michael, 2010. *The Enlightenment of Sympathy*. Oxford: Oxford University Press.

Friedmann, Jeffrey, 1996. "Introduction: Economic Approaches to Politics." In *The Rational Choice Controversy*, ed. Friedmann, 1–24. New Haven, CT: Yale University Press.

Friedrich, Carl J., 1968. *Constitutional Government and Democracy*. 4th ed. Waltham, MA: Blaisdell Publishing.

Fryde, E. B., and Edward Miller, eds., 1970. *Historical Studies of the English Parliament*. 2 vols. Cambridge, UK: Cambridge University Press.

Galston, William, 2010. "Realism in Political Theory." *European Journal of Political Theory* 9, no. 4: 385–411.

Garrett, Don, 2007. "The First Motive to Justice: Hume's Circle Argument Squared." *Hume Studies* 33, no. 2 (November): 257–88.

Gauthier, David, 1979. "David Hume, Contractarian." *Philosophical Review* 88, no. 1 (January): 3–38.

Gay, Peter, 1966. *The Enlightenment: An Interpretation*. Vol. I: *The Rise of Modern Paganism*. New York: W. W. Norton.

Geisel, Theodor Seuss, 1969. "The Glunk That Got Thunk." In *I Can Lick 30 Tigers Today! And Other Stories*. New York: Random House.

Geuss, Raymond, 2005. *Outside Ethics*. Princeton, NJ: Princeton University Press.

———, 2007. *Philosophy and Real Politics*. Princeton, NJ: Princeton University Press.

Goodin, Robert E., 1976. *The Politics of Rational Man*. London: John Wiley & Sons.

———1980. *Manipulatory Politics*. New Haven and London: Yale University Press.

Le Gout Des Autres, 2000. Directed by Agnès Jaoui. Canal+. Motion picture.

Griffith, J.A.G., and Michael Ryle, with M.A.J. Wheeler-Booth, 1989. *Parliament: Functions, Practice and Procedures.* London: Sweet & Maxwell.

Gutmann, Amy, and Dennis F. Thompson, 1996. *Democracy and Disagreement.* Cambridge, MA: Harvard University Press (Belknap Press).

Haakonssen, Knud, 1981. *The Science of a Legislator: The Natural Jurisprudence of David Hume and Adam Smith.* Cambridge, UK: Cambridge University Press.

———, 1993. "The Structure of Hume's Political Theory." In Norton 1993, 182–221.

Habermas, Jürgen, 1987. *The Theory of Communicative Action.* 2 vols. Trans. Thomas McCarthy. Boston: Beacon Press.

Hamilton, Alexander, James Madison, and John Jay, 2001 (1788). *The Federalist.* Gideon Edition. Ed. George W. Carey and James McClellan. Indianapolis, IN: Liberty Fund.

Hampsher-Monk, Ian, and Andrew Hindmoor, 2010. "Rational Choice and Interpretive Evidence: Between a Rock and a Hard Place?" *Political Studies* 58: 47–65.

Hampshire, Stuart, 1989. *Innocence and Experience.* Cambridge, MA: Harvard University Press.

Hampton, Jean, 1986. *Hobbes and the Social Contract Tradition.* Cambridge, UK: Cambridge University Press.

Hanley, Ryan Patrick, 2009. *Adam Smith and the Character of Virtue.* Cambridge, UK: Cambridge University Press.

———, 2011. "David Hume and the 'Politics of Humanity.'" *Political Theory* 39, no. 2 (April): 205–33.

Hanvelt, Marc, 2012. *The Politics of Eloquence: David Hume's Polite Rhetoric.* Toronto: University of Toronto Press.

Hardin, Russell, 1982. *Collective Action.* Washington, DC: Resources for the Future/Baltimore: Johns Hopkins University Press.

———, 1995. *One for All: The Logic of Group Conflict.* Princeton, NJ: Princeton University Press.

———, 1999. *Liberalism, Constitutionalism, and Democracy.* Oxford: Oxford University Press.

———, 2003. *Indeterminacy and Society.* Princeton, NJ: Princeton University Press.

———, 2007. *David Hume: Moral and Political Theorist.* Oxford: Oxford University Press.

Harriss, G. L., 1975. *King, Parliament, and Public Finance in Medieval England to 1369.* Oxford: Clarendon Press.

———, 1981. "The Formation of Parliament, 1272–1377." In Davies and Denton 1981, 29–60.

Hartz, Louis, 1955. *The Liberal Tradition in America.* New York: Harcourt, Brace & World.

Hayek, F[riedrich] A., 1966. "The Legal and Political Philosophy of David Hume." In *Hume: A Collection of Critical Essays,* ed. V. C. Chappell, 335–60. Garden City, NY: Doubleday & Company (Anchor Books).

Hayward, John, 1610. *The First Part of the Life and Raigne of King Henrie the IIII.* London: John Windet. (False imprint: London: John Wolfe, 1599.)

Herdt, Jennifer A., 1997. *Religion and Faction in Hume's Moral Philosophy.* Cambridge, UK: Cambridge University Press.

Hicks, Philip, 1996. *Neoclassical History and English Culture: From Clarendon to Hume.* Houndmills, UK: Macmillan; New York: St. Martin's Press.

Hirschman, Albert O., 1977. *The Passions and the Interests.* Princeton, NJ: Princeton University Press.

Hiskes, Richard P., 1977. "Has Hume a Theory of Social Justice?" *Hume Studies* 3, no. 2 (November): 72–93.

———, 2005. Review of Whelan (2004). *Hume Studies* 31, no. 1 (April 2005): 181–3.

Hobbes, Thomas, 1971 (1681). *A Dialogue Between a Philosopher and a Student of the Common Laws of England.* Edited with an Introduction by Joseph Cropsey. Chicago: University of Chicago Press.

———, 1991 (1651). *Leviathan.* Ed. Richard Tuck. Cambridge, UK: Cambridge University Press.

Holmes, Stephen, 1988. "Precommitment and the Paradox of Democracy." In *Constitutionalism and Democracy,* ed. Jon Elster and Rune Slagstad, 195–240. Cambridge, UK: Cambridge University Press.

Holmes, Stephen, and Cass Sunstein, 1999. *The Cost of Rights: Why Liberty Depends on Taxes.* New York: W. W. Norton.

Holt, J. C., 1981. "The Prehistory of Parliament." In Davies and Denton, 1981, 1–28.

Honig, Bonnie, 1993. *Political Theory and the Displacement of Politics.* Ithaca, NY: Cornell University Press.

Hont, Istvan, 1994. "Commercial Society and Political Theory in the Eighteenth Century: The Problem of Authority in David Hume and Adam Smith." In *Main Trends in Cultural History,* ed. Willem Melching and Wyger Velema, 54–94. Amsterdam and Atlanta: Editions Rodopi B.V.

Hont, Istvan, and Michael Ignatieff, eds., 1983. *Wealth and Virtue: The Shaping of Political Economy in the Scottish Enlightenment.* Cambridge, UK: Cambridge University Press.

Hunt, Lynn, 2007. *Inventing Human Rights.* New York: W. W. Norton.

Huntington, Samuel P., 1968. *Political Order in Changing Societies.* New Haven, CT: Yale University Press.

———, 1981. *American Politics: The Promise of Disharmony.* Cambridge, MA: Harvard University Press (Belknap Press).

———, 1991. *The Third Wave.* Norman: University of Oklahoma Press.

Immerwahr, John, ed., 1989. *The Science of Man in the Scottish Enlightenment: Hume, Reid and their Contemporaries.* Edinburgh: Edinburgh University Press.

———, 1990. "On Reading Hume's *History of Liberty.*" In Capaldi and Livingston, 1990, 1–23.

———, 1992. "Hume on Tranquillizing the Passions." *Hume Studies* 18, no. 2 (November): 293–314.

Kalyvas, Andreas, and Ira Katznelson, 2008. *Liberal Beginnings: Making a Republic for the Moderns.* Cambridge, UK: Cambridge University Press.

Kirchheimer, Otto, 1969. "Changes in Political Compromise." In *Politics, Law, and Social Change,* ed. Frederick S. Burin and Kurt L. Shell, 131–59. New York: Columbia University Press.

Korsgaard, Christine M., 1999. "The General Point of View: Love and Moral Approval in Hume's Ethics." *Hume Studies* 25, nos. 1–2 (April/November): 3–41.

Kramnick, Isaac, 1968. *Bolingbroke and His Circle: The Politics of Nostalgia in the Age of Walpole.* Cambridge, MA: Harvard University Press.

Krause, Sharon R., 2004. "Hume and the (False) Luster of Justice." *Political Theory* 32, no. 5 (October): 628–55.

Krause, Sharon R., 2008. *Civil Passions: Moral Sentiment and Democratic Deliberation.* Princeton and Oxford: Princeton University Press.

Kreps, David M., 1990. "Corporate Culture and Economic Theory." In *Perspectives on Positive Political Economy*, ed. James E. Alt and Kenneth A. Shepsle, 90–144. Cambridge, UK: Cambridge University Press.

Krishnakumar, Anita S., 1998. "Reconciliation and the Fiscal Constitution: The Anatomy of the 1995–96 Budget 'Train Wreck.'" *Harvard Journal of Legislation* 35 (Summer): 589–622.

Lagerspetz, Eerik, 1995. *The Opposite Mirrors: An Essay on the Conventionalist Theory of Institutions*. Dordrecht, The Netherlands: Kluwer Academic Publishers.

Lasswell, Harold, 1936. *Politics: Who Gets What, When, How.* New York: McGraw-Hill.

Lecaldano, Eugenio, 2008. "Hume's Theory of Justice, or Artificial Virtue." In Radcliffe 2008, 257–72.

Lewis, David, 1969. *Convention: A Philosophical Study.* Cambridge, MA: Harvard University Press.

Lind, Michael, 1995. *The Next American Nation: The New Nationalism and the Fourth American Revolution.* New York: Free Press.

Livingston, Donald W., 1976. "Introduction." In *Hume: A Re-Evaluation*, ed. Donald W. Livingston and James T. King, 1–19. New York: Fordham University Press.

———, 1984. *Hume's Philosophy of Common Life.* Chicago: University of Chicago Press.

———, 1990. "Hume's Historical Conception of Liberty." In Capaldi and Livingston 1990, 105–53.

———, 1991. "Hayek as Humean." *Critical Review* 5, no. 2 (Spring): 159–77.

———, 1995. "On Hume's Conservatism." *Hume Studies* 21, no. 2 (November): 151–64.

———, 1998. *Philosophical Melancholy and Delirium: Hume's Pathology of Philosophy.* Chicago: University of Chicago Press.

Livingston, Donald W., and James T. King, eds., 1976. *Hume: A Re-Evaluation.* New York: Fordham University Press.

Locke, John, 1960. *Two Treatises of Government*, ed. Peter Laslett. Cambridge, UK: Cambridge University Press.

Luce, R. Duncan, and Howard Raiffa, 1957. *Games and Decisions: Introduction and Critical Survey.* New York: Wiley.

Luhmann, Niklas, 1998. "*Quod Omnes Tangit*: Remarks on Jürgen Habermas' Legal Theory." In *Habermas on Law and Democracy*, ed. Michel Rosenfeld and Andrew Arato, 157–73. Berkeley: University of California Press.

Lyotard, Jean-François, 1984. *The Postmodern Condition: A Report on Knowledge.* Trans. Geoff Bennington and Brian Massumi. Minneapolis: University of Minnesota Press.

Machiavelli, Niccolò, 1996 (1531). *Discourses on Livy.* Trans. Harvey C. Mansfield and Nathan Tarcov. Chicago: University of Chicago Press.

MacIntyre, Alasdair, 1978. "Hume on 'is' and 'ought.'" In *Against the Self-Images of the Age*, 109–24. Notre Dame, IN: University of Notre Dame Press.

———, 1984. *After Virtue.* 2d ed. Notre Dame, IN: University of Notre Dame Press.

———, 1988. *Whose Justice? Which Rationality?* Notre Dame, IN: University of Notre Dame Press.

Mackie, Gerry, 1996. "Ending Footbinding and Infibulation: A Convention Account." *American Sociological Review* 61, no. 6 (December): 999–1017.

Macleod, Alistair, 1981. "Rule-Utilitarianism and Hume's Theory of Justice." *Hume Studies* 7, no. 1 (April): 74–84.

MacQueen, Daniel, 1990 (1756). *Letters on Hume's* History of Great Britain (originally *Letters on Mr. Hume's* History of Great Britain). With a new introduction by John Valdimir Price. Bristol, UK: Thoemmes Antiquarian Books Ltd.

Madicott, J. R., 1981. "Parliament and the Constituencies, 1272–1377." In Davies and Denton 1981, 61–87.

Manzer, Robert A., 1996. "Hume's Constitutionalism and the Identity of Constitutional Democracy." *American Political Science Review* 90, no. 3 (September): 488–96.

———, 2001. "A Science of Politics: Hume, *The Federalist*, and the Politics of Constitutional Attachment." *American Journal of Political Science* 45, no. 3 (July): 508–18.

Mayhew, David, 2000. "Political Science and Political Philosophy: Ontological Not Normative." *PS: Political Science and Politics* 33, no. 2 (June): 192–3.

McArthur, Neil, 2005. "David Hume and the Common Law of England." *Journal of Scottish Philosophy* 3, no. 1: 67–82.

———, 2007. *David Hume's Political Theory: Law, Commerce, and the Constitution of Government.* Toronto: University of Toronto Press.

Marongiu, Antonio, 1961. "Q.o.t., Principe fondamnetal de la Démocratie et du Consentement, au XIVe siècle." In *Album Helen Maud Cam: Studies Presented to the International Commission for the History of Representative and Parliamentary Institutions* 24: 101–15.

Miller, David, 1981. *Philosophy and Ideology in Hume's Political Thought.* Oxford: Clarendon Press.

Miller, Eugene F., 1990. "Hume on Liberty in the Successive English Constitutions." In Capaldi and Livingston 1990, 53–103.

Miller's Crossing, 1990. Directed by Joel Coen. Circle Films. Motion picture.

Montesquieu, Charles de Secondat, baron de, 2000 (1721). *Considérations sur les causes de la grandeur des Romains et de leur decadence.* Oxford: Voltaire Foundation, 2000.

Moore, James, 1977. "Hume's Political Science and the Classical Republican Tradition." *Canadian Journal of Political Science/Revue canadienne de science politique* 10, no. 4 (December): 809–39.

Moshe et al., 1611. *The Holy Bible.* Ed. James Stuart. London: Robert Barker. Many reprintings.

Mossner, Ernest Campbell, 1980. *The Life of David Hume.* 2d ed. Oxford: Clarendon Press.

Müller, Jan-Werner, 2003. *A Dangerous Mind: Carl Schmitt in Post-War European Thought.* New Haven and London: Yale University Press.

Nagel, Thomas, 1995. *Other Minds.* Oxford: Oxford University Press.

Norton, David Fate, ed., 1993. *The Cambridge Companion to Hume.* Cambridge, UK: Cambridge University Press.

Oakeshott, Michael, 1975. *On Human Conduct.* Oxford: Oxford University Press (Clarendon Press).

Oakley, Francis, 1983. "Legitimation by Consent: The Question of the Medieval Roots." *Viator* 14: 303–35.

O'Neill, Daniel I., 2010. "Review Essay: Whither Democracy?" *Political Theory* 38, no. 4: 564–75.

O'Neill, Onora, 1996. "Kant on Reason and Religion." The Tanner Lectures on Human Values, Harvard University, April 1–3. Accessed at http://www.tannerlectures.utah.edu/lectures/documents/oneill97.pdf, 8 September 2010.

Oren, Ido, 2009. "The Unrealism of Contemporary Realism: The Tension between Realist Theory and Realists' Practice." *Perspectives on Politics* 7, no. 2 (June): 283–301.

Penn, William 2011. *Winter King: Henry VII and the Dawn of Tudor England*. New York: Simon & Schuster.

Phillipson, Nicholas, 1981. "The Scottish Enlightenment." In *The Enlightenment in National Context*, ed. Roy Porter and Mikuláš Teich, 19–40. Cambridge, UK: Cambridge University Press.

———, 1989. *Hume*. Avon, UK: Bath Press; New York: St. Martin's Press.

Philp, Mark, 2007. *Political Conduct*. Cambridge, MA: Harvard University Press.

Pitkin, Hanna Fenichel, 1967. *The Concept of Representation*. Berkeley: University of California Press.

Pocock, J.G.A., 1971. *Politics, Language, and Time*. New York: Atheneum.

———, 1975. *The Machiavellian Moment*. Princeton, NJ: Princeton University Press.

———, 1983. "Cambridge Paradigms and Scotch Philosophers." In Hont and Ignatieff 1983, 235–52.

———, 1985. *Virtue, Commerce, and History*. Cambridge, UK: Cambridge University Press.

———, 1987. *The Ancient Constitution and the Feudal Law*. A Reissue with a Retrospect. Cambridge, UK: Cambridge University Press.

———, 1999. *Barbarism and Religion, Vol. 2: Narratives of Civil Government*. Cambridge, UK: Cambridge University Press.

Pollock, Frederick, and Frederic William Maitland, 1968 (1898). *The History of English Law before the Time of Edward I*. 2d ed. 2 vols. London: Cambridge University Press.

Popper, Karl, 1988 (1982). *The Open Universe: An Argument for Indeterminism*. London and New York: Routledge.

Porter, Roy, and Mikuláš Teich, eds., 1981. *The Enlightenment in National Context*. Cambridge, UK: Cambridge University Press.

Post, Gaines, 1964. "A Romano-Canonical Maxim, *Quod Omnes Tangit*, in Bracton and in Early Parliaments." In *Studies in Medieval Legal Thought*, 163–238. Princeton, NJ: Princeton University Press.

Potkay, Adam, 2001. "Hume's 'Supplement to *Gulliver*': The Medieval Volumes of *The History of England*. *Eighteenth-Century Life* 25 (Spring): 32–46.

Prestwich, Michael, 1988. *Edward I*. Berkeley: University of California Press.

Price, John Valdimir, 1965. *The Ironic Hume*. Austin: University of Texas Press.

Przeworski, Adam, 1986. "Some Problems in the Study of Transition to Democracy." In *Transitions from Authoritarian Rule: Prospects for Democracy*, ed. Guillermo O'Donnell, Philippe C. Schmitter, and Laurence Whitehead, 47–63. Baltimore: Johns Hopkins University Press.

———, 1998. "Deliberation and Ideological Domination." In *Deliberative Democracy*, ed. Jon Elster, 140–60. Cambridge, UK: Cambridge University Press.

Przeworski, Adam, and Henry Teune, 1970. *The Logic of Comparative Social Inquiry*. New York: Wiley.

Radcliffe, Elizabeth S., ed., 2008. *A Companion to Hume*. Oxford: Blackwell.

Raphael, D. D., 2001. *Concepts of Justice*. Oxford: Oxford University Press.

Rawls, John, 1996. *Political Liberalism*. Paperback edition with a New Introduction. New York: Columbia University Press.

Raz, Joseph, 1979. *The Authority of Law*. Oxford: Clarendon Press.

Ridge, Michael, 2003. "Epistemology Moralized: David Hume's Practical Epistemology." *Hume Studies* 29, no. 2 (November): 165–204.

Ringer, Fritz, 2004. *Max Weber: An Intellectual Biography.* Chicago and London: University of Chicago Press.

Robertson, John, 1983. "The Scottish Enlightenment and the Limits of the Civic Tradition." In Hont and Ignatieff 1983, 137–78.

Roskell, John, 1970. "Perspectives in English Parliamentary History." In Fryde and Miller 1970, 2.296–323.

Russell, Bertrand, 1945. *A History of Western Philosophy.* New York: Simon & Schuster.

Sabl, Andrew, 2001. "Looking Forward to Justice: Rawlsian Civil Disobedience and its non-Rawlsian Lessons." *Journal of Political Philosophy* 9, no. 3: 307–30.

———, 2002. "When Bad Things Happen From Good People: Hume's Political Ethics of Revolution." *Polity* 35, no. 1 (Fall): 73–92.

———, 2006a. "Hume's Moral Psychology of Party." Paper presented before the Annual Meeting of the Hume Society, Koblenz, Germany, 7–10 August.

———, 2006b. "Noble Infirmity: Hume on Love of Fame." *Political Theory* 34, no. 5 (October): 542–68.

———, 2009a. "The Last Artificial Virtue: Hume on Toleration and its Lessons." *Political Theory* 37, no. 4 (August): 511–38.

———, 2009b. "New Models and Orders: Hume's Cromwell as Modern Prince." In *The Arts of Rule*, ed. Sharon R. Krause and Mary Ann McGrail, 245–65. Lanham, MD: Lexington Books.

———, 2011. "History and Reality: Idealist Pathologies and 'Harvard School' Remedies." In *History and Political Philosophy: On the Political and Ethical Significance of the Past*, ed. Jonathan Floyd and Marc Stears. Cambridge, UK: Cambridge University Press.

Schelling, Thomas C., 1980 (1960). *The Strategy of Conflict.* Cambridge, MA: Harvard University Press.

———, 2006a. *Micromotives and Macrobehavior.* New edition. New York: W. W. Norton.

———, 2006b. "Strategies of Commitment." In *Strategies of Commitment and Other Essays*, 1–26. Cambridge, MA: Harvard University Press.

Schlesinger, Arthur, 1973. *The Imperial Presidency.* New York: Houghton Mifflin.

———, 1998 (1949). *The Vital Center: The Politics of Freedom.* New Brunswick, NJ: Transaction Publishers.

Schliesser, Eric, 2009. "Hume's Attack on Newton's Philosophy." *Enlightenment and Dissent* 25: 167–203.

Shklar, Judith N., 1987. *Montesquieu.* Oxford: Oxford University Press.

Shulman, Alix Kates, 1998. "A Marriage Disagreement." *Dissent* (Winter): 36–46.

Siebert, Donald T., 1990. *The Moral Animus of David Hume.* Newark: University of Delaware Press.

Simpson, Matthew, 2008. Review of Hardin 2007. *Ethics* 188, no. 3 (April): 549–53.

Skinner, Andrew, 1993. "David Hume: Principles of Political Economy." In Norton 1993, 222–54.

Skinner, Quentin, 1969. "Meaning and Understanding in the History of Ideas." *History and Theory* 8: 3–53.

———, 2002. *Visions of Politics. Volume I: Regarding Method.* Cambridge, UK: Cambridge University Press.

Smith, Adam, 1981 (1776). *An Inquiry into the Nature and Causes of* The Wealth of Nations. Ed. R. H. Campbell, A. S. Skinner, and W. B. Todd. 2 vols. Indianapolis: Liberty Fund. Cited by book, chapter, part (where present), and paragraph number.

Smith, Rogers, 1997. *Civic Ideals: Conflicting Visions of Citizenship in U.S. History*. New Haven, CT: Yale University Press.

Starr, Paul, 2007. *Freedom's Power: The True Force of Liberalism*. New York: Basic Books.

Stears, Marc, 2005. "The Vocation of Political Theory; Principles, Empirical Inquiry and the Politics of Opportunity." *European Journal of Political Theory* 4, no. 4: 325–50.

———, 2007. "Liberalism and the Politics of Compulsion." *British Journal of Political Science* 37, no. 3 (July): 533–53.

Stein, P. G., 1988. "Roman Law." In Burns 1988a, 37–47.

Stewart, John B., 1963. *The Moral and Political Philosophy of David Hume*. New York: Columbia University Press.

———, 1992. *Opinion and Reform in Hume's Political Philosophy*. Princeton, NJ: Princeton University Press.

Stockton, Constant Noble, 1976. "Economics and the Mechanism of Historical Progress in Hume's *History*." In Livingston and King 1976, 296–316.

Taylor, Charles, 1989. *Sources of the Self*. Cambridge, UK: Cambridge University Press.

———, 1994. "The Politics of Recognition." In Charles Taylor, K. Anthony Appiah, Jürgen Habermas, Steven C. Rockefeller, Michael Walzer, and Susan Wolf, *Multiculturalism: Examining the Politics of Recognition*, ed. Amy Gutmann, 25–73. Princeton, NJ: Princeton University Press.

Taylor, Robert S., 2004. "Self-Realization and the Priority of Fair Equality of Opportunity." *Journal of Moral Philosophy* 1, no. 3 (2004): 333–47.

Thomas, Peter D. G., 1996. *John Wilkes: A Friend to Liberty*. Oxford: Clarendon Press.

Todd, William B., 1982. "Foreword" to Hume, *History of England* (see above under Hume): xi–xxiii.

Tolonen, Mikko, 2010. "Hume's Case for Monarchy." Paper presented before the Annual Meeting of the Hume Society, Antwerp, Belgium, July 6–10.

Tsebelis, George, 1990. *Nested Games: Rational Choice in Comparative Politics*. Berkeley: University of California Press.

Tucker, Robert C., 1970. "The Theory of Charismatic Leadership." In *Philosophers and Kings: Studies in Leadership*, ed. Dankwart A. Rustow, 69–94. New York: George Braziller.

Twain, Mark, 1917. *A Connecticut Yankee in King Arthur's Court. The Writings of Mark Twain*, vol. 16. New York and London: Harper & Brothers.

van Holthoon, F. L., 2008. "Macaulay and Hume: A Question of History." *European Journal* 9, no. 2 (December): 1–3.

Vieira, Monica Brito, and David Runciman. 2008. *Representation*. Malden, MA and Cambridge, UK: Polity Press.

Waldron, Jeremy, 1987. "Theoretical Foundations of Liberalism." *Philosophical Quarterly* 37, no. 147 (April): 127–50.

———, 1994. "The Advantages and Difficulties of the Humean Theory of Property." *Social Philosophy and Policy* 11 (1994): 85–123.

———, 1999. *Law and Disagreement*. Oxford: Oxford University Press.

Walzer, Michael, 1973. "Political Action: The Problem of Dirty Hands." *Philosophy and Public Affairs* 2, no. 2 (Winter 1973): 160–80.

Watner, Carl, 2005. "*Quod Omnes Tangit*: Consent Theory in the Radical Libertarian Tradition in the Middle Ages." *Journal of Libertarian Studies* 19, no. 2 (Spring 2005): 67–85.

Weber, Max, 2004. "Basic Sociological Concepts." In *The Essential Weber: A Reader*, ed. Sam Shimster, 311–58. London: Routledge.

Weinbrot, Howard D., 1993. "Politics, Taste, and National Identity: Some Uses of Tacitism in Eighteenth-Century Britain." In *Tacitus and the Tacitean Tradition*, ed. T. J. Luce and A. J. Woodman, 168–84. Princeton, NJ: Princeton University Press.

Wennerlind, Carl, 2008. "An Artificial Virtue and the Oil of Commerce: A Synthetic View of Hume's Theory of Money." In *David Hume's Political Economy*, ed. Carl Wennerlind and Margaret Schabas, 105–26. London and New York: Routledge.

Wertz, S. K., 1975. "Hume, History, and Human Nature." *Journal of the History of Ideas* 36, no. 3 (July–September): 481–96.

———, 1996. "Moral Judgments in History: Hume's Position." *Hume Studies* 22, no. 2 (November 1996): 239–368.

Wexler, Victor G., 1979. *David Hume and the* History of England. Philadelphia: American Philosophical Society.

Wharton, Edith, 2008 (1920). *The Age of Innocence*. Charleston, SC: Forgotten Books.

Whelan, Frederick, 1985. *Order and Artifice in Hume's Political Philosophy*. Princeton, NJ: Princeton University Press.

———, 1995. "Time, Revolution, and Prescriptive Right in Hume's Theory of Government." *Utilitas* 7, no. 1 (May): 97–119.

———, 2001. "Hume and Smith on Perverse Effects in Political Life." Paper delivered at the conference, Political Economy and Scottish Culture, Arlington, VA, June.

———, 2004. *Hume and Machiavelli: Political Realism and Liberal Thought*. Lanham, MD: Lexington Books.

Williams, Bernard, 2005. *In the Beginning Was the Deed: Realism and Moralism in Political Argument*. Princeton, NJ: Princeton University Press.

Wolin, Sheldon, 1954. "Hume and Conservatism." *American Political Science Review* 48, no. 4 (December): 999–1016.

Index

CPSIA information can be obtained
at www.ICGtesting.com
Printed in the USA
LVHW08s0745050818
585984LV00005B/492/P